Value Profit Chain: Treat Employees Lik...
James L. Heskett, W. Earl Sasser, Leonard A. Schlesin...
658.8

C 2003

*f*P

Also by Heskett, Sasser, and Schlesinger

THE SERVICE PROFIT CHAIN

The Value Profit Chain

Treat Employees Like Customers and Customers Like Employees

James L. Heskett
W. Earl Sasser, Jr.
Leonard A. Schlesinger

THE FREE PRESS

New York   London   Toronto   Sydney

THE FREE PRESS
A Division of Simon & Schuster, Inc.
1230 Avenue of the Americas
New York, NY 10020

Manufactured in the United States of America

10 9 8 7 6 5

Library of Congress Cataloging-in-Publication Data
Heskett, James L.
    The value profit chain : treat employees like customers and customers like
employees / James L. Heskett, W. Earl Sasser, Jr., Leonard A. Schlesinger.
        p. cm.
    Includes index.
    1. Customer services. 2. Consumer satisfaction. 3. Organizational effectiveness.
4. Communication in marketing. 5. Employee loyalty. I. Sasser, W. Earl.
II. Schlesinger, Leonard A. III. Title.

HF5415.5 .H473 2003
658.8'12—dc21   2002027162
ISBN 0-7432-2569-4

WE ARE INDEBTED to a number of people for their ideas and their patience in testing ours.

First are those practicing managers from whom we have learned important lessons. They include Colleen Barrett, Pete Blackshaw, John Bogle, William Bratton, Charles Cawley, Scott Cook, Cliff Ehrlich, Bill Hybels, Herb Kelleher, James Kinnear, Bruce Nelson, Alan O'Dell, William Pollard, Jamie Priestley, Frederick Reichheld, Hal Rosenbluth, Don Soderquist, Tom Watson, Mel Warriner, Jack Welch, and Lorenzo Zambrano. Gary Loveman and John Morgridge, who divide their time between the "real world" and the academic, have been valued sources of ideas.

On the academic side, over the years we have benefited especially from an exchange of ideas with current and former colleagues, including Jim Cash, Roger Hallowell, Luis Huete, Tom Jones, Robert Kaplan, John Kotter, Christopher Lovelock, David Maister, Robert Miles, Miguel Ochoa, and Jeffrey Rayport.

Field casework and research have yielded a number of insights in support of this work. We are particularly indebted to those who have helped us in these efforts. They include Ken Carrig, Alan Grant, Norman Klein, Lucy Lytle, Dan Maher, James Mellado, Dan O'Brien, Kenneth Ray, and Jeffrey Zornitsky.

Laura Berkman Coleman served as our research associate on this effort. This involved everything from fact checking to tracking down elusive sources of information. We are indebted to her for her creative detective work.

The dean of the Harvard Business School, Kim Clark, and the School's Division of Research provided important sources of support for our work. Bruce Nichols was very helpful in shepherding our manuscript through the various steps to publication. We also owe a special debt of gratitude to our longtime friend and editor, Bob Wallace, who as always provided encouragement as well as detailed comments and advice at critical moments in our project.

Finally, we are grateful for the understanding and forbearance of our spouses and partners, Marilyn, Connie, and Phyllis, for our work together over the years.

James L. Heskett
W. Earl Sasser, Jr.
Leonard A. Schlesinger

Contents

Preface   x

Introduction   xv

PART I   Achieving Value-Centered Change   1

  1. The Value Profit Chain   5
  2. Rethinking the Business Using Value-Centered Concepts   34

PART II   Getting Management's Attention   51

  3. Measuring and Communicating Customer Lifetime Value   53
  4. Measuring and Communicating Employee Value   75
  5. Mobilizing for Change: Challenging Strong Cultures   95

PART III   Engineering Value Profit Change   109

  6. The Performance Trinity and the Value Profit Chain   113
  7. Employee Relationship Management
        Treating Employees Like Customers   136
  8. Customer Relationship Management
        Treating Customers Like Employees   166
  9. Managing by Value Exchange   184
 10. Leveraging Value over Cost   200

PART IV   Cementing the Gains   223

 11. Identifying and Revisiting Core Values   227
 12. Developing Value-Centered Measurement and Recognition   245
 13. Hardwiring Performance   260
 14. Leading the Organization to Learn and Innovate   275

Afterword   *295*

Appendix A: *Compendium of Value Profit Chain Research*   *301*
Appendix B: *The Value Profit Chain Audit*   *318*
Appendix C: *Calculating the Lifetime Value of a Customer*   *338*

Notes   *345*
Index   *361*

OUR RESEARCH over the past three decades has led us to conclude that winning organizations:

1. Have strategies encompassing well-aligned cultures as well as market and operating foci designed to deliver results and process quality (versus products and services) to important constituencies.

2. Achieve results and process quality through the following:

   ■ adherence to promoting relationships in what we call a value profit chain, one designed to foster customer, employee, partner, and investor loyalty, trust, commitment, and ownership.

   ■ reliance solely on those measurements and incentives that reflect primarily the means of achieving the strategy and, secondarily, the goals of the strategy.

   ■ establishment of strong cultures (based on widely shared values) that foster adaptive behavior as well as the development of ideas and people.

3. As a result, achieve superior "brand" franchises, encompassing all those things that contribute to an organization's long-term status as the preferred seller, buyer, employer, neighbor, or place to invest.

This work, which was inspired by scholars we cited at the time, stimulated many other researchers to test our conclusions in a variety of business settings. More than 40 examples of this effort, all based on empirical research, are reviewed in Appendix A. All but two supply evidence supporting our conclusions concerning one or more of the links in the value profit chain. We believe we can provide possible explanations for the exceptions.

Ideas embodied in the value profit chain are regularly employed today by consulting organizations large and small. One of the most comprehensive of these efforts, supported by findings from detailed analyses of a large database of experience, is even touted as a "total blueprint for worldwide capital."[1]

Our homework in support of value profit chain thinking began with the introduction of a new course, Management of Service Operations, into the Harvard Business School curriculum by Earl Sasser in 1972. This inspired other research that resulted in the publication of three books.[2] The first of these essentially laid out the hypotheses that would later evolve into value profit chain concepts. The second examined ways in which these concepts were being applied to create what we called service breakthroughs. The last provided, through research in more than 200 large corporations, factual evidence about the kinds of strong corporate cultures that did—and did not—support outstanding long-term performance.

The work continued with the publication of a *Harvard Business Review* article, "Putting the Service Profit Chain to Work," in 1994 and a book that expanded on the theme.[3] The article and the book presented evidence to support a set of relationships accounting for much of the corporate profitability and growth that we had been observing throughout a collective experience of nearly 100 years of teaching, consulting, and managing. It was intended to provide a fact-based roadmap for leaders of for-profit and not-for-profit service organizations wishing to upgrade the performance of their organizations, based on a pattern of experiences observed in the very best service organizations, ranging from Southwest Airlines (from shortly after its founding to the present) to the New York Police Department (under then-commissioner William Bratton).

Our goal was to set forth an organizing framework that was simple, workable, measurable, and memorable—all essential to effective implementation. The service profit chain and its related concepts served the purpose on all counts. It was so simple and intuitive that it has been labeled obvious by some of our critics, a label we regard as the ultimate compliment. In a sense, our goal was to provide a cookbook intended to demystify a number of overly complex management concepts, not unlike what Julia Child achieved in simplifying and providing wide access to the intricacies of French cooking in her writings and television programs.

Our past work, concentrated primarily in the service sector, raised more questions than it answered, among them the following: (1) Can these ideas that have worked well in greenfield start-ups provide the basis for transformational change in ongoing enterprises? (2) Can they be applied in manufacturing as well as service-providing firms? (3) Assuming the ideas are applicable, where does one start in introducing change into an existing large organization? (4) Regrettably, more recently, how do these ideas hold up in the face of a massive "discontinuity," such as the terrorist attacks of September 11, 2001, or economic contractions associated with a recession? Over the past 5 years, we have had an opportunity to come up with responses to these questions, albeit responses that may lead to yet other questions.

Value is the uniting theme running throughout our recent observations and measurements and those of others. We are speaking here of value for all major constituents of an organization: its clients, its employees, its suppliers, its investors, and its communities, among others. This includes value for organizations that are manufacturers or service providers. It also includes value for important stakeholders in both for-profit and not-for-profit organizations.

The goals are to (1) maximize value in a web of relationships and (2) ensure that value is distributed in ways that are perceived as fair. Value improperly apportioned among important stakeholders leads to eventual failure, as so many Internet start-ups demonstrated in recent years. In an attempt to impress potential customers with free or nearly free goods and services, the start-ups, under the "get big fast" mantra, neglected value for many investors and employees. Unless value generates value for all important players in the chain, there is no fuel to drive the next cycle of the socioeconomic internal combustion engine.

It is easy to assume that everything is managed for value of some kind. Who wouldn't attempt to achieve it? If this is the case, however, why are only a few organizations able to deliver on the promise and many more of their competitors unable to do so? Further, surprisingly few organizations are capable of completely rethinking their businesses. Fewer yet identify with any enthusiasm and creativity the core values that guide the enterprise. Finally, only a select circle of managers has the mind-set and skills to manage the change required. What can be done about this are issues to be addressed here.

We know much more now than we did only several years ago. For instance, we have learned that organizations achieving what is described earlier:

1. Don't have to trade off objectives of achieving low cost or a differentiated position in the minds of customers (something Collins and Porras in their landmark book, *Built to Last,* have labeled "avoiding the Tyranny of the OR, and embracing the Genius of the AND.")[4]

2. Know no bounds, either in terms of geography or organizational reach; they can organize and lead entire supply chains.

3. Can achieve astounding size, encompassing a million employees or more.

We have also learned that the concepts set forth in *The Service Profit Chain* are not confined to the creation of greenfield organizations we have studied closely—the Southwest Airlines, the Cisco Systems, and the Wal-Marts—whose founders and leaders understood them (and continue to understand them) well. They can be employed in rethinking and remaking organizations—in managing organizationwide change, either under the pressure or in anticipation of crises, as we have seen in organizations as diverse as IBM, Alcoa, Office Depot, and the Willow Creek Community Church,[5] or they can be employed to reenergize organizations to sustain outstanding performance, as at General Electric.

The last 20 years, beginning with the publication of Tom Peters' and Robert Waterman's book, *In Search of Excellence,* have produced a myriad of "roadmaps" for managers. A veritable blizzard of disparate ideas, such as economic value added, culture change, differentiation, the profit zone, customer relationship management, the value chain, knowledge transfer, supply chain management, and the balanced scorecard, confronts the thoughtful manager today. The intensity of interest in these ideas has been heightened by the speed with which organizations have experienced such phenomena as globalization, deregulation, and privatization. The technological advances leading to the so-called New Economy have given new emphasis to the need for speed in management decision-making and implementation. The turn of the century—ushered in with a visible increase in terrorism-inspired reflection on personal values, lifestyles, and work styles—is prompting much speculation about the nature of the twenty-first-century company. Without an organizing concept based on empirical research and fact, today's leaders are faced with a daunting, somewhat confusing, ideologically biased, and potentially disruptive body of ideas. The value profit chain is just such an organizing concept. It provides the missing link between many of these management roadmaps.

SUCCESS DRIVEN AND SUSTAINED by value profit chain thinking starts with attention to what we call the "performance trinity," comprising leadership and management, culture and values, and vision and strategy. The third of these elements is "hard" in character but the easiest to formulate. The real challenge is in the first two "soft" elements. The performance trinity is implemented in the context of a world of sociological, technical, regulatory, and economic change. While providing the starting point for sustainable change, it is also a backdrop for other value profit chain concepts. It is the foundation for achieving five value profit chain virtues—leverage, focus, fit, trust, and adaptability—leading to a sixth, value for customers, employees, partners, and investors. Of these, trust and adaptability result from winning cultures and values. Leverage, focus, and fit are largely achieved through vision (goals) and strategy (ways of achieving the goals), something we call the strategic value vision.

The strategic value vision targets customers for which value is to be created, primarily through the vehicle of a "value concept"—a business definition—based on results and the way they are to be attained (process quality), not products or services. The value concept is achieved with maximum benefit for customers, employees, partners, and investors through an operating strategy that seeks to leverage results over costs by means of such factors as organization, policies, processes, practices, measures, controls, and incentives. All this is supported by a value delivery system comprising elements of an organization's infrastructure.

The virtues of leverage, focus, fit, trust, adaptability, and value are achieved through an array of levers. Foremost among these are information technology, knowledge transfer, supply chain management, value exchange, operating strategy, and such financial concepts as economic value added, all representing important elements of operating strategy in the strategic value vision. The relationships between elements of the performance trinity, value profit chain virtues, strategic value vision, and these levers are illustrated in Figure 1. The levers in turn fuel the value profit chain itself.

The value profit chain, core to sustaining outstanding performance, is shown in Figure 2. It is based on "value equations" for customers, employees, partners, and investors. For customers, the appropriate value equation is

$$\text{Value} = \frac{\text{Results} + \text{Process Quality}}{\text{Price} + \text{Customer Access Costs}}$$

For employees, it is adapted to read:

$$\text{Value} = \frac{\text{Capability} + \text{Work Place Quality}}{1/\text{Wages} + \text{Job Access Costs}}$$

Similar adaptations are shown for partners and investors in Figure 2.

Important to this thinking, which is based on empirical research, is that elements of the cycle are self-reinforcing. Employee value leads to the satisfaction, loyalty, and productivity that produces customer value, satisfaction, loyalty, trust, and commitment. Satisfied, loyal, trusting, and committed customers are the primary driver of company growth and profitability, important determinants of investor value. Finally, the fruits of growth and profitability are reinvested in value for partners (suppliers, communities, and others), employees, customers, and investors.

Some of the best examples of value profit chain thinking are organizations that were established on the basis of many of these ideas. They include Southwest Airlines, Wal-Mart, the Vanguard Group of mutual funds, ServiceMaster, and Shouldice Hospital, organizations from which we have learned a great deal firsthand. What about leaders of organizations that were not founded on these ideas, organizations seeking to become more than just merely good? How do they cut into these seemingly self-contained, self-reinforcing relationships? Where do they start in the process of developing sustainable performance excellence? How do

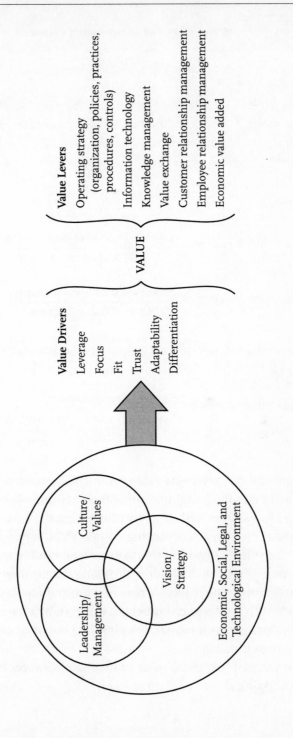

Figure 1 FACTORS IN VALUE PROFIT CHAIN SUCCESS

Value Levers
Operating strategy
(organization, policies, practices,
procedures, controls)
Information technology
Knowledge management
Value exchange
Customer relationship management
Employee relationship management
Economic value added

VALUE

Value Drivers
Leverage
Focus
Fit
Trust
Adaptability
Differentiation

Culture/
Values

Vision/
Strategy

Leadership/
Management

Economic, Social, Legal, and
Technological Environment

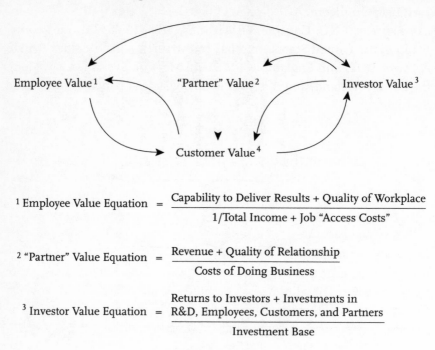

■ Figure 2 The Value Profit Chain

^{1} Employee Value Equation $= \dfrac{\text{Capability to Deliver Results + Quality of Workplace}}{1/\text{Total Income + Job "Access Costs"}}$

^{2} "Partner" Value Equation $= \dfrac{\text{Revenue + Quality of Relationship}}{\text{Costs of Doing Business}}$

^{3} Investor Value Equation $= \dfrac{\text{Returns to Investors + Investments in R\&D, Employees, Customers, and Partners}}{\text{Investment Base}}$

^{4} Customer Value Equation $= \dfrac{\text{Results + Process Quality}}{\text{Cost (Price) + Customer Access Costs}}$

those organizations achieving value profit chain excellence sustain their positions in a rapidly changing competitive environment?

Further research as well as practical experience since our earliest writing suggests some very clear starting points. The few quantitative studies of cause and effect support practical experience and management intuition. Change begins with a leadership team capable of creating value for employees, among other factors centered around employees' capability to deliver results to valued customers. It is driven by a reevaluation of culture and values just as importantly as it is by new visions or strategies. It is led, not merely managed.

In just the past few years, value profit chain concepts have been used as an underlying driver of change to one degree or another in a wide range of organizations, including Harrah's Entertainment, Au Bon Pain, Taco Bell, Omnicom, AC Nielsen, Office Depot, Limited Brands, American Express, PNC, Continental Airlines, Sears, SYSCO, and Loomis Fargo in the United States. In other countries, the list includes British Airways, BUPA (in England), CEMEX (in Mexico), Swedbank (Sweden), the Bank of Ireland, and the Nova Rede division of Banco Comercial de Português.

■ Organization of the Book

We begin by revisiting the remarkable accomplishments of two organizations that have delivered value to customers, employees, partners, and investors for years—Wal-Mart Stores and the Vanguard Group of mutual funds. Both have risen to leadership positions in their respective industries by maintaining a strict adherence to value profit chain thinking. Because these organizations were based on value profit chain concepts from the outset of their development, we next turn to companies such as IBM that have more recently realized growing success through a transformation based on this kind of thinking.

The process of leading change requires either the presence or the creation of dissatisfaction with the status quo within an organization. Without this, the foes of change—stasis and equilibrium—continue to prevail. The second section of the book suggests ways leaders can disturb the equilibrium and develop such dissatisfaction, ways we have found useful in our work. The first of these, addressed in Chapter 3, is the estimation and communication of information about customer lifetime value, a process that often yields astounding information and a wake-up call to management to reduce customer defections. The second, the subject of Chapter 4, is an estimation and communication of employee value, a process that inevitably elevates the importance of retaining productive talent in an organization. Finally, in Chapter 5, we address ways of mobilizing for change by challenging strong, often nonadaptive, cultures. Here the experiences of James Kinnear, then president and CEO of Texaco Inc., are both remarkable and instructive.

Once awareness of the need for change has been created, it is important to turn to ways of engineering value profit change through superior models and processes for action. The starting point is a reengineering of the performance trinity. The experiences at Office Depot, the world's largest office supply organization, suggest that there is a hierarchy within this trinity in which leadership and management first influence culture and values and then develop a vision and strategy, all of which have a high degree of "fit" with one another.

The final four chapters of this section deal with levers for change. Chapters 7 and 8 deal with two important stakeholders that drive performance, employees and customers. They argue that in working with employees we can learn a lot from insights about how to treat customers, as is the case in organizations as different as Cisco Systems and the Willow Creek Community Church. The reverse is also true, as we see in a subsidiary of one of the largest global providers of marketing communications and services. Chapter 9 concentrates on the long-term significance of a very simple but powerful concept, *value exchange*— what an organization gets for what it gives in relating to customers, employees, and others by utilizing the levers of information technology and knowledge transfer. Experiences at Capital One, a leading practitioner of the concept, help us understand how it must extend to all links in the value profit chain to be truly effective. Finally, Chapter 10 reviews other important levers for achieving value (leveraging results and process quality over cost) in the chain, utilizing what we have learned over 27 years of contact with Southwest Airlines, during which time we and our colleagues have prepared several case studies of the organization.

Once value is achieved for employees, customers, partners, and investors, the primary challenge is to cement the gains and sustain performance. This involves revisiting the core values, those shared beliefs that provide the heart of an organization's culture, in ways illustrated by IBM, Johnson & Johnson, Cisco Systems, and others, our concern in Chapter 11. It argues for the development of measures and methods for recognizing performance on important dimensions of the value profit chain through balanced scorecard concepts, as illustrated by experiences at Mobil, Sears, and others that are described in Chapter 12. Next, performance can be "hardwired" by redefining the very purpose of an organization in terms of solutions, then guaranteeing their delivery to customers.

Efforts at CEMEX (for ready-mix concrete), Intuit (personal financial software), and eBay (the "people's" trading exchange), described in Chapter 13, provide important examples to suggest the potential in this concept.

The book concludes with the ultimate method for sustaining organizations that set the pace in their fields of activity over long periods of time through listening, learning, teaching, best practice, and knowledge transfer, all behaviors requiring enlightened leadership that is all too rare these days. Here, rich examples from the Omnicom Group, a global advertising and marketing communications firm, and GE help shed light on the complex set of efforts needed to make "the corporate brain" function effectively.

■ A Final Note

In the process of exploring the value profit chain we have learned something about what we still don't know. Others have tested our ideas and discovered complexities in the relationships that we may not have described fully. We have been able to collect much more data and many more examples to suggest conditions in which the process of unlocking value in the value profit chain is particularly applicable.

Most important, we have become convinced that the thinking behind the value profit chain provides a basis for sorting and organizing the confusing array of ideas for managers being advanced today. It helps bring order out of chaos while providing a basis for benchmarking an organization against best practice on various dimensions of the chain, as suggested in the audit we have included as Appendix B to the book.

There has been a long-running debate about whether more value is created out of the formulation or implementation of strategy. A parallel debate has centered around strategy as primarily (1) a question of positioning an organization against competitive forces and the needs and relative power of important constituencies, or (2) a process of identifying and developing core competencies in capitalizing on a "position." Neither of these is a particularly useful debate because strategy formulation means so many different things to different people—everything from defining a business to setting goals to doing deals—and because of the overlap in strategy formulation and implementation or positioning and core competencies. To the extent that successful implementation requires the proper definition of the business in the first place by means of what we call a strategic value vision, we discuss strategy formulation in this book.

However, you won't find us telling stories about how a clever, all-seeing CEO was able to switch his company out of one business and into another. (Why is it that only CEOs are credited with doing this in the popular write-ups when in fact it requires leaders at all levels?) Instead our primary interest is in documenting, through both stories and empirically based research, ways in which value profit chain thinking can be used to lead change in existing businesses in ways that significantly increase value for customers, employees, shareholders, and others while moving them from the ranks of the "merely good" to those of business sector leaders.

PART I

Achieving Value-Centered Change

M OST DECISIONS made by managers either destroy long-term value or don't create any. This includes both tactical and strategic decisions, and it includes decisions made by well-meaning, intelligent, and even well-trained managers. It's hard to believe this is the case in an era in which new concepts and how-to's for planning, strategic development, and decision-making are trumpeted at a rate unknown in the past.

To be fair, most managers today don't have a fighting chance to create value. They are often forced to plan, decide, and act without clear, coherent, or comprehensive roadmaps. They substitute goals for plans and strategies. They lose strategic focus in an effort to extend the reach of the organization, confusing products and services with results. Once the focus is lost, it becomes more difficult to know how (and even which) results are to be leveraged over costs, thereby resulting in misallocation of resources. They must operate without appropriate value-centered measures to tell them where they've been, what has worked well in creating value, and what is possible. Too often, they must move forward without agreed-on shared values that anchor a culture, itself an important element in a value-building strategy. As a result, they hire the wrong people for the wrong reasons, paying a frightful price not only in terms of lost time and progress, but in terms of strict limits on sustainable growth. Of course, to the extent that they are responsible for ensuring that this doesn't happen, well-meaning managers are rightly held accountable for their own demise.

Some destroy value by failing to react to changes in the competitive, social, economic, or legal environment. Ironically, they are sometimes victims of their own past success. There is a strong temptation to resist significant change in a winning strategy.

Still others destroy value out of sheer greed and arrogance, as we witnessed in the recent fall of Enron. They are assisted in this process by inactive boards of directors who often provide insufficient oversight over accounting and other matters, as well as nonvocal shareholders who merely vote with their feet rather than hold management and directors accountable for their actions. They may parade their values in front of employees, but managers in these organizations are recognized whether or not they adhere to them. Fortunately, they represent a minority. In the process, however, they adversely impact customers and employees as well as investors, in fact all constituencies having anything to do with an organization.

There are significant exceptions. A handful of organizations have been created in recent years that are literally value-creating machines. It's hard to believe, but many of them—FedEx, Cisco Systems, Home Depot, Microsoft, Wal-Mart, SAS, Vanguard Financial Services, and Southwest Airlines—all leaders in their respective industries, essentially are products of the last 30 years. They were built on elements of a value-centered framework that has stood the test of time. The concepts it encompasses are those underlying much of what we regard as success in today's rapidly changing business environment. They work for constituencies both internal and external to the organization. They produce results for both nonprofit and for-profit enterprise, and they can stimulate a complete rethinking of the business, one that results in a new vision and mission.

These organizations were the product of people with both vision and the latitude to follow through on the vision. What about organizations that don't have the luxury of starting from a blank page, those whose histories go back far beyond an era in which we've begun to make significant progress in understanding the true roots of value creation, or, in some cases, those saddled with the baggage of past mistakes? Here the task is much harder, but not impossible, as demonstrated by such organizations as IBM, Office Depot, and Texaco.

Chapter 1

The Value Profit Chain

A HANDFUL OF ORGANIZATIONS have created extraordinary value for customers, employees, investors, and others. The way they've done it follows identifiable patterns. The remarkable thing is not how successful they've been. It is rather the fact that there are so few who've done it.

■ Advocate for the Investor

The Vanguard Group[1] of mutual funds was founded on the premises that mutual fund investment managers (1) through their investment decisions destroy as much value for investors as they create and (2) through their behaviors destroy value for investors by running up high management fees, in part for their own enrichment. In response, its strategy, since its founding, has been to (1) avoid to the extent possible making investment decisions for its investors and (2) through a variety of policies and practices, minimize costs and management fees incurred by its mutual funds. The results have been nothing short of remarkable. They have been achieved by an organization that its founder, John Bogle, describes grandly as embodying "the majesty of simplicity in an empire of parsimony."[2]

As an investor, if you check the management fees associated with various mutual funds, you will find that those of the Vanguard Group of mutual funds are invariably lower than the average for all others, in fact lower by a factor of 3 or 4, depending on the type of fund. On this score, there is no comparison. As a result, even though many of the Vanguard funds perform in the middle of the pack in terms of investment performance, comparatively low fees add so much to the compounded value of Vanguard's customers' holdings that they invariably are found near the top on this measure. It requires that an investor hold the fund long enough to reap the advantages of low costs. This is all right with Vanguard's management; it doesn't encourage short-term investors to invest in its mutual funds. In fact, it institutes various policies designed to discourage them from investing with Vanguard. This is part of a process by which Vanguard delivers superior value to the customers it seeks, at the same time growing at the fastest rate of any major mutual fund group in the industry over the past decade.

As you might imagine, Bogle, Vanguard's first chairman and CEO, is not popular in the mutual fund industry. He has refused consistently to join the club of high-cost, high-fee competitors. As a result, it has been more than a decade since he was asked to address the industry's top managers. The head of at least one high-profile competitor hasn't spoken to him in years.

Vanguard's rapid growth rate attests to the fact that it is perceived as delivering investment results to investors. With such low operating costs, however, one might assume that Vanguard's service is compromised, or that employees display dissatisfaction with lower salaries, nonpalatial facilities, and the like. After all, they all must fly coach while in the company's employ and forgo reserved parking spots, leased autos, and an executive dining room—unheard of in the world of financial services. In fact, Vanguard's base compensation levels, although not published, are probably no greater than the industry average, but employee dissatisfaction and turnover are much lower. Why? Because the company also delivers high value to its employees by treating them with respect, rewarding them with substantial bonuses for saving money for investors, and providing a stable, positive working environment in a growing organization.

■ Agent for the Customer

A visit to the weekly management meeting at Wal-Mart Stores in Bentonville, Arkansas, is noteworthy in many ways.[3] The first is probably the day and time, Saturday morning at 7:30. One reason for this is that Wal-Mart's operating executives are thought to generate little value holed up in their offices all week. Hence, they spend nearly every week on the road from Monday morning through Thursday evening, reserving only Friday and Saturday morning for meetings in Bentonville.

The second thing a visitor notices is the size of the meeting room, filled with nearly a thousand people. The big room is necessary because of the relatively broad criteria for who may attend: members, their relatives, and invited friends of the Wal-Mart "family," a word still used frequently in an organization that now includes more than a million employees and several million family members. Third is the circus-like atmosphere of the meeting, with "ringmaster" and since retired Chief Operating Officer Don Soderquist (who happened to be leading the meeting that one of us last observed) introducing vendors with new merchandise, interacting in a somewhat orchestrated fashion with selected guests in the audience, and leading the Wal-Mart cheer (one of several programmed during the morning). The cheer, at one point given by the latest graduating class of young management trainees from the the company's Walton Institute—"Give me a W, give me an A, give me an L, give me a squiggly (with a roll of the hips) . . ."—culminates in the shouted question, "Who's number one?" "THE CUSTOMER!"

Of even greater significance is that in the midst of this hoopla a great deal of information about the week's, month's, and year's performance is communicated, decisions are actually made, and a visitor comes away from the meeting with a sense that there is truly a family spirit to the meeting. Both retired and active managers are in the room. Employees have brought their children and parents with them. Exchanges among audience members are encouraged along with questions put to senior executives gathered near the front of the auditorium. A meeting that one of us witnessed began with the introduction by Don Soderquist of a store manager we'll call Bill Smith, manager of Wal-Mart store number 1038 located somewhere in Washington. Bill had been invited to the meeting with expenses (including a ride to and from Bentonville in a corporate aircraft) arranged by his regional manager so that his accomplishment of increasing soft goods sales by 20% over the previous 6 months could be recognized. As Bill stood up and reported his results, someone in another part of the auditorium requested a "roving" microphone to say, "Bill, I used to work with your dad, and I can tell you he wouldn't be satisfied with a 20% increase." Whereupon Bill replied, "I couldn't agree more, Joe; this is just the beginning." (A host provided assurance that the exchange between managers hadn't been rehearsed.)

Maudlin as this behavior may sound, a sense of pride and belonging actually seems to pervade the group as it files from the room at the conclusion of the meeting, with knots of attendees remaining behind to exchange greetings and converse with one another, not unlike a congregation at the conclusion of a church service.

Perhaps the most telling clue to the continuing success of Wal-Mart is the massive tote board extending much of the way across one side of the large room. The board's flashing lights report a huge updated number every second. What is it? Sales? Profits? Number of employees? It's none of these. Instead, the number reports the amount of money saved for its customers by Wal-Mart during the year. The board is an icon of one of the organization's most important core values, "serving as agent for the customer," a core value that spurs Wal-Mart's buyers to get the best value from their vendors, something done in the name of the customer, not the company. This helps explain why Wal-Mart's vendors describe what its buyers are like in such terms as "tough," "brutal," and "demanding" (but also "fair"). When negotiating on behalf of customers—a selfless endeavor—buyers can be very tough and demanding.

When an organization serves as the agent for the customer, value pervades everything it does. For example, one of the things many people remember about a visit to a Wal-Mart store are the employees at the door, often senior citizens, who greet customers and bid them good-bye. Most customers regard this as a "nice touch" that doesn't cost the company too much money. In fact, its greeters were placed there originally in part to save the company money in the form of reduced shoplifting. The idea originated from a 1980 visit to a Wal-Mart store in Crowley, Louisiana by erstwhile company founder Sam Walton and one of his senior executives, Tom Coughlan, when they were greeted by an elderly gentleman stationed at the door by the manager. According to Coughlan,

> The store, it turned out, had had trouble with shoplifting, and its manager was an oldline merchant named Dan McAllister, who knew how to

take care of his inventory. He didn't want to intimidate the honest customers by posting a guard at the door, but he wanted to leave a clear message that if you came in and stole, someone was there who would see it.[4]

True, it's unlikely that any of these elderly gentlemen and ladies could stop a shoplifter, but their mere presence at the door seems to have repaid their wages many times over. Thus, Wal-Mart enhances customers' perceptions of its service while reducing its costs and enabling it to deliver merchandise at even lower prices.

Other shoppers may remember the Wal-Mart slogan, "Everyday Low Prices." Again, a policy that appears designed primarily to deliver low prices to customers also produces lower costs for the company. By avoiding the sales peaks and reduced margins resulting from periodic price promotions, Wal-Mart is able to create regular flows of merchandise that save inventory carrying costs for both itself and its suppliers.

Wal-Mart works with its suppliers in other ways as well. Several major suppliers, such as Procter & Gamble and General Electric, have joint agreements under which sales and inventory information is exchanged on a constant basis, shipment is made in carload quantities to storage points maintained by the supplier, the transfer of ownership of shipments to Wal-Mart is delayed to the last possible moment, and payment for shipments is actuated instantaneously by suppliers at the point of transfer, thereby reducing the costs of accounts receivable for them. As a result, costs are minimized for Wal-Mart, its customers, and its suppliers.

What about employees? Surely they don't work for Wal-Mart because of plush offices (relatively small spaces in a converted warehouse), high salaries and wages, or lavish perquisites. Although wages at Wal-Mart are not high, all employees are given an opportunity to participate in a plan offering ownership of the company's stock. This perhaps explains the presence of a daily posting of Wal-Mart's stock price in all of its stores, a reminder to both customers (many of whom are shareholders) and employees of the company's performance. In some organizations, this emphasis on stock price could lead to short-term behavior or, even worse, a potential loss of savings. At Wal-Mart, it seemed to create a spur to better performance during a period of several years when the stock price plateaued. As a matter of fact, Wal-Mart has the lowest rate of turnover of its employees in the large general merchandise discount retail chain business.

This is a value-centered organization at work. Value is created for customers, to whom Wal-Mart directs its efforts. Value is created for the right kind of employee, those who place the sense of family that the organization tries to create ahead of high wages. Value is certainly created for investors (including many employees), who have received handsome total returns on their investments during most of Wal-Mart's years as a publicly listed stock. Value is created for vendors, with whom Wal-Mart's management has helped work out ways of preserving profitable relationships while reducing the prices charged the company for its merchandise.

In its pursuit of value, Wal-Mart has been criticized for destroying value in the communities it serves by putting small competitors out of business and sucking the life out of traditional downtown retail centers by locating its facilities where it can obtain the large tracts of land needed to accommodate 250,000-square-foot stores and the parking that they require. Others have argued that good retailers offering customized service and close relationships with customers have survived against Wal-Mart's competition, that Wal-Mart makes good retailers better, that city centers were in a state of decline before the company's arrival, and that Wal-Mart creates jobs to replace those lost by retailers unable to compete with it. The issue is one to which the company's leadership is sensitive. It represents one more challenge to be addressed through the value creation process.

■ Important Concepts in the Search for Value

The search for *value,* what you get for what you pay, is the primary motivation for the actions of customers, employees, suppliers, and others with whom an organization interacts. It has spawned several generations of investors whose poster boy is Warren Buffett, chairman of Berkshire Hathaway, an investment company emphasizing value in all its investments. It has created an entire consulting "industry" around the concept of economic value added, and it is what most customers seek when purchasing goods and services. Value means many things to many people and is a highly subjective, personal matter, but its pursuit has fueled durable business success. It is both a driver and a reflection of several important phenomena that we are only beginning to understand and act on. We have characterized these phenomena previously in terms of several evolving concepts, concepts we now refer to as the strategic value vision, the value profit chain, and the customer value equation. The Vanguard and Wal-Mart experiences help us illustrate them in a quick of review of each.

THE STRATEGIC VALUE VISION

The strategic value vision is a framework for strategic planning based on several assumptions:

1. People buy results and process quality (the way results are achieved), not products or services—something we term a value concept, very useful in forming a business definition.

2. To know what results and process qualities are sought, targeted customers must be carefully delineated, in both demographic (age and income, for example) and psychographic (such as lifestyle, needs, and fears) terms. Just as important, an effort must be made to describe customers that are not being targeted.

3. The primary goal of an organization should be to leverage results and process quality over costs. This is achieved through a focused, internally consistent operating strategy comprising policies, procedures, organization, controls, incentives, and an organization culture designed to do just that.

4. The operating strategy is supported by information systems (sometimes more popularly known in Internet-based retailing today as "clicks"), locations, technology, and the "bricks and mortar" comprising a value delivery system.

5. Value results from both market and operating focus. Through focus, both superior results for customers (often termed "differentiation" by scholars of strategy) and low costs can be achieved.

6. The vision is applicable not only to customers but to employees and other important constituents of a firm as well.

The strategic value vision is illustrated diagrammatically for Vanguard and Wal-Mart in Figures 1-1 and 1-2, respectively.

Target Market Vanguard seeks to deliver results for investors desiring long-term financial return and good service. At the same time, it typically shuns the establishment of mutual funds featuring highly volatile securities. It has, for example, been a pioneer in lower-risk funds such as those based on indexes of large numbers of stocks. This makes it particularly attractive for employers offering 401(k) workplace savings plans to employees. At the same it discourages another group of potential investors seeking higher returns (with commensurately higher risks). By invoking penalties for the rapid turnaround (purchase and sale) of mutual fund shares, Vanguard discourages the short-term investor as well.

By locating its stores originally in secondary markets, including towns of 10,000 or even less, Wal-Mart was founded on relationships with non-urban customers. This has, of course, changed for reasons ranging from real estate to customer "mentality," but Wal-Mart continues to shun the centers of large cities for its stores. Although it targets certain geographic markets through its locations, the store serves people with a wide range of incomes in every community in which it operates. The one thing they have in common is a search for value.

Value Concept Vanguard delivers results to customers measured, among other things, in total return on investment over longer periods of time, not just 1 or 2 years. At the same time, its emphasis on customer service is quite high. It does this under the motto "advocate for the investor." Because the Vanguard Group is operated on a "mutualized" basis, its investors are also its owners, enjoying the dual benefit of value through their investments and through the much lower cost structure that results from not having internal expenses "marked up" by managers who have ownership stakes in the substantial profits they earn by managing their funds. It also provides its own employees "crew members" with

■ Figure 1–1 The Strategic Value Vision for The Vanguard Group

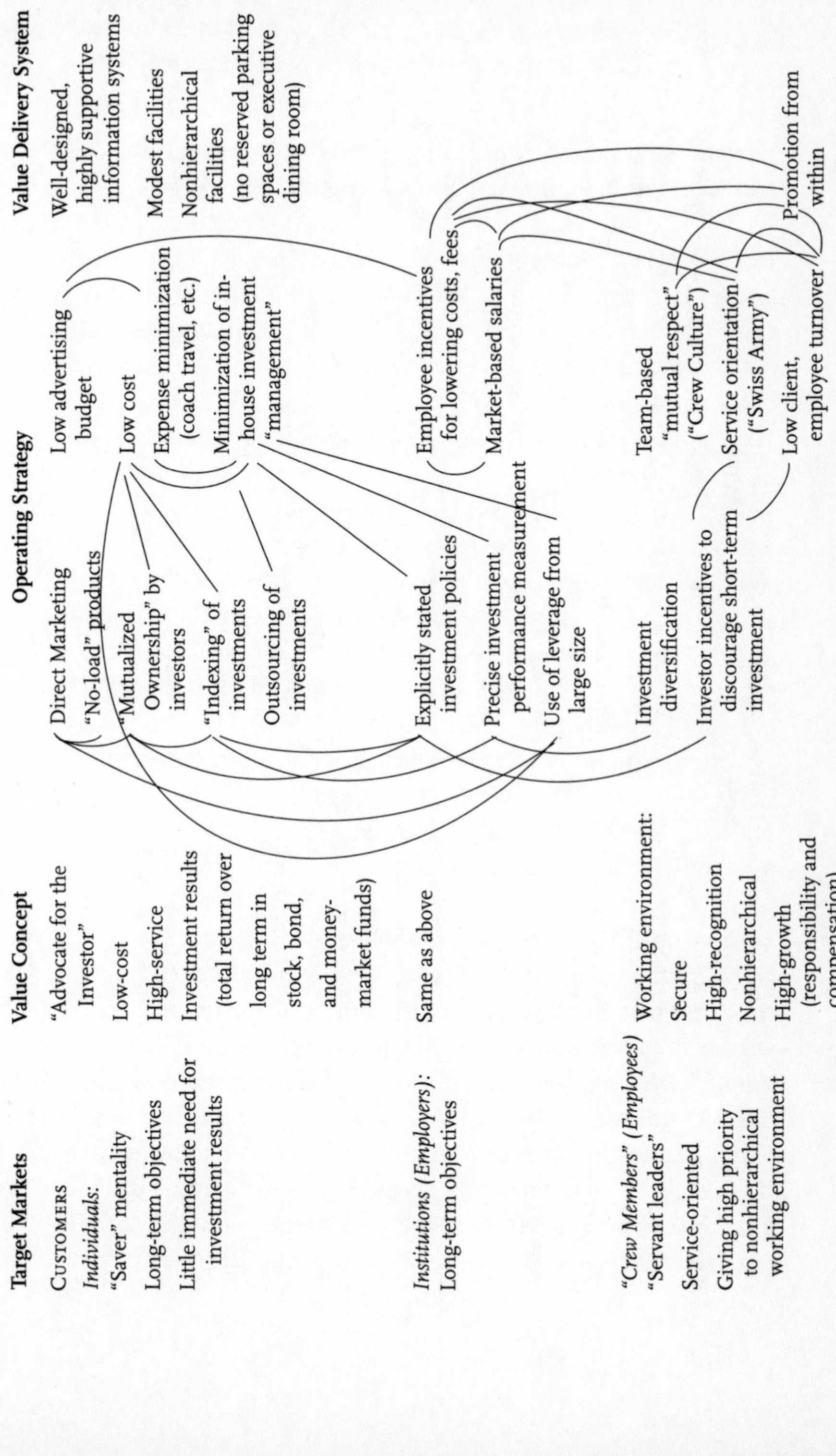

Target Markets

CUSTOMERS
Individuals:
"Saver" mentality
Long-term objectives
Little immediate need for investment results

Institutions (Employers):
Long-term objectives

"Crew Members" (Employees)
"Servant leaders"
Service-oriented
Giving high priority to nonhierarchical working environment

Value Concept

"Advocate for the Investor"
Low-cost
High-service
Investment results (total return over long term in stock, bond, and money-market funds)

Same as above

Working environment:
Secure
High-recognition
Nonhierarchical
High-growth (responsibility and compensation)

Operating Strategy

Direct Marketing
"No-load" products
"Mutualized" Ownership" by investors
"Indexing" of investments
Outsourcing of investments

Low advertising budget
Low cost
Expense minimization (coach travel, etc.)
Minimization of in-house investment "management"

Employee incentives for lowering costs, fees.
Market-based salaries

Explicitly stated investment policies
Precise investment performance measurement
Use of leverage from large size

Investment diversification
Investor incentives to discourage short-term investment

Team-based "mutual respect" ("Crew Culture")
Service orientation ("Swiss Army")
Low client, employee turnover

Value Delivery System

Well-designed, highly supportive information systems
Modest facilities
Nonhierarchical facilities (no reserved parking spaces or executive dining room)

Promotion from within

■ **Figure 1-2** The Strategic Value Vision for Wal-Mart Stores, Inc.

Target Markets	Value Concept	Operating Strategy	Value Delivery System
Customers	"Agent for the customer"	"Everyday low prices"	State-of-the-art information systems (data warehouse)
Value-oriented	Lowest possible prices	Use of leverage from large size	Well-designed distribution centers (with extensive "cross-docking")
Mobile	Wide assortment	Leveling of logistics flows	Strategically located stores
Wide income range	Quality merchandise	Store-level operating merchandising latitude	Frugal store, office design
	Friendly, knowledgeable service	Extensive "partnering" with suppliers	High-capability communication systems
	Convenient hours	Low advertising budgets	Large aircraft fleet
	A successful, pleasant shopping experience	Emphasis on "family-oriented" culture	Large company-owned truck fleet
Employees	Stable employment in a "family-like" exciting working environment	Hiring "nice" people	
"Nice" people	Personal and financial growth	Keeping managers close to customers	
"Servant leaders"		Creation of exciting workplace for managers, employees (contests, etc.)	
	Large, steady "base" of demand at acceptable overall profit	Promotion from within	
Suppliers		Low employee turnover	
Dependable		Heavy reliance on stock ownership for incentives	
U.S.-based (when possible)		Daily sharing of store-level performance	

stable, secure employment in a high-recognition, nonhierarchic working environment in which they can achieve above-average earnings for jobs in Vanguard's suburban Philadelphia labor market.

Wal-Mart's formula for results for customers is, in the words of Sam Walton, nothing more than "a wide assortment of good quality merchandise; the lowest possible prices; guaranteed satisfaction with what you buy; friendly, knowledgeable service; convenient hours; free parking; a pleasant shopping experience."[5] It achieves this, in large part, by serving as an agent for the customer, a mission remarkably similar to that for the Vanguard Group. In a sense, however, Wal-Mart also serves as agent for the employee, offering stable employment in communities where it is not always available, variable hours (often on a part-time basis), a "familylike" culture, and opportunities for personal (and financial) growth. To its suppliers, it offers a large, steady source of demand not disrupted by promotional peaks and valleys, representing a good "base" customer on which other higher margin business with less dependable customers can be built. To its investors, it has represented one of the more stable long-term investments available among retailing organizations.

Operating Strategy   The ways in which Vanguard leverages value over cost embrace John Bogle's philosophy, quoted earlier, of "the majesty of simplicity."[6] On the investment side, each fund has explicitly stated investment policies and precise performance measurement standards (against peer indexes of investment performance). Portfolios are broadly diversified and conservatively managed. In fact, to the extent possible, Vanguard avoids managing equity funds in-house that require investment decisions, preferring to outsource them, often at very low rates in exchange for the vast amounts of capital that Vanguard can deliver to outside fund managers. The objective is for its investors to achieve the largest possible share of the returns for an asset class across the market.

The other half of the process of delivering value to clients is frugality in the manner in which the organization goes about its business, as we have seen earlier. Roger Hallowell has attributed the extremely low operating expense ratios of the Vanguard funds to cost savings (representing 43% of the difference between Vanguard and the industry average) and the fact that Vanguard's investors are its owners, thereby eliminating margins needed to deliver profits to noninvestor owners (representing the other 57% of the difference).[7] The company's product policy, known for featuring *index funds,* those whose portfolios are determined on a formula designed to emulate the performance of large groups of individual securities, minimizes the need for high-priced investment managers. By targeting long-term investors, Vanguard avoids the high turnover and tax costs associated with large numbers of transactions generated by investors who constantly alter their portfolios. These investors expect Vanguard to practice frugality, as exhibited by the number of complaints received by investors when they receive duplicate mailings of announcements or statements. According to one report, Bogle noted that even this expense irritated investors, commenting that "Vanguard shareholders cannot tolerate the idea of waste."[8]

At Vanguard, the turnover of employees, members of the "crew," is lower than industry averages. This is likely achieved more through a stated policy of "mutual respect" than through high salary and wage structures. Vanguard offers performance incentives, however, that enable employees to earn up to 30% of their annual compensation. The incentives are diametrically opposed to those in existence at most of Vanguard's competitors. They reward results that produce favorable comparisons between Vanguard's cost structure and returns delivered to investors (vs. increased profits or share of market) and those of its competitors. Given the company's adherence to a mix of money market, bond, and stock funds featuring relatively conservative investment policies, it enjoys less pronounced fluctuations in assets under management, offering stable employment.

Wal-Mart's leverage is achieved through the company's immense buying power, which yields the lowest costs for merchandise of any category. This leverage has been used to foster supply chain partnerships with such major suppliers as Procter & Gamble and GE that have eliminated many steps in the supply chain through a sharing of information, an efficient allocation of responsibilities for various tasks and risks, and the creation and maintenance of high levels of trust between the partners.

It takes more than low cost to achieve the merchandise assortments desired by customers. This requires an intimate knowledge of buying preferences on the part of merchandising and other headquarters personnel. It helps explain why offices are so small; they are rarely occupied. Instead, a management job at headquarters is an invitation to 4 days of travel per week, time spent relating to customers and employees on the front line, a practice personified by the admonition to visiting executives to do something personally for at least one customer during every store visit. Wal-Mart's Everyday Low Price policy is more than an effort to build an image of economy and value in the mind of the customer. It implies a policy of no or few "sales," thereby providing little incentive to delay or speed up purchasing patterns. This reduces the need for poorly used, high-cost peak capacity in warehouses and improves the company's "in-stock" merchandise performance record. It also eases supply problems with vendors, giving Wal-Mart yet another justification for lower prices on the goods it purchases.

The company's culture, propagated by "nice" people, advocates competition and fun at all levels. Most of this activity, however, has a dual purpose, both to foster involvement in the Wal-Mart "family" and to boost sales. For example, headquarters executives regularly choose merchandise items that they will "sponsor" in sales contests implemented through cooperation by store managers. This requires that senior executives, who spend most of their time in the stores, maintain close contact with both customers and store management in an effort to get their "sponsored" items promoted and sold. Some might view this as wasted valuable time. As a result, however, Wal-Mart's senior management maintains an unusual sensitivity to merchandising and store operating problems while enjoying a business-fostering competition. This may help explain Wal-Mart's unusually low turnover rates in both frontline and management ranks, because employees become caught up in the excitement generated by the constant activity created by the contests and other events, getting to know management better than in most general merchandising organizations.

Note the large number of mutually reinforcing ideas and practices embodied in the operating strategies of both these organizations, as shown by the connecting links in Figures 1-1 and 1-2. The more numerous these relationships, the more internally consistent and focused we have found operating strategies to be.[9]

Value Delivery System   Value delivery systems for both these organizations support their strategies. Real estate and location decisions play a role. As mentioned earlier, Vanguard's location in suburban Philadelphia helps it maintain economic compensation patterns. Its facilities are functional but not extravagant, thereby communicating to all employees the company's main purpose, to deliver value to investors. Its information support systems, recently upgraded to state of the art for the industry, enable frontline service personnel to have immediate access to investor files sufficient to provide well-regarded service. The telephone system can be switched as needed to support Vanguard's "Swiss Army" policy of training people at all levels to take customer service calls during particularly busy periods. Many investments in technology have been designed to lower waste and cost, such as the elimination of duplicate mailings to investors.

Similarly, Wal-Mart's location of stores on the outskirts of cities and towns gives it a real estate cost advantage while providing space for the ample parking required by its highly mobile customers. Its inventory "smoothing" practices and rapid movement of merchandise across its well-designed distribution center shipping docks mean that it can operate with minimal distribution center capacity. These practices would be impossible without the operation of a "state-of-the-art" inventory system, one operated from one of the largest "data warehouses," containing information about customer buying patterns, in existence today. A large company-operated truck fleet further contributes to both reduced cost and precise control over shipments. To connect members of its far-flung "family," Wal-Mart for years has operated one of the most sophisticated in-house teleconferencing and broadcasting networks, one used constantly in communicating with people in its stores from its Bentonville headquarters. In addition, it operates an extensive fleet of aircraft to enable its managers to spend as much time as possible close to customers. High utilization is the watchword for all of these assets, and all are operated with a spirit of frugality characterized by the company's spartan facilities, beginning with the CEO's small, somewhat cluttered office.

THE VALUE PROFIT CHAIN

The value profit chain comprises a series of interrelated phenomena organized according to the following assumptions:

1. Customer loyalty and commitment are the primary drivers of growth and profitability.

2. Customer loyalty and commitment emanate from customer satisfaction compared to competition.

3. Customer satisfaction results from the realization of high levels of value compared to competitors.

4. Value is created by satisfied, committed, loyal, and productive employees. Its perception by customers (both internal and external to the organization), suppliers, and other important constituents of an organization is enhanced most by the satisfaction levels of those employees in direct contact with constituents.

5. Employee satisfaction results from several factors, the most important of which are the "fairness" of management; the quality of one's peers in the workplace; the opportunity for personal growth on the job; *capability,* the latitude within limits to deliver results to customers; levels of customer satisfaction achieved in customer-facing jobs (the so-called mirror effect); and monetary compensation, often in that order according to a number of studies of the phenomenon. It is at the heart of efforts to build the organizational capability to deliver both high value and low costs.

6. Relationships between elements of the value profit chain are self-reinforcing. They can work for or against organizational performance.

When organizations get elements of the value profit chain right, the results are dramatic. For example, data describing how Vanguard and Wal-Mart rated against their major competitors on various value profit chain components in the year 2000 are shown in Figures 1-3 and 1-4, respectively.[10] We review them by starting at the performance "source"—

■ **Figure 1–3** COMPETITIVE VALUE PROFIT CHAIN PERFORMANCE:
THE VANGUARD GROUP VERSUS MAJOR MUTUAL FUND FAMILIES*

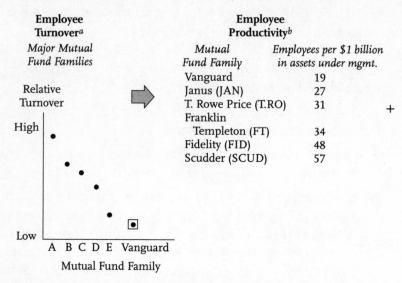

Employee
Turnover[a]

Major Mutual
Fund Families

Relative
Turnover

High

Low

A B C D E Vanguard

Mutual Fund Family

Employee
Productivity[b]

Mutual Fund Family	Employees per $1 billion in assets under mgmt.
Vanguard	19
Janus (JAN)	27
T. Rowe Price (T.RO)	31
Franklin Templeton (FT)	34
Fidelity (FID)	48
Scudder (SCUD)	57

[a] Based on the results of a survey conducted by Roger Hallowell, 1995.

[b] *Sources:* Company annual reports, The Investment Company Institute, company public relations offices, and *Dun's Business Rankings, 1996* (Bethlehem, PA: Dun and Bradstreet, Inc.).

[c] *Source:* Vanguard-supplied industry data.

[d] *Sources:* Lipper Analytical Services, Inc., and Vanguard.

[e] *Sources:* Vanguard, *The Vanguard Advantage, 1996,* based on data provided by Lipper Analytical Services, Inc.

[f] Adapted from Roger Hallowell, *Dual Competitive Advantage in Labor Dependent Services,* doctoral dissertation, Harvard Business School, 1997, p. 44.

[g] Based on 1994 data supplied to Roger Hallowell by the U.S. Securities and Exchange Commission.

[h] *Sources:* ICI and Libber Analytical Services, Inc. in *The Future of Money Management in America: 1995 Edition* (New York: Stanford C. Bernstein & Co., 1996).

* This figure is adapted from material presented in Roger Hallowell, *Dual Competitive Advantage in Labor Dependent Services,* doctoral dissertation, Harvard Businesss School, 1997.

employee satisfaction, commitment, loyalty, and productivity—and working our way toward profit and growth.

Employee Satisfaction, Commitment, Loyalty, and Productivity   The process starts with selection and continues with training, the development of support systems, and the implementation of measures and incentives for performance against organization goals.

Advertising Expenses[c]

Advertising as a %
of Average Assets

Mutual Fund Family	1994	1992
Vanguard	0.5	0.7
Franklin Templeton	2.3	2.9
Dreyfus	4.8	6.2
Fidelity Investments	1.6	3.8
Scudder	2.8	2.9
T. Rowe Price	3.9	5.7
Janus	3.7	2.5

Mean Expense Ratios, 1995[d]

	Vanguard	Industry mean
All Equity	40	153
All Bonds	22	103
Domestic Equity	38	144
International Equity	49	185
Money Market	23	61
Taxable Bonds	23	113
Municipal Bonds	20	93

Fund Performance (Return), 1995[e]

Percent of Funds
Outperformed by Vanguard Funds

Fund Type	1 Yr.	5 Yrs.	10 Yrs.
Equity Funds	74%	62%	56%
Balanced Funds	91	83	79
Fixed-Income Funds	84	80	91
Tax Exempt Funds	71	88	97
Money Market Funds	93	95	100

Relative Cost and Service Positions of Major Direct-Market U.S. Mutual Fund Families[f]

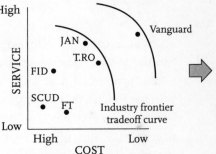

Dual competitive advantage trade-off curve

High · SERVICE · Low

JAN · T.RO · FID · SCUD · FT · Vanguard

Industry frontier tradeoff curve

High · COST · Low

Customer Satisfaction Complaints, 1994[g]

Complaints to U.S. Securities
and Exchange Commission

Mutual Fund Family	Service Complaints per $B in assets*	Performance Complaints per $B in assets*
Vanguard	0.08	0.01
Fidelity	0.33	0.02
T. Rowe Price	0.33	0.10
Scudder	0.47	0.25
Dreyfus	0.49	0.07

Annual Growth Rates, 1986–1994[h]

	Annual Growth Rates 1986–94
Fidelity	20%
Vanguard	22
Dreyfus	9
T. Rowe Price	15
Scudder	17
Franklin Templeton	16

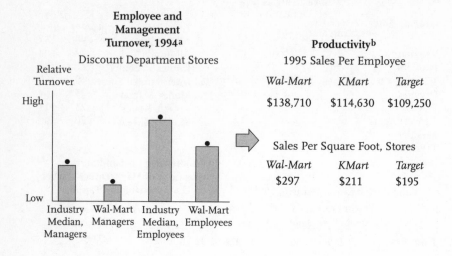

■ **Figure 1–4** COMPETITIVE VALUE PROFIT CHAIN PERFORMANCE:
WAL-MART STORES, INC. VERSUS DISCOUNT DEPARTMENT STORES*

Employee and Management Turnover, 1994[a]

Discount Department Stores

Relative Turnover

High

Low

Industry Median, Managers | Wal-Mart Managers | Industry Median, Employees | Wal-Mart Employees

Productivity[b]

1995 Sales Per Employee

	Wal-Mart	KMart	Target
	$138,710	$114,630	$109,250

Sales Per Square Foot, Stores

	Wal-Mart	KMart	Target
	$297	$211	$195

At Vanguard, the effort centers around "crew members," the 10,000 "honest-to-God, down-to-earth human beings, each with their own hopes and fears and financial goals" employed by the organization.[11] People are selected first on their ability to treat everyone with respect in an organization with no management perquisites. Given Vanguard's careful selection and training efforts as well as the effective support systems that it provides its frontline crew members, it is possible to increase their latitude to make decisions on behalf of clients. The rule is: "Do what's right. If you're not sure, ask your boss."[12] Recognition for individual effort is provided through the nonmonetary Award of Excellence, based on recommendations from peers. The organization's Partnership Plan recognizes group performance by enrolling every employee as a partner on the first day of work, entitling the partner or "crew member" to share in the organization's *earnings,* defined as a combination of (1) the difference between Vanguard's expenses and the expenses that would prevail if its average expense ratio equaled those of its largest competitors and (2) the extra returns (net of any return shortfalls) earned for shareholders by its funds and portfolio managers.

As shown in Figure 1-3, Vanguard's employee turnover rates, a signifi-

Operating Margins[c]

Firm	1994	1993	1992
Wal-Mart	7.1%	7.5%	7.5%
Target	5.4	5.6	5.5
KMart	2.4	3.8	5.9

Consumer Ratings[d]

Chain	Value*	Service ("Sales Help")
Wal-Mart	5	4
Meijer	4	3
Target	5	2
ShopKo	3	2
Bradlees	3	1
Venture	4	1
Montgomery Ward	3	2
Fred Mayer	3	2
KMart	3	1
Caldor	3	1
Ames	2	1

**Growth, Profit, and Return on Equity,
1985-1995[e]**

Company	Average Annual Growth in Sales	Average Annual Growth in Profit	Return on Equity
Wal-Mart	27.0%	23.6%	24.2%
Target	10.3%	.9%	14.3%
KMart	4.4%	negative	8.6%
Sears	negative	3.4%	9.2%

[a] *Sources:* Wal-Mart company data, "1995 Senn Delaney Employee Turnover Study," and "1995 Multi-Outlet Retailer Compensation Survey Results, William M. Mercer, Inc." All data are for 1994.

[b] *Source:* Margaret Gilliam and John Seitz, "Wal-Mart Stores, Inc.," CS First Boston Equity Research, August, 1995.

[c] *Sources:* Company annual reports; George C. Strachan, "The Discount Store Industry Paradox: Consumed by an Appetite for Growth," Goldman Sachs U.S. Research, 1995; and George C. Strachan, "The State of the Discount Store Industry," Goldman Sachs U.S. Research, 1994.

[d] *Source: Consumer Reports,* November, 1994, p. 721; 5 is the highest rating and 1 the lowest.

[e] Computations based on data from Compustat.

* This figure is adapted from material presented in Roger Hallowell, *Dual Competitive Advantage in Labor Dependent Services,* doctoral dissertation, Harvard Businesss School, 1997.

cant measure of loyalty, are substantially below those of its major competitors in the industry. Commitment is not measured formally, but the large
volume of letters received annually in the CEO's office expressing commitment to the organization's role as "advocate for the investor" and its simple
Golden Rule–like primary core value of "respect for each individual" suggests its presence. This—in addition to the strategy to which Vanguard
adheres in delivering value and the policies, practices, and processes it
employs in implementing the strategy—accounts for much of the reason
that Vanguard's employee productivity is at least 30% higher than that of
any major competitor and more than twice the industry average.

Wal-Mart's "family" of associates had grown to more than 1.2 million
by the end of 2001. The primary criterion according to which associates
are chosen is simply "niceness." Nice people are then trained in "the Wal-
Mart way" by the company's experienced managers. This ranges from
various aspects of the physical job to be done to ways of greeting and
treating customers. A particular emphasis is then placed on the recognition of associates by their managers, with a constant effort made to maintain associate commitment through the extensive sharing of store-level
performance data, daily meetings to discuss matters needing attention,
and in-store contests and awards. Wages for Wal-Mart's store managers
and associates are only on par with those for comparable organizations,
but everyone is eligible for a stock purchase plan that enables them to
buy Wal-Mart at a 15% discount to market. Roughly 50% of all associates
do so. The appreciation in the stock has accounted for much of the
wealth found throughout the organization. These are among the contributors to Wal-Mart's unusually high associate satisfaction, commitment,
loyalty, and productivity, even as the company has moved into larger markets, with more than half its stores now in nonrural markets.

The results? At Wal-Mart, productivity, as measured by sales per employee or by square foot of operating space, outstrips discount superstore
competitors significantly, by up to 20% more than its nearest competitor,
as shown in Figure 1-4. It is a factor in Wal-Mart's superior productivity
in its use of space, typically 30% greater than its nearest competitor, a
critical factor in explaining its performance in an industry with huge
fixed costs tied up in retail "bricks." Both these figures are in part products of the organization's lower employee turnover rates, as measured

against the industry, at both the store manager and frontline employee levels.

Customer Satisfaction and Loyalty   Vanguard's goal of high long-term return to investors requires a high degree of investor loyalty if the goal is to be achieved. Its other goal of good, dependable customer service is intended to help the organization achieve the first goal. Together, they have produced outstanding results, as shown in Figure 1-3. U.S. Securities and Exchange Commission data, collected regularly for all financial institutions, indicates that Vanguard's performance complaints from clients (per billion dollars of assets) are about half those of its nearest competitor, the Fidelity Group, and lower than that of other fund groups by several orders of magnitude. Similarly, complaints about service are a fraction of those of its nearest competitor. Judging from the money flowing into and out of fund groups in recent years, it appears that Vanguard's investors are much more loyal as well.

Wal-Mart typically has ranked at or near the top of ratings by the *Consumer Reports* survey of customers' perceptions of value and sales help for various discount department stores and mass merchandisers.[13] Individual surveys conducted by independent researchers from time to time have tended to confirm these findings.[14] Consumer-unaided feedback to the organization is more frequent and generally more positive than that for its major competitors, according to data compiled by PlanetFeedback, a market monitoring organization.[15] The organization operated in many communities without serious competition for many years, but that has changed. Despite growing competition, Wal-Mart has been able to maintain relatively high levels of sales per associate and per square foot of store space, admittedly a poor but nevertheless suggestive measure of the organization's ability to retain its customers' loyalty.

Growth and Profitability   Given what Vanguard has achieved on other dimensions of the value profit chain, it should be no surprise that its growth rate has been the highest among large fund groups in recent years, as shown in Figure 1-3. Because the organization is operated on a mutual basis, with investors as owners, profitability might be thought of as a concept foreign to Vanguard. In fact, however, it has real meaning, because it is used to calculate bonuses for crew members. It is based, in part, on the improvement in the difference between ratios of expenses to funds under management between Vanguard and its competitors. On this basis, Vanguard's expenses declined by 10 to 60%, depending on the class of assets, between 1985 and 2000. Those of the industry as a whole increased from 15 to 30% over the same period of time. This performance has yielded Vanguard's crew members substantial annual bonuses during this entire period.

In the decade between 1990 and 2000, despite its size, Wal-Mart sales grew at an average rate of 20.6% to a size exceeding all but one U.S. corporation in revenues (which it has since surpassed). Its margins regularly exceeded those of its major competitors, and its growth in profits and stock price performance outpaced them as well, as shown in Figure 1-4.

THE VALUE EQUATION

Value to customers, suppliers, investors, and other important constituencies can be characterized by four elements, arrayed in the following manner:

$$\text{Value} = \frac{\text{Results} + \text{Process Quality}}{\text{Customer Access Costs} + \text{Price}}$$

Value is a watchword at Vanguard. It is measured for desired investors in terms of overall long-term investment results after management fees. There is an equally strong emphasis on the quality of service provided to Vanguard clients, although on this score the organization is faced with a much more daunting task of maintaining superiority over other large fund organizations that are also noted for good customer service and state-of-the-art service technologies. Nevertheless, as we saw earlier, Vanguard has managed to achieve lower complaint levels than its major competitors on both performance and service dimensions. One reason for lower performance complaint levels may be Vanguard's reluctance to emphasize short-term investment gains in its promotional message, on which the organization spends a fraction of the amount spent by its competitors when measured against assets under management, as shown in Figure 1-4. Vanguard instead relies on word-of-mouth (viral) marketing, to which good service is an important contributor. As a result, client access to fund administrators and service personnel has a high priority, as suggested by the deployment of Vanguard's Swiss Army of executives and crew members to provide peak-load client service when necessary. Finally, Vanguard has been, in a sense, a price leader in the mutual fund industry, pioneering the concept of "no load" funds, those sold with no sales charge. This has required that the organization place a heavy reliance on direct marketing because of an unwillingness to pay sales charges incurred by competitors to encourage brokers and other sales representatives to employ "push" marketing techniques—as opposed to Vanguard's "pull" strategy.

Value for crew members results from a combination of base pay and cost-based incentive compensation, high-quality information support systems, values that emphasize respect for the individual and the absence of perquisites for crew members of various rank, latitude (within limits) to deliver results to clients, frequent recognition, and stable employment in an organization with steadily growing opportunity. Vanguard's location in suburban Philadelphia is easily reachable, thereby reducing access costs. The company also provides various low-cost, on-site support services, such as the subsidized company "galley" where everyone eats together.

Similarly, Wal-Mart's stated policy of Everyday Low Prices provides a strong appeal for value-oriented customers. Merchandise selection and availability, engineered by a cadre of "area directors" responsible for merchandising various departments in each store, is also considered an important element of the results delivered to customers. Area directors are responsible as well for customer service. The importance of this task is emphasized frequently and is underscored by the practice of visiting Wal-Mart executives who personally help customers during every visit to a store. Although this is a somewhat symbolic gesture, it is an effective way to remind everyone of the importance of customer service even in an organization emphasizing everyday low prices. Wal-Mart also turns customer access costs to its advantage by providing store locations that are convenient for those customers it seeks and offering them ample free parking as well. Finally, Wal-Mart's costs, not only for merchandise, but for operations, are the lowest in the industry. Tremendous bargaining leverage ensures that no competitor receives a lower cost. Wal-Mart's merchandisers make one good buy after another, and the logistics organization coordinates shipments to maximize truckload economies for shipments that are often "cross-docked," that is, moved through shipping facilities without going into inventory, and perhaps financed by large suppliers with whom Wal-Mart has partnerships. Finally, advertising, as at Vanguard, comprises largely of no-cost, word-of-mouth "viral" promotion on the part of loyal customers.

Associates similarly must see value in working at Wal-Mart, given the organization's generally lower rates of associate turnover than its competitors. The results for frontline associates are represented by a combination of modest pay, flexible working hours, and opportunities to invest in company stock at a discount. Just as important, though, is a culture centered around the selection of "nice" people as associates, frequent recognition, a concern for "family" (both on and off the job), and an atmosphere of excitement on the job. Managers assert that every manager is a human resource manager at Wal-Mart. The "people representative" at each store not only organizes hiring and employee scheduling but also maintains "open-door" access to any employee in the store having trouble with their manager. Process quality is reinforced for associates by the policy of sharing store-level financial information with everyone on a regular basis, a policy that also provides everyone with an idea of how their efforts influence performance. The goal is to provide a sense of "ownership" on the part of everyone. As one manager put it, "This is their store. That's the way it should be. They have responsibility and ownership."[16] Don Soderquist, at the time chief operating officer, provided a top-level view of the value equation for associates at Wal-Mart when he said, "We believe we can only make customers happy when our associates are happy."[17]

Much of what is described here does not cost much. In fact, if it contributes to the higher productivity levels attributed to Wal-Mart's operations, it represents a significant competitive advantage. Although mass merchandisers do not release separate figures for labor costs as a proportion of sales, the catchall category of "operating, selling, and general and administrative" costs largely comprises salaries and wages. As a proportion of sales at Wal-Mart, it is typically 20% below that of its competitors, suggesting that a combination of higher productivity and nonmonetary features of workplace quality deliver much lower labor costs for Wal-Mart than for its closest competitors. Clearly, this value package does not appeal to all prospective employees. Wal-Mart's management understands what makes the company and its jobs appealing and selects its employees accordingly.

Wal-Mart generates results for vendors through the large volumes of merchandise it can sell in relatively short periods of time. Even though the company has a reputation for tough negotiating practices, it is generally regarded as fair. It has achieved this reputation through practices designed to result in low prices while creating opportunities for higher margins for its suppliers. By supplying superior, current sales information to suppliers, for example, Wal-Mart enables them to manage inventories more efficiently. Under some of its contracts, Wal-Mart provides immediate payment for product shipped from nearby warehouses as compensation for the extra expenses incurred in providing special replenishment services to the organization.

As noted earlier, there are differing views about the results that Wal-Mart has created for the communities in which its stores are located. On the plus side are the high-value (not high-priced) merchandise brought to residents; the fact that in many areas of low population concentration a Wal-Mart store attracts customers from outside a community's normal trading area; and of course the jobs brought to the community as well as the increased taxes received from Wal-Mart and its employees. On the other hand, Wal-Mart has been criticized for putting small stores out of business and contributing to the decline of the traditional business centers of many communities. Others have argued that it has merely hastened a trend already in motion while making it possible for the best small retailers to survive by fashioning merchandise and service offerings to avoid direct competition with the giant.

All this helps explain why Wal-Mart generates extraordinary value for investors. In the decade beginning in 1982, for example, Wal-Mart stock provided the highest returns to investors of any stock in the Standard & Poors 500 index. In the 20 years beginning in that same year, it has produced the highest total return to investors of any company in its industry.

Several factors deserve comment here.

First, not for a moment do we believe that the outstanding performance measures of these two organizations that we have presented here are coincidental. Nor do we believe that an organization can perform very well on one of these dimensions without performing well on others.

Second, there is a direct relationship between the conceptual elements shown here. Increasing amounts of evidence, which we discuss in greater detail later, point to employee capability leading to satisfaction, commitment, loyalty, and productivity as the drivers of much of what outstanding organizations are able to achieve. This does not occur in a vacuum. It is the product of effective leadership and clear, positive values that are aligned with an organization's mission, one that is itself both clear and highly focused.

Third, sustained industry leadership is not a product of a vision and strategy completely thought out at the outset by one or even a group of visionaries. The primary reason that Sam Walton adopted the small-town strategy for Wal-Mart was not a vision that carefully avoided positioning Wal-Mart against larger competitors or markets. It was because his wife, Helen, refused to move to a town with more than 10,000 in population when Walton lost the lease on his original store.[18] As another example, Helen Walton is credited by her husband with the idea for establishing benefits and profit sharing at Wal-Mart long before the company first issued its stock publicly and encountered its first attempt on the part of unions to organize associates. In Helen Walton's words,[19]

> We were on a trip, driving someplace, and we were talking about the high salary that Sam was earning, and about all the money and benefits that he was paying the officers of the company in order to keep his top people. He explained that the people in the stores didn't get any of those benefits, and I think it was the first time I realized how little the company was doing for them. I suggested to him that unless those people were on board, the top people might not last long either. I remember it because he didn't really appreciate my point of view at the time.

Similarly, Vanguard might be a somewhat different organization today if John Bogle hadn't been fired by the board of the Wellington Management Company (eight years after he had undertaken an unwise merger of the two organizations) because of differences in view about the direction for the organization (although in all fairness he had given a great deal more thought to an ideal overall position and strategy than had Sam Walton).

There are many more similarities than contrasts between these two organizations. Note the significant parallels on which their successes have been built:

1. Both were founded on a value-centered philosophy for customers—"advocate for the investor" in one case and "agent for the customer" in the other—a philosophy extended to employees and investors as well.

2. Both developed a strategy aimed at a clearly focused customer group.

3. Both gave explicit attention to relationships between elements of the value equation—results, process quality, customer access costs, and price.

4. Both rely on customer and employee loyalty, important elements of the value profit chain, as focal points of a successful business formula.

5. Both have identified the shared values on which these businesses are based and have employed these shared values in everyday decision-making.

6. Both have put together operating strategies comprising policies, practices, procedures, and processes that reinforce the shared values while leveraging value over cost—operating strategies that provide operating focus for everything these organizations do.

7. Both achieve profitability and high growth, not by targeting them, but as a by-product of efforts to provide value for customers, employees, and others.

One analyst's report sums up succinctly the parallels between Vanguard and Wal-Mart:[20]

The similarity between their market share progressions is striking. Both organizations seek to exploit good service and brand-name products using a structurally lower expense base. The share gains these companies have achieved have bred continued and greater cost advantages.

■ Questions for Managers

Among questions raised by the material presented in this chapter are the following. Some are incorporated into the value profit chain audit presented in Appendix B.

1. What is your organization's "business"? Is it defined in terms of value and results versus products and services?

2. How is your organization positioned against the needs of preferred customers and in relation to the capabilities and offerings of competitors and suppliers?

3. How carefully has your organization defined who it will serve and who it will not serve?

4. By what means—policies, practices, processes, organization—is value leveraged over costs for customers, employees, and others?

5. How focused are your organization's views of preferred customers and employees on the one hand and operating strategies for leveraging value over cost for them on the other?

6. To what degree does your organization's value delivery system (bricks and mortar, systems, networks, and so on) enable its operating strategy to leverage value over costs?

7. To what extent do you measure and track elements of the value profit chain?

8. To what extent are managers and employees recognized and rewarded on the basis of achieving value profit chain measures?

9. What do customers and employees seek on various value equation dimensions? How do you know?

The common theme running through the conceptual relationships presented here is value. Value is the constant at the heart of all important ideas concerning strategy and management. Given the myriad concepts set forth with a wide variety of terminology in today's communication-rich society, it is easy to forget this. Managers need a unifying fact-based framework to utilize the multitude of management concepts being proposed today, too many on the basis of little systematic evidence. Here we have reviewed one such fact-based comprehensive framework that has been under development for nearly two decades, one based on the strategic value vision, the value profit chain, and the value equation. Two familiar but comprehensive examples, those of Vanguard and Wal-Mart, who have so dissociated themselves from traditional competition that they are more likely to benchmark themselves against each other than companies in their respective industries, are used here to illustrate the concepts. These are familiar examples drawn from greenfield start-ups facing little need for basic changes in direction throughout highly successful and extended periods of growth and profitability. What about firms facing the need for change?

Chapter 2

Rethinking the Business Using Value-Centered Concepts

THE ADMONISHMENT TO RETHINK a business based on the needs of various important constituencies sounds so simple. If that's the case, though, why are so few organizations able to do this over long periods of time? Even some of the more successful, at least in the intermediate term, lose this ability as internal pride based on past success turns to external arrogance, something customers sense very quickly. Worse yet, they lose the ability to listen to the needs of customers, suppliers, and others and to import ideas from successful practitioners both inside and outside the organization. Consider what happened at IBM.

■ Value-Focused Transformation at IBM

At IBM, the task of new leadership in 1993 was made measurably more difficult or easier, depending on how you look at it, by the fact that the company was in the process of losing $8 billion in 1 year and was feared by many to be a candidate for dismemberment or takeover. Louis Gerstner, IBM's new CEO and the first without a pedigree forged by years of service with the company, didn't have to create dissatisfaction with the status quo among its employees. The feeling already hung heavily over what was once one of the proudest companies in the world.

The causes of IBM's downward spiral were many. They included a failure on the part of management to reinforce values that had made the company great (an issue we revisit in Chapter 11), the failure to redefine the company in the face of a rapidly changing environment that no longer placed a heavy reliance on mainframe computing, a devotion to an outmoded product strategy, and an arrogance reflected in the organization's inability or unwillingness to listen to the changing needs of customers.

Only 8 years later, basic changes made as part of a value-centered transformation at IBM were beginning to pay off. The company that CEO Louis Gerstner had encountered upon taking over in 1993 was in many ways unrecognizable from the IBM of 2001.

Take business software, for example: the company was internally producing hundreds of applications but garnering a small market share and making very little money.[1] IBM's software-producing competitors were serving clients through partnerships that enabled them to remain much more flexible while bringing new products to market with significantly greater speed than IBM. The company clearly had to play a game of catch-up. While closing or selling most of its internal software development capability, IBM entered into 50 strategic partnerships with some of the largest software developers during 2000, essentially outsourcing much of the development as part of its effort to sell total solutions. The same was occurring throughout the company. In fact, a third of its revenue was attributable to partnerships in 2000, a sharp contrast with 5% in 1993.

Although hardware sales remained flat at IBM in 2000, its International Global Services division (IGS) continued to be the company's consistent growth engine. This was not the result of an inspirational decision to provide support services for IBM's products; these had always been offered. Rather, it was the result of efforts to emphasize service as a business rather than as a means to sell hardware, particularly the mainframe computers for which the company had been famous. This meant that increased emphasis would be placed on "turnkey" contracts under which IBM took on full responsibility for managing a customer's information-processing facility. The decision was made to focus on services that could in some cases hasten the demise of IBM's legendary mainframe computers, the backbone of the company's success for decades. The services were designed to help IBM clients reorient their information systems to the Internet, including the use of distributed computing through many small computers rather than one large one.[2] It required petitioning a federal judge to lift the terms of a consent decree handed down in 1956 that forced IBM to operate its service business on an arm's-length relationship with product divisions to prevent the company from exercising monopoly power over competitors. This effort was successful in 1994.

Much of this is taken for granted today. Only a few years ago, however, this would have been considered heresy at IBM. What happened? An exasperated board of directors, harried by investors and concerned about IBM's future, brought in new leadership from outside the company. To make matters worse, the new CEO, Louis Gerstner, had no background in technology, coming instead from a background in consumer products and services. This represented a break with a proud 79-year history of success and a series of internally developed leaders.

At the time, IBM's leadership was desperate for solutions. It even resorted to the first early retirement program in the company's history, designed to shed 35,000 employees. To the surprise of management, 50,000 decided to accept the early retirement incentives, in part because things were going so poorly. To the surprise of no one, however, John Akers, then the company's CEO and a lifetime IBM employee, repeatedly reaffirmed the company's primary commitment to mainframe computers as the core of IBM's future strategy. Under this strategy, service support was regarded primarily as a means to sell computers, a matter that was reflected in the relatively unprofitable service contracts into which the company was entering. Things were so bad at the company that even the increasingly invasive attitude of arrogance ascribed to many of its employees was on the decline. In a sense, the way was paved for a transformation by new management.

Among the many decisions that Gerstner and his team made upon taking over at IBM, two stand out for their importance. While maintaining that he didn't have a vision for IBM, a comment that received wide publicity and criticism at the time, Gerstner began the implementation of a vision. First, he announced shortly after assuming his job, "We must become the premier solution-provider to our customers."[3] Note the absence of reference to products (especially mainframe computers) or services. The emphasis was on results. In each of IBM's businesses, customer need for solutions became the focus of attention, requiring that the company's management spend much more time with customers. (The company's partnering strategy for software, described earlier, was a direct descendant of this philosophy. By 2001, it was managed by means of a giant "solutions map," a grid breaking down the world by industry, geography, customer size, type of computer system running a customer's software, and the type of business problem addressed by the IBM "consortium" of partnerships.)[4]

To become a primary solutions provider, IBM's leadership made a second momentous decision. It reversed a decision that had been made by Gerstner's predecessor to break up the organization into several self-contained "Baby Blues," a derivation of IBM's "Big Blue" nickname. After all, how could the company become a solutions provider through a group of decentralized, uncoordinated subsidiaries? Gone were the service contracts written with little or no profit margin as a means to sell mainframe computers. In their place were business arrangements designed on the basis of the lifetime value of the total stream of revenue from a customer relationship, regardless of product or service source.

The execution of this strategy of course required many additional decisions. These included the further reduction in the size of the organization, a move carried out in accordance with one of IBM's forgotten core values, "respect for the individual," a core value that many had interpreted as implying the guarantee of lifetime employment at IBM, something never envisioned by the company's founder.[5] Even more important were increases in importance for stock option incentives in the company's compensation plans, the tying of compensation in varying degrees to overall company performance as opposed to that for product or service lines, the abandonment of "management by consensus" that required lengthy meetings of many people, an increasing emphasis on function over form (even including a lowered emphasis on the importance of the quality of the "foils"—overhead transparencies—used in company presentations), and a change in behaviors related to dress and other practices. All seem logical in retrospect. However, all represented distinct departures from previous practice.

By 2001, IBM had regained its footing as a major provider of information systems solutions to a wide range of clients. Its International Global Services division was in the midst of a 5-year plan to double its size by adding $30 billion in revenue, an accomplishment that would make it IBM's largest unit, with 46% of its revenues. Perhaps most exciting of all, the company announced an overarching initiative, Project Eliza, to encompass efforts by many of IBM's business units to achieve something called autonomous computing, the development of computers capable of managing and fixing themselves. This is a potential solution to one of the greatest problems of all, finding enough skilled workers to manage increasingly complex technology involving larger amounts of hardware and software produced from a number of different sources.[6]

Note what happened at IBM. The need for change was born out of an acute need for action generally recognized by employees, investors, customers, and others. A model for change was required. The one advanced by Lou Gerstner and his associates was centered around the provision of results to important constituencies, both outside and inside the IBM organization. They then set about, through various processes for change, to do more with less, increasing the value delivered to these important constituencies. All this represented such a compelling and logical response that it overcame whatever vestiges of opposition that may have existed in the organization.

IBM today is characteristic of an organization in an advanced state of change. Others have not progressed as far, but they are following a progression of steps important for managers in all organizations.

■ Successfully Rethinking the Business

We are seeing a sea change in the visions being fashioned for many large organizations, in response to either stagnant performance or a change in leadership. Such efforts are taking on identifiable patterns.

From Products to Services

Nearly all net new jobs in the U.S. economy in the past 20 years have been created in the service sector. This is true of nearly all highly developed economies in the world. In contrast to popular belief, it is not a new phenomenon, as those who deplore what they call the "burger-flipping" economy would have us believe. The last decade in which jobs in manufacturing establishments exceeded those in service establishments in the U.S. was that beginning in 1890.[7]

The shift in emphasis from products to services has taken several forms, depending on management intent. Producers of higher technology products, for example, have found that it is impossible to maintain a competitive posture without a full range of support services, a necessary component of a competitive product service package.[8] Such organizations have tended to organize the delivery of services as an arm of a product-oriented organization.

Others have found such profit potential in services that they have reorganized to highlight service as a separate business venture. For example, Hewlett-Packard's Worldwide Customer Support Operations endeavors to provide seamless 24 hour, 7 day per week service on a global basis from service centers located strategically across the world's time zones in a range of languages reflecting HP's worldwide customer base. This organization, operating as a separate business capable of servicing customer networks encompassing other vendors' equipment, now produces 15% of the company's revenue.[9]

A third and even more strategically important form of the trend from product to service typically involves companies whose products have become "commodities," difficult to differentiate from those of competitors. In a fast-moving world of product development, technological change, and high performance expectations, it has become harder and harder to make competitive returns from the manufacture of basic commodities—coal, sulfur, and even certain chemicals, as well as durable goods (computers, appliances, autos, and even software)—sold to business users and consumers. There is growing agreement that even technology is not immune to "commoditization." In many such industries, it has been found that significantly higher margins await the firm willing either to service the products it manufactures or literally to convert its products into components of overall services.

There is a natural bias in most manufacturing firms toward making things. The shift in emphasis from manufacturing as an end in itself, with services provided mainly to support the product, to a strategy of manufacturing as a component activity designed to provide products and services to customers has often been difficult and traumatic. Many of these firms were founded by engineers and appeal to people with a fondness for things as opposed to more intangible services.

The notion of a shift to a significant emphasis on services is not usually rejected out of hand so much as it is subtly ignored, at least until the managers responsible for services focus attention by proposing that their activities be regarded as stand-alone businesses supporting not only products sold in-house but competitors' products as well. It is as if successful goods-producing organizations were being asked to engage in "foreign" behaviors: to work with ideas rather than things, to desert the factory to spend time with customers. Nevertheless, as the gap in margins between manufacturing and service-providing activities has widened, it has become painfully clear, even to the most hardened manufacturing advocates, where the money is being made.

Ask anyone, for example, to define Otis Elevator's business and most people would say, of course, elevators. However, several important trends in the industry forced Otis's own management to rethink this definition some years ago. First was the realization that margins on the manufacture and sale of elevators were dropping to the point at which they were negligible. Installation carried with it higher margins, but Otis typically shared these with contractors who were responsible for buildings in which Otis's equipment was installed. The real money was in the service of these machines. Over time, elevator design and manufacture came to be seen as a necessary vehicle to obtain elevator service contracts, the source of nearly all of Otis's profit. It sounds simple on paper, but the process of changing the mentality of the organization from a product to a service orientation was very difficult. Even today, managers are caught occasionally reverting to the old product mentality.

Given the importance of the cost of elevators in the overall cost of a building, it became more and more important that Otis design products that could be operated with greater efficiency and dependability. This required more instrumentation, eventually leading to the installation of what we now would regard as a computer with medium to large applications involving two or more elevators. It raised the potential of greater service costs associated with more complex technology, but it also provided the opportunity for Otis to design elevators that today can be monitored electronically, with problems diagnosed through a remote elevator monitoring (REM) system connecting an elevator with the OTISLINE Center. This enables some problems, such as door opening times, to be adjusted remotely. For others, a decision can be made to send a technician already armed with a diagnosis to the site. This further enhances Otis's ability to deliver profitable service in an economic way.[10]

Similarly, a number of chemicals producers have found that the standardized nature of their output has forced them to turn to services as a source of differentiation. After all, you get little credit for trying to differentiate yourself from a competitor by developing a compound of H_2SO_4 and trying to sell it as an improved form of sulfuric acid (H_2SO_3). In fact, at least one producer of sulfuric acid, a company at the time called American Cyanamid, considered exiting the business because of increasingly lower margins on the product. At times it seemed that only a psychological dedication to a business on which the company had been founded prevented its management from exiting the business.

In fact, a way of rescuing the business was prompted by a critical need on the part of customers for increased value. Users of sulfuric acid were beset with increasing problems of recycling spent acids in ways that complied with more and more stringent environmental laws. It wasn't until American Cyanamid's management decided to respond to the needs of their customers by developing a sulfuric acid recycling service that the business completely turned around. This required the development of spent acid recycling stations, where spent acids could be reconstituted to their original condition, as well as the rescheduling of delivery trucks to enable them both to deliver new acids and to pick up spent acids. American Cyanamid exited the sulfuric acid business in favor of the sulfuric acid service business. Similar high-value services are being performed at relatively low cost and substantial margins by other chemicals producers as well. It literally has saved several businesses.

The transition has been much more difficult in industries such as auto manufacture, distribution, and sale, the endeavors of traditionally run manufacturing firms and the auto dealerships they have created. For years, factory-authorized auto dealers were trained to run their businesses according to strictly organized accounting systems. The systems were structured to encourage dealers to charge all overhead costs of their dealerships (such as those associated with occupancy, utilities, and telephone) to the service side of the business with the goal of breaking even financially on service. Whatever they made on sales, having covered the sales overhead costs with margins on service, was considered profit. It provided an easy "rule of thumb" for managing the business, but it led over the years to the assumption among dealers that profit was made on the sales of product, not service. The quality of service in many dealerships reflected this assumption.

The mentality among those manufacturing autos was little different. In the U.S., sales executives were always ranked more highly on the salary structure than those in charge of service activities. The U.S. industry maintained the practice of reporting sales every 10 days. There were no comparable measures for service. Without such measures, it was impossible to recognize either corporate executives or dealerships for outstanding service.

Today, all this has changed. Accounting systems recommended for dealer use now attempt to break out costs to reveal the true profit of sales and service at the dealer level. Dealers are encouraged to meet standards of excellence in their service activities. They are also encouraged to sell service, as evidenced by the emphasis placed on the sale of long-term service contracts along with the sale of the vehicle, service contracts carrying an average margin several times that for the auto itself. Unfortunately, it took life-threatening performance declines and foreign competition (that demonstrated the importance of high-quality service in relationships with customers) to bring industry executives and dealers to their senses.

Even relatively new manufacturing endeavors, such as those for e-commerce software, are being redefined to emphasize services. By providing contracts to supply, service, and operate software on a monthly rental basis, so-called application service providers claim the ability to greatly shorten the time needed by clients to install new systems, train employees in their use, and make them fully operational and dependable. This has been particularly attractive to e-commerce ventures for which speed has taken on added value, given the warp speed at which competition moves and change occurs. Such firms as Verizon, with its traditional business core in the communications industry, have begun offering packages that include computing capability from one or more suppliers, e-commerce software configuration, network creation, the design of business processes, and day-to-day system management. Even at rental fees that represent significant savings in cash flow for their clients, software service firms like Verizon can improve the margins they could otherwise realize from simply selling the software. More importantly, they have created more steady cash and earnings flows associated with servicing rather than selling the software, an element of predictability valued by investors.

In recent years, with high-profile announcements of strategies to make service businesses a more important component of their activities from such organizations as IBM and General Electric, it has become almost fashionable to give services prominent billing in information supplied by many manufacturing organizations to investors. Ironically, in both these firms, services have long played prominent roles in their profit models. For IBM, service was such a formidable component of the company's competitive juggernaut that it was, as we have seen, forced in 1956 by the U.S. Justice Department to operate its data processing services division on an arms-length basis from its manufacturing units. At General Electric, the company began financing the appliances it sold as early as 1932,[11] thus providing the foundation for a GE Financial Services organization that today is the world's largest financial institution and the source of over 40% of GE's profits.[12]

What's different about the recent emphasis on services at IBM, GE, and others? It is the establishment of entire businesses to provide services formerly performed largely in support of company products. Further, it is characterized by a systematic effort to find and develop the service component of every manufacturing endeavor in which the organization engages.

As dramatic as the shift from an emphasis on products to services has been in many organizations, it is only the first step in the progression toward value-centered management that we will witness in the coming years, one characterized at its next stage of development by an emphasis not on products or services but on results.

FROM PRODUCTS AND SERVICES TO RESULTS

There is an old marketing saw that goes, "Customers don't buy quarter-inch drills; they buy quarter-inch holes." The implication is that a manager thinking he is in the quarter-inch-drill business is likely to be blindsided by a competitor who develops a totally different, better, less expensive way of making holes. The drill is a product. Drill repair is a service. The payoff comes when a company defines its business in terms of results.

Redefining a business in this manner can also lead to greatly expanded opportunity, to which managers of a small, successful, family-owned grass seed processing company in Central Ohio several decades ago could attest. The company, which had realized $2 to $3 million in sales and comfortable margins for decades before World War II, found itself with a new generation of family managers following the war. The search for expanded opportunity led management to bring in expert outside consultants, to no avail.

Then one day the company's senior management made its annual call on its banker to obtain the seasonal inventory financing required in a business producing its product in the fall and selling it in the spring. As usual, they began to present its carefully prepared spreadsheets to support the loan request when the banker said, "Put the spreadsheet away. You've always repaid your annual loan. You've got the money. What I'd really like to talk about is how to get rid of those brown spots in my backyard."

After explaining what the banker could do to deal with his problem and beginning the short walk back to the company's headquarters, it suddenly occurred to its managers what business they were in. It was not grass seed.

Taking the banker's cue, they concluded that they were in the business of green lawns. From that moment on, the business was transformed. To achieve a green lawn, the ordinary gardener needs not only seed for various soil and moisture conditions, but also seed for sunny and shady areas. In addition, fertilizers and weed control chemicals are needed, along with telephone hotlines and newsletters to enable lonely gardeners to obtain advice and share their misery with others. Customers giving themselves over wholeheartedly to the idea of achieving the most beautiful green lawns also offer good potential for the sale of seed and fertilizer spreaders as well as well-engineered lawnmowers and other gardening equipment.

By redefining its business in terms of results versus products or services, the management of the company, well-known in many parts of the world as O. M. Scott & Sons, was able to expand the company's sales by many times in the process of creating an industry-leading brand for its product and service line.

It found, though, that the exercise of rethinking the business, fully understanding the strategic direction, must be undertaken at every important strategic juncture. At O. M. Scott & Sons the entire process had to be repeated as Monsanto and other petrochemical companies entered the competition for green lawns by offering synthetic products, such as Astro-Turf. As a result of its reevaluation, O. M. Scott's management redefined the business as "natural green lawns," establishing a more heavily staffed professional division to sell to stadium owners, golf courses, and other major users of natural turf.

The transition from products and services to results has had a profound impact on the manner in which business units at General Electric have plotted their course. Near the outset of his tenure as CEO in 1981, Jack Welch challenged all GE businesses to become No. 1 or No. 2 in their respective industries or to become candidates for being fixed, closed, or sold.[13] This was intended as a wake-up call for business leaders who had become self-satisfied with their success. All responded, but some in less effective ways than others. In Welch's words, ". . . as a hard and fast rule, it is too easy to get around. What this bureaucracy of ours had been doing was simply redefining markets narrowly enough to make sure that we came out No. 1 or No. 2."[14]

Although Welch was aware of the problem, it was a U.S. Army colonel serving as a lecturer at the U.S. Army War College who, while addressing a middle management class at GE's Crotonville Management Institute, inspired a suggested remedy.[15] According to Welch, "the . . . [class] recommended a 'mind-set change' They said we needed to redefine all our current markets so that no business would have more than a 10 percent market share. That would force everyone to think differently about their businesses."[16]

What in fact happened was that many businesses became redefined in terms of results, suggesting greatly expanded opportunities in both products and related services needed to deliver an overall result to customers.

This led to an increased emphasis on services at GE. More important, it shifted attention to the potential for delivering results to important customers. For example, the company's aircraft engines business was redefined to become one of providing "thrust service," involving the sale of contracts for a guaranteed level of engine use. Included in such a contract, in addition to the engines, are parts, repairs, and financing.

In recent years, much the same thing has happened at Boeing, CEMEX, and the New York Police Department. Late in 2000, for example, with its core manufacturing businesses of commercial aircraft and defense hardware slowing to 5% annual growth rates, Boeing elevated to full business unit status relatively new businesses that finance aerospace equipment transactions, provide software and hardware for air traffic management, deliver Internet service to aircraft, and provide aircraft servicing. Several months later its chairman, Phil Condit, announced a repositioning of its businesses to "'open new frontiers' by becoming a rounded provider of 'aerospace solutions.'"[17]

It is quite possible that one source of motivation for Boeing's redefinition was its relationship with GE, a supplier of engines for some of its aircraft (often to the specifications of the aircraft purchaser). In 1999 GE concluded a partnership agreement with Boeing under which GE would supply all engines to Boeing's newest jet as part of a package to offer its thrust service contracts to Boeing's aircraft customers.

Lorenzo Zambrano, chairman and CEO of Mexico-based CEMEX, the third largest cement producer in the world, asks, "Who wants a sack of cement? You want a home or a bridge or a runway."[18] He has refocused his organization on delivering results as a means of differentiating a commodity.

What works in the private sector is equally applicable to the social sector. William Bratton, who led a revolution in police work around the world as police commissioner for New York City, did it by admonishing his organization to manage for results—reduced crime levels—rather than efforts such as answering emergency calls. It was something unheard of at the time, but it has been proven to work. In New York City alone, major crimes in 2001 were only 60% of what they were when Bratton assumed his job at the outset of 1994, a far greater decline than in any other large U.S. city.[19]

From Results to Value

Redefining a business from products and services to results recognizes that customers don't buy services or products, they buy results as well as the way they are delivered, something we refer to as *process quality*. It is in essence a repositioning of a business in relation to new or existing customers and competitors through a metamorphosis from price to value, as shown in Figure 2-1.

The next step in achieving a value-centered organization requires not only repositioning but a rethinking of shared values, policies, practices, procedures, and processes in a manner that leverages results over costs for customers, employees, and other important constituencies. This is the focus of the remainder of the book.

■ **Figure 2–1** Evolution in Value-Centered Thinking

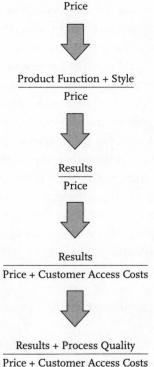

Price

$$\frac{\text{Product Function} + \text{Style}}{\text{Price}}$$

$$\frac{\text{Results}}{\text{Price}}$$

$$\frac{\text{Results}}{\text{Price} + \text{Customer Access Costs}}$$

$$\frac{\text{Results} + \text{Process Quality}}{\text{Price} + \text{Customer Access Costs}}$$

■ Patterns in Organization Behavior on the Road to Value

Note several parallels in the examples described here. At IBM, crisis triggered the business rethinking process. The experience of managements at O. M. Scott & Sons, American Cyanamid, Otis, GE, and others suggests that it doesn't have to happen that way.

Some of the most powerful ideas have led to the expansion of a business from a product-based manufacturing capability and customer franchise. Many have involved a discovery or a rediscovery of the profit opportunities for services offered in conjunction with products by traditional manufacturers. Nearly all have led to the provision of many additional products and services necessary to deliver results to customers. All have resulted in significant increases in revenue growth and profitability.

These experiences suggest that customers place a much higher value on results than on products or services—and they are willing to pay for them.

At the same time, however, the most sweeping of these business redefinitions have required significant organizational change, including new measures of performance and incentives. Most often, they have provided justification for policies and practices to encourage close ties between separate businesses producing related products, parts, services, and financing, whether or not they are operated as separate profit centers.

Trends toward the outsourcing of nonstrategic capabilities by many businesses in an effort to achieve greater operating focus offer added opportunities for value-added, results-centered offerings by suppliers.

The relatively small number of organizations in the "late stages" of the progression in scope of output from products and services to results and total value suggests that the phenomenon is still in its early stages. The phenomenal success of those who have advanced the furthest suggests that the rush to value has just begun.

■ Questions for Management

Those just beginning the journey to total value may well want to ask themselves the following questions:

1. How long has it been since your organization's management conducted a comprehensive review of its business definition?

2. Did this review result in a definition centered around results desired by important customers? How do you know?

3. To what extent does the business definition address the needs of constituents other than customers?

4. Has this led to a review and/or reaffirmation of shared values, the core of the organization's culture?

5. Has it produced appropriate changes in organization, particularly the introduction of mechanisms to ensure coordinated delivery of components of a results- and value-centered offering to customers?

6. Has it required changes in policies (for example, regarding the latitude within limits with which frontline personnel can deliver results to customers) and practices (appropriate performance measurement and incentives)?

Rethinking a business involves creating a new vision or model for change and also a process for achieving the vision. Today, dramatic new means exist for doing this. Many are technology driven and have become synonymous with the information-rich "new economy," which, even though it is now in its post-fad stage among business pundits, does exist. On the one hand, they represent new business opportunities in and of themselves. More important to us, they provide effective ways of leveraging results over costs while improving process quality and customer access, all elements of the value equation.

Without leadership, it is impossible to achieve anything. Getting the attention and support of leadership is the first step in the process of change. This is our next concern.

PART II

Getting Management's Attention

THE PATH to sustainable improvements in value is being mapped. Despite this, a surprisingly small number of firms have ventured beyond widely accepted economic value added (EVA) measures to explore nonfinancial concepts for improved value creation. Why have intelligent and well-meaning managers been so slow in adopting these concepts?

Typically, organizations continue to do what they do best or maintain biases toward what they have always done. Thus, a designer and manufacturer of computers is inclined to pass the task of service to others. It may even outsource the manufacture of components, assuming that it can add more value by concentrating on the development of new designs and computing processes. It almost certainly will take little responsibility for educating buyers in the use of its products, relying instead on the preparation of hard-to-follow instruction guides that do not help the buyer unlock the full value of the purchase. This leaves the customer to enlist the assistance of amateur instructional "word of mouth" that attends the introduction of many high-tech products, with the resulting high variability in quality of instruction, learning, and usage.

Second, those who are making an effort to utilize value-centered concepts in laying out and implementing strategies have discovered that the process takes time, sometimes more time than impatient investors allow.

Third, although the concepts are straightforward, the actions behind them are complex. Changing or, just as important, reaffirming the shared values comprising the core of an organization's culture requires a sensitive ear and close attention to process. Changing an organization takes time if existing strengths are to be preserved as change is engineered. The way in which an organization positions itself in relation to its customers and competitors cannot be changed overnight. The changes in operating strategy needed to support a repositioning effort must often be extensive if internal consistency in the elements of the operating strategy are to be achieved.

Managers desiring to convince others of the importance of value-centered concepts often ask us how to get the attention of their bosses and peers. The material in this section is our answer. It consists of developing estimates of the value of both customers and employees, as well as the financial consequences of the continued neglect of such ideas.

The purpose of these efforts is not to establish a precise measure of value for each customer or employee but to convince management that such matters are worth high priority on its agenda. Of course, getting the attention of senior managers is only the first step and must be backed up by a plan for the implementation of value-centered concepts. The effort has to begin somewhere and somehow, however. This is where it begins.

Practitioners of change know that it is difficult to achieve change without an acute sense of dissatisfaction with the status quo, an outstanding model for change, and effective processes for change. When an acute sense of dissatisfaction with the status quo does not exist, one must be created. A common method is to close plants and lay off employees. One of the best means of getting the attention of a complacent group of managers and their employees, however, short of mass layoffs, is the measurement and communication of the value of both customers and employees. This paves the way for further efforts to search outside the organization for value-enhancing ideas by means of benchmarking, and it encourages everyone to exchange ideas regarding best practice already existing within the organization.

Chapter 3

Measuring and Communicating Customer Lifetime Value

C ARL SEWELL, the owner of a group of auto dealerships in the Dallas area, has estimated the lifetime value of one of his luxury auto customers as $332,000.[1] This includes both purchases of new autos and the stream of services and parts associated with their maintenance. Is this the lifetime value of every one of his firm's customers? No. Does it apply to all types of autos he sells? No. Is it an unchanging estimate over time? No. Then why go to the bother of calculating such a figure? Sewell maintains that the rough estimate has influenced greatly the way he designs and runs his businesses. It has resulted in his customers being introduced to mechanics who will eventually service their autos, to the service areas of his dealerships being maintained like hospitals, and to his salespeople being compensated so well that they stay with the firm and develop longer relationships with customers.

Phil Bressler, the erstwhile owner of some 20 Domino's Pizza outlets in the Baltimore area, used to discourage his employees from thinking of an individual customer's order for one pizza as representing $8. Instead, he impressed upon them the importance of thinking of the lifetime value of a frequent pizza eater as being more like $4,000, the product of ten years of consumption of roughly a pizza per week. Is this lifetime of ten years typical of all loyal pizza customers? No. Is this the exact lifetime value for a frequent, loyal consumer of pizzas? No. It spurred Bressler to action, though. It prompted him to say to his employees, "Think of the customer as having $4,000 pasted on his forehead, which you peel off $8 at a time. Then act accordingly."[2] He then rewarded employees whose customers evidenced the smallest number of complaints.

The management of a large company manufacturing transaction processing equipment did not fully realize the importance of customer lifetime value in managing customer relationships until its ATM division several years ago failed to bid on a low-margin contract, to the dismay of its supplies and services divisions, both businesses that could have made a lot of money from the contract. Given the SBU-oriented organization of the company, there was limited realization at the time of true customer lifetime value across business units. This necessitated the creation of mechanisms for coordinating the estimation of lifetime value as an important input to the bidding process for products, supplies, or services. Further, it facilitated the rethinking of its customer relationship management organization, procedures, and policies.

The concept of customer lifetime value has taken on a life of its own over the past decade. It has spawned a growing body of research designed to provide relatively exact calculations of the discounted value of various types of customers over time.[3] Much of this research, however, has dealt with only a portion of the costs and value important in a customer relationship.

Our interest in customer lifetime value is somewhat different. To convince senior managers of the importance of lifetime value and the strategies and actions that flow from it, we need only gross approximations requiring a totally different approach. The estimates, we have found, are often so astounding that even if they are off by a magnitude of 2 or 3, they still provoke the desired response, a decision to lead an initiative to increase the customer value proposition.

■ Customer Value over Time

The first step in establishing awareness of the importance of lifetime value is to understand the hierarchy of relationships with customers, shown in Figure 3-1. It suggests that establishing customer satisfaction is only the first stage in a relationship that progresses to loyalty, in which a customer not only expresses an interest in repurchasing but begins to devote a larger and larger share of the total "wallet" to a given brand. Next comes commitment, in which customers attempt (either successfully or unsuccessfully) to influence others to purchase. Finally, over time, a sense of ownership is established in which customers actually endeavor to provide product or service improvements by taking the trouble to complain or provide a continuing stream of suggestions.

■ **Figure 3–1** HIERARCHY OF CUSTOMER BEHAVIORS

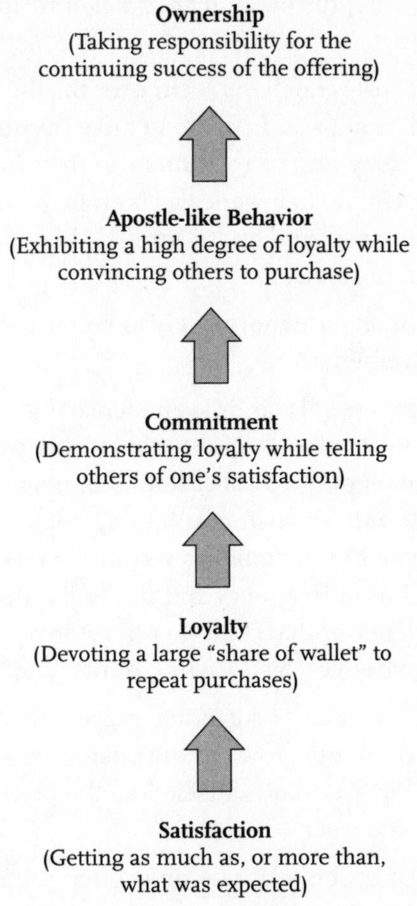

Ownership
(Taking responsibility for the
continuing success of the offering)

Apostle-like Behavior
(Exhibiting a high degree of loyalty while
convincing others to purchase)

Commitment
(Demonstrating loyalty while telling
others of one's satisfaction)

Loyalty
(Devoting a large "share of wallet" to
repeat purchases)

Satisfaction
(Getting as much as, or more than,
what was expected)

The hierarchy of customer relationships provides the underlying rationale for the customer lifetime value patterns shown in Figure 3-2, a stylized diagram based on actual data:

1. For many products or services, breakeven may require 1 year or more after the establishment of a customer relationship to offset customer acquisition costs.

2. Margins and profits on existing items in a line of products and services may decline over time, but loyal customers are willing to pay higher margins on (and are quicker to adopt) new products and services.

3. Significant cost reductions occur over the life of a customer relationship as vendor and customer alike become better "trained" in how to carry on the relationship; in some cases, loyal customers contribute to lower costs both by participating in the delivery of a service[4] and by "training" other customers in the use of a product or service.[5]

4. Loyal customers are more likely to recommend product or service improvements.[6]

5. Profits from referrals become an increasingly significant proportion of the the total value of the relationship over time.[7] They vary with the tendency of a loyal customer to make referrals, the influence of referrals on customer buying behavior, and the relative desirability of the customer to whom the referral is made (measured in terms of frequency and size of purchases and the subsequent tendency of that customer to refer yet others, termed the "loyalty ripple effect" by Dwayne Gremler and Stephen Brown).[8]

6. Over time, the value of customer suggestions for product or service improvements grows as the customer assumes an ownership mentality based on satisfaction, the perception of preferred treatment, and trust.

7. The last year of the relationship is often the most profitable for the vendor; by extending the average lifetime of customer relationships by 1 year, from 5 to 6, profit levels can be increased by from 25 to 85% according to one study.[9]

At the core of a change process designed to enhance value based on customer lifetime value concepts is the need to measure and communicate the importance of these relationships to employees at all levels in the organization.

■ **Figure 3–2** FACTORS CONTRIBUTING TO CUSTOMER LIFETIME VALUE

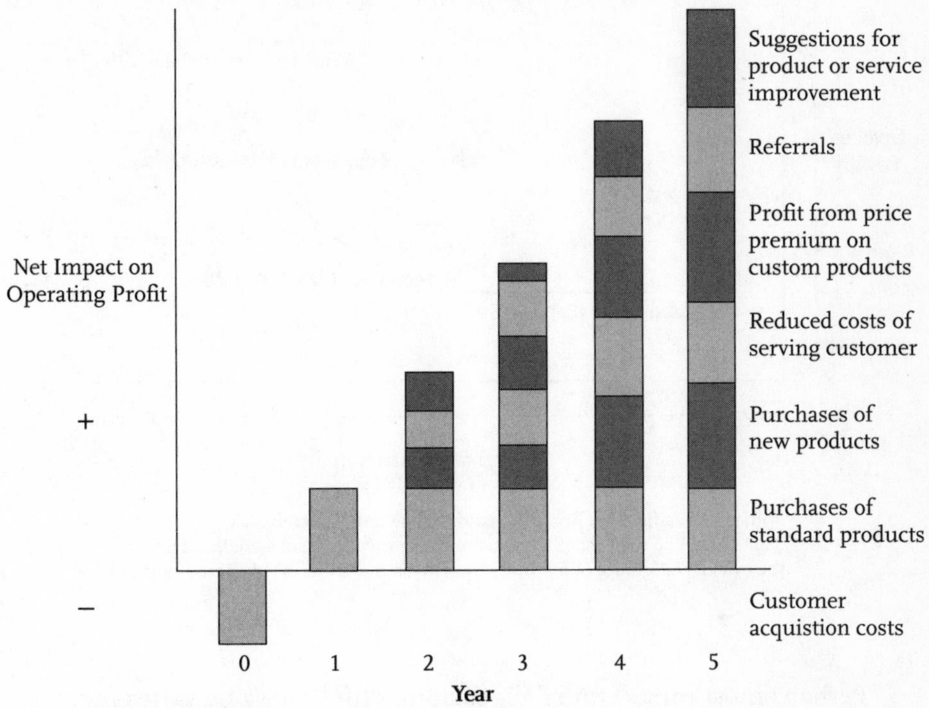

Suggestions for product or service improvement

Referrals

Profit from price premium on custom products

Reduced costs of serving customer

Purchases of new products

Purchases of standard products

Customer acquistion costs

Net Impact on Operating Profit

+

−

Year

0 1 2 3 4 5

Source: Adapted from Frederick F. Reichheld and W. Earl Sasser, Jr., "Zero Defections: Quality Comes to Services," *Harvard Business Review*, September–October, 1990, p. 108.

■ Value in a Portfolio of Customers

All customers do not have the same lifetime value. Value can vary according to the volume of purchases. For many products and services, for example, so-called heavy users comprising no more than 15% of all customers buy as much as 85% of the offering, as is the case for beer sold in the United States. Value can also vary according to the level of a customer's loyalty, the "share of wallet" garnered by any one vendor. Loyalty, as shown in Figure 3-3, is a function of a customer's level of satisfaction.

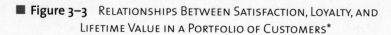

Figure 3-3 Relationships Between Satisfaction, Loyalty, and Lifetime Value in a Portfolio of Customers*

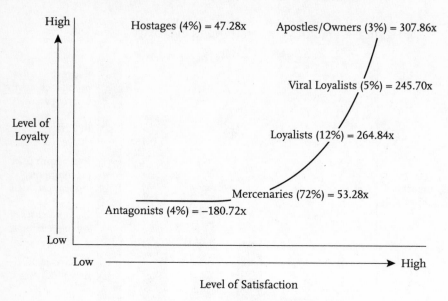

* Values in this figure reflect calculations shown in Appendix C.
** This should be read as: of 100 customers in the portfolio, 4 are hostages; they yield 47.28 units of lifetime value, measured in terms of operating profit.

Perhaps most important of all, customer lifetime value varies most widely by the likelihood that a customer will voice his or her satisfaction to others (the customer's "viral behavior") and the level of influence a customer has over others, factors determining the customer's "referral value."

Differences between lifetime values in a portfolio of customers are diagrammed in Figure 3-3:

1. The value of customers varies widely, ranging from large negative values for *antagonists,* those who are not only dissatisfied with a product or service but also are active (in current terminology, *viral*) in telling others about their dissatisfaction, to large positive values for *viral loyalists,* especially *apostle/owners* who exhibit posi-

tive viral behavior and who also have unusually great influence over friends, which distinguishes them from viral loyalists.

2. Together, apostle/owners and viral loyalists are capable of fostering significant revenue growth through referrals of potential customers, typically those who are followers in the adoption of new products and services. They play a pivotal role in marketing strategies.

3. Both apostle/owners and viral loyalists tend to exhibit ownership behavior, communicating a stream of constructive complaints and suggestions back to their "partners."

4. Between antagonists and apostle/owners is a wide range of intermediate players exhibiting varying behaviors. These include *hostages*, dissatisfied customers with nowhere to turn for alternatives, some of who may also be antagonists; *mercenaries*, those who switch from one product or service to another, often based on lowest price; and *loyalists*, those who remain loyal to a product or service but rarely tell others of their loyalty.

It's important to note several other aspects of Figure 3-3. First, modest lifetime value is assigned to hostages. This is a composite for all hostages, including those who are terrorists and those who aren't. However, hostages often are highly viral, complaining to others about their lack of alternatives—for electric power, a convenient grocery store, or a source of industrial material. This is often exacerbated by the perception that "price gouging" is being practiced. Thus, the negative value of relationships with hostages may offset some of the positives.

The hostage problem was brought most forcefully to our attention by a visit to a Big Three U.S. auto manufacturer, where it was pointed out that it, too, had hostages, something rather surprising in a highly competitive market for automobiles. Who were these hostages? Most unfortunately, they were its own employees, who had been given attractive price incentives to buy their employer's autos but who were dissatisfied with the autos' performance. In this case, the cost of selling to hostages took on added negative value, bringing into question the very practice of providing price incentives in this case. Thus, one admonition that might be made to organizations with hostages as customers is "free the hostages" by giving them viable alternatives for meeting their needs. (For the auto manufacturer, valuable competitive information could have been gained by providing equally attractive incentives for employees, particularly engineers, to drive competing makes of autos.)

Second, note the wide differences in lifetime value between mercenaries and loyalists. Few organizations that we've studied make any money from dealing with mercenaries. Even though they may represent more than 70% of an organization's customer base, mercenaries represent nearly profitless sales volume in most cases. The most one can hope for in many of these cases is to break even on such sales, thereby providing a base volume of sales to cover fixed costs. As long-distance telephone service providers discovered as a result of the "phone wars" that swept the U.S. in the 1990s, the cost of acquiring mercenaries who regularly switched phone service providers, sometimes as part of a strategy to obtain free service, far outweighed the lifetime value of their business.

Third, there is a similarly wide difference in lifetime value between loyalists and apostle/owners, suggesting the importance of incentives for somehow encouraging loyalists to tell others, including providers, how they feel about a product or service. In fact, in several industrial, business-to-business settings, we have found that loyalists are quite willing to give such testimonials—if only they are asked. Too often, protective sales representatives try to discourage such requests for fear that they will disrupt a successful relationship. Ironically, just the reverse may be true. Loyalists often become even more loyal when asked to provide referrals to prospective customers.

Fourth, although not shown in Figure 3-3, our experience has suggested that it is very difficult to recruit loyalists from among the ranks of mercenaries without first segmenting the mercenaries according to the reasons for their behavior. The motives and buying psychologies of members of the two groups are for the most part different. However, within the ranks of mercenaries, there are usually customers whose behaviors may be influenced by reasons other than price, suggesting the potential for a conversion.

The profile shown in Figure 3-3 represents the sum of several customer characteristics: quantity of purchases, loyalty to a particular supplier, likelihood of telling others (viral character), and degree of influence over others (*marquee effect*). As they converge, as shown in Figure 3-4, these characteristics create a customer "sweet spot," one on which effort can be concentrated in preserving relationships. At the same time, it suggests several contiguous areas (in the diagram in Figure 3-4) of a high potential for enticing additional customers into the sweet spot. Each may require a different kind of effort, to which we return in a later chapter.

Although the example shown in Figure 3-3 is based on a composite of actual experiences, it nevertheless reflects what we have found in a variety of companies and products. The results are dramatic. Among other things, loyalists—whether viral and influential or not, representing 20% of the customer portfolio in our example—produce more than 100% of the lifetime value from the sale of a product or service. An apostle/owner, a loyalist who is both viral and influential, represents more than

■ **Figure 3-4** THE CUSTOMER "SWEET SPOT"

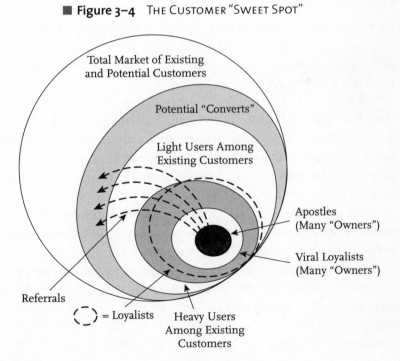

138 times the lifetime (in this case, 10-year) value of a mercenary. The way in which these numbers were calculated, as well as the assumptions under which they were prepared, are shown in Appendix C.

Wide differences in the lifetime value of various types of customers suggest the importance of first profiling the customer portfolio before assigning values to various groupings of customers.

■ Profiling the Customer Portfolio

Having identified characteristics influencing lifetime value, the next step in a change-producing process is the development of a profile of the customer portfolio. Most important to this process is the establishment of criteria for defining groupings of customers, shown in Figure 3-3. Such criteria are unique to each organization.

BUSINESS-TO-BUSINESS CUSTOMER PROFILING

Given the heavy concentration of sales in a relatively small number of customers for most business-to-business organizations, the profiling process can be confined to, say, the largest hundred customers. It often produces a surprisingly diverse profile.

Sources of information used in this process start with sales information. Because the sales information contained in a vendor's files may contain only a portion of the total purchases by a customer, it requires estimates of market share by the sales representatives responsible for each account. Given this information, loyalty indices can be established for each customer.

Sales representatives may be the best source of information about terrorists: salespeople are closest to the market and are able to observe negative customer attitudes and behaviors.

Indexes identifying hostages are typically based on measures of customer satisfaction, often collected periodically, and levels of loyalty discussed earlier. High levels of loyalty combined with low levels of customer satisfaction are almost certain indicators of the presence of a hostage.

Business-to-business customers are often asked to provide referrals to potential customers. Records of these referrals, perhaps combined with information from new customers regarding major influences on their decisions, provide indicators of the viral nature of each account, as well as the degree to which each is truly an apostle, what is sometimes referred to as a marquee account. Such marquee accounts are relatively easy to identify in business-to-business settings, thus providing a basis for the final assessment needed to complete the profile.

CONSUMER CUSTOMER PROFILING

Organizations relating to large numbers of relatively small customers have a somewhat different set of challenges in profiling a customer base. They require a reliance on survey-based sample data as well as input from various types of "listening posts." Increasingly, however, with the advent of Internet-based methods of communication, the profiling of large numbers of customers in more reliable fashion is becoming a reality.

So-called customer satisfaction surveys must go beyond merely the question of satisfaction if they are to yield the data necessary for profiling the customer base. They must also establish the level of commitment of a customer to a product or service, as well as the viral character of the customer. Three survey questions provide a basic tool for this:

1. How satisfied are you (with the product or service)?

2. How likely are you to repurchase?

3. How likely are you to tell someone else about your experience?

Additional questions identify behaviors that go beyond intent and establish level of commitment, viral character, influence, and ownership:

1. How many times have you purchased (all products or services of this type) in the past 6 months (or some other period of time reflecting purchase frequency for a product or service category)?

2. How many times have you purchased (this product or service) from (our company) in the past 6 months?

3. How many others have you told about your experience (with this product or service) in the past 6 months?

4. How many of those that you have told in the past 6 months have, to your knowledge, also purchased (the product or service)?

5. How many times have you offered constructive criticism or suggestions for product or service improvements over the past 6 months?

Increased emphasis on the profiling of customers is reflected in changing marketing survey techniques such as these. In addition, services have been created that either track consumer purchasing behavior through the use of "membership" cards offering incentives to identify individual purchases or provide the capability of actually dialoguing with individual customers about their purchase and usage experiences through the use of the Internet. For example, recent business start-ups have been created to facilitate the creation of on-line "sessions" in which consumers can trade reactions to products or services, sometimes under the direction of a session leader who can encourage the kind of in-depth feedback associated with much more expensive face-to-face focus groups.

Similarly, efforts have been made to focus on customers who provide feedback concerning products and services in the belief that they are often heavy users, invested in the success of their suppliers, viral in character (by virtue of their willingness to act on their positive or negative feelings), and psychological "owners." Customers of this type not only are invaluable to product improvement efforts, they are quite likely to be the core of those who drive "word-of-mouth" marketing phenomena. This has led to the creation of C2B (consumer to business) "feedback spaces" among Internet-based service providers. Pete Blackshaw, after observing the importance of viral customers at Procter & Gamble, set out to create one such service.[10]

Blackshaw, cofounder of P&G Interactive, the company's Internet-based marketing organization, on a special assignment consulting with P&G's Consumer Relations Department, found that consumers who provided feedback via the Internet were the most viral, that is, most willing to talk with others about products. Those who identified themselves through the feedback process as satisfied P&G product users passed on an average of 16 full-sized P&G product samples to friends when given the chance. Just as important, fully 85% of consumers offering negative product feedback were found to be prepared to switch brand allegiance after making a complaint.

On the other hand, only 1 in 25 consumers inclined to give feedback were found to do so. Reasons for not doing so included lack of time, inconvenience, little or no knowledge about whom to contact, cynicism about the possibility that it would matter, and the passing of the "feedback moment."

As a result of this experience, Blackshaw and several colleagues founded a company, PlanetFeedback, with the intention of fixing the "corroded pipe" between a business and its customers. They created a Web site structured to provide free assistance to users wishing to write letters to individuals or organizations. PlanetFeedback helps them structure their letters, allows them to send copies to others (thus exhibiting viral behavior), ensures that the letters and copies get to the right place, and even provides follow-up to determine whether the letters generate a response. In the process, it collects information that provides an early warning system to businesses, ideas for new product or service features, and a better understanding of customers occupying the sweet spot in Figure 3-4.

Estimates of customer lifetime value are often critical in convincing the leadership of an organization that its business needs to be rethought from top to bottom. The rethinking may include processes for producing products and delivering services, organization, measuring and evaluating performance, compensation practices, and even the criteria for selecting new employees.

So how is customer lifetime value measured? The process we describe, although perhaps not up to the standard of more analytic, exacting research, is one that is adequate for our purposes, convincing leaders of the need for change and encouraging the more effective allocation of resources in moving customers up the lifetime value ladder. We return to a more complex framework of analysis when we examine value exchange in Chapter 9. Our purpose here is to provide a "quick and dirty" process for estimating value as a means of jump-starting the change process.

■ Measuring Customer Lifetime Value

The elements of customer lifetime value estimates are discussed here. More detailed examples, as well as access to an Internet-based estimation program, are described in Appendix C.

LENGTH OF RELATIONSHIP

What is the typical length of a customer relationship? At an Internet service provider experiencing a 20% annual customer defection rate, it is effectively 5 years. At MBNA, a credit card issuing and servicing organization, it is now up to more than 10 years after a concerted drive by management to provide outstanding customer service and stimulate renewed card usage, an effort stimulated by a calculation of customer lifetime value similar to this one.[11] At USAA, an organization founded on providing financial services to commissioned military personnel and their families over one or more lifetimes—and a company with one of the most loyal customer bases among all U.S. businesses—the assumption is that a customer will use the organization's financial services for an average period of 50 years.

Once the length of the relationship has been estimated or calculated, the kind of chart shown in Figure 3-2 can be begun. In the example for Acme Household Products, a fictitious company with experience based on a composite of actual research findings described in detail in Appendix C, the length of the relationship ranges from 1 year for terrorists (who nevertheless continue to discourage new customers for 3 years more after their defection) to 10 years for loyalists, viral loyalists, apostles, and owners.

ACQUISITION COSTS

A major consumer goods manufacturer may spend $100 million per year for advertising for a new product. A good part of that may be spent with the intent of retaining current customers, but all but a small portion of it is probably intended to attract potential new customers. If the manufacturer is able as a result to add 500,000 new users, we generally assume that the cost of acquisition is $200 per new customer. Companies relying on a sales force to develop new customer accounts typically spend much more for acquisition costs. For example, the sales cycle for the adoption of a new medical device may be 6–12 months, over which time the sales effort devoted to the relationship may exceed $100,000. At the far end of the spectrum, defense contractors may spend millions of dollars in the preparation of a bid for a new contract. Because of the way in which cost accounts are maintained, many organizations find it relatively easy to estimate customer acquisition costs.

RELATIONSHIP COSTS OVER TIME

Activity-based costing coupled with customer profitability accounting techniques have in recent years allowed more careful tracking of customer relationship costs.[12] Because such costs may (and probably should) vary greatly from one customer to another, it is useful to break them out separately from other operating costs in estimating lifetime value. This is particularly true for business-to-business relationships in which the relationship costs per customer may be substantial and vary greatly from one customer to another. Remember, though, the object is not to estimate costs to the penny; it is to get a general idea of how costs in support of a customer relationship vary over time.

MARGINS ON BASE SALES (BASE RETENTION VALUE)

Business-to-business relationships are centered around the purchase of products and services that are basic to the product line. Similarly, consumer product and service suppliers provide multiple offerings containing items that are purchased over and over, meeting basic needs. Often, these products and services over time are offered at lower and lower margins as price becomes an important differentiating factor in their purchase.

MARGINS ON RELATED SALES

Product or service innovation, although costly in its own right, is often regarded as a primary source not only of future survival and success but also of profit. Margins on new products or services are typically much higher than those for base sales. Further, loyal customers are often less price sensitive than others and also more likely to be among early adopters for new products or services. For these reasons, it is useful to develop separate estimates for new product revenue in the overall line of items offered to the customer.

The net result of sales patterns, relationship costs, and margins on sales can be expressed in terms of one number, overall margins on sales, for an individual customer or portfolio of customers, as shown for our fictitious company, Acme Household Products, in Appendix C.

VALUE OF REFERRALS

An important contributor to lifetime value often overlooked by those researching the phenomenon is value from referrals. This requires an estimate of the number of referrals made by existing to potential customers, the likelihood that the referral is acted upon, and the subsequent nature of the referred customer's purchasing behavior. Thus, it is a function of the viral behavior of a current customer as well as that customer's expertise or reputation, as perceived by those who are the target of the referral.

In business-to-business situations, referrals can be tracked for each account, often because they are initiated by the maker of the product or service being referred. For consumer products or services, referrals are more ephemeral. As we mentioned earlier, they can be estimated from time to time through survey techniques. Online customer-to-business feedback services can track specific consumer referrals through a feature allowing those writing feedback letters to copy others of their choice. Again, the purpose here is to develop estimates, not precise measures.

Referrals are only of value if they produce action. Subsequent sales data for business-to-business situations will document the value of referrals. In consumer situations, greater reliance may have to be placed on estimates by those making the referrals. To the extent that such estimates may be inflated along with an individual's estimate of his or her level of influence, they may need to be discounted. Of course, with the development of more sophisticated tracking devices, such as membership cards providing electronic identification of consumer purchases, as well as the development of ways of analyzing the contents of more sophisticated customer databases or "data warehouses," actions taken by those receiving referrals can be tracked more accurately.

The assumptions regarding referrals associated with the Acme Household Products example in Appendix C reflect actual situations we have observed. They assume that loyalist customers who are not viral do not tell others of their satisfaction and therefore do not produce a margin stream from referrals. Viral loyalists, on the other hand, tell others but may not have a sufficient level of credibility to have a maximum impact on potential customers. They are assumed in the example to "convert" one additional customer per year to the Acme customer portfolio. Apostles (or marquee loyalists), on the other hand, succeed in converting three additional customers per year, adding significantly to their lifetime value.

VALUE OF SUGGESTIONS

Because very few organizations incorporate it into their business strategies, little or no effort has been devoted to the measurement of the value of customer suggestions. However, the processes used by a number of organizations to recognize and reward employee suggestions can be applied to customer value as well. Remember, our purpose here is not to recognize and reward customers but to provide the basis for an estimate of the premium to be assigned to the value of customers who assume the "ownership" mantle that motivates them to provide feedback.

OVERALL CONCLUSIONS FROM THE ANALYSIS

The customer lifetime value estimates shown for Acme Household Products in Appendix C are dramatic. However, in our experience they are not unusual. In summary, they suggest that loyalists, viral loyalists, and apostle/owners, representing only 20% of Acme's customer base, produce all of the margin on which profit potential is based. Further, an individual apostle/owner is worth roughly 70 times more than a mercenary in total margin over the length of the relationship.

These conclusions are roughly the same regardless of whether the raw data produced by the lifetime value estimates is discounted for the time value of money. The results would be dramatic even if the estimates for loyalists, viral loyalists, and apostles were inaccurate by a factor of 100%. In short, they are sufficiently significant to serve the purpose of stimulating senior management to action in identifying and courting potential apostles. What kinds of actions are most appropriate?

■ Actions Based on Customer Lifetime Value Measurements

The estimation of customer lifetime value can trigger several types of actions, including those involving communication of the information, identification and tracking of customer behavior, organization in response to customer behaviors, and the allocation of resources to foster lifetime value.

COMMUNICATING LIFETIME VALUE

The mere communication of customer lifetime value estimates to members of an organization can have a profound impact on the behavior of customer-facing personnel. For example, in Phil Bressler's Domino's Pizza organization, described earlier, delivery personnel were encouraged not to argue with customers about whether deliveries failed to meet the 30-minute delivery guarantee in place at that time (and therefore qualified for free product). Instead, they were given the latitude to give the customer the benefit of the doubt in the hope that it would produce viral behavior in the form of stories about Domino's great service.[13]

When accompanied by changes in policy or incentives to reflect the importance of customer lifetime value, communication of the information can have an especially great impact on employee performance. Just making employees aware of the information typically influences behavior as well.

IDENTIFYING AND TRACKING CUSTOMER BEHAVIOR

The example presented earlier suggests that customer behaviors produce an array of lifetime value estimates. It follows that it is important to establish mechanisms for not only identifying behavior patterns in a portfolio of customers but also tracking behavior over time. This literally can be done on a customer-by-customer basis in most business-to-business enterprises. For example, customer satisfaction levels and incidents that might affect them are tracked for every one of Cisco Systems' customers, representing a wide range of purchasers of data and voice routing equipment for intranet and Internet applications. Each night, customers thought to be at greatest risk of being alienated are identified. Each is assigned for personal contact by a senior member of management, including the CEO.[14]

Tracking behavior patterns for consumer products and services may be done for groups of customers as well as on a one-on-one basis. Market share trends may be established through a number of data collection services providing such information, but they really represent symptoms of potential problems, the results of past actions.

Increasingly, customer-centric organizations serving consumers are establishing a variety of listening posts for tracking behaviors as well as customer concerns producing behavioral changes. Typically, these may include a customer service organization prepared not only to solve customer problems but also to collect ideas for product or service improvements. Increasingly, they involve the regular use of focus groups, Internet chat rooms, and Internet-based feedback devices to detect and provide an early-warning system to trigger actions to address customer concerns proactively.

Organizing for Customer Relationship Management

Customer relationship management, for which lifetime value estimates provide strong justification, requires a customer-centric organization. An enterprise organized around products or services inevitably creates the possibility for multiple points of contact with a customer. Each may involve an opportunity to influence the quality of the relationship. As in the example cited earlier, a business unit experiencing low margins may elect to pass up an opportunity for a relationship representing significant opportunities for other business units in the same organization, either out of ignorance of the total opportunity or because of a reward system that provides no incentive to take customer lifetime value into account.

An organization comprising separate business units marketing to the same customers can benefit from (1) efforts to communicate estimates of organizationwide lifetime value for potential customers, (2) policies assigning lead marketing responsibility for a particular relationship to the business unit with the earliest sales opportunity or greatest margin opportunity, and (3) measurement and recognition practices that distribute rewards among business units realizing varying margins from products or services sold to the same customer.

ALLOCATING RESOURCES

Based on the estimates produced for Acme Household Products, both in this chapter and in Appendix C, it is easy to jump to the conclusion that nearly all marketing resources should be redirected to the task of converting mercenaries to loyalists and even apostle/owners. However, a limited amount of research suggests that only a relative small proportion of customers exhibiting price-sensitive mercenary behavior have the mind-set or the economic means to become loyalists. Here customer psychographics (the mind-set) probably outweighs the demographics (economic means). After all, demographics are much more likely to change than psychographics. Marketing research designed to identify not only current satisfaction and behavior of mercenaries but also future commitment (through such responses as "I plan to repurchase," or "I plan to tell others of my satisfaction with the product") may enable an organization to target potential loyalists.

The negative margin flows associated with antagonists and hostages also deserve attention in the allocation of marketing resources. At the very least, efforts should be expended to neutralize such customers. Often, recognition of the situation and the solicitation of feedback from them is a more successful way of doing so than some kind of product or service giveaway, particularly when the customer already registers dissatisfaction with the current product or service.

Perhaps the best investment of marketing funds for retention purposes is that devoted to the development of virality among loyalists and eventually the expansion of the pool of apostle/owners. Once they are identified, steps can be taken to involve them as partners in the marketing effort by providing them with additional information useful in fostering the viral process. Product samples can be made available for distribution to potential customers at their suggestion. Through frequent contact, they can be made to feel that they are special emissaries of the company, members of a club or community of like-minded customers. This kind of investment, for example, has done as much as anything to foster the resurgent success of the once moribund producer of Harley-Davidson motorcycles. Harley-Davidson has organized a fanatical group of owners and fans by catering to their latent willingness to serve as apostles for the product. This investment has greatly expanded the "sweet spot" for the company's products.

Of course, some customers over time assume a sense of "ownership." One of our favorite examples of this phenomenon is provided by frequent flyers at Southwest Airlines, who are regularly invited to assist the company's staff in selecting new cabin and counter attendants for the airline. When asked why he had taken time off from work to help Southwest, one frequent flyer told us that he wanted to see how a successful organization selected new employees and thought that it would be fun to spend a day finding out. Then, after pausing for a moment, he added, "Besides, it's my airline." That kind of customer is priceless.

■ Questions for Managers

Among questions raised by our discussion of customer lifetime value are the following:

1. Has your organization profiled its customer base by the groupings shown in Figure 3-3?

2. How is loyalty defined among your organization's customers?

3. What proportion of your organization's total customer base and overall operating profits is represented by loyalists, viral loyalists, and apostle/owners?

4. What are you doing to communicate this information to your employees?

5. How has this information influenced training methods, job latitude (in delivering results to targeted customers), recognition policies and/or performance incentives in customer-facing jobs, and overall allocation of marketing and customer service expenditures in your organization?

Customer relationship management (CRM) is a concept in name only without an understanding and estimation of customer lifetime value. The latter provides not only the rationale for CRM but also the basis for marketing strategies designed to maximize profit and growth through the reallocation of greater amounts of effort and funds to customer retention and the development of loyalists, apostles, and owners. Once management has identified the 20% of its customer base that produces all of its profits, significant change begins to happen in the management of relationships with both existing and potential customers. The primary lever in achieving this successfully is ERM, employee relationship management, our next concern.

Chapter 4

Measuring and Communicating Employee Value

T HE CORNERSTONE OF HUMAN RESOURCE MANAGEMENT is employee value, not a vague set of concepts or actions with unmeasured outcomes. It is enhanced through policies and practices that build continuity and commitment among employees, outcomes that can be measured, our primary concern here.

When an experienced automobile salesperson is replaced by a novice, it has been estimated that the cumulative cost to a dealership in lost productivity can exceed $300,000 in auto sales. When Oracle loses a software engineer, the cost is several times that of hiring and training a replacement. This cost also includes the value of ideas and methods lost as well as damage to the process by which knowledge is transferred in the organization. When Merrill Lynch loses a productive broker to a rival, the cost of the loss of clients more loyal to their broker than to the firm literally can be in the millions.

Such costs are the result of several relationships in the service profit chain. They start with management's commitment to the development of factors contributing to employee satisfaction. High employee satisfaction reduces turnover and increases profit growth, often resulting in twice the rate of profit growth in organizations with highly satisfied employees as opposed to employees with low satisfaction levels.[1] The effects can be even more dramatic.

In the wake of the September 11, 2001, terrorist attacks on the U.S., only one of the seven largest airlines, when permitted to fly, resumed its regular flight schedules and did not lay off employees. This was Southwest Airlines.

At least one report of these actions, which required the use of some of Southwest's large cash balance, focused on the airline's desire to grab a larger share of the market for airline travel from higher-cost rivals.[2] Of course this is true, but the article missed a more important point. One of the primary reasons that Southwest was in a position to do this was because of nearly three decades of enlightened efforts to build value for its employees as well as customers, based on a high regard for the lifetime value of both.

These efforts created an exceptionally long average "life" of Southwest employees with the company. This, in turn, is an important reason that Southwest had a substantial cash balance that could tide it and its employees over a difficult and stressful time in the industry. By the end of 2001, Southwest was actually flying more daily flights than on September 10, 2001.

The strategy, both pre- and post-September 11, has created extraordinary value for Southwest's shareholders, many of them employees. For a period of time after September 11, the market value for Southwest's stock was greater than that for the other six largest airlines combined. We will look at Southwest's value-creating strategy in greater detail in Chapter 10.

■ The Importance of Employee Continuity

Clearly, the loss of an employee involves much more than the hiring and training costs traditionally attached to such an event. For example, Cliff Ehrlich, former head of human resources at the Marriott Corporation, pointed out to us years ago that nearly two-thirds of the cost of the loss of a manager at the company's Roy Rogers fast-food subsidiary at that time could be attributed to the subsequent loss of productivity.[3]

Although replacement and training costs may be a fraction of the annual employment costs for highly skilled personnel, the loss of business resulting from a shortened association with an individual may result in costs to the organization of several times the annual employment costs.

Customer lifetime value concepts, largely unknown at the time of our first book, are now common knowledge and practice. They are the handmaidens of the rush to embrace ideas concerning customer relationship management (CRM), a field in which entire careers appear to be blossoming. However, until recently concepts of employee value have received limited attention.

In fact, employee turnover may be the largest single category of cost to some organizations, for example those providing professional services. How often have you heard the comment, "In our company, the assets walk out the door every night"? Unfortunately, having recognized this, too many managers do too little about it, primarily because they don't understand employee lifetime value. The effort to do so can be a primary driver of change in employee relationship management (ERM), practices as well as throughout the organization.

The unintended loss of a previously highly valued employee is an often unrecognized tragedy. Efforts are made to rationalize the loss: "He hadn't been performing up to his full potential lately," "We couldn't compete with the offer she received," and "Fortunately, we have plenty of depth in the skills that he possessed." Interestingly, these are all views, whether sincere or not, intended to rationalize the loss of the individual to the organization, too often by deprecating the value of the departing person. No matter how the event is rationalized, however, it's a tragedy. Just how great a tragedy is our concern here.

Note that our focus here is on measuring the value of the employee to the organization. In Chapter 7, when we turn to issues of employee relationship management, we talk about how to increase employee lifetime value, revisiting issues of employee retention and the value equation through the eyes of the employee.

Consider, for example, a retailing organization that we'll call Richards Foods, with $8 billion in sales, $300 million in earnings before tax, and 60,000 frontline (store and warehouse) employees, each representing an average of $30,000 per year in total costs (salary as well as fringes and overhead), with an annual "defection" rate of 80% per year, two-thirds of which (or 32,000 in number) is unplanned by management. This figure for defections may appear to be extraordinarily high, but there are well-known retailers experiencing it today. If the benchmark defection rate for the best-performing retailer in the industry, the "employer of choice," is half that of Richards Foods, the potential for improvement is dramatic. Using an estimate of one-third the annual compensation for the cost of the unplanned departure of a customer-facing employee, an assumption that we justify later, the cost for each of the 32,000 employees in question is $10,000. Assuming that the best-performing competitor (or the best-performing store in the chain) enjoys a defection rate only half this number, the potential improvement for the firm in question is 16,000 × $10,000, or $160 million before tax, a potential 40% improvement in pretax profits.

The estimate of the potential for improvement doesn't end there. Let's assume that through improved hiring procedures, the rate of planned employee departures from the organization could be cut in half as well. This would reduce the number of planned departures from 16,000 to 8,000 per year. Assuming that planned departures cost $5,000, or half as much as those that are unplanned, the resulting improvement would reduce costs by another $40 million, or 10% of pretax profit.

As we will see, given the improvements we have described, revenue will not remain the same. It will increase. Even if it is assumed that it doesn't, the operating margins for the firm in question will increase by $240 million, or 3.0 percentage points, a dramatic improvement for a retailer realizing only 3.75% returns on sales before taxes.

Of equal significance alongside possible cost savings or revenue enhancement are the constraints that poor hiring and employee retention practices place on strategic options. How often have you heard managers say that they are constrained by a shortage of management talent? Or that expansion could be planned at the rate of 20% rather than 10% if there were only enough available people and the time to train them?

To paraphrase a popular advertisement, improvements in hiring and retention leading to increased employee lifetime value are achieved one employee at a time. First it is necessary to estimate their value in order to call top management's attention to the value-adding opportunity.

■ The Two Faces of Employee Continuity

High rates of employee turnover may be costly, but extremely low rates may also result in costs of a different kind. Thus, employee continuity may have its downside as well. Over time, employees may reach peaks in job satisfaction and productivity, after which effort may wane, attitudes toward customers harden, and revenue and profit production decline. When this happens despite an organization's efforts to provide stimulation through continued training, new assignments, and other incentives, the individual and the organization may best be served by severance of the relationship. Such "planned turnover" (which of course is never truly planned) is a fact of life in all organizations.

Employee satisfaction and productivity may follow varying patterns over the life of an association with the organization. For example, the previously mentioned study by The Service Management Group found that in multiunit retail companies, the satisfaction level of new employees is usually found to be 9 on a scale of 10 after 1 month of employment, and 5 to 11 months later it dips to a level of 6. For those remaining on the job, however, it then begins a steady incline to a level of 9 after 4 years or more.[4] This suggests the importance of measuring and understanding employee satisfaction and productivity cycles so that appropriate efforts to help employees through "troughs" in their job experiences can be timed appropriately, thus averting some amount of planned turnover.

Planned turnover requires careful management attention to the needs and performance of individuals and their impact on the performance of the organization as a whole. One approach to the challenge is to force a planned turnover rate. At General Electric, for example, managers are required to identify the 10% of the people in their organizations who are their poorest performers. Failing a positive response to added training or reassignment, these employees are given assistance in finding employment outside GE. Such policies are controversial, but they reflect the need for planned turnover in even—and perhaps especially—the best run organizations.

Thus, the goal of the value-driven organization is not zero employee defections. It is instead zero unplanned employee defections.

■ Traditional Cost Estimates of Employee Defections

Traditionally, it has been assumed that the cost of employee defections comprises recruiting and training costs, period. Typically, these may range from 5 to 15% of annual total employment costs, including wages and salaries, for a particular job in organizations choosing to do their own hiring. At the other end of the scale, executive recruiting firms may charge up to 40% of the first year's salary for hard-to-find senior executives. Estimates of the value of retention traditionally have ended here, primarily because of the ready availability of these types of information to human resource managers. In reality, however, these costs represent only the tip of the iceberg of the total costs of employee defection.

■ Changing Assumptions Regarding Employee Lifetime Value

In recent years, organizations managing what we have termed the "Bermuda Triangle" of employee-customer relationships, shown in Figure 4-1, have become sensitized to the extraordinary costs of losing employees who enjoy ties to both their customers and their employer. Those whose customers leave with them, as is often the case in many professional services such as investment brokerages, represent immediate defection costs of $1 million or more. One study of hundreds of customers found that more than half who had left their brokerage firms had defected because their brokers had left. Further, they tended to be the more profitable customers. The broker with the highest profit margin at the time of the study—more than twice the industry average—was A. G. Edwards. It was also found to have the lowest broker defection rate, less than half the industry average.[5] It is probably no coincidence that A. G. Edwards was named as one of the best places to work in 2001 in the *Fortune* survey for that year.[6]

Although a customer may not follow his favorite Starbucks counter person to a new employer for his morning cup of coffee, nevertheless the loss of a familiar face (and name) behind the counter may increase the probability of the future loss of the customer to a conveniently located competitor such as Peets or a favorite regional brand. The Bermuda Triangle exists to some degree in all customer-facing jobs.

Further, the time required to replenish the lost base of business through personal relationships and the cumulative loss of business during the employee "replenishment" process are often substantial. Efforts

■ Figure 4–1 THE "BERMUDA TRIANGLE" OF
EMPLOYEE-CUSTOMER RELATIONSHIPS*

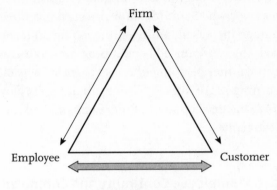

High-Risk Scenario

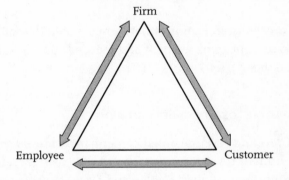

Balanced Scenario

Note: Width of arrow = strength of relationship.

*This concept was first brought to our attention by a former colleague, D. Daryl Wyckoff.

to hire several inexperienced employees to replace the one who has left
the organization are constrained by the talent available to train increasing numbers of newcomers successfully.

Given the escalation in salaries required to hire new talent, in part a
function of the need to provide an incentive for a talented employee (particularly a professional) to make a move, the person brought into the organization to replace the departing talent invariably inflates the wage
costs of the organization.

In total, employee replacement costs often dwarf the amounts that organizations spend to retain valued talent of all types.

This helps explain why professional service firms in particular have gone to extraordinary lengths to retain experienced professionals. It helps explain as well why Starbucks provides such incentives as stock options to encourage increased tenure on the job for all its employees and why McDonald's has announced benefit programs to increase the retention rates for its counter personnel.[7] It also suggests why other organizations are becoming more interested in estimating employee value as a steppingstone to the development of more enlightened human resource management strategies.

■ The Impact of Employee Continuity and Commitment on Lifetime Value and Profitability

Employee continuity and commitment impact both the top and bottom line through revenue enhancement and reduced costs. Just how they do so is reflected in Figure 4-2.

BEYOND EMPLOYEE LOYALTY TO COMMITMENT

Cost reductions and revenue enhancement are achieved through what students of human resource management increasingly refer to as employee "commitment." Robert Kaplan and David Norton have described this as the degree to which employees "understand the organization's goals and are committed to helping the organization achieve them."[8]

Employee commitment goes beyond loyalty. It involves, for example, an understanding of and identification with the values and strategies of an organization. It can be measured, of course, in these terms, but an even more effective measure is the frequency with which an employee refers others for employment with the organization. This is perhaps the ultimate act of commitment. It also helps reduce recruiting costs, particularly if referrals are handled under the assumption that high-productivity employees are likely to associate with and recommend potentially high-productivity friends, the "winners begetting winners" philosophy.

■ **Figure 4–2**   SOURCES OF EMPLOYER LIFETIME VALUE*

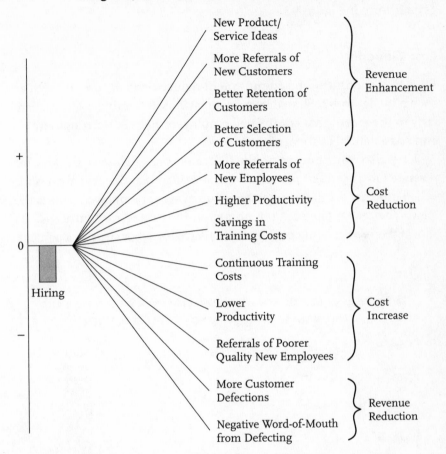

Source: Adapted from Frederick F. Reichheld, *The Loyalty Effect* (Boston: HBS Publishing, 1996), p. 100.

Again, survey results provide evidence to support these beliefs. According to the previously mentioned study by The Service Management Group, less than 30% of employees expressing either dissatisfaction or neutral feelings about their place of work expressed a willingness to recommend it to others. In contrast, 39% of satisfied employees and 75% of very satisfied employees expressed a similar willingness to recommend their organization to others for employment.[9] These results are shown in graphic form in Figure 4-3.

Cost Reduction

Employee continuity and commitment reduce costs in several ways, as shown in Figure 4-2. First, they provide savings in training costs, particularly to the extent that committed employees help in training new recruits as a natural element of their work.

They also contribute to productivity increases that pave the way for revenue enhancement per employee, provided that the organization is scaled properly to reflect increased productivity per employee. This is the "fewer/better employees" phenomenon illustrated in Figure 4-4. As shown there, as revenue per employee increases, labor costs as a percent-

■ **Figure 4–3** RELATIONSHIP BETWEEN EMPLOYEE SATISFACTION AND WILLINGNESS TO RECOMMEND AS A PLACE TO WORK

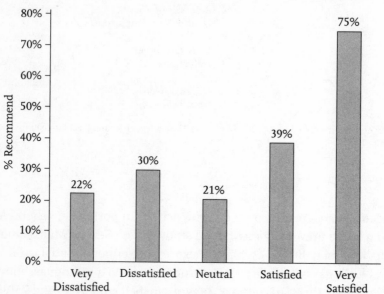

Source: Data from a national retailer, collected by The Service Management Group, 1999.

■ **Figure 4–4**   ECONOMICS OF THE "FEWER BETTER" EMPLOYEE PHENOMENON

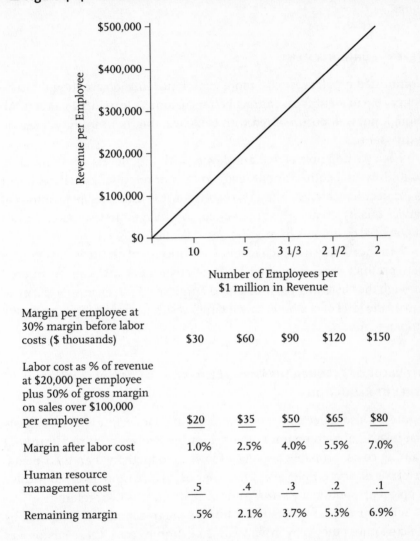

Margin per employee at 30% margin before labor costs ($ thousands)	$30	$60	$90	$120	$150
Labor cost as % of revenue at $20,000 per employee plus 50% of gross margin on sales over $100,000 per employee	$20	$35	$50	$65	$80
Margin after labor cost	1.0%	2.5%	4.0%	5.5%	7.0%
Human resource management cost	.5	.4	.3	.2	.1
Remaining margin	.5%	2.1%	3.7%	5.3%	6.9%

age of gross margin before labor decline, even if 50% of the margin on increased sales is devoted to employee compensation.

In addition, the referral of new employees by committed employees helps reduce hiring costs, at the same time carrying a high probability that the referred potential employee may become as committed as the person referring them, a reflection of the adage that "winners attract winners."

REVENUE ENHANCEMENT

Committed employees with more experience in a job are thought to be better able to identify and attract better customers to an organization. Although not well-documented with evidence, this assumption makes intuitive sense.

What we do know is that employees with high levels of satisfaction, continuity, and commitment foster customer retention, a critical factor in profit enhancement. They also contribute to customers' perceptions of service quality, creating an atmosphere in which more frequent referrals of potential customers by existing ones take place.

Yet a fourth way in which revenue enhancement occurs is through the new product ideas proposed by loyal customers that can be filtered through the "listening post" of a loyal employee. In a sense, this is a measure of the level of customer "ownership" resulting from a high-continuity employee model.

THE VALUE OF PLANNED TURNOVER: ELIMINATING COST INCREASES AND REVENUE REDUCTION

Figure 4-2 also reflects the negative value of poor performers. It suggests that instead of helping train others, they themselves require continuing training costs, probably because of lower productivity than their peers. Referrals of new employees, when they occur, are more likely to involve people representing the same kinds of challenges as their referrers.

Where poor performers really hurt an organization is represented by the customers they may drive away. In extreme cases, these customers may become what we call "terrorists," communicating their dissatisfaction to other actual or potential customers.

Revenue enhancement and cost reduction opportunities vary by job category. For our purpose, which you will recall is a way of providing a rough estimate of the value of employee continuity and commitment as a way of calling top management's attention to the importance of value profit chain relationships, it is useful to take into account the varying nature of job responsibilities for estimating purposes.

■ Factors in Estimating Employee Value

An investment broker will have a very different lifetime value profile from that of a housekeeper in a motel chain. The profiles for both, as well as the methods of estimating them, will differ from those for someone in the "back office" of an organization providing support to those in direct contact with customers, suppliers, or lenders. Estimates can be developed around what we call job factors and individual factors.

JOB FACTORS

Job factors have been used by many organizations to estimate value for pay purposes since at least 1943, when a former bank executive, Edward N. Hay, founded a compensation consulting company based on a system he had developed for evaluating the importance of various jobs. Under his system, "Hay points" were assigned to jobs based on such factors as the size of the budget administered and levels of responsibility. This system was weighted heavily toward one additional measure, the number of people found reporting to a person in a particular position. Other things being equal, the more people reporting, the higher the suggested pay. The natural result was to encourage organization building leading to greater hierarchy and larger bureaucracies, not exactly the kind of side effect intended by its users.

Other more appropriate job factors, given little or no attention in the so-called Hay system, could have included (1) the potential value resulting from the maintenance of external relationships (with customers and others), (2) the relative importance of attitude and skills for the job, (3) the degree of standardization of the job, (4) the training time required to bring a manager or employee to full productivity, (5) the interconnectedness of the job with other jobs in the organization, including responsibilities for the success of others, and (6) the potential overall impact of the job on the performance of the organization.

INDIVIDUAL FACTORS

Factors influencing the value of a particular individual, regardless of the job, may include (1) the attitudes, skills, and level of judgment brought to the job, where this is deemed important, (2) interpersonal, intraorganizational skills, and (3) the ability of an individual to "make the numbers" or achieve other goals. This is the stuff of the typical performance review, with a heavy emphasis placed on the third quality.

Less frequently are individuals evaluated on such factors as their ability to (1) manage according to the shared values making up the culture of the organization or (2) attract and retain desired employees from both within and outside the organization.

For our purposes of estimation, individual factors are important only for the most senior members of management. Other yardsticks serve our purpose in directing top management's attention to the importance of employee relationship management issues.

■ Estimating Rules of Thumb

Any estimate of employee value should be based, when possible, on existing methods of measurement in an organization. Fortunately, a growing number of organizations are beginning to collect information regarding employee turnover. Generally, this is divided into turnover rates for exempt (management) and nonexempt (hourly) employees. In some cases, it differentiates planned from unplanned employee defections, an important distinction considering the fact that unplanned defections often represent a much greater loss of value than that for planned turnover.

For our purposes, it is useful to expand on this taxonomy. We propose establishing a third category, encompassing managers in the top two levels in the organization. Within each of the resulting three categories, we sort out those jobs with responsibilities for dealing directly with customers both external and internal to the organization. This results in a categorization shown in diagrammatic form in Figure 4-5.

■ **Figure 4–5** REPLACEMENT COSTS PER EMPLOYEE (THE DOLLARS AND PERCENTAGE OF ANNUAL EMPLOYMENT COSTS), RICHARDS FOODS

	Unplanned Replacements		Planned Replacements	
Employees Without "Customer-Facing" Premium ($30,000 per year in employment costs)	Hiring and Training: Revenue and productivity enhancement: (or $4,800)	12% 4% 16%	Hiring and Training: Revenue and productivity enhancement: (or $2,400)	12% (4%)* 8%
Employees With "Customer-Facing" Premium ($30,000 per year in employment costs	Hiring and Training: Revenue and productivity enhancement: (or $15,000)	30% 20% 50%	Hiring and Training: Revenue and productivity enhancement: (or $7,500)	30% (5%)* 25%
Middle Management ($100,000 per year in employment costs)	Recruiting and Training: Revenue and productivity enhancement: Replacement salary "premium": (or $100,000)	40% 50% 10% 100%	Recruiting and Training: Revenue and productivity enhancement: Replacement salary "premium": (or $40,000)	40% (10%)* 10% 40%
Top Management	Unique to each individual		Unique to each individual	

*Assuming a negative contribution to revenue and productivity enhancement for planned replacements.

VALUE OF A 1-PERCENTAGE-POINT CHANGE IN EMPLOYEE RETENTION

For jobs encompassing large numbers of employees, the goal is to provide an estimate of the value of a 1-percentage-point change in employee retention. For this purpose, we turn once again to our fictitious retail chain, Richards Foods, an organization with 60,000 frontline employees.

Based on our earlier calculations, a reduction in employee defection rates from 80 to 40% per year would result in cost reductions of $160 million for unplanned defections (making up two-thirds of departures) and $40 million for planned departures (with each costing the organization half as much as an unplanned defection). Thus, a 1-percentage-point reduction results in cost reductions of $4 million for unplanned defections and $1 million for planned departures. Assuming no change in the mix of unplanned defections and planned departures, the 1-percentage-point reduction would equal cost reductions of $5 million, realized for the entire length of time that the turnover rate could be suppressed by 1 percentage point, adjusted periodically for changes in the size of the organization. By itself, this would probably be enough to catch the attention of top management in an organization realizing $300 million pretax income on its sales.

THE "CUSTOMER-FACING" PREMIUM

Not all jobs have an equal impact on an organization's revenues or costs. In particular, those jobs that have a real influence on customer loyalty carry a value premium, whether those customers are external or internal to the organization. Here the value equation once again becomes helpful:

$$\text{Value to Customer} = \frac{\text{Results} + \text{Process Quality}}{\text{Access Cost to Customer} + \text{Price}}$$

Thus, at Richards Foods, perhaps half of the 60,000 frontline jobs are of critical importance in the delivery of good results (product availability and knowledgeable employees), good process quality (friendly, efficient employees), and low access costs (good store layout, product availability, and employees able to assist in locating products). Naturally, they carry a replacement cost higher than the average for all unplanned defections, as shown in Figure 4-5.

At Richards Foods, the hiring and training costs of a customer-facing frontline employee represents more than twice that of, say, a warehouse employee, or about 30% versus 12% of annual employment costs. In addition, a 20-percentage-point premium for revenue and productivity enhancement through customer service brings the estimated replacement costs for customer-facing employees to 50% of annual employment costs, resulting in an average of a 33% cost rate for all frontline employees, the rate used in our overall calculations earlier in the chapter.

The 20-percentage-point premium is calculated from customer surveys indicating that 22.5% of Richards Foods customers cite customer service and friendly employees as the primary reasons for shopping at the company's retail outlets. This represents $1.8 billion of Richards' $8 billion in annual sales. If the gross margin on sales is 10%, this represents a $180 million annual value collectively provided by Richards' 30,000 customer-facing employees, or 20% of their annual employment costs of $900 million (at $30,000 per employee). This can be translated as a 20-point-premium on the percentages that employee value represents as a proportion of annual employment costs for this group of employees.

Similarly, both managers and front-of-the-store employees at Richards Foods rely on others within the organization to ensure their ability to deliver on the promise of the customer value equation. Those occupying particularly critical jobs in the Richards internal supply chain also have higher than average replacement costs because of their potential impact not only on the stores' physical performance but also their impact on general employee morale and the quality of the workplace.

THE MANAGEMENT PREMIUM

Unplanned turnover of managers carries with it not only much higher replacement costs than for frontline employees but also collateral costs resulting from adverse impact on the rest of the organization.

Managers may be replaced because of their adverse effects on the organization. As a result, the cost of making a planned replacement may be low (in contrast to the cost of the "hiring mistake" leading to the employment of the manager being replaced). For this reason, the differential between unplanned and planned turnover for this group of employees may be much greater than for frontline employees.

For example, at Richards Foods, employing 1,000 managers below the top two levels in the organization, the average turnover rate is 30%. As shown in Figure 4-5, the all-in cost of an unplanned replacement is $100,000, including recruiting and training, lost productivity for the organization, a replacement salary "premium," and potentially damaged customer relations. That for a planned departure is $40,000, largely for the recruiting and training of a replacement.

If one-half of manager turnover is unplanned, the annual management turnover at Richards Foods would comprise 150 managers whose departure is unexpected and 150 who have been asked to leave. The total annual cost would be 150 × $100,000 + 150 × $40,000, or $21 million. Stated another way, it would represent $700,000 in cost per percentage point change.

The essence of management is its impact on others in an organization. As shown in Figure 4-5, however, some management positions may have a special impact on external or internal customer relationships as well, thus warranting the "customer-facing" premium for this group of employees.

THE TOP MANAGEMENT PREMIUM

Because of their importance and individuality, management jobs comprising the top two levels in an organization should be treated as special cases. Here the costs, risks, and rewards are much greater than for other positions. A promotion or hiring mistake can have a profound impact on both performance and cost.

Among this group, the severance costs associated with planned departures can be very large. The replacement salary premium also appears to be escalating, especially for chronically difficult-to-fill positions. All this underscores the importance of decisions to hire, promote, and disengage in this select group of individuals.

Given these considerations, the severance costs associated with a planned departure can cost an organization just as much as the adverse impact on customer relations associated with an unplanned defection. In total, the costs may approximate several times the annual employment costs associated with an individual position.

Because top management continuity and commitment are so important to the leadership of an organization, it is a vital part of the job of the CEO, who is often more fully aware of the significance of turnover at this level than at other levels of the organization. Thus, it's probably not as important to quantify costs and benefits at this level (as opposed to other levels in the organization) as a call to action for more effective employee relationship management in the organization.

■ Employee Satisfaction, Continuity, and Commitment as Barometers of Future Performance

Repeatedly we have observed that employee lifetime tenure resulting from job satisfaction, continuity, and commitment has a direct impact on customer satisfaction. Further, organizational continuity is invariably associated with profitability and knowledge retention. If the resulting organizational stability is also associated with the hiring of individuals whose attitudes enable them to adapt and remain open to new ideas, such organizations provide good testing grounds for new products and ideas.

Employee lifetime, as measured by retention and defection rates, should be an important piece of information for prospective employees and customers. As a barometer of future performance, it is of vital importance for prospective investors. For these reasons, the results of employee relationship management must be regarded as the most important indicators on top management's "dashboard" of measures. Such indicators are represented by trends in employee turnover as well as referrals of high-potential employment candidates by employees at various levels in the organization (a measure of commitment).

Typically, organizations periodically ask employees how satisfied they are with their jobs. Unless accompanied by questions designed to elicit information about continuity and commitment, this has little value. Increasingly, organizations that focus on the measurement of employee value are asking such questions as (1) to what degree does your job allow you to fully utilize your capabilities? (2) to what degree does your job fulfill your need for personal development? (3) how high is your regard for the quality of your manager? (4) how high is your regard for the quality of your peers? and (5) how willing would you be to refer a valued friend or relative to this organization for possible employment? Answers to these questions can provide predictive measures of employee continuity and commitment.

■ Questions for Managers

Among the questions raised here for managers are the following:

1. Have you established categories of jobs for which employee satisfaction, loyalty (planned and unplanned turnover rates), and commitment are tracked regularly?

2. Do you establish total costs—including those of recruitment, training, the cost of damaged relationships with external and internal customers, wage escalation, and impact on the effectiveness of the organization—associated with the replacement of an employee?

3. Are these costs calibrated for important categories of frontline employees, middle managers, and top managers as well as customer-facing employees?

4. Has your organization estimated the bottom-line impact of a one-percentage-point increase in employee retention?

5. Where it is of particular importance, what steps are you taking to manage relationships along all three sides of the Bermuda Triangle connecting the firm, its customers, and its customer-facing employees?

6. How, if at all, have answers to these questions influenced efforts to extend employee "life" on the job?

Employee retention, when viewed in the context of the value profit chain, may represent the greatest source of value-added to customers and investors, not to mention the employees themselves. Fortunately, we have learned a great deal about best practice in building loyal, productive organizations. This is our prime concern in Chapter 7.

Chapter 5

Mobilizing for Change: Challenging Strong Cultures

A FIRE CAUSED BY A LIGHTNING BOLT on March 17, 2000, in Philips Electronics NV's Albuquerque, New Mexico, semiconductor plant required fast action on the part of cellular telephone companies relying on the output to meet heavy demand for their products at the time. How two competitors reacted, Nokia Corporation of Finland and Telefon AB L. M. Ericsson of Sweden, both the most important companies (in terms of market value) in their respective countries, provides insight into ways in which organizations with strong cultures can be mobilized for value-focused change.[1]

Nokia and Ericsson, both important customers of Philips "who together bought about 40% of the plant's production," were alerted to the fire on March 20.[2] Both were informed that production of RFCs, radiofrequency chips—essential components in both Nokia's and Ericsson's hottest cellphone products—would be disrupted for perhaps a week but that they were on Philips' list of companies with top priorities for semiconductors as soon as production resumed.

According to one account, at Nokia, the news traveled immediately to the person responsible for keeping Nokia's supply lines open, Pertti Korhonen, and to the company's top management. Korhonen immediately initiated daily communications with the Philips plant as well as order-tracking procedures. Both soon suggested that the problem was worse than originally thought. "Within 2 weeks, a SWAT team of 30 Nokia officials had fanned out over Europe, Asia, and the U.S." to find alternative suppliers, redesigned at least one of the necessary components so that it could be produced more easily by Philips and other suppliers, and arranged meetings between the managements of both companies to review production capabilities and reroute Philips' capacity from other plants to meet Nokia's needs.[3] A project already under way at Nokia to design ways of speeding up production of the chips was accelerated and implemented at the New Mexico plant, allowing it to supply a portion of the chips when it came back on-line after the fire.

At Ericsson, the original notice was treated as a low-level matter and not communicated up the line. Even after it appeared that the matter was more serious than originally thought, middle managers did not pass the information higher until early April. By then it was too late. Alternative sources had already been contracted by Nokia. And Philips had already initiated joint projects with Ericsson's competitor.

As a result of these events and responses at a critical time of increasing demand, Nokia managed to meet demand for its cellphones but Ericsson did not.

This event, or something like it, could not have been predicted on the basis of the strength of these companies' cultures. Both have strong cultures, in part reflecting national pride and the importance of each of these companies to their country's respective economies. It's clear, however, that the behaviors fostered by these strong cultures gave Nokia an advantage over its rival across the Baltic Sea. It quite likely helps explain why Nokia's management listened to what was happening among its suppliers, immediately shared intelligence at all levels, and acted on a carefully planned contingency strategy, fanning out all over the world to fashion alternative sources of components.

A comparative analysis of value profit chain comparisons might have predicted that these two competitors would have had different responses, if not these particular responses, to this disaster.

For example, other things being equal (which they never are), the value profit chain suggests that smaller, more productive organizations are able to achieve the results they do because they hire the right people, train and support them effectively, and then give them greater latitude to do whatever is necessary to meet customer needs, serve other parts of the organization, or whatever they are tasked to do. It would thus be reasonable to expect that Nokia's organization achieves much greater revenue per employee than Ericsson's. At the time of the Albuquerque fire, the two competitors were realizing almost the same volume of revenue, in Nokia's case $27.7 billion in sales and, for Ericsson, $28.5 billion.[4] The product mix of the companies' sales were not the same (with Nokia much more heavily into cellphone sales and Ericsson realizing much more of its sales through networking equipment), but these differences probably did not account for the fact that Nokia's 60,000 employees were achieving roughly the same revenue as Ericsson's 100,000. It is important for any major product designer and manufacturer to know that a combination of smaller size and greater latitude for decision makers can make a formidable competitor.

One would expect as well that the levels of employee satisfaction and loyalty weigh in Nokia's favor, although Scandinavian companies in general enjoy high levels of employee loyalty. Nevertheless, Nokia's employees are known for their almost fanatical devotion to the company, in part fostered by some of the most enlightened human resource policies in the world.

It would also be useful to know the relative levels of satisfaction of each company's suppliers and customers, as well as the longevity of relationships with each. Given the manner in which Nokia's management worked with Philips to help it meet at least a portion of its orders, one suspects that Nokia is held in high regard by Philips executives, who couldn't help notice the way two of its important customers responded to the same event.

On the customer side, events like the March 2000 disruption in supplies and Ericsson's subsequent inability to meet demand for its products suggest that its customer satisfaction levels also took a hit, whether or not they were declining up to that point. What we do know is that in the ensuing year following the disruption in the supply chain, there was a three-percentage-point gain in market share for Nokia and a similar loss for Ericsson.[5] In the longer term, this may have contributed to a decision by Ericsson's management the following January to discontinue the production of cellphones entirely.

In short, this was an expensive lesson for Ericsson's management. It also represented a huge opportunity for a self-examination of its procedures, its organization, its performance appraisal practices, and even its values and culture.

Change is threatening, to leaders and especially to those being led.

This is why truly significant change requires planting the seeds of dissatisfaction with "business as usual." There is no better way of doing this than through the development of comparative yardsticks that signal opportunities for improvement, as well as organized efforts to respond to the symptoms communicated by the yardsticks.

Such yardsticks range from a pattern of incidents or stories like this to more formal measures obtained from benchmarking, peer competitor tracking, best-practice initiatives, or organization self-audits. In total, they provide ways of alerting top management to the need for change, as well as mobilizing an often reluctant organization around the need for the changes it has identified. If implemented properly, they provide tools for making a bottoms-up case for change, with higher probability for success in implementing necessary initiatives.

Both the symptoms and the causes of superior performance must be the focus of efforts by management to establish, apply, and communicate results from comparative yardsticks. What is done to improve processes, policies, and organization of effort with the help of these measurements is the subject of later chapters. The way in which the "call to action" is sounded is our concern here. What has to be done to sound this call to an underperforming organization? What challenges must outstanding organizations meet daily in maintaining their leadership? How do they do it?

■ Dealing with the Downside of Success: Overcoming the "Not Invented Here" Syndrome

For years, it was thought that success bred strong cultures, which in turn enabled successful organizations to maintain leadership positions over long periods of time. One extensive study of over 200 large U.S. corporations that examined this phenomenon found this to be true—and false.[6] In fact, strong cultures were just as often found, at some point in an organization's history, to inhibit success. Often, it was the point at which organizations looked to their own successes rather than external challenges as guidelines for action.

After searching in vain for a relationship between the strength of an organization's culture and its long-term success, the researchers decided to find out why companies with strong cultures do so well and so poorly. They visited and studied some of each, carefully paired by industry and other characteristics to eliminate explanations other than differences in their cultures. One story from the collection of field data, as told to one of the authors, will suffice.[7]

It concerns Texaco Inc., a proud vertically integrated petroleum refiner and retailer founded in 1902, that had blazed its way to the top of its industry in the 1950s through an emphasis on close to perfectly balanced volumes of production, refining, and retailing capacity and a penchant for cost control. By 1960, Texaco's stock was second only to IBM's among stocks held by mutual funds.

Texaco was regarded as a "loner" in the industry, rarely participating in industry activities. The company's strategy required highly centralized management, led by Augustus C. (Gus) Long for nearly twenty years. His emphasis on cost control was legendary.

An example of the company's careful management of expenses (and its cloistered culture) was that only three Texaco executives were permitted to belong to Houston's famed Petroleum Club at any one time, a number far fewer than at Texaco's competitors. This was put in perspective by one senior executive who said, "There was no need to belong. Texaco people kept their own counsel. There was a Texaco way and a wrong way of doing things."[8]

Oil industry analysts characterized the Texaco culture during this period as "cost concious, mean, nasty, cold, slow to change, too centralized, militaristic, authoritarian and oppressive," practicing "a total disregard of trends in the industry" and "absolute arrogance." Texaco senior executives, while somewhat kinder in their comments, labeled the organization as "very independent, highly structured, not very well-liked in the industry, inward-looking, straightlaced, honest, formal, focused on saving a nickel and proud of it."[9]

But in the late 1970s, the strategy for Texaco had become undone. Petroleum reserves declined. Some, such as those in Iran, were expropriated. Refineries and retail service stations alike had become small and outdated by industry standards (which Texaco ignored). The stations didn't reflect trends to self-service and the marketing of non-petroleum convenience goods. By 1978, Texaco's return on equity was the lowest in the industry.

Fortunately for the company, Gus Long's successor, John McKinley, made the first move to change Texaco's culture in 1980 by restructuring the company around profit centers, requiring new policies regarding the sharing of internal profit information. When James Kinnear assumed the CEO's job two years later he moved quickly to change the company's culture and performance. One of his more significant actions was his support for quality improvement initiatives in the company's outmoded refineries. This required a significant change in management's willingness to compare its performance with other organizations. By 1989, the initiatives had gained corporate-wide acceptance through what became known as the Texaco Quality Process.

Using IBM's guiding principles as a starting point, management then formalized its culture with a statement that "preserved the old values . . . but stated them in a way 'as alive as today's news.' "[10] Emphasizing "quality, customer service, shareholder-return, inspired leadership, corporate-responsibility, respect for the individual, highest ethical standards, teamwork, communication, and technological leadership," it was carried to the far reaches of the global organization by Texaco's leadership.

After a difficult turnaround, by 1992 Texaco's leadership had once again restored the company's performance, albeit on a smaller scale than during its mid-century heyday.

One common characteristic of company managements with strong cultures and poor performances in the decade of the 1980s—including IBM and Texaco—was their failure to look outside the walls of their own organizations to those doing things differently. Each defined quality according to its own standards, not those of its customers. Managers were encouraged to distance themselves not only from competitors but also from all practices foreign to accepted practice within the companies.

This study found that the shared values at the heart of an organization's culture do influence profitability and growth. Strong cultures based on shared values that encourage such factors as employee-centric and customer-centric behaviors support profitability and growth, particularly when those values are given high visibility and regularly influence strategic decisions.

■ Developing Comparative Yardsticks

An important way of getting management's attention regarding the need for change is the development of comparative yardsticks against which an organization can be compared with those engaged in "best practice." Rather than describe a range of widely known procedures by which this can be done in detail, we suggest ways in which value profit chain thinking can influence benchmarking, competitor tracking, best practice, and self-auditing initiatives.

Benchmarking, peer group or competitor analysis, the search for best practice, peer group or competitor analysis and tracking, and self-auditing are close cousins in the family of management concepts. They all have aspects, as David Altany has put it, of "learning from others . . . simply sharing."[11] They all involve knowledge transfer—the lifeblood of change—either within or between organizations.

Although there has been some argument about the terms, they all represent means of developing comparative yardsticks that provide ways of expanding management minds and encouraging continuous improvement in processes, practices, and policies. Most important, all are means of sensitizing management to the need for change. The questions are what to look for and by what means.

WHAT TO LOOK FOR

Comparative yardsticks start with the identification of symptoms and move to causes.

Symptoms.   Take the case of Nokia and Ericsson. The mere fact that Ericsson's management was not able to respond as rapidly as Nokia's in a supply crisis was itself a symptom. Similarly, other comparisons developed around elements of the value profit chain, cited in the example, provide additional symptoms. For example, that Nokia's employees are more productive is important for both companies. By itself, it could be used as a spur to Ericsson's management to reassess its use of personnel and its design of jobs, a spur to change that could eventually lead to increased value not only for Ericsson's customers but for its employees and investors as well.

Organizations that are open to change track competitors and resist the urge to rationalize unfavorable trends or gaps in performance. In fact, a few have tied executive incentive compensation to an organization's performance relative to a "peer group" of organizations, whether they are direct competitors or not. Most measures used for this purpose are financial, but if taken seriously by a management and its board, they can be useful stimulants of dissatisfaction with the status quo as well.

A particular form of comparative management, peer group profiling, has grown in recent years, most often as a means for providing incentives for an organization's top management. Once again, it measures the results achieved by various organizations on dimensions contributing to overall financial performance. It is usually based on financial and operating measures that can be obtained from published reports. The top management group may be appraised and rewarded based on its performance against the published accomplishments of a single peer company or a composite of the best performers on each of several measures. It provides a call to action without any particular indication of just how improvement is to be achieved.

Causes.   Comparative measures yield symptoms. To get to causes of these symptoms requires much closer examination of a wide range of practices thought to be contributing to the symptoms. This is where benchmarking, best practice, and self-auditing techniques come in.

By What Means

Given an indication that employee morale and satisfaction with the job appear low, one organization could of course identify another inside or outside its industry with which to consult about policies and practices. It may or may not find the right organization, and it may or may not ask questions that elicit useful information. Benchmarking, best practice, and self-auditing techniques grew as more formal, organized responses to this need to obtain ideas from other organizations.

Benchmarking.   Benchmarking was all the rage in the late 1980s and early 1990s. It received added support with the initiation of the Malcolm Baldrige National Quality Awards in the U.S. in 1987, as well as its national counterparts from the U.K. to the Philippines. All are programs that fostered self-examination and the subsequent initiation of continuous quality improvement processes in many organizations. It was pursued with an almost fanatical devotion to form, sometimes at the expense of substance. More recently, organizations in the public sector have benchmarked their activities against successful commercial organizations. For example, over the last several years the U.S. Marine Corps has used its observations of supply chain systems at such organizations as UPS, Wal-Mart, and Unilever to help it substitute information for up to $200 million in excess inventory in an effort to revamp its logistics.[12]

Whether carried out in the private or public sector, within an industry or on a "global" basis, the concept of benchmarking provides an orderly approach to previously disparate efforts. It can be carried out on a standalone basis or as one of the techniques of continuous improvement, a favorite "umbrella" vehicle for stimulating organization change.

In the U.S., the Xerox Corporation was the first most visible practitioner of benchmarking. Dr. Robert Camp, a Xerox executive, subsequently wrote "the book" on the subject, although others have followed.[13] The Xerox method involves the following 10 steps: (1) identify business activities and underlying processes most critical to business success, (2) identify comparative organizations, either best competitors or those thought to be "best in class" regarding various functional activities, such as handling accounts receivable or receiving goods at warehouses, (3) determine appropriate data collection methods, whether involving internal information, information from the public domain, or original research and investigation, often through field site visits to "best in class" practitioners, (4) determine the "competitive gap" between best in class and the current practices inside an organization, in terms of both the nature of the gap and practices contributing to it, (5) project future performance levels or achievable goals, based on the likelihood and speed of potential change resulting from the process, (6) communicate the findings, conclusions, and resulting goals in ways intended to gain acceptance for change, (7) establish more detailed functional goals at operational levels in the organization, (8) develop action plans, (9) implement specific actions and monitor progress, and (10) recalibrate, ensuring continuous improvement centered around repeated benchmarking, thereby incorporating thinking characterized by benchmarking into the very culture of an organization.[14]

Recently, benchmarking has acquired a more controversial reputation. One survey of 500 CEOs, designed by Gary Hamel and conducted by the Gallup Organization, concluded that competitive strategies were becoming more alike, raising the question of the extent to which benchmarking was responsible for the lemming-like behavior of organizations seeking to identify and implement best practices.[15] These kinds of conclusions are suspect to the extent that benchmarking is done on a global basis without respect to industry. It also ignores the major benefit of benchmarking (and other efforts to establish comparative yardsticks): getting an organization to look outside its boundaries as a prelude to change.

Benchmarking most frequently has involved the identification of functional processes most critical to a business, such as billing, order picking, or payroll processing, and the prioritization of effort according to the importance of each process to the overall performance of the organization. When applied in this manner, it can yield somewhat fragmented conclusions and actions that may or may not fit an overall strategy.

It can be carried out at a more strategic level as well, however, addressing elements of a proven strategic model—one supported by empirical research—such as the value profit chain. At this level, comparative analysis leading to idea sharing and self-improvement can address broader phenomena, such as employee productivity and loyalty, the latitude afforded employees in decision making, and incentives for the successful use of such latitude. For example, one study of 60 companies found that companies capping (putting limits on) the bonuses of their managers created much less market value than those not doing so.[16]

If the principle objective is to foster dissatisfaction with the status quo and deal a blow to management complacency, benchmarking is one of several useful ways to do this. There are others.

■ **Figure 5–1** RELATIONSHIPS BETWEEN EMPLOYEE CAPABILITY AND CUSTOMER SATISFACTION, REGIONS OF A EUROPEAN BANK

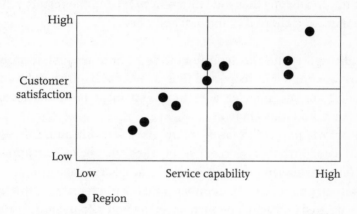

Internal Best Practice. Organizations comprising a number of operating units performing essentially the same tasks—whether exhibiting movies, operating minimills for steel production, or fixing mufflers— invariably have found differences in productivity, profitability, and other measures between the best and worst that sometimes reach a magnitude of four or five times, as suggested by comparative data for several regions of a European bank shown in Figure 5-1.

Multiunit or multibusiness organizations have the luxury of being able to foster best practice on an internal basis by creating frequent opportunities for business unit managers to share ideas (with appropriate incentives to do so). This is knowledge transfer of a highly useful nature, and it helps ensure continuous management ferment and improvement. However, it requires the establishment of comparative yardsticks, the continuous widespread communication of performance on those yardsticks, and the expectation that unit-level managers will become proactive in exchanging ideas needed to improve performance. At GE, for example, if a business unit manager boasts of a new idea to a member of senior management, the first question asked is, "Which other (business unit) managers have you told about it?" Given the GE culture of "boundaryless" behavior, "nobody" is the wrong answer.

Organizations comprising various types of businesses often find that certain functions performed by each may be quite comparable, again leading to conclusions that wide differences exist in the results achieved and the methods followed by the best and worst.

Self-Auditing.　One shortcoming of the techniques just described is that most are limited in scope and thus do not have sufficient breadth of impact on an organization's leadership and management, at least for the purpose of stimulating change.

One answer to this is a family of organizationwide audits developed for a variety of purposes in recent years. Those that have been applied so extensively that "normative" results can be scaled for cross-company and cross-industry comparison are most valuable in identifying the "gaps" between desired and actual performance, the first step in stimulating initiatives for change.

One of the earliest of these "standardized" self-audit devices was created as part of the Malcolm Baldrige National Quality Award program. It was designed to enable an organization to appraise its processes, measures, and results for individual determinants of quality against standards implied by audit questions. Responses prepared by organizations participating in the program are then reviewed by a national panel of experts, with feedback provided both in writing and (for finalists) through site visits to certify the quality of responses leading to possible recognition through awards. It is important to note that most organizations implementing Baldrige Award processes do not formally enter the award program. They gain the benefit of the self-audit process without doing so.

Other self-audits have been developed and standardized on the basis of extensive research and application. They have the advantage of covering much broader themes than audits addressing only quality improvement. If the purpose is stimulating management to action, they do the job quite well.

One such self-audit is based on the findings of James Collins and

Jerry Porras, as reported in their book, *Built to Last*.[17] Another is based on the findings we reported elsewhere.[18] An updated version of this self-audit is included in Appendix B. Both can be used to perform "gap analyses" between a management's self-perceived performance levels on a given dimension and its perceived importance of each. Those items regarded as most important by management on which management perceives its actual performance to be low (against the benchmark descriptions contained in the audit) automatically receive the highest priority for change and improvement.

■ Questions for Management

Some of the most basic questions for management raised by this discussion include the following:

1. Do the shared values at the core of your organization's culture suggest the importance of activities—listening to customers and employees, innovation, and continuous value creation, among others—that ensure productive change?

2. What organizationwide umbrella initiatives, such as customer relationship management, continuous quality improvement, knowledge transfer, or total customer satisfaction, does your organization have in place for encouraging continuous change?

3. Does your organization regularly employ peer competitor tracking as means of gauging the need for change and ways of achieving it? If so, to what extent does it track elements of the value profit chain?

4. Do you benchmark regularly to identify ways of closing the gaps on value profit chain dimensions between your organization, its competitors, and world-class practitioners?

5. What is done to communicate throughout the organization the results of benchmarking and internal and external best-practice thinking and action?

6. How does your organization encourage the exchange of good ideas among its operating units and recognize those who take the lead in doing this?

7. What are you doing regularly to discourage the complacency and external arrogance that often result from the success that fosters strong, proud cultures?

One or more techniques may be used by management to counter a sense of complacency often born of success, overcome the not-invented-here syndrome, and generally foster an urgency for change in already successful organizations that are nevertheless performing at a "merely good" level. Our concern here is less with the particular technique selected. It is instead that one or more be in place, be given high visibility, and be used as a constant spur to the organization to seek ways of increasing value. The use of the output of these efforts to emphasize the need for value-enhancing change is our next concern.

PART III

Engineering Value Profit Change

IF THERE IS A COMMON THEME to our experience, it is that profit and growth are linked directly to customer and employee satisfaction and loyalty. They are driven by the value delivered to each of several important constituencies, including customers, employees, and shareholders. There is a growing body of evidence to support all these claims.

This conceptual framework, which we have called the value profit chain, provides a powerful starting point for engineering change. Organizations managed by the value profit chain invariably represent high levels of performance in a variety of industries against which others can benchmark what they are doing and achieving.

Those who have studied the management of change cite a simple equation to illustrate the challenges facing managers who attempt to do it.[1]

Probability of change   =   Dissatisfaction (with status quo) × Quality of the Model for Change × Quality of the Process for Change > Cost of Change (to those who must endure it)

Several features of this model are worth noting. First, the perceived cost of change is nearly always high. This means that the product of dissatisfaction, quality of model, and quality of process for change must be high. The components of the formula are multiplicative, however. Thus, a low value for any one dimension greatly diminishes the likelihood of success in achieving significant change. This explains why so few change management efforts actually succeed. A recent example is that of Rick Thoman, hired by Xerox to do what he had done previously at IBM's faltering personal computer division—turn it around. His effort as CEO lasted only 13 months before he was replaced. In his words, "The difference is that I.B.M. people were ready for change. They weren't ready at Xerox."[2]

Those who have been successful at managing change have either benefited from an already high level of dissatisfaction among members of the organization or have been able to foster it, often through restructuring, layoffs, ultimatums, or benchmarking against more successful competitors and others. It is often the most distasteful step in the process. Once this step is achieved, however, the service profit chain provides both a model and a process for change. To the extent that its adherents have succeeded in rising to the top of their respective industries, it also supplies the benchmarks that can be used to eliminate management complacency and create dissatisfaction with the status quo.

The relationships comprising the service profit chain are more definitive. They imply cause and effect. We have come to believe that if you know what your employee satisfaction levels are today in important customer-facing jobs, you can predict tomorrow's levels of customer satisfaction and loyalty and the growth and profit of the organization "the day after tomorrow." The evidence supporting this position includes perhaps the most comprehensive test of these ideas, which was carried out at Sears several years ago, to which we will return.

This has governed the sequential organization of topics in this portion of the book. It is why we start with managers and progress to employees, a choice that in itself runs counter to the practices in most organizations seeking to achieve significant change. The tendency is rather to seek ways of improving customer satisfaction in the shortest period of time through pricing, improved service, or improved accessibility of a product or service. This flies in the face of most evidence suggesting that long-run customer satisfaction and loyalty are impossible to achieve unless they are preceded or accompanied by improvements in employee satisfaction and loyalty. The "trail of the money" leads back to its source: satisfied, loyal, productive managers and their employees. Let's start at the source.

Chapter 6

The Performance Trinity and the Value Profit Chain

A "performance trinity," in which value profit chain concepts are central, comprises leadership and management; culture, values, and intangible assets based largely on trust; and vision and strategy, as shown in Figure 6-1.

At its core are leaders and managers. Without them, there would be no culture, no values, no vision, and no strategy. There would be no high-capability frontline employees. Leaders and managers create and too often destroy value. The process by which they do this is complex. However, David Glass, former CEO of Wal-Mart, has succinctly stated what our evidence has demonstrated. He has said in many presentations, "Give me fewer, better trained, better paid people and they'll win every time."[1] This works at all levels of an organization, but the key to this belief is the meaning of the phrase "better qualified."

All our work suggests that *better qualified* means much more than the possession of leadership and management skills. Of greater importance is the degree to which leadership attitudes and behaviors reinforce strong and adaptive shared values at the very heart of the organization's culture.

■ The Performance Trinity

The critical roles of leadership and management are those of identifying and fostering value-building cultures, values, visions, and strategies while implementing change-reinforcing processes intended to establish and align the three components of the performance trinity, represented by the degree of overlap in the three intersecting circles in Figure 6-1.

■ **Figure 6–1**   THE PERFORMANCE TRINITY

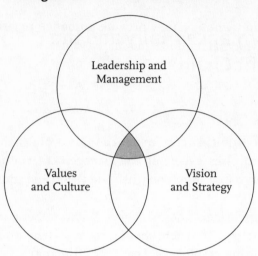

= Degree of alignment in the components of the performance trinity.

At various times during the past two decades, attention has shifted from one to another of the elements of this "trinity." Michael Porter's widely known work, comprehensively set forth in his book *Competitive Strategy,* provided a structured approach to the analysis of strategy, with primary emphasis on the so-called external aspects of strategy encompassing the sources of an organization's leverage in its relationships with other players in its competitive environment.[2] Whether or not it was Porter's intent, this was accompanied by only limited attention to culture, values, organization, or change-inducing processes, even though no strategy would be complete or even achievable without them.

Edgar Schein, in his highly regarded work, shifted attention to another element of the performance trinity.[3] He defined an organization's culture as encompassing both values shared by most members of an organization and group behavior norms—commonly held beliefs about how to act in a given organization. Group behavior norms may change from time to time, but shared values rarely do.

Work in which one of us has been involved has concluded that strong cultures are important determinants of success—and failure.[4] What is really important is whether the shared values ensure sensitivity to the needs of important constituencies—customers, employees, investors, and others—and whether they provide guidance regarding accepted norms of behavior that reinforce the shared values.

Strategy and culture may strongly influence organizational structure and the kinds of talent, skills, and knowledge hired or developed by an organization. The capability of the resulting organization will exert strong limits on the strategy, however, including growth from both internal and external sources. How often have you heard top management say, "It's what we ought to do, but we don't have the people to pull it off"? In a very real sense, what we're addressing here are ways of throwing off the constraints of human resources to enable entire organizations to achieve their full capability, thereby removing an important limit to sustainable growth and profit.

There's more. We're talking about ways of building value. According to Baruch Lev, a professor on the faculty of the Stern School of Business at New York University, the assets listed on the balance sheets of public companies in the U.S. are falling because "intangibles are fast becoming substitutes for physical assets."[5] In recent years, physical assets accounting for most of the book value of corporations have fallen to around one-third of market value, which is assumed to value both tangible assets and "intangibles." These intangibles, what some call franchise value, comprise such factors as brands, information, technology, customer relationships, the quality of employees, and the quality of an organization's leadership and administration. Given the often astronomic lifetime values of customers, managers, and employees that we examined earlier, it is easy to see why defections erode these intangible sources of value.

Elements of the performance trinity itself can be thought of as part of a comprehensive strategy formulated and implemented in the context of a broader environment. Clearly, there are complex, ambiguous relationships between elements of the trinity that defy description and provide the grist for endless debate over semantics, particularly concerning the nature of strategy. This too is suggested by the areas of overlap in Figure 6-1.

The trinity encompasses components that too often have been labeled "hard" (vision and strategy) and "soft" (culture, values, and intangible assets). Outstanding leaders have concluded that the most difficult elements to get right—and those that require the most time and are most difficult to emulate—are the soft elements.[6]

Internal consistency among components of this performance trinity is just as important as the responsiveness of the trinity to its environment. Truly innovative initiatives within the trinity can in fact change elements of the environment, what we have previously termed "changing the rules of the game."[7] The trinity itself represents a framework around which outstanding models and processes for change, critical to the successful change management model that we discussed in the introduction to this section, can be formulated.

All, however, would be impossible without the right leadership and management, suggesting the highest priority of leaders bent on change. A recent comprehensive study of leaders who led the transformation of their organizations from good to great performance provides broader support for the notion:

> We expected that good-to-great leaders would begin by setting a new vision and strategy. We found instead that they first got the right people on the bus, the wrong people off the bus, and the right people in the right seats—and then they figured out where to drive it.[8]

As Andrea Jung, incoming CEO of Avon Products, said recently, "I literally spent the first 60 days getting the right people—those who embrace change—into the top 100 jobs."[9]

Relationships between the elements of the performance trinity are reflected in recent efforts to reverse the fortunes of Office Depot, the largest purveyor of office supplies in the world.

■ The Performance Trinity at Office Depot

Office Depot's success was one of the more remarkable stories in business in the 1990s.[10] Its founders, noting the early success of a New England office supply retailer, Staples, set out to emulate its strategy of creating a "category killer" for office suppliers in creating Office Depot in 1986. Although Office Depot was second into the business, its aggressive strategy of leasing locations at a prodigious pace, then building and opening large "big box" stores of up to 30,000 square feet, particularly in the Southeast and West Coast of the U.S., soon propelled it past Staples in size. At the time, one factor thought by Office Depot executives to account for this was the more cautious and deliberate leadership, particularly at the board level, of its chief competitor. There was also more than a little preoccupation at Florida-based Office Depot with proving that it could outcompete the New Englanders at Staples. In the process, Office Depot established itself as one of the first retailers in history to hit $10 billion in annual sales within 13 years of its founding, much less time than Wal-Mart needed to reach the same milestone.

Both organizations grew rapidly. Office Depot, however, under the astute leadership of David Fuente, maintained its lead by its aggressive development of the business of contracting with large organizations to become their sole supplier of office supplies. It maintained its lead by implementing its strategy in other countries through both partnerships and wholly owned subsidiaries. It developed a large catalog-direct-sales capability. It strengthened that lead by its early entry into the on-line retailing and contract sales of office supplies. In fact, its executive vice president of e-Commerce, Monica Luechtefeld, could recall a successful negotiation leading to a contract with MIT (in the Staples "backyard") in 1995 that included faculty member Tim Berners-Lee, one of the "fathers" of the Internet. Office Depot quickly became one of the largest on-line retailers in the world.

Then Office Depot "hit a wall," particularly in its North American retail business, at the time accounting for a large portion of its sales and profits. Its leadership at the time attributed this in large part to the fact that the retail market for office suppliers had become saturated and Office Depot, being the largest, had hit the wall first. Its stock began to fall. An effort to merge with Staples was halted by the U.S. Justice Department. In the process, the companies' leaders were once again reminded of their former differences. Office Depot was generally thought to have lost a great deal of momentum while trying to complete the deal. There was "catching up" to do. This was engineered in part by the hiring of new, highly regarded talent and the rapid opening of new stores. As it turned out, however, some of the new managers were more intent on making the numbers at all costs than ensuring that the needs of employees were being met. Many of the new stores, often with two or three established, competing stores in a given market, proved to be too little, too late. The result was several quarters of disappointing results in which the numbers were not met, employee morale sagged, and the company's stock price sagged even more. It was in this context that the board decided in July 2000 to bring in a new CEO, Bruce Nelson, who had joined Office Depot two years earlier with its acquisition of Viking International, a catalog direct marketer of office products that Nelson headed at the time.

LEADERSHIP AND MANAGEMENT

In some respects, Nelson's chances for success were enhanced by Office Depot's problems, which had created a high level of dissatisfaction within the organization. Questions remained about his chances, however. His management style, with an emphasis on the "soft" elements of the performance trinity, differed markedly from that of his predecessor, who spent a great deal of time on things he enjoyed, such as deal making and the formulation of strategies designed to outwit the competition. Nelson began raising eyebrows among those furthest from the action by his early decision to begin replacing what were perceived as Office Depot's "hard-driving, highly talented" senior executives.

Nelson was very deliberate, some would say too deliberate, in selecting replacements. For example, it took him several months to find Jerry Colley, a senior operating executive from AutoZone, to take over the North American retail stores. Colley, known for his "down-home" sayings, whose style was to spend most of his time in the stores working alongside retail employees, was regarded as the direct opposite of his predecessor. He propagated the best ideas being practiced in individual Office Depot stores, ideas such as Showtime. Showtime comprises those hours of heaviest traffic in the stores when all store employees are expected to drop other duties to serve customers and Office Depot managers are prohibited from contacting stores.

Similar appointments were announced for the leadership of the contract and commercial, international, and catalog businesses, who joined the head of e-commerce at the heart of the organization. A new chief financial officer and head of human resources were named. Inside Office Depot, the word began coming up through the organization that these were the right moves.

CULTURE AND VALUES

There had been little time during Office Depot's meteoric growth to devote to culture and values. They naturally evolved from a "can-do" spirit. "Whatever it took" would be a good way to characterize them.

As a result, Nelson and his colleagues had to spend time thinking about the core values that reflected their beliefs. They tested their ideas with a broad range of employees. Given the size of the company's organi-

■ **Figure 6–2** OFFICE DEPOT VALUES AND DIMENSIONS ON WHICH THEY ARE MEASURED

Values	Dimensions
Respect for the Individual	• We value diversity across the Company. • We praise publicly and provide constructive feedback privately. • We listen; we understand and we are responsive to each other. • We treat every employee, customer and supplier with honesty, dignity and respect. • We provide a safe place to work for our employees and to shop for our customers.
Fanatical Customer Service	• We impress our customers (internal and external) so much that they want to buy again. • We give higher priority to people than to tasks. • We do it right the first time but "wow" our customers on recovery when we miss.
Excellence in Execution	• We will consistently increase shareholder value. • We consistently involve employees at all levels toward the relentless improvement of our business. • We hold ourselves and our teammates accountable for results. • We strive for perfect execution every day. • We reward innovation and intelligent risk taking. • We celebrate the wins.

Source: Office Dept, 2002

zation, now 48,000 strong, they decided to make sure that they were simple. The result? Three core values: respect for the individual, fanatical customer service, and excellence in execution. Each of the three had several dimensions, as shown in Figure 6-2. The dimensions prescribed both beliefs (such as "We value diversity across the company") and behaviors (such as "We praise publicly and provide constructive feedback privately").

Vision and Strategy

The strategic vision adopted for the company was one reflected in the culture and values. It was simply to become "the best place to work, shop, and invest." Note the order of the objectives. Reflecting the findings of value profit chain research, it placed the employees first. Office Depot was not the first to adopt this vision; Sears had pursued it, for example, in the mid-1990s.[11] For a variety of reasons, however, Sears' management had not been able to deliver on its promise, as described in Chapter 11. The company's leadership was determined to make sure that this didn't happen at Office Depot.

So-called stretch goals were developed for each of the elements of the vision: (1) become one of the top 100 companies to work for in 2 years, (2) become the fastest growing company in each of its business segments (retail, commercial, catalog and Internet, and international), and (3) provide outstanding returns to its investors.

To reinforce the vision and goals, a scorecard reflecting each dimension of each of the three values was developed. Managers at all levels of the organization were encouraged to convene their employees to develop similar measures most appropriate for their area of responsibility. For example, the measures extended down into the stores for the retail business. They were developed for each of the company's 24 U.S. distribution centers and each of its call centers for direct sales via catalog and the Internet. Sample measures from the scorecard are shown in Figure 6-3.

COMMUNICATION AND IMPLEMENTATION

Among the more important decisions made by Office Depot's management team were those concerning the "rollout" of its ideas. The first decision was to involve all 48,000 employees in a process designed to communicate the values, vision, and strategy to everyone and to challenge them to think about what needed to be changed if these were to be achieved, what would be needed to do it, and how it would have to be done. Each was asked to think about barriers to change that would have to be eliminated and what he or she would have to do differently.

The second was to try to accomplish this process of communication faster—within 2 months if possible—rather than more slowly. This was achieved through a "cascade" process of overlapping work groups extending down to all levels of the organization.[12]

RESULTS AND CHALLENGES

By the end of 2001, only 18 months after taking over, Bruce Nelson and his colleagues could point to significant accomplishments. Poorly performing stores had been closed. New international retail, commercial, and Internet services had been initiated. The company's growth had enabled it to avoid a layoff in the wake of a deepening recession and the terrorist attacks on the U.S. Measures of customer and employee satisfaction and loyalty had shot up. The company's stock had risen by 160% during the year. Transformation utilizing value profit chain ideas had worked so far.

For example, employees were becoming more innovative in ways supportive of the values and goals. These "best practices" were being communicated through such vehicles as the company's annual global management meeting. At the most recent meeting, films featuring accomplishments included shots of a Phoenix store manager inviting a customer to participate in the store's daily preopening employee kickoff meeting to suggest ways in which the store could improve. They included a California warehouse manager describing the language program instituted to bridge the gap between Spanish- and English-speaking employees. The former were learning English; the latter were learning Spanish.

■ **Figure 6–3** RETAIL BALANCED SCORECARD (WITH FIGURES INTENTIONALLY LEFT BLANK)

(Dollars in thousands unless otherwise noted)

	2nd Quarter This Year	3rd Quarter This Year	4th Quarter This Year	4th Quarter Plan	4th Quarter Last Year	Year-to-Date This Year	Year-to-Date Plan	Year-to-Date Last Year
Compelling Place to Invest								
Asset Management								
Inventory turns								
Obsolete inventory reserve (debit) credit								
Sales per total store sq ft (in whole $'s)								
Profitability								
Comparable sales % change								
Average transaction size (in whole $'s)								
Comparable transactions %								
Comparable IMU growth								
Labor (operating) % to sales								
Operating profit (without preopening) %								
Advertising Costs								
Advertising (without co-op) % to sales								
General and Administrative Costs								
G&A % to sales								

Compelling Place to Shop

	2nd Quarter This Year	3rd Quarter This Year	4th Quarter			Year-to-Date		
			This Year	Plan	Last Year	This Year	Plan	Last Year
Fanatical Customer Service								
Retail Customer Service Index								
Complaints								
Product Selection and Availability								
Average outs per store								
Top 500 outs*								
Ad outs†								

Compelling Place to Work

	2nd Quarter This Year	3rd Quarter This Year	4th Quarter			Year-to-Date		
			This Year	Plan	Last Year	This Year	Plan	Last Year
Employee Turnover								
Management								
Hourly								
Employee Engagement Index								
Employee Diversity Index								

*Stockouts among 500 most popular items.
†Stockouts among advertised items.
Source: Office Depot, 2002. This scorecard is typical of those created for each business unit within the company.

As a result, the warehouse had acquired the reputation as a great place for Hispanics to work. The film included shots of employees of the New Orleans distribution center, who had taken over much of the responsibility for the center's performance, including its high rate of pilferage, resulting in a rise from seventeenth to fourth place in performance among Office Depot's distribution centers, talking about how they did it.

Questions remained. Little or no growth in the North American retail market, still the cornerstone of the company's business, would require that it look elsewhere for the growth that the market expected. Significant margin increases had resulted from new cost-cutting ideas suggested by employees at all levels, but how long could this be continued? Could the soft elements of the performance trinity really differentiate Office Depot in ways that would be difficult for competitors, with lookalike merchandise, businesses, and even brands, to emulate? How could the company learn from and avoid the pitfalls that had beset Sears in its attempts to do much the same thing? For example, would it be able to disengage from managers who consistently "made their numbers" while abusing the shared values?[13]

Nevertheless, Office Depot's management had already achieved a great deal of progress. Note how this was done. First it required that the right people be in place, people prepared to manage by the agreed-on shared values. Next, a strategic value vision was articulated, one designed in this case to shake up the organization and deliver results rather than merely products or services. The culture and strategy enabled the company's leadership to define the talents, attitudes, and behaviors it needed to seek and encourage in its managers to implement the strategic vision in ways compatible with the culture and values. All had to be developed simultaneously by means of convincing models and processes for change, each of which had to be tested and proved workable in order to overcome natural resistance to change. In short, the performance trinity was falling into place.

Office Depot's experience is echoed by a small handful of companies, all outstanding performers in their industries, many of which we have had a chance to observe over the past two decades. It is fully consistent not only with tenets of the value profit chain but also with the managerial behaviors required to fuel the profit chain. What outstanding performers have told us about how they are able to achieve what they do provides a literal handbook for organizational reengineering, critical to the management of change and the creation of value.

■ "Reengineering" Organizations, Leaders, and Managers

As in other efforts to manage change, an organization must first understand how far under its potential it is actually performing. The best way to make the point is to benchmark practices and outcomes against world-class performers. These are easy to identify in the lists of best places to work that are prepared periodically by interested business publishers. Of course, not all great places to work are outstanding performers among their competitors, but the relationship is quite strong, as shown in an analysis of the relative economic performance of publicly listed companies named by *Fortune* magazine as Best Places to Work, presented in Figure 6-4. It suggests that the best places to work achieved growth rates in sales and profits that were substantially higher than a broader base of companies represented by the Standard & Poor's 500 list. One might argue that success contributes to great workplaces; nevertheless, these performances suggest the power of the relationship between employee satisfaction and performance. Efforts to examine how they do what they do can be eye-opening to an organization quite satisfied with its "merely good" practices and accomplishments, a matter we explore further in the next chapter.

Organizational reengineering without serious disruption takes time, but not as much time as most managers think they require. In fact, the longer that B and C players, to use GE's terminology, exist among the ranks of A players in an organization, the higher the likelihood that A players will find other sources of employment where they can work with other A players.[14]

The actions described here are not necessarily sequential; nor are they sufficient without the added initiatives described in the next chapter. Rather, progress must be made on many fronts simultaneously to achieve the desired result.

What we have found in our visits to a number of high-performing or-

■ **Figure 6–4** COMPARISON OF PERFORMANCE MEASURES, FORTUNE'S 100
BEST PLACES TO WORK VERSUS COMPANIES IN THE STANDARD & POOR'S 500, 1998–2001

Year	Avg. Growth in Revenue		Avg. Growth in Profits		Avg. Growth in Market Value	
	100 Best*	S&P 500	100 Best*	S&P 500	100 Best*	S&P 500
1998	14%	8%	116%	6%	31%	35%
1999	14%	4%	55%	9%	30%	28%
2000	24%	12%	66%	21%	96%	21%
2001	25%	13%	228%	9%	121%	5%

*The list of the 100 top employers is drawn from *Fortune's* Top 100 Employers. For each year, only those firms among the top 100 employers who are publicly owned and/or publish results are included. Therefore, the number varies year to year, including 32 companies for 1998; 29 companies for 1999; 28 companies for 2000; and 28 companies for 2001.
Source: S1 *Research Insight.*

ganizations, both for-profit and not-for-profit, were patterns of management beliefs and behaviors that were quite different from those of their merely good counterparts.[15] These organizations and their managers march to a different beat. They create fewer, more significant jobs, extending spans of control; give those jobs only to those who buy into the organization's performance trinity; force change in leadership and management behavior; measure, recognize, and reward the delivery of results by means of a "balanced score card" of value profit chain measures; pay more in order to pay less; deliver value from the center as well as on the front line; and move fast.

The remarkable thing about these best practices is that we found few organizations following them. In fact, conventional practice argues against most or all of them. Further, we found that merely good managers have a tendency to implement only certain of these practices. They search for the "one best idea" that provides the key to performance turnaround. As a result, they achieve no significant results. In many cases, their results are worse than average, leading us to conclude that there is no destination halfway in this journey. Managers must buy it all or seek out some other vehicle for managing change.

Create Fewer, More Significant Jobs—Extending Spans of Control

As A players are moved into position and B and C players replaced, jobs can be combined and reconfigured, leading to a reduction in force. Remember David Glass's admonition that "fewer, better trained, better paid employees . . . win every time"? This action often leads to dissatisfaction among B and C players. It has the reverse effect on A players, who now see everyone pulling their weight in the organization. It is only one of the factors influencing increased satisfaction.

This process can literally change the shape of the organization. It challenges long-held beliefs about limits on the span of control over which an individual can manage effectively at the same time that it leads to a rethinking of the management task.

For example, such organizations as FedEx, Xerox, and Taco Bell, in an effort to reduce administrative costs while expanding the capability of their frontline employees, have created management positions to which numbers of people report that represent several times the limit formerly thought possible. At CEMEX, the world's third largest multinational supplier of cement and related products, the demand for management to accommodate growth is so great that former country manager jobs are being replaced by positions with responsibility for the management of several countries or a region, freeing talent for deployment elsewhere in the world and relaxing a serious constraint on growth.[16]

GIVE THE JOBS ONLY TO THOSE WHO BUY INTO THE PERFORMANCE TRINITY

Upon assuming responsibility for the New York Police Department in 1994, Commissioner William Bratton had first to identify the focal point for operating responsibility in the department and then identify the people he wanted in jobs located at the focal point, people who believed passionately in a vision for change.[17]

Responsibility was focused on the commanders in charge of each of the city's 76 precincts. The essence of the vision was that from that point forward the department would be managed for results (a lower major crime rate) rather than effort (the number of responses to 911 emergency calls). Candidates were asked whether they believed that crime could be, in effect, "managed," and with what results. Three of four failed the test, either because they believed (along with many students of the subject) that their actions could have little or no impact on crime levels. They were moved aside and replaced with those who believed in the vision. The results these successors produced exceeded all expectations and literally changed life in the city for the better for years.

The story is repeated in organizations that have succeeded in reengineering themselves. The proportions of those managers failing the new tests posed by the initiative are also remarkably similar to those experienced by Bratton and his team at the NYPD.

FORCE CHANGE IN LEADERSHIP AND MANAGEMENT BEHAVIORS

The creation of fewer, more significant jobs with greater spans of control, if done decisively, can force important changes in leadership and management behavior, literally sorting out those capable of such change from those unable to make the transition.

The nature of the management task—at Office Depot, CEMEX, FedEx, or Taco Bell—has been changed from that of command and control over subordinates to that of consulting and cheerleading with associates who are largely responsible for governing the limits of their actions and meeting certain nonnegotiable core standards in their work. As a result, these organizations have fewer layers of management than in the past and far fewer managers than before, pay higher individual salaries for management talent, and have achieved lower administrative costs than were previously thought possible.

For example, with responsibility for the performance of managers overseeing 60 restaurants, market managers at Taco Bell had no time for conventional oversight tasks.[18] Instead, they had to apply their skills in helping their direct reports formulate market strategies for the restaurants in their respective market areas as well as ensuring that best practice ideas are communicated among restaurant managers. They had to serve as consultants and cheerleaders to managers reporting to them.

Perhaps the most extreme version of this practice is one of telling managers that, provided their organizations achieve certain nonnegotiable minimum standards, they can do whatever else they deem necessary to increase the performance of their organizations. This was implemented in the late 1980s at Au Bon Pain, the chain of French bakery cafes, by one of us under the belief that if you treat employees like adults, trust them, and reward them properly, they can achieve extraordinary results. This proved to be the case at Au Bon Pain, where managers who rose to the occasion were able to double and triple the profits of their stores, thereby increasing their compensation levels by three or four times through a system that allowed them to split profits above goals negotiated with the company.

This is consistent with what research has told us—that you achieve outstanding results by prescribing outcomes, not methods, then helping talented managers and employees achieve the outcomes by whatever means they see fit, within prescribed limits of corporate policy.[19]

Notice that we have not used the most overworked and misused word in the English business language here, the one that starts with "e" and contains the word *power*. The concept of maximum latitude within limits trumps that one every time.

Hire and Promote with "A Player" Input

Organizations that have been most successful in reengineering themselves have engendered strong cultures based on strongly shared values and behavior norms. They often become "cultlike," with a great deal of informal coaching regarding accepted norms as well as the ability of frontline managers to act in response to immediate needs for decisions, confident that their knowledge of the culture will lead them to make acceptable decisions and take acceptable actions.

This argues, however, for heavy reliance on existing employees in decisions to hire and promote within the organization. Typical of such organizations is a relatively high percentage of new employees, sometimes as much as a third, hired on the recommendations of existing employees. Further, management inputs in promotion decisions are taken particularly seriously. All of these recommendations are discounted on the basis of the quality of the source. Why? Because research and common sense suggest that managers and employees most often associate with and attract others like themselves. A players attract (and most often recommend) A players; B players attract B players. Furthermore, A employees are more likely to recognize A behaviors in prospective employees as well as managers when they see them.

Measure and Reward the Delivery of Results

Performance-based reward systems based on the delivery of results define in part the employee "talents" needed by an organization. They attract "scorekeepers," who are able to rise to the challenge of frequent measurement and comparison.

The frequency of measurement, comparison, and reward of course depends on the nature of behaviors being encouraged. At MBNA's customer service call center, for example, hundreds of employees provide personalized service to the holders of credit cards issued by the company.

In an effort to maintain the highest levels of service in the industry as a means of achieving the highest level of cardholder usage and loyalty, MBNA measures customer satisfaction from these interactions daily. Scores are posted and rewards accumulated on a daily basis. The rewards themselves are paid monthly. The intent here is to give each "team" of service personnel a fresh start daily toward winning a reward. It requires an assiduous effort to track customer satisfaction, a useful by-product of the initiative.[20]

More complex tasks require more complex measurement and compensation systems. For some, a "balanced scorecard" similar to that implemented at Office Depot, including both financial and nonfinancial measures, may be appropriate.

REDUCE UNPLANNED MANAGEMENT DEFECTIONS

Outstanding performers engineer a certain amount of turnover into their human resource strategies. The most systematic way in which this is done is to dismiss periodically a stated percentage of the lowest performers. Others are less dogmatic about this, but all regard zero turnover as a warning signal.

Having said this, every effort is made to retain all others in the organization, leading to unplanned turnover that is often less than that of competitors by a factor of 2 or 3. This is in part a natural by-product of actions discussed earlier, but it requires constant, frequent attention to the needs of individuals from those who are nominally responsible for "managing" them. In fact, winning managers are often characterized by their systematic, proactive efforts to devise ways of interacting with each of the people who report to them, ensuring that the needs of both the organization and the individual are met.

PAY MORE IN ORDER TO PAY LESS

Witness the results from the implementation of this concept at organizations from Taco Bell to General Electric.

The creation of market management positions responsible for as many as 60 restaurants at Taco Bell enabled the restaurant chain to eliminate two layers of management occupied by district and regional managers in a traditional organizational pyramid with spans of control of roughly eight at each level. This in turn enabled the company to hire from the ranks of MBAs, paying up to $120,000 in salary and incentives, much more than had been paid to previous district or regional managers. By eliminating many of these jobs, Taco Bell was able to attract a new caliber of talent to the industry while reducing its overall management compensation.[21]

Over the 20-year period from 1980 to 2000, GE's average compensation per employee for all businesses except GE Capital Services, increased by 142%.[22] However, compensation as a percentage of sales for the corporation actually fell by more than half.

At the highest levels of the GE organization, the goal has been to build a team of A players by a number of means, one of which is compensation. In recent years, for example, the list of managers receiving stock options has been greatly expanded to include more than 20,000. By building the capability of this cadre of leaders within the organization, GE has received a high return on its investment in salaries and incentive compensation. In the process, it has provided a convincing illustration of the importance of paying more in order to pay less.

Paying more in order to pay less also reduces overall employment costs to the extent that it contributes to the reduction in unplanned management defections.

Deliver Value from the Center

A primary motive for many of the behaviors that describe GE's leadership is the determination to prove that the center of this highly diversified company delivers value that justifies not breaking the company into more homogeneous pieces.[23] This is achieved at GE through many nonfinancial means, such as the development of management talent among (rather than within) business units; the identification and leadership of cross-business initiatives, such as Six Sigma Quality, Workout, and others; a concentration on knowledge transfer through not only the corporatewide business initiatives but also the operation of the premier management development center in the business world at Crotonville,

New York; and the provision of world-class support systems for the provision of legal, human resource, and financial services.

GE's headquarters management must provide continuing evidence that it delivers value because of the diversified nature of the firm, but it sets an example for less diversified organizations as well, particularly those that practice decentralization to the point that it actually destroys value through the creation of intracompany barriers among profit centers. GE's form of enlightened decentralization, which imposes distinct limits on the latitude of profit center managers, serves as an example for many other organizations. It requires careful management of the highest quality. It is also an antidote to the value destruction that occurs at the center of companies whose pieces are worth more than the market value of the entire organization.

MOVE FAST

After having led the complete rethinking of General Electric's performance trinity and the reengineering of its organization between 1981 and 1985, reducing GE's employment headcount by 30% through company divestitures and downsizing, Jack Welch expressed his single biggest regret. He hadn't moved fast enough. In his words,[24]

> I don't think I have moved fast enough. I don't think that I have moved as decisively as I should have in some areas. . . . These incremental nudgings and coaxings in a world that is moving in nanoseconds (are) absolutely not acceptable in leading corporate change today. I was too cautious and too timid. I wanted too many things, too many constituencies on board. I believe that.

■ The Results? Higher Productivity, Growth, and Profitability

Many managers start here. In high-capability organizations it is instead a result, the product of the initiatives described earlier. But it is an end that also serves as a means to other accomplishments.

Consider once again GE's experience between 1981 and 2001. During this period of time, the company's employee base went from 402,000 to 313,000 while its sales increased 370%, an increase in productivity (measured in sales per employee, adjusted for inflation) of 189%, or nearly 8% compounded annually. This contrasts with a compounded rate, adjusted for inflation, of less than 2% during the previous 10 years under GE's universally lauded leadership.[25]

This has provided the company greater latitude in the more competitive pricing of its products and services while increasing its profitability (again, adjusted for inflation) nearly sevenfold. At the same time, many of GE's businesses have pursued strategies that differentiate their products and services from competitors. It suggests that the product of the actions described here enables an organization to have it all—product or service differentiation, more competitive prices, and higher profits. This, in the words of Robert Collins and Jerry Porras, authors of the influential book *Built to Last,* represents avoiding "the Tyranny of the OR," and embracing "the Genius of the AND."[26] As they go on to point out, "We're not talking about balance here. 'Balance' implies going to the midpoint, fifty-fifty, half and half. . . . A visionary company doesn't seek simply balance between idealism and profitability; it seeks to be highly idealistic and highly profitable."[27]

■ Questions for Managers

The observations and evidence presented in this chapter raise several questions for managers seeking value-centered change in their organizations:

1. Are you sure that you have the right people in place before launching efforts to change the trajectory of performance for the organization?

2. When necessary, how will you capitalize on—or create if necessary—discontent with the status quo to overcome opposition to change?

3. Do you have a clear vision and a series of processes for accomplishing change in your organization?

4. Do you devote enough time to the task of making the soft elements of the performance trinity—values, culture, leadership, and management—hard?

5. To what extent does your organization:

   a. Create fewer, more significant jobs, extending spans of control?

   b. Give those jobs only to those buying into the performance trinity?

   c. Thereby force change in leadership and management behaviors?

   d. Hire and promote with A player input?

   e. Measure and reward the delivery of results?

   f. Reduce unplanned management defections?

   g. Pay more in order to pay less?

   h. Deliver value from the center?

   i. Move fast in organizational reengineering efforts?

6. Have you made an attempt to identify, retrain, and, if necessary, dismiss those members of management who are not able to manage by the values, regardless of their ability to make their numbers?

7. To what degree have you implemented the concept of a "balanced paycheck" that reflects important elements of the value profit chain, such as employee and customer satisfaction, commitment, and loyalty, as well as growth and profitability?

Experiences at Office Depot and a select group of other high-performing organizations suggest that much of what works for managers holds for employees as well. The process of building high-capability frontline organizations, whether in manufacturing or service industries, for-profit or not-for-profit, can be characterized as employee relationship management. At its core, it involves treating employees like customers.

Chapter 7

Employee Relationship Management: Treating Employees Like Customers

*T*HE CUSTOMER COMES SECOND is the eye-catching title that Hal Rosenbluth and Diane McFerrin Peters chose for their book several years ago.[1] Data from value profit chain research supports this notion. Experiences at organizations as diverse as Cisco Systems, Alcoa, and the Willow Creek Community Church help illustrate it.

One of the strongest proponents of employee relationship management (ERM) is Cisco Systems, the Internet networking equipment and solutions provider that fell on relatively hard times with the decline of its markets in the wake of the bursting of the telecommunications "bubble." Hard times for Cisco, however, even at the nadir of its particular recession in 2001, meant revenue per employee of nearly $600,000, more than double that of its competitors. In fact, few organizations in any industry, no matter how healthy their markets, achieve a significant fraction of those numbers.[2]

The philosophy of treating employees like customers contributed in no small measure to Alcoa's performance under Paul O'Neill, who would later become Secretary of the Treasury under President George W. Bush. According to one account,[3]

> On his first day, he told Alcoa's executives that . . . the only way to improve the company's fortunes was to lower its costs . . . [through] the cooperation of Alcoa's workers . . . [by showing] them that you actually cared about them . . . [by establishing] as the first priority of Alcoa, the elimination of all job-related injuries (a major concern of aluminum industry workers). Any executive who didn't make worker safety his personal fetish—a higher priority than profits—would be fired.

Pastor Bill Hybels and his team at Willow Creek Community Church understand the notion clearly in engaging the hearts and souls of hundreds of volunteers.[4] At Willow Creek, like many social-sector organizations, customers and employees (often volunteers) may be one and the same. Nevertheless, in many ways Willow Creek's success, which has produced the fastest-growing church in the world, is due to its attempts to understand the needs of potential members as well as its volunteers. These needs are then reflected in church operating policies. As one remarkable example, Willow Creek only creates *ministries*, groups of church members and volunteers providing critical services of various kinds, when a member of the organization evidences a strong desire to lead them. Thus, ministries reflect the interests of volunteers as much or more than the needs of the community. The organization understands the importance of leadership to the success of any venture, and it understands the importance of treating employees like customers.

■ Treating Employees Like Customers: Cisco Systems

Cisco's employee relationship management initiatives have not been very visible in the blizzard of publicity surrounding the company and its efforts to exhort potential customers to "do as it does." This involves capitalizing on the "Internet ecosystem" to implement Internet-based applications connecting the company to customers, suppliers, and others—of course, using Cisco's routers and other hardware and software products and services to do so. Employee relationship management was one of the first functions networked at Cisco in 1995 through the creation of an intranet site.

This emphasis helps explain why Cisco has been at or near the top of the list of best places to work in the U.S. It has achieved this through, among other things, enlightened workplace policies, significant employee benefits, a strong culture intended to strengthen internal relationships, and generous use of options awarded on the first day of employment (as opposed to unusually high salaries, which would violate the company's emphasis on frugality).[5]

The company has relied for its sustainable growth on both the increasing productivity of its existing employees and the potential for future productivity embodied in those numerous smaller organizations that it has acquired. During the days of the company's heady growth, potential acquisitions were evaluated primarily in terms of strategic fit (with a heavy emphasis on compatible cultures), creative new product ideas, and cost per acquired professional. They were also evaluated in terms of their size, measured in people. Because it paid top dollar for these people, it had to ensure that it could engage and retain them. This meant restricting the size of each acquisition so that acquired employees could be oriented quickly to Cisco's very strong culture and well-defined management policies. As a result, it had to excel at bringing new employees into the organization. Mimi Giroux, who herself had been an employee of a company acquired by Cisco in a badly implemented integration in 1994 and was engaged to assist in improving the process, commented, "My standard rule is, I'm going to keep those people whole."[6] Recent critics of the company's practices have claimed that despite such efforts the heads of many of the companies acquired by Cisco have long since departed the company.[7] Even in the face of its problems, however, Cisco's management claimed to have been able to maintain a voluntary departure rate of no more than 12% through the end of 2001, significantly lower than that of other Silicon Valley high-tech firms.

Repeatedly, we have encountered in high-capability organizations the firm belief that there is a limit to the relative number of new (versus existing) employees that an organization can absorb each year. This is true at Cisco. In recent years, the company's leadership has repeatedly rejected acquisitions that would position it more strongly in the lucrative Internet service business because it would require the addition of literally thousands of employees producing annual revenues of less than $200,000 per employee to have the same impact on growth and profitability of smaller, higher-tech acquisitions. The numbers of new employees would be just too great to absorb.

One practice by which Cisco maintains a controllable growth rate of its organization and high revenue per employee is by outsourcing more people-intensive activities, such as assembly and product service, a practice moderated only during slow-growth periods. For those hired or added to the organization by acquisition, the drive to retain valued employees at Cisco starts before they arrive. Compatible culture is a prime factor in the decision either to hire or to make an acquisition. The company's values—focusing on dedication to success, innovation and learning, partnerships, teamwork, and doing more with less (with an emphasis on frugality)—provide the criteria.

The effort continues on the first day of employment at Cisco. Upon arriving at work, a new employee finds that she already has an active account on the Cisco Employee Connection (CEC), one that provides constant access to all personal files describing benefits and other information as well as a medium for filing expense reports, accessing such things as the calendars and photographs of colleagues, and communicating with others in the company. The goal is to allow every new hire to be productive in the job on the first day without the distraction of having to resolve personal details. Employment itself entitles an employee to stock options. The value of those options is calculated constantly and is immediately available to the new employee. Despite this, the company found that employees preferred other portals to the CEC, especially My Yahoo! To increase the use of CEC, Cisco arranged with Yahoo to set up a customized My Yahoo! Web site just for Cisco employees, allowing them to view sports scores, weather, and news in addition to Cisco-only information. As a result, employees were given the content they wanted along with the content the company wanted them to have.[8]

Employment does not carry with it the assumption of a lifetime association with Cisco. Far from it. Even though the company has regularly pruned its poorest performing employees from its rolls and was forced to lay off 8,500 of its 48,000 employees during the 2001 downturn, Cisco, even at the height of the technology boom, was able to achieve an unplanned employee defection rate that was less than half that of its major competitors for talent in the Silicon Valley. This is perhaps the most important reason that the company was able to grow at rates of more than 50% per year on a sustained basis before the downturn.

■ Treating Employees Like Customers: Alcoa

CEO Paul O'Neill determined what employees wanted most at Alcoa—safety on the job—and made sure that he had the right management team to help them create what was termed by one report "the world's safest place to work."[9] It required replacing those managers who didn't believe the results could be achieved. No one believed that safety alone would ensure that Alcoa achieved its profit targets. It was used to prove to the entire organization what they could do, however. If they could all but eliminate accidents on the job, they could apply the same processes and effort to reduce costs.

In the process, the organization was flattened and more and more responsibility shifted to the front line. This proved to be too much for some managers at all levels who were not comfortable with the degree of latitude being given to those reporting to them. O'Neill and his colleagues literally launched a war on hierarchy, selling Alcoa's prestigious downtown Pittsburgh office building and moving into much more modest quarters where office design did not reflect rank. The same profit-sharing plan was created for both managers and employees.

Over time, the results were dramatic. During O'Neill's 12 years at the helm of Alcoa, his belief in the employees paid off handsomely. The company's profits reached $1.5 billion in 2000 from a low of almost nothing in 1993. Its stock appreciated 33 times over the same period of time.[10]

■ Treating Employees Like Customers: Willow Creek Community Church

There are few employees in the traditional sense at Willow Creek Community Church, an evangelical religious organization located in Barrington, Illinois,[11] but there are many members and volunteers, the lifeblood of the church. Before they were members, they were believers. Before that they were seekers, "unchurched Harrys and Marys," in the lingo of the organization. Willow Creek's genius has been its ability to attract the unchurched through a seven-step process that begins by sorting out seekers from believers, a concept based on research by Pastor Bill Hybels. According to Hybels, he found that people had given up on organized religion because it was boring, didn't address the needs of modern families, and was always asking for money. His answer was to create a seekers service that was entertaining, that linked the teaching of the Bible to issues facing modern Americans, that did not involve religious icons, and that did not ask for contributions. At the same time, he created a separate believers service focused on important messages from the Bible in a more conventional religious setting for those convinced that Willow Creek was the church for them. Believers subsequently were invited to bring seekers to subsequent seekers' services and to try to get acquainted with those seekers attending out of curiosity. The result was explosive growth for a church that now attracts more than 20,000 to its Sunday services.

Explosive growth would be regarded as heaven-sent by most religious organizations. At Willow Creek, it created important challenges in an organization seeking to treat its volunteers and staff members like customers.

The numbers of seekers showing up at Willow Creek's doors unaccompanied by believers became so great that believers, members, volunteers, and staff members began to feel overwhelmed. More important, the seekers couldn't be properly introduced to the Church or informed of the process by which one might associate with it in more significant ways. Some may have regarded it as the best form of entertainment—its music and drama had become that professional—on a Sunday morning in suburban Chicago.

As a result, Willow Creek's leadership actually decided in the early 1990s to discourage rampant growth in the church's size until it could rethink its strategy, focusing on the needs of its members, volunteers, and staff, eventually enabling it to better serve its clientele of seekers and believers. For a period of some months, Willow Creek may have been the only church in the world not seeking to grow in reach, influence, and membership.

This reappraisal, in addition to clarifying the ecclesiastical foundation of the church's strategy, led to more effective ways of introducing seekers into the church, decisions to increase the number of "ministries" and services within the church that could involve larger numbers of believers in more significant activities, a division of the organization into teaching (preaching) and administrative tasks, and an outreach program akin to franchising that would allow the church to grow through its Willow Creek association. The association is designed to help congregations around the world create their own version of Willow Creek, often under different names, by making available operating manuals, the texts of sermons, and even the forms used to encourage comment on and control the quality of their church's activities. The appeal of the association has been as great as that of the mother church. As of late 2001, it had over 7,200 member churches worldwide.

Even given this reappraisal of strategy and the resumption of growth of Willow Creek, policies are still in place designed to maximize the success of the experience for members, volunteers, and staff. For example, staff are surveyed regularly regarding the value that they derive from their association with the church. The more than 100 "ministries" within the church, ranging from food relief to car repair, are still maintained only if and as long as there are members willing to lead them: no leadership, no ministry, regardless of need.

Clearly, Willow Creek is what we would call customer oriented, but it just as firmly treats its volunteers and staff like customers as well. Along with Cisco Systems and Alcoa, it has achieved high capability, measured by staff members' ability to create value, by treating employees like customers. What exactly does this mean?

■ What We Are Learning: Breaking the Cycle of Mediocrity

Let's start by reviewing what we and others have learned in the past few years of remarkable progress in understanding what makes high-capability organizations tick. For us, much of it started in organizations like Au Bon Pain, where one of us had a chance to experiment with his own human resource management initiatives,[12] and the Fairfield Inn division of Marriott International, where Mel Warriner changed our thinking about expectations for people and the excellence that can be achieved by setting expectations high. Mel's story is in many ways the most interesting.[13]

In the mid-1980s, Warriner, a human resource management maverick, was ready to experiment with counterintuitive ideas about how to mobilize an organization. He was in the right place at the right time, a perfect choice to join a small team charged by Bill Marriott to find itself some office space outside Marriott headquarters and come up with a plan to get the company into the economy lodging business fast to counteract competitors like Hampton Inns that had a five-year head start in the business. The team was led by an individual described by one team member as a "visionary without discipline," perfect for the job. To Bill Marriott's credit, he was sure that if the team members didn't get out of headquarters, their ideas would be suffocated by the conventional wisdom—collected over many years and reinforced by the fact that most senior management had graduated from only a handful of hotel schools—about how to design and run a hotel. He was years ahead of his time in employing a strategy to combat a "disruptive technology," one characterized by fewer services at much lower prices, represented by economy lodging, the fastest growing segment of the industry.[14]

The resulting Fairfield Inns were designed to deliver only two things, the friendliest employees and the cleanest rooms anywhere, all for a price at the time of no more than $39.95 per night. Facility design was simple, omitting such complex elements as a restaurant or an elaborate pool area and making it easy to staff the hotel with only two groups of people, those at the desk performing administrative tasks and those cleaning the rooms. The facility and staffing plan were the least innovative aspects of the plan that Warriner and his colleagues came up with.

The plan turned conventional wisdom upside down concerning hotel employees and how to motivate and reward them. It focused on the housekeepers, not the "front of the house." To deliver on the promise of "cleanest rooms anywhere," Warriner needed to attract housekeepers who were best in class. He wanted fewer of them, to be paid better and to be more comfortable in responding to performance measurement and incentive rewards than other housekeepers. They had to be obsessive about cleanliness, "scorekeepers" who enjoyed being compensated based on open competition, and able to relate to guests: quite a combination. As Warriner learned later, it described about 1 in 24 who applied for the job. To find them, he called in the Gallup Organization to structure a selection strategy around "life themes" that defined such factors as a person's obsessions, interests, and behaviors.[15] Never had so much attention been given to selecting a hotel housekeeper.

Warriner needed this kind of housekeeper because of his plan to measure performance with electronically gathered guest opinions about cleanliness and friendliness, collected at the time of checkout with a computer-aided touch screen device called SCORECARD. He needed them because of his intent to post the scores publicly on a weekly basis and pay bonuses based on the level of guest satisfaction levels with the cleanliness of their rooms. He also needed them because, under his plan, housekeepers would be visible members of the staff, at the forefront in guest relations. Many would be asked to manage a guest amenities budget, allowing them to spend a modest amount of money at their own discretion to make sure that frequent guests, especially "road warriors" covering a regional business territory, might occasionally be wowed by the personally selected food items waiting for them in their rooms upon their arrival, a process often managed by the housekeeping staff. The plan would only work, of course, if housekeepers were given the latitude to perform their jobs, recognized as important members of the team, and rewarded sufficiently to encourage them to remain on staff long enough to become acquainted with frequent guests and their preferences.

With the help of his consultant, Warriner devised ways of finding this rare breed by measuring those factors that distinguished outstanding housekeepers in other hotels from those who were only average. Many of these differences had to do with attitudes toward their work, measurement and incentives, and interacting with guests. They also had to do with an ability and willingness to take responsibility not only for their actions but those of others, because Warriner instituted an "attendance bonus," granting extra days of "earned leave" to those who saw that their jobs were staffed by either themselves or other qualified housekeepers with whom they had made arrangements in advance.

In short, Warriner had to find adults who were expected to be treated as adult members of a functioning team, taking responsibility for their own actions and those of others. He did it, in the process opening our curious eyes about revolutionary ways of managing frontline human resources while freeing up managers from "babysitting" supervisory tasks to enable them to do more important work.

Warriner and others like him have broken what we have termed the "cycle of mediocrity," shown in Figure 7-1, in which frontline customer-facing jobs are designed down to their lowest component so that little training is required to perform them. Of course, these jobs then warrant little compensation. Little surprise then that employers face high rates of turnover in such jobs. They assume that, since training costs are low, the cost of turnover is low, completely ignoring the adverse impact of high turnover on customer satisfaction. Managers have little opportunity to relate in any way to such employees, instead spending most of their time overseeing a revolving door staffing process. Mel Warriner reversed the

■ Figure 7–1   THE CYCLE OF MEDIOCRITY*

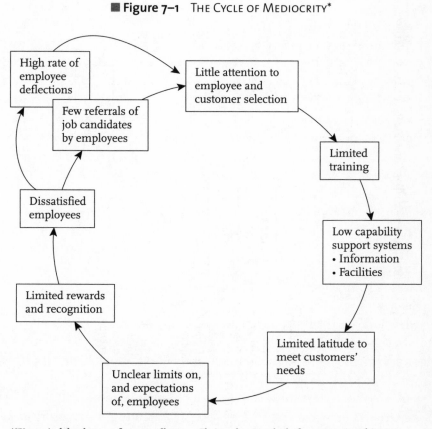

*We are indebted to our former colleague, Christopher Lovelock, for suggesting this term.

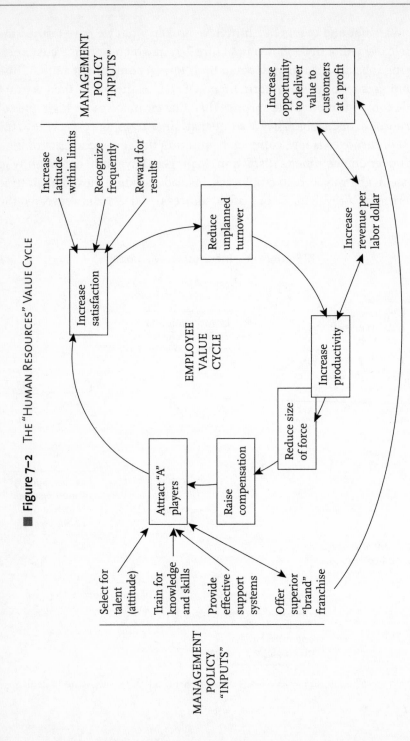

■ **Figure 7–2**   The "Human Resources" Value Cycle

direction of the cycle, creating the human resources value cycle shown in Figure 7-2. His actions reflect those we've seen repeatedly in high-performing organizations.

■ Steps in Breaking the Cycle of Mediocrity

High-capability organizations are built from the ground up, starting from the identification of business mission or objectives, the general targeting of people needed to deliver them, and the selection of individual employees. Great organizations select for attitude and train for skills. They regard personal development as both ends and means. They follow this with the creation of outstanding support systems, both human and technical. This allows them to broaden the latitude with which employees can solve problems for customers, always within limits. They then measure, recognize, and reward those who deliver such results with attendant process quality. Some then completely reverse traditional ideas of "limits" by allowing employees to do anything to achieve long-run benefits for the company as long as they fulfill a core set of expectations. All this can be achieved only with substantial costs of the loss of those unable to adjust to the challenges of these practices, the retraining of others, and the development of support systems necessary to make the delivery of desired results a routine matter. These initiatives are preceded by efforts to identify the business mission and target the labor market.

IDENTIFY A FOCUSED BUSINESS MISSION

Had Fairfield Inn's planners not first identified a focused business mission, they would not have been able to profile the kinds of people needed to achieve it. Typically, organizations try to be too many things to too many people. Fairfield didn't have time to do everything in its efforts to catch its competitors, led by Hampton Inn. Its management specified only two targets based on the most important needs of economy lodging patrons, clean rooms and friendly employees.

Southwest Airlines attempts to deliver only a few things to its customers: on-time arrivals, frequent departures, empathetic employees, fun, and a cost that is as low as or lower than traveling by automobile. This dictates a selection process that focuses on hiring empathetic employees who enjoy doing things a little differently. For this reason, candidates for the job of cabin attendant at Southwest are asked to participate in large group interviews in which each is asked to stand up and relate his or her most embarrassing moment. Interviewers not only watch the person doing the reciting. They also watch others to see whether they are empathizing with the person in the spotlight, selecting only those who are.

TARGET THE LABOR MARKET

Just as desired customers are targeted in deliberate marketing strategies, so too must an enlightened human resource strategy target labor markets. This requires knowing just what characteristics are sought for various positions, à la Mel Warriner, and taking steps to make sure that the ordinary temptations of everyday hiring aren't allowed to subvert the plan.

The targeting process is often based on a measurement of the characteristics shared by successful practitioners of the job to be filled. It requires inventorying existing employees for this purpose through the interviews and questionnaires designed to unearth basic beliefs and behaviors, for example. This is what Fairfield Inn's management set out to do. Once targets are established, the next step is to "hire for attitude," a term that reflects a propective candidate's ability to identify with the needs of customers and fellow employees as well as the shared values of the organization as a whole.

HIRE AND FIRE FOR ATTITUDE

The selection of managers and employees is the most important decision made in an organization. Those who are most successful in the large sample of organizations we have studied devote at least as much attention to attitude as to skills in making their selections.

In reporting these findings and conclusions, we have encountered frequent doubters. Among our most vocal critics were practitioners of medical services, who derided us for even thinking about hiring doctors on the basis of first attitude, then skills. Only 10 years later, with the publication of evidence showing that the vast majority of malpractice lawsuits against doctors could have been avoided through displays of improved attitude on the part of caregivers, medical administrators are coming around to the notion that the practices apply even to their profession.[16]

Challengers of these ideas should take very seriously the work of Buckingham and Coffman, given the vast amount of data on which it is based.[17] They sought to differentiate great managers from their average (or worse) counterparts. What they found turned upside down much of the conventional wisdom concerning frontline management. Among other things, they found that great managers pick the right people, trust them, don't overpromote them, never pass the buck, and make very few promises to their people but keep them all.[18] Nothing too revelatory here—but there's more.

They found that great managers select primarily for talent (including attitude) because they know that it is largely a waste of time to try to correct this kind of shortcoming in an employee once he or she is hired. Talent is defined for each job by studying the behaviors of the best-performing employees already on that job; the objective is to replicate the talent.

This work is consistent with ours on almost all dimensions, but it refines it significantly, particularly in terms of priorities for hiring. We have repeatedly found great organizations hiring for attitude and training for skills, but Buckingham and Coffman speak about great managers "hiring for talent," something that, in contrast to knowledge and skills, cannot be taught. Their definition of talent includes how people strive (why they do what they do), think, and relate (to others). Different combinations of talent are required for various jobs. The key is in establishing the fit between talent sets and jobs. It is found by studying the talents of the best-performing individuals in each job and then hiring others on that basis.

The process must start with a management resolve both to hire and to "weed the ranks" of managers and employees in critical roles on the basis of talent: in the words of Buckingham and Coffman, "striving, thinking, and relating" behaviors. In their terminology, this requires an identification of the kinds of "talent" (including attitude) required for critical jobs, a process in which outstanding performers in those jobs play a vital role.

However, success in hiring (and firing) for desired talents demands an understanding of the culture and strategy of an organization as well as the requirements of the job. It requires an examination of the talents possessed by those most able to fill the needs of a job while fitting into the organizational culture and strategic game plan. Those unable to fit the culture and manage by the values of the organization have to go, regardless of their ability to make their numerical goals. This was an important conclusion reached in the early 1990s at GE, for example, where so-called "Type IV" managers, those who delivered on their commitments, making their numbers, but didn't share the organization's values, began to be relieved of their jobs.[19]

For those not possessing needed talents, great managers claim that it is a waste of time trying to help people attain them. Either they "manage around" them, by teaming managers with complementary talents, or terminate the manager based on the conclusion that one shouldn't "waste time trying to put in what was left out."[20]

An important element of talent at the outset of a change effort is belief in the ability of the organization to make significant change and in one's ability to manage in the new environment. It requires a reassessment of existing managers to determine their attitudes toward change and the possibility of achieving significantly higher goals. Such reassessments typically result in a categorization of managers into three groups: the third who accept higher goals and the change they imply, the third who accept higher goals and are willing to make the significant effort needed on their part to adapt to a changed environment, and the third who are unwilling or unable to be a part of the change. In our experience, the ratios are surprisingly constant across organizations as diverse as Taco Bell, Xerox, and the New York Police Department, all of which have undertaken the task.

TRAIN FOR KNOWLEDGE AND SKILLS—FOR THE JOB AND FOR LIFE

Leading organizations are finding that an important way of keeping the managerial talent they require is to make sure that valued people feel that they are developing themselves personally. This has become particularly critical in an age of personal versus organizational responsibility for one's career, increasing talk of individuals as "brands," and the death of the idea of lifetime employment with one organization.

Development occurs through shifting job assignments as well as more formal educational initiatives. This requires that top management take a special interest in the progress and needs of valued individuals. It takes time.

While he led General Electric, Jack Welch spent nearly half his time overseeing the process by which the top 750 managers in the organization were assigned, developed, evaluated, and rewarded. According to Welch, "We always told our business leaders, 'You own the businesses. You're renting the people.'"[21] It is a significant factor in explaining how the company was able to have a number of potentially outstanding successors ready to fill every important job, including that of CEO. In the most recent selection of Welch's successor, Jeffrey Immelt, the company's board had the luxury of choosing from among three finalists who were identified from among as many as a dozen possible candidates. In fact, in 1995 when Welch underwent emergency heart bypass surgery, *The Wall Street Journal* was able to identify 17 possible successors for his job.[22]

Employers today are expected to make available opportunities for acquiring knowledge and skills on a regular basis. All provide training necessary for on-the-job success, but leaders differentiate themselves from the pack by offering increasing opportunities for the development of knowledge and skills for success in life, those that make it easier for an individual to negotiate an increasingly complex environment.

Provide Outstanding Support Systems

Improved support, ranging from information systems to just-in-time inventory systems to remote service capabilities, is transforming the nature of many jobs today. Unless accompanied by first-rate training for knowledge and skills in its use, many of the benefits of such systems go unrealized, something that it has taken American industry years to realize.

The primary goal of the most successful of these systems—support systems that not only deliver promised results but are adopted by their intended users—has been to better enable users to deliver results to intended clients, usually with less effort. The latter is important in encouraging the use of new systems, no matter how much they eventually increase the capabilities of their users.

Take, for example, the experiences at CEMEX, the world's third-largest producer of cement and related products, headquartered in Monterrey, Mexico. Its chairman and CEO, Lorenzo Zambrano, a techie by undergraduate training, immediately began "wiring" the company when he assumed the top job in 1985 after having been frustrated by the lack of information as a manager for 18 years for the company. In fact, he had been forced to purchase his own computer when his boss turned down his request for funds to do so.[23]

Zambrano set out with a vengeance to create a communications and information system based on a single standard for hardware and software, spending nearly $200 million in 2000 and 2001 for an integrated platform that today connects 300 servers and 10,000 personal computers and allows managers all over the world to exchange information and ideas while enabling headquarters to track performance on a daily basis. The goal has been to enable each of CEMEX's business managers to walk into a new office on the first day of a new job, regardless of global location, and be comfortable immediately with the information system.

Information technologies support the company's global e-trading businesses as well as local operations. As Zambrano points out, it would have been nearly impossible for CEMEX to become a global competitor in the past nine years without these systems. It would have been impossible for the company to achieve 20% annual growth in EBITDA (earnings before income tax, depreciation, and amortization) with only a 4% annual growth in staff between 1990 and 2001.

Expand Latitude, Within Limits, to Deliver Results

Having made progress on other initiatives intended to break the cycle of mediocrity, the latitude afforded each employee to deliver results to customers, the operational definition of organizational capability, can be expanded, always within stated or implied limits. At the Ritz-Carlton organization, any employee can commit the organization to up to $2,000 in costs to fix a problem involving a customer, an explicit limit. At Southwest Airlines, employees are admonished to "do whatever you feel comfortable doing for a customer," an implicit limit. This works particularly well at Southwest because all employees with more than six months of service are members of the company's profit-sharing plan and thus indirectly shareholders in the company.

RECOGNIZE AND REWARD FOR RESULTS

Results, whether measured in terms of improved profits or improved customer satisfaction and loyalty, are the sine qua non of successful organizations. Extensive research has shown that frequent recognition for achieving these results is just as important as rewards. For example, one look at Southwest Airlines' monthly employee magazine, LUVLines, gives the impression that recognition for delivering results is one very important function of management. Awards are numerous, and they're given often. The magazine is a sea of pictures of employees whose achievements are being recognized. "War stories" of outrageously good service to customers, other employees, or the communities served by Southwest are related not only in the magazine but every day on the company's flights and at its service counters.

■ What Employees Want

David Maister, in perhaps the most extensive study of employee relationship management and its impact on profitability, provides additional insights into ways in which the "cycle of success" is fostered.[24] The nature of his analysis enabled him to determine cause and effect. Maister's findings, summarized in Figure 7-3, indicated that financial performance was driven in the organizations he studied primarily by quality and client focus, which in turn was a function most importantly of employee satisfaction and high standards. Maister concluded, based on his data, that raising employees' survey responses to only four statements concerning

■ **Figure 7–3** MAISTER'S MODEL OF CAUSE AND EFFECT IN THE
VALUE PROFIT CHAIN*

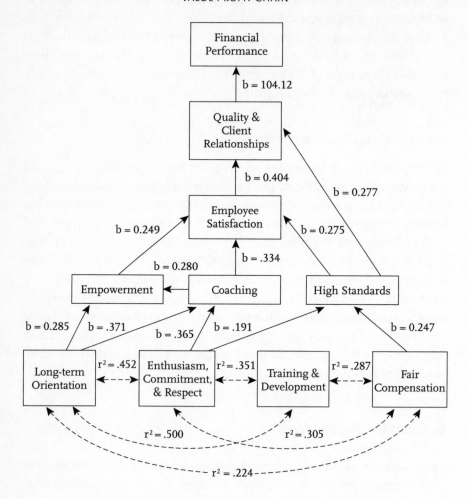

Source: David H. Maister, *Practice What You Preach: What Managers Must Do to
Create a High Achievement Culture* (New York: The Free Press, 2001), p. 79. This analysis
is based on data from more than 5500 respondents from 139 offices operated by 29
separate firms owned by the same publicly held marketing communications company.
"b" values signify the amount of change in the caused variable (the pointed end of the
arrow) that would result from a one-unit change in the "causing" variable (the blunt end
of the arrow). "r²" values signify the percentage variation in one value that can be explained
by variations in the other.

their satisfaction from a 4 to a 5 on a 6-point scale would have caused a 42% improvement in financial performance in the organizations he studied:

1. I am highly satisfied with my job.
2. I get a great sense of accomplishment from my work.
3. The overwhelming majority of the work I'm given is challenging rather than repetitive.
4. I am committed to this firm as a career opportunity.

The experiences of managers whom we have observed have inspired more organized forays into the relationship between frontline employees and those who manage them. A composite of these findings leads to some clear conclusions.

Based on our study of a number of high-capability organizations, we have found some remarkably consistent patterns of behavior among managers and those who work with them that contrast sharply with those in "merely good" organizations. If you work through the complexity of a much greater number of measures, employees repeatedly provide some variation on the following responses to the question, "What is most important to you in your job?" They are, in varying orders of importance, except for the sixth: (1) the "fairness" of my manager, (2) the degree to which my work is recognized, (3) working with "winners," (4) the opportunity to solve problems for (or deliver results to) customers, (5) opportunities for personal development, and (6) appropriate compensation.[25]

When employees use the term "fairness" in assessing a manager, they really are commenting on the quality of critical decisions—hires, promotions, rewards, and dismissals—made by managers. In other words, managers are on display at all times, with every decision, large and small, in view and under appraisal by employees.

Recognition is an important element of fairness. Are the right people recognized? Are they recognized for the right behaviors, that is, those that really contribute to capability? Is the recognition itself appropriate to the accomplishment? In essence, this is another comment on the quality of leadership.

Whether or not one is working with winners also relates to the quality of critical managerial decisions. Of course, every assessment is made "in the eye of the beholder" and is therefore somewhat subjective. High performers repeatedly tell us, however, that they like to work with other winners. They often are reluctant to talk about "losers," but the implication is that employees are prone to sort out their colleagues along the lines of high and low capability and make judgments about which they prefer working with.

The opportunity to solve problems for customers, whether internal or external to the firm, is the essence of capability in the eyes of employees. It's worth a lot. It has, for example, transformed the quality of working life at the U.S. Social Security Administration, where many aspects of the job, including compensation, are strictly controlled. Of course, capability is built over time through the steps outlined in the previous section. It starts with selection and training. For those working in customer relations at the Social Security offices around the country, it has been facilitated by improved information technology and other support systems, as well as greater latitude, within the limits of the law, in processing customer questions and responses. It has been accompanied by greater attention paid to customer satisfaction and recognition for those cited as the best problem solvers.

Fifth, but increasingly not fifth, is opportunity for personal development. Particularly in an age in which employees have concluded that they are responsible for their own careers, careers that are less and less likely to be realized within one organization, opportunities for both job- and life-related personal development become an increasingly important criterion for attracting and keeping high-capability people.

Last, and really last, among these six factors is compensation. Typical of high-capability employees is a sense of confidence in their ability to earn sufficient income, either now or in the future. They are often willing to forgo current income in situations where they sense a rapid rate of personal development, either on the job or in educational programs. If anyone doubts this, witness the hundreds of thousands of young, confident dot-com'ers who were willing to work incredibly long hours for little monetary compensation in exchange for challenging jobs and the promise of future wealth. Few realized the wealth, but few with whom we have talked spoke with regret about having taken the jobs.

A seventh factor that has engendered a great deal of debate in recent years is that of employment (not necessarily job) continuity. On the one hand are scores of organizations with high levels of long-term performance that emphasize the importance of stability and continuity in the workplace and at all levels of the organization. At the same time, skeptics of the validity and importance of this phenomenon for the future point to the growing magnitude of change in competitive forces causing an impermanence in organizations, with the attendant need for employees to take charge of their own careers regardless of employer. The data still speaks for itself. It is hard to find long-term success built on short-term expediency in hiring and laying off employees among the highest-performing organizations anywhere. Recognition of the value of continuity is high at Cisco Systems, for example, where CEO John Chambers has, when making certain acquisitions, agreed that no employee would be let go without the consent of the CEO of the acquired company.

■ The Value Equation for Employees

Note how these factors map onto the value equation for employees, shown in Figure 7-4. Capability and the opportunity for personal development represent results. Process quality is represented by the fairness of leadership, the recognition of accomplishments, the presence of winners on the team, and continuity in the life and leadership of the organization. Compensation is the inverse of "price" in this formula: the higher it is, the better. Access costs, although not making our list of the top seven, may be logistical or psychological, depending on the workplace and its location, and can be a determining factor in whether an organization is able to attract talent, even in economies where the mobility of talent is high.

The value equation for employees is linked directly to that for customers and investors. The linkage for customers is primarily through the greater value delivered by enthusiastic, involved, capable, and loyal employees. The linkage for investors is reflected primarily in productivity—the ability to achieve more with less—made possible by a well-thought-out value equation for employees, as investors in companies like Cisco Systems and Alcoa (as well as organizations discussed in other chapters, such as IBM and Wal-Mart) have realized over the years.

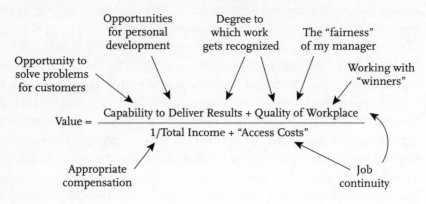

■ **Figure 7–4**   WHAT EMPLOYEES WANT, EXPRESSED IN TERMS OF THE
EMPLOYEE VALUE EQUATION

Observations combined with more analytic work have helped us formulate a set of guidelines for highly effective management behaviors as
well as action steps necessary in developing a high-capability frontline
organization. They can be added to many of those outlined in Chapter 6
that apply equally to managers and employees.

■ How Employees' Wants Are Met: Organization Culture as Brand

Organizations repeatedly identified by their employees as the best places
to work (1) make it easy for prospective employees to self-select themselves into or out of the organization, (2) set high standards and expect a
lot, (3) go out of their way to encourage managers to listen, learn, teach,
and communicate, (4) make few promises and keep them all, (5) compensate fairly as part of a value package, and (6) seek continuity in management as well as employment. When despite these efforts, employees
leave or are asked to leave, every effort is made to treat the employee as
one would a prospective customer, which many of them may become,
particularly in businesses serving other businesses.

These are all aspects of an organization's core shared values, the core
of its culture. Outstanding employers regard organization culture as

their "brand." The communication of this brand to existing and prospective employees is regarded as a high-priority activity.

FACILITATE SELF-SELECTION INTO OR OUT OF AN ORGANIZATION: CULTURE AS BRAND

Organizations go out of their way to communicate in ways that enable potential customers to decide on purchases of products or services. Unfortunately, the same is not always true for an even more important marketing task: making accurate representations to prospective employees that enable them to select themselves into or out of a job. The task is even greater for organizations generally perceived to be great places to work, because they tend to attract a wide range of applicants of whom only a portion represent a good fit with the organization's culture. At Capital One, a high-performing provider of credit card and other services that we learn much more about later, CEO Richard Fairbank says, "At most companies, people spend 2 percent of their time recruiting and 75 percent managing their recruiting mistakes."[26] At Capital One, top executives spend 20% of their time recruiting in an organization that has devised a number of methods for helping prospective employees select themselves into or out of the organization.

Several years ago, the leadership at Claydon Heeley Jones Mason (CHJM), a London-based marketing communications agency operating in Europe and Asia, undertook to answer the question, "What will it take to make this a great place to work?"[27] It appointed a senior account manager, Jamie Priestley, as "Doctor of DNA" and member of the management board, entrusted with the tasks of sharpening the organization's core values, encouraging management to practice them, and communicating them in ways that distinguished CHJM from many other organizations offering similar services. Given CHJM's fact- and performance- based culture, everything that Priestley did would have to be measurable.

Priestley developed a "cultural calendar" for the year, including a coherent plan for cultural "pulses" (such as subsidized trips to the theater) and "spikes" (big company meetings and parties). A "people's collective," reflecting the irreverent, quirky attitude encouraged among staff, was formed to ensure that ideas, especially for cultural pulses, were kept fresh. Among many others, ideas included the creation of a satirical internal magazine and such institutions as "duvet day," one day a year on which employees could call in and say they just didn't feel like coming to work.

A spike typically occurred with a new acquisition, with an event planned to welcome newly merged employees into the CHJM culture. Priestley also became "tone cop" for all information provided to the public, including potential new hires. The word rapidly spread that CHJM was a different place to work, as creative internally as the nature of its work was for clients. Its challenge became one of convincing even some good people attracted to the company—who doubled in numbers—that it was not right for them. Revenue and profit doubled over a two-year period after the launching of the initiative.

Enabling prospective employees to more effectively self-select is a first step toward establishing the high level of trust discussed later. As one respondent to Maister's survey put it,[28]

> We get high trust scores from our people because when we hire them, we are honest about the situation that they are entering, including workload, salary, bonus, responsibilities, and everything else. We deliver or exceed on our promises to people . . . and their job is precisely what we said it was going to be.

Set High Standards and Expect a Lot

The "Pygmalion effect," characterized by the high expectations of Professor Henry Higgins for Eliza Doolittle in the George Bernard Shaw-inspired musical, *My Fair Lady,* is alive and well in high-value performers today. It's characterized by the concept of organizing around fewer, more capable people with larger, more highly compensated jobs.

It's also characterized by a constant weeding out of those uncomfortable in this kind of working environment. This practice has characterized the thinking at Cisco Systems, for example. As Barbara Beck, senior vice president for human resources, has put it, "The decision of who to let go has nothing to do with length of service or level. It's 'are you adding value?' or 'do you fit the culture?'"[29]

Encourage Managers to Listen, Learn, Teach, Serve, and Communicate

At ServiceMaster, a provider of a range of support services for commercial establishments and homes and an employer of nearly 200,000 frontline service workers, one of the guiding values is that of helping employees develop their full potential. The relevant guideline is "Don't ask someone to do something until you've helped him or her be somebody."[30] This is done not only through training programs that help them perform their jobs better but through other efforts, such as language instruction, that help them achieve a better way of life. This requires that managers listen, learn, teach, serve, and communicate, setting an example by their actions for others. As Bill Pollard, erstwhile chairman and CEO of the company, puts it, "Anyone not able to learn, teach, and serve is not a candidate for management success at ServiceMaster."

This sounds like a platitude or truism, but many managers, as they climb the traditional organizational ladder, forget how to listen, learn, and serve as they spend more time talking, acting, and being served. Pollard, in his own way, has constantly communicated expectations to others at ServiceMaster. How else can one explain the day that one of us observed him on his knees cleaning up a cup of coffee that he had spilled on the carpet at a ServiceMaster board meeting—and not attracting extraordinary attention from other board members.

Emphasize Trust: Make Few Promises and Keep Them All

At Cisco Systems, where the mission is to create "unprecedented value and opportunity for our customers, employees, investors, and ecosystem partners," only a few promises—a dedication to innovation, learning, change, stretch, frugality; emphases on partnering and teamwork; and the opportunity to have fun while changing the way people work, live, play, and learn—are implied in the values. At IBM, one of its three core values promises respect for the individual. This is the primary promise of the company to its employees.

Adherence to promises requires a continuing review of strategic and tactical decisions in the context of such promises and the core values of the organization. The operative motto regarding trust and promises in organizations that deliver high value to their employees is, "use them or lose them."

Compensate Fairly as Part of a Value Package

Organizations we've highlighted in this chapter are not the highest pay-ing companies in their respective industries if salaries, are the only crite-rion. However, all provide high value of a nonmonetary nature by emphasizing the quality of leadership, other employees, and the work-place itself. Most offer an opportunity for all (as at Cisco, Southwest, or Capital One) or many (as at GE) employees to participate in the spoils of success through opportunities for ownership in their organizations.

Achieve Organization Continuity

In the 123-year history of the General Electric organization it has had only nine CEOs, including the recently appointed Jeffrey Immelt, who, based on precedent, can reasonably be expected to be CEO for some years. This has to have played a role in the organization's long-term suc-cess. It has provided a stable "performance trinity" (leadership and man-agement, culture and values, and vision and strategy) to which people can relate. Further, it has given each leader of the GE organization suffi-cient time to place his stamp on the company and carry out his vision. It is reflected at all levels in the remarkable capability of this organization to develop talent and to keep many of the people it develops.

How do organizations achieve such stability? In part they do it by en-gaging in practices that attract, develop, and retain great leaders, man-agers, and employees. Management practices that achieve this have been the object of a study by Buckingham and Coffman in recent years.[31] They have found that great managers define outcomes (results) and then let their employees reach them by their own methods, within the limits of corporate policies and other constraints. They found that great managers focus on strengths, assigning their best people to the best business oppor-tunities. They spend the most time with their best people, not their worst. They search for ways of expanding jobs without giving in to the temptation merely to promote high achievers into jobs they may not be good at, as is the case when managers promote high performers in customer-facing jobs, often away from customers. In all these facets of management, the great ones systematically believed and acted differently from average managers. Perhaps even more significantly, they believed and acted differently from conventional human resource management wisdom.

CREATE WINNING PROCEDURES FOR EMPLOYEE TURNOVER

Great marketing organizations, when they lose a customer, try to do so in ways that make future sales to that customer not only possible but likely.

Dismissing people is much more difficult than hiring them, as nearly every manager learned during the sharp economic downturn of 2000–2001. The task is regarded by value profit chain advocates as an opportunity. And in fact, an informal survey of such managers suggests that they have taken significantly different approaches to the task than suggested in press reports of recent actions in other organizations.

Many employees, once a decision is made to dismiss them, are treated like pariahs by management. By doing so, managers miss an important source of information about the organization. Worse yet, they communicate unfortunate signals to those remaining on the job about the quality of the workplace. As one respondent to Maister's survey put it:

> In the past, . . . bad treatment of those leaving had a hugely negative impact on those who stayed. It was like a double standard. If you were leaving, all of a sudden you were treated as less than a human. People realized that if they were to leave too they would get that treatment from "their firm" as well.

> That part of our culture has changed. Now we treat people who leave respectfully and with appreciation for what they have done for our firm. We have goodbye parties, sending people away respectfully, with their contributions highlighted. The result is that we have former employees who actually want to come back.

This process works well for those choosing to leave an organization on their own, as well as for those failing to meet standards of the job. It works as well for organizations facing significant reductions in business. Jamie Priestly, "Doctor of DNA" of Claydon Heeley Jones Mason, whose accomplishments we described earlier, related how the company, operated under value profit chain principles, reacted when faced with a 67% loss of its client base in 2001 due to the misfortunes of many of its dot.com clients. Actions taken included (1) early and accurate dissemination of bad news to employees, (2) fanatical renewed emphasis on customer satisfaction, (3) explicit reaffirmation of the objective of generating risky, inspiring work, (4) preservation of internal activities designed to preserve the DNA of the company (a quirky, fun culture), scaled down appropriately to meet lower budgets, (5) every effort possible to avoid layoffs, including voluntary salary cuts among senior people to save more junior jobs, (6) taking extreme care—such as providing career counseling references, and indefinite use of office space—with all people laid off, and (7) creating an alumni club to maintain contact with those forced to leave.[32]

There is another important bonus here. Many organizations may find that former employees control future purchase decisions in customer organizations. The goodwill engendered by a successful departure can influence future revenues and relationships. This helps explain why a growing number, such as Procter & Gamble and Microsoft, are creating "alumni" networks similar to that at Claydon, Heeley, Jones, Mason, linked by Internet web sites, to maintain contact with employees who have departed.

■ Questions for Management

In total, the findings on which this chapter is based prompt several questions for management:

1. To what extent do your organization's revenue and profit growth rates outpace the growth of the organization's head count?

2. What steps is your organization taking to reinforce the "cycle of success" among employees and between frontline employees and customers?

3. What are you doing to facilitate the self-selection process by communicating clearly focused values to both current and potential employees?

4. How are managers encouraged to establish relationships with employees necessary to convince them that personnel decisions are made on the basis of the best information?

5. What are you doing to meet the personal development needs of potential "free agents" increasingly willing to take responsibility for their own development?

6. Are you taking steps to ensure that winners are able to work with winners on the job, including

   a. The effective pruning of the organization?

   b. Careful consideration of job candidates referred by winners currently in the organization?

7. Do you give employees the latitude (within limits) to deliver results and process quality to customers both inside and outside the organization?

8. Do you compensate—based on abilities to deliver results and process quality to customers—in both frequent recognition as well as rewards?

9. Have you carefully thought out processes for disengaging employees from the organization in ways that produce useful feedback and encourage the continued loyalty of both those leaving and those staying?

In the organizations we have described here employees are nurtured like customers. Their full value is known. Their unintended loss is regarded as a tragedy. Employee relationship management is just as important as customer relationship management, to which we turn next.

Chapter 8

Customer Relationship Management: Treating Customers Like Employees

ORGANIZATIONS THAT BEGIN to treat customers like employees—through careful selection, training and support, evaluation, recognition and reward, and even dismissal—experience a significant change in their relationships with customers and employees alike. We're not talking about insignificant change. This is nothing less than a transformation that can enhance an organization's reputation with its customers while becoming an employer of choice among its people.

Managers in many of Omnicom's advertising agencies and diversified marketing services companies have come to believe that to serve their clients well while retaining valued professionals in an industry with a reputation for high rates of turnover, they must select and develop clients with care. This has enabled them to extend the length of their relationships with valued clients. It has also enabled them to avoid difficult clients with whom relationships often lead directly to the loss of talent or the loss of reputation. The strategy has paid off in relationships that provide more challenging work to highly talented employees, better results for selected clients, and an impressive bottom line.

Customer selection and training may be thought to be more feasible in organizations marketing to businesses rather than consumers, but it is the very basis of a phenomenon called "permission marketing."[1] Consider, for example, the Successful Money Management Seminars program at SMMS, Inc., a subsidiary of ING's U.S. Financial Services Group, a provider of a full line of insurance and investment products. It has literally altered insurance from a product that has to be sold ("pushed," often by commissioned agents, through a process regarded as painful and postponable by prospective policyholders) to one that is bought. Those who enroll in an SMMS program participate in classes in personal finance. As part of the program, they pay a fee to receive extensive education on financial issues and solutions through multi-session seminars. In the process, they are exposed to generic financial product solutions. At the conclusion of the program, more than half of program participants purchase one or more products they have selected as right for them on the basis of what they've learned. As a representative of SMMS put it, "A core value at SMMS is that all sales conversations are permission based."[2]

Though the financial advisors using the SMMS marketing platform represent multiple companies, their own perception of ING as a provider of consumer education is so compelling that when it comes time for specific product solutions, they often recommend ING products. In addition, the consumer's perception shifts from a cost/price mindset to one of solution/value. Of products purchased as a result of SMMS seminars, the vast majority of those sales that are tracked by ING are proprietary sales, regardless of comparative price. Why? At least in part because of the trust built up between those presenting a program perceived to be offered with high integrity and a group of self-selected customers with a high level of interest at the beginning of the relationship.

These examples illustrate for us concepts that we explore in greater depth in this chapter. They include the customer value equation and customer/vendor relationship management—ways in which customers can be successfully treated like employees through selection, training, support, recognition and reward, and, yes, dismissal.

■ The Customer Value Equation

Value, what one receives for what one pays, is second nature to customers. However, it is so often forgotten by those serving them that it holds the key to successful competitive opportunities designed to differentiate products and services. Consider the case of Mobil's Speedpass, developed in 1996 under the leadership of Joe Giordana, then a marketing manager for the company. It became one of the most successful innovations in the history of petroleum retailing.

For years, petroleum marketers have sought solutions to the problem of gassing up cars, a process their marketing research had told them repeatedly was regarded by customers as a necessary evil—second only to dental work—to be minimized if at all possible. One by one, they sought to eliminate what customers hated most. Thus self-service was almost immediately successful, most commonly thought to be because of lower prices offered for do-it-yourselfers. As a matter of fact, just as many consumers valued the elimination of waiting time and the interaction with service station employees. Self-service still required a payment process that many customers found inconvenient, however, that is, until Speedpass, a device the size of a key chain that is waved at a reader on a gas pump for gasoline and used for other purchases in service station stores, which are then billed to a credit card. It sounds simple—but it wasn't.[3]

First, Mobil had to identify those who would be most likely to try Speedpass. In its tests, it found that they were likely to be more tech friendly, time constrained, educated, and affluent than average consumers. Then Mobil had to prove that Speedpass worked, speeding up an undesirable task while providing accurate, timely billing as well as access to other products and services. In tests, Speedpass reduced the average time to gas up, roughly 3.5 minutes, by 30 seconds. Unless it resulted in more sales, however, it would be hard to convince service station and convenience store owners to pay for the Speedpass technology, costing $15,000. These fears were eased when it was found that Speedpass users visited Mobil stations one more time per month than other customers. Thus, Speedpass was found to be a device for leveraging value over cost for both customers and retailers.

Once the convenience of Speedpass was proven to the early innovators, larger groups of potential users had to be exposed not only to Speedpass but to the way in which it could be used, a task for a massive television advertising program. By 2001, Speedpass was regularly being used by 5 million consumers. Of these, many were thought to have switched allegiance from another brand of gasoline in an industry in which customer allegiance was thought to be influenced largely by price and convenience rather than brand. Further, Speedpass users, because they were more likely to concentrate their purchases at Mobil stations and to include nongasoline items in those purchases, were found to spend significantly more per month than other customers.

The customer/vendor value relationship for Speedpass is shown in

Figure 8-1. It suggests that nearly everything about the relationship was changed by an innovation based on deep knowledge about customer behavior.

■ Customer/Vendor Relationship Management

The decade of the 1990s saw a rush to embrace concepts of CRM, customer relationship management.[4] But just as vendors began applying more sophisticated tools for managing relationships with customers, however, the explosive growth of the use of the Internet by customers occurred. As a result, customers achieved greater potential power to manage relationships with their vendors by gaining access to more transparent product, price, and service information that enabled them to

■ Figure 8–1 CUSTOMER/VENDOR VALUE RELATIONSHIPS AFTER THE INTRODUCTION OF SPEEDPASS INTO THE PETROLEUM PRODUCTS MARKETING PROCESS

Mobil

$$\text{Value} = \frac{\text{More Sales and Profits} + \text{Higher Dealer and Customer Satisfaction} + \text{Faster Payments Processing}}{\text{Lower Costs for Payment Processing} + \text{Access to More Consumer Data}}$$

Dealer

$$\text{Value} = \frac{\text{More Sales and Profits} + \text{Higher Dealer and Employee Satisfaction} + \text{Less Hassle On the Job}}{\text{Lower Costs for Transaction Processing} + 1/\text{More Frequent Customer Visits; Greater Access Frequency}}$$

Customer

$$\text{Value} = \frac{\text{Faster Purchases} + \text{Less Interaction With Others}}{\text{Less Expenditure of Time} + \text{Easier Access to Gasoline and Other Products}}$$

begin playing off one vendor against another. This was thought by some to sound the death knell for customer relationship management. Ironically, it hasn't turned out that way, but the growing potential for vendor relationship management on the part of customers represents an equally important lever for managing change, as we will see.

CUSTOMER RELATIONSHIP MANAGEMENT

Relationships with customers are achieved, in part, according to one extensive study of service quality, by satisfying generic customer needs for dependability, timeliness, empathy, authority, and tangible evidence.[5] In this terminology, dependability and timeliness mean "doing what you say you will do when you say you will do it." Empathy means "doing it by putting yourself in the customer's shoes." Authority means "doing it in a way that says you know what you are doing," and tangible evidence means "leaving behind some evidence that you have done what you said you would do." Intended primarily for the design and delivery of services, the findings have relevance as well for products.

More lasting relationships, leading to increased customer loyalty and advocacy for products and services, are formed, according to researchers at the Gallup Organization, through a four-stage process reflecting what customers want from a relationship.[6] The process is not unlike Maslow's hierarchy of needs, from basic food and shelter to higher needs for self-esteem. Gallup's hierarchy of customer needs, according to Marcus Buckingham and Curt Coffman, starts with the need for accuracy, the ability of an organization to do what it says it will do. It then proceeds to the need for availability, one that addresses customer concerns about convenience as well as access, especially in time of need for such services as cash dispensing. These factors are, however, only the entry to the game for providers of many products and services.

Longer-term customer loyalty and advocacy depend on whether two additional needs, those for partnership and advice, are met. Of course, customers seek partnerships and advice only for certain products and services representing high levels of perceived financial, psychological, or physical risk or payoff. For the business, the commitment of resources to a new information technology platform represents such a risk. Among consumers, purchases of real estate, automobiles, or upscale home furnishings—representing not only expensive purchases but also social statements—meet these criteria. Similarly, many services, such as medical or financial, whose quality cannot be known in advance, do as well.[7]

This hierarchy of needs parallels in some respects the hierarchy of customer behaviors presented earlier in Figure 3-1.

Customers with the greatest perceived risks and payoffs—those with the greatest needs for accuracy, availability, partnership, and advice—are often the most willing to pay for solutions to their needs, to invest the effort needed to develop a successful relationship, and to prove loyal to those providing effective solutions. This is the cornerstone of our argument for treating customers like employees as a means of introducing significant change into the customer relationship management process. How is this done? By selecting them as carefully as key employees, providing them with the training and support necessary for a successful relationship, evaluating them, recognizing and rewarding them, and, when absolutely necessary, firing them.

Selection and Self-Selection.   Marketers of products, services, or technologically based solutions requiring substantial changes in customer behavior understand the importance of customer selection. As Everett Rogers found years ago, it is important to identify innovators who are willing and even anxious to be the first to try many innovations.[8] As we saw earlier, it is useful to select even among these early innovators those who are most influential in spreading the word of their experiences. They are the first to undergo the training necessary to produce the successful experiences leading to word-of-mouth referrals so critical to most innovations.

Client relationship management begins with careful selection at Merkley Newman Harty, a New York–based advertising agency and subsidiary of Omnicom. "Like so many good things," said President Parry Merkley, "we 'stumbled into' [a model for selecting clients] during a partners' off-site management meeting."[9] The model reflects MNH objectives, embodied in the "4 Cs": creative, culture, client, and cash. It has proven effective in identifying ideal new business prospects.

Basically, it involves the preparation by MNH management of a cur-

■ **Figure 8–2** "4C" DIAGRAMS FROM THREE CURRENT ACCOUNT REVIEWS, MERKLEY NEWMAN HARTY

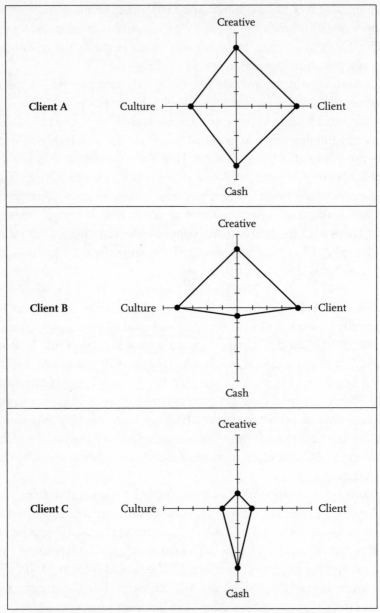

Source: "The Balanced Scorecard, The Four 'C's: Creative, Culture, Client, Cash," a case written by Dan Maher and Dan O'Brien under the guidance of Tom Watson, Executive Vice President of Omnicom. Copyright 2000 by Omnicom University and the Omnicom Group, Inc.

rent account review diagram reflecting the "shape" of each prospective client, as shown in Figure 8-2. To prepare it, MNH principals ask four questions, rating a prospective client on each:[10]

1. Creative: What are the chances we'll be able to deliver fabulous, cutting-edge creative work to this client?

2. Culture: Do we like who they are? Do we think they're interesting and good at what they do? Is our agency culture appropriate to their culture? Basically, do our cultures match?

3. Client: How do we feel about adding this client to our roster? Do we feel excited? Would we want to become partners with this client? Would we be willing to stay late and work weekends for this client?

4. Cash: Do we think that we will be paid an appropriate amount of money for the services we will provide to this client? What are the chances of getting a price premium? Of getting only "minimum wage?" Will they try to take advantage of the agency?

Such a process communicates several messages. To employees it says that the organization is interested in obtaining work that is both challenging and beneficial to personal development. To prospective clients it says that Merkley Newman Harty—like the U.S. Marines searching for a "few good men"— is not looking for just any kind of business. To management it emphasizes the need to achieve a balance of profit and creative potential in its work for clients.

Training and Support.   There is ample research to support the proposition that perceived product or service quality is a function of the degree to which products or services perform up to the level or in excess of what was expected.[11] Thus training plays an important role in setting customers' expectations.

Training is important in the use of a product or service. The infamous VCR, used for making and playing video recordings, is a notorious example, but it is illustrative of a wide range of products. For years, many users of VCRs have received a small portion of the potential benefits they've offered. Most have learned only to use them to play commercial videos. They've been unable to learn to set them properly to record broadcast or cable material. Many haven't even learned how to reset the digital clock following a power outage. Witness the number of jokes about flashing "12:00s" on VCRs. This spawned an opportunity for new products, such as coding systems intended to simplify the recording process, but it also reduced the value of the product to consumers.

The same is true of any product or service that may require out-of-the-ordinary behaviors of their customers. For example, many first-time flyers with Southwest Airlines are put off by the idea of no assigned seats, no meals, and the attempted humor of Southwest employees. Those who are willing to undergo the training necessary to appreciate what is going on by flying Southwest more than once often become apostles. As Colleen Barrett, now president of the airline, puts it, "Once customers fly on us three times they're hooked."[12] Those unwilling to do this may turn to the Internet "gripesite" for Southwest, typical of those for many organizations that focus on certain customers but sometimes attract customers falling outside the field of focus. But the benefits of focus and education far outweigh the negative reactions of a few.

High-tech product and service support has been so notoriously poor that most users enjoy little of the value such products and services promise. For example, how much of the software capability provided by your computer operating system do you use? How much do you know how to use? How much do you even know is available? Most damning of all, how often have you received outstanding support in learning how to use it?

Realization of the need for customer training and support has just begun to dawn as well on e-commerce purveyors of products and services. Research has shown that a large proportion of those visiting commercial Internet sites log off without buying anything. Worse yet, many of these visitors log off after having spent more than 5 minutes at the site, adequate time to get well into the ordering process. Data from PlanetFeedback, a web-based customer satisfaction monitoring service, suggests the greatest sources of frustration among Web site visitors are "confusing" navigation, an overabundance of promotions, slow download speeds (stemming from too many graphics), and "site errors," all of which contribute to poor "overall experiences."[13]

As a result, a growing number of leading e-tailers are making available shopping assistants with the click of a keyboard key. Other even more advanced services provide assistants on standby alert who monitor customer shopping patterns, notice Web site shopping behavior suggesting customer frustration, and come online to offer their assistance.

Evaluation.   Client evaluation at Merkley Newman Harty doesn't stop with prospective clients. It worked so well that it was extended to the existing stable of clients being served by the firm. The result of the individual appraisal of each client by MNH staff was a scatter diagram similar to that shown in Figure 8-3. Creative potential was determined by the di-

■ **Figure 8–3**   A Scatter Diagram of Results of a Client Portfolio Appraisal at Merkley Newman Harty*

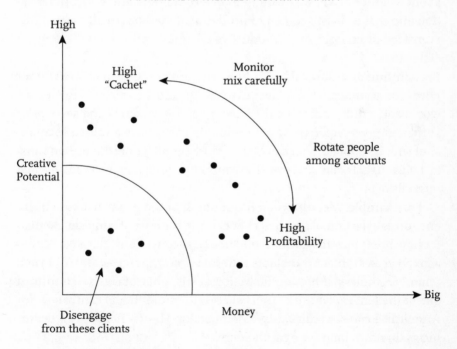

* Showing hypothetical plots.

mensions of creative, culture, and client in the MNH 4C objectives. The economic dimension reflected cash in the appraisal scheme.

By preparing the diagram shown in Figure 8-3, MNH was able to get a helicopter view of its existing client base to address questions of whether it represented a proper balance between economic and creative potential, money and "cachet."

Having done this, MNH took the process one more step by inviting clients to evaluate its teams on the same four dimensions. To do this, the questions had to be revised slightly: Is our creative work effective (creative)? Do you like who we are (culture)? What does it feel like to be a client of our agency (client)? How much value for money are you receiving (cash)?

The results from a test of this initiative were instructive. On the one hand, it forced clients to quantify their levels of satisfaction in ways they hadn't been forced to do in the past. On the other, it raised questions about whether MNH was willing to invest the time and effort in a relationship that a client seemed to think was necessary. In all cases, however, it led to a clearer, more productive relationship.

Recognition and Reward.   To Buckingham and Coffman's customer needs for accuracy, availability, partnership, and advice, cited earlier, we would add a fifth, membership. Customers for products and services of sufficient perceived risk want to think that they have a valued relationship with a supplier. This can be the most significant influence on satisfaction, longer loyalty, and even the commitment that produces unsolicited referrals of others.

For example, Merrill Lynch has found that the greatest single influence on satisfaction of its retail clients is the number of contacts, no matter how brief, they have with their "financial consultant" (broker) during a given year. Contact translates into membership in the Merrill Lynch "club," regardless of how exclusive it really is. This, of course, prompted one of the longest-running, most successful promotional campaigns for American Express credit cards, "Membership Has Its Privileges," featuring well-known long-time cardholders.

In putting together recognition and reward initiatives, organizations can do worse than to ask themselves what would constitute membership in the mind of valued customers. The answer is influenced by the degree to which it is already employed in a particular industry. For example, among airline travelers, it is now more than frequent flyer miles. Based on findings from a number of studies, it may require no more than the use of travel records to recognize problems that valued travelers encountered, with personalized follow-up letters expressing apologies.

Decisions regarding recognition and reward have important economic consequences. We return to this matter in the next chapter, dealing with value exchange.

Dismissal. When absolutely necessary, outstanding organizations dismiss clients—or, more bluntly, they fire them. Herb Kelleher, when he was CEO at Southwest Airlines, said, "We don't say that the customer is always right. That's an abdication of a company's responsibility to its employees. A customer can be abusive to your people. That customer is not right. We say to them that we don't ever want to see them again."[14]

When confronted with such a customer, every attempt is made at Southwest to fire them publicly, if possible in front of other employees as an affirmation of management's support. There is a parallel here between the public way that Southwest attempts to fire customers and the manner in which dismissals of managers unable to manage by the values are announced at such organizations as GE. As Jack Welch has put it, "When we find the bad apples, we make a huge public event out of it . . . we never say 'left for personal reasons.'"[15]

If properly implemented, a "silver bullet" policy for firing customers in the hands of employees, who understand that it can be used only in extreme cases, sends a strong message about the quality of the work environment, one that is repeated frequently until it becomes a part of organization lore. It is totally consistent with an emphasis on customer selection, training and support, evaluation, and reward and recognition—in short, with managing customers like employees.

More typically, customers may be encouraged to end a relationship because they don't meet the objectives of an organization's strategy. For example, at ING Direct, a rapidly growing subsidiary of ING North America delivering selected banking services via phone and the Internet to customers in the United States and Canada, processes have been designed to produce the lowest possible transaction costs for those customers who transact business through nonpersonalized channels. In return, the company regularly offers the highest rates of interest in the United States on such products as CDs and money market accounts. Further, there are virtually no charges assessed for maintaining an account or carrying out transactions. The bank's slogan, "Great rates, no fees, no minimums," stresses the simplicity of its strategy, embodied by a "broad vision" of "leading Americans back to saving" by attempting to be "best in class" for each of the limited number of services it offers.

ING Direct provides a cadre of highly skilled service representatives capable of selling products and servicing the needs of clients in need of help, but excessive use of the representatives triggers an advisory note suggesting ways in which a client might make more effective (and lower-cost) use of the service. Failure to change client behavior results in a "Dear Customer" letter advising the client that with no future change in behavior, the account will be closed and service terminated. Arkadi Kuhlmann, head of ING Direct, commented recently:[16]

> Clearly setting a customer's expectations as to what we can and cannot do allows us to practice a bit of . . . tough love. When confronted with behavior that goes against the expectations customers almost always volunteer to change, understand the rationale, and almost always turn into brand evangelists. This . . . has a profound impact on our employees who step by step gain faith in the fairness and even-handedness of dealing with our customers in a uniform way.

Firing customers, if accompanied by a rational explanation and an opportunity to change buying behaviors of customers to be fired, may not create "antagonists." It may also be a necessary cost of a strategy aimed at providing the maximum value to a group of targeted clients, those with both purchase potential and the willingness and ability to buy and use products and services in ways that are designed as part of the strategy. To the extent that such clients at ING Direct must subsidize the behaviors of those for whom the bank's products and services are not designed, their value equation is compromised.

Jamie Priestley, of Claydon Heeley Jones Mason, whom we met in Chapter 7, takes issue with the term "firing clients":[17]

"Firing clients" is misleading because it implies adjectives like smug, macho, impulsive. The truth is that every fibre of a professional service firm [such as Priestley's employer, a marketing communications agency] wants to solve its clients' problems, no matter what obstacles are in the way. . . . We're no different—except that we have a formal process in place not just to review client satisfaction but also to assess how much good our clients are doing us . . . [because] . . . Without motivated staff all our business aims are 100% academic. Every three months the [management] board assesses the overall value of each client to the agency. . . . The decisive questions for us are: . . . To what extent does this client provide a learning environment and fun? . . . Will our creatives and planners want the work in their portfolio? . . . Does this client help nurture our agency ambitions?

[For example] . . . In 1994, we decided to resign a major blue-chip client which was worth 15% of our revenue. We were scoring 4 or 5 out of 5 on all client satisfaction criteria and were happy we were doing the best possible job . . . [but] . . . Our team was increasingly pessimistic about the account ever becoming more challenging, and we concluded that short-term income would stand in the way of our longer term ambitions. Since then we've deliberately shed between 7% and 20% of our revenue each year. . . . In every instance where we've fired a client, we've been rewarded with more energized staff, net gains in revenue within 4 months and stronger credentials for new business.

VENDOR RELATIONSHIP MANAGEMENT

Customers treating vendors like employees experience many of the same benefits as we've just discussed. In fact, this is a cornerstone of enlightened vendor relationship management today, and it could well serve as an example for vendors seeking to serve their customers better.

As a result of successful vendor relationship management, customers are obtaining a wide range of services and capabilities from their vendors. This is perhaps no more true than among a range of organizations that have implemented extensive outsourcing programs. At Cisco Systems, for example, a network of customers, vendors, manufacturers, service providers, and company facilities is linked by the Internet to provide a smooth flow of Internet equipment and service from manufacturers to customers, most often without any hands-on contact by Cisco personnel with the product. This can only be achieved by a seamless Internet system backed up by substantial personal or Net-based sales effort and Net-administered quality control processes. It has proved so successful that Cisco today accomplishes excellent supply chain service while realizing more than 80% of revenues through its Cisco MarketPlace Internet site, relying on five contract manufacturers for nearly 60% of final assembly and testing and 100% of basic production and carrying out or coordinating 85% of its product support services by means of the Internet. This is referred to at Cisco as a "single enterprise." As Carl Redfield, Cisco's senior vice president for manufacturing, pointed out, "We develop the entire process, and we know what every supplier is doing every moment."[18]

With the sharp decline of the market for Cisco's products in 2001, the company found that it had to pull some of its manufacturing away from its contract manufacturer vendors. It did so in a way that would enable it to reinstitute the relationships at a later date with a recovery in the market.

One of the more innovative vendor relationship programs is that which has been in place for at least 20 years at the Fiat Corporation in Italy. Fiat regularly invests money in vendors whom it has identified as potential developers of innovations for its products. The program has paid off in a number of innovations that would have been hard to encourage inside the bureaucracy of Fiat's sprawling organization.

■ Impact of a Weak Economic Environment on Value Profit Chain Principles

These principles may all be well and good when times are good, but what are the implications of value profit chain principles—managing employees like customers and customers like employees—in a weak economic environment? We would like to say that the effects of a weak economic environment are mitigated by value profit chain management, that organization downsizing is minimized by the enhanced ability to retain desired clients. However, we are only now beginning to gather data from the most recent 2000 downturns to explore these questions.

Based on a cursory survey of organizations we know to have utilized the value profit chain to implement change several years before the economic downturn, we can advance several opinions:

1. Value profit chain management influences how responses to weak economic conditions are handled, not whether necessary action is taken. For example, layoffs occur; they are managed more sensitively with an eye to retaining the loyalty of former employees.

2. Because of the value profit chain, organizations have a much clearer view of how to prune the organization—who should stay and who should go.

3. There is a greater tendency to preserve jobs during bad times in these organizations through such vehicles as job sharing or reduced compensation.

4. Employees are much more amenable to job sharing or wage reduction as a means of preserving jobs.

5. There is a natural tendency to relax client selection criteria. However, continued attention is given to the need to maintain a balance of clients to preserve the opportunity for employee development in knowledge jobs.

6. Fewer client firings occur, but employees continue to hold the "silver bullet."

7. Every employee and customer relationship is managed with an eye to economic recovery; there is a continued sensitivity to the need for loyalty and commitment.

Again, Jamie Priestley provides more detailed commentary regarding a situation in which his organization lost 44% of the clients for its marketing communication services during 2001, most of them dot-com'ers who suffered serious cutbacks:[18]

Claydon Heeley Jones Mason [Priestley's employer] really cashed in on its previous investment in a strong culture. . . . A clear strong culture meant that the [management] board did not have to debate how it should behave. Managers already knew that, for staff, frankness and clear vision were the most important management qualities.

The results for this organization have been as remarkable as its actions. In 2001, 70% of all "pitches" for new business were won. Fully 60% of all revenues as of December 2001 were new to the agency during the year. During that year the agency also produced some of its best work, according to client feedback and awards received. A survey of those released (enrolled in CHJM's Alumni Club) also revealed that 55% of them would come back if offered a job, even though many had already relocated.

■ Questions for Management

In treating customers like employees, provocative questions are raised for managers:

1. Does your organization have explicit criteria for selecting customers? Did employees responsible for customer-facing tasks have a hand in drawing up the criteria?

2. What amount of training and support do your customers require in using your products or services? How do you know? For example, has this been determined by actual observations of the products or services in use?

3. How easy is it for your customers to obtain the support they need to use your products or services?

4. How are valued customers recognized and rewarded? To what degree are they given the sense that they are valued members of a "club"?

5. Are there procedures in place for disengaging from unproductive or even destructive customer relationships? To what extent

do employees have a voice in determining or applying the procedures?

The experiences described in this chapter suggest the value of treating customers like employees—selecting them carefully (for attitude, with an attendant payoff of more highly satisfied, loyal employees capable of delivering improved results and process quality), training them (for skills, with a payoff of reduced costs to both parties in the relationships), providing them with support systems to make the relationship more successful, recognizing and rewarding them for their performance (often with lower prices), and, when absolutely necessary, firing them (in the interests of employees and the long-term reputation of the organization among other customers).

The very close relationship between customer and employee satisfaction, which we have termed the mirror effect,[19] may be most extensively observed in service organizations but is present in every business in which large number of employees occupy customer- or supplier-facing jobs. It argues strongly for policies and procedures that build customer relationship management strategies around an extended view of customer lifetime value that includes the customer's (or the supplier's) impact on the culture and continuity of an organization. Relationship lifetime value (a product of customer and employee value, discussed in Chapters 3 and 4, respectively) provides the foundation for a growing adherence to strategies centered around a concept called value exchange in shaping relationships with customers, suppliers, and other partners in the supply chain. This is why we next focus on the matter of value exchange.

Chapter 9

Managing by Value Exchange

Procter & Gamble calculates the risk and reward of an investment in a supply chain partnership with Wal-Mart designed to eliminate steps in the handling and documentation of product flows while improving in-store stock availability. SAS carefully decides how to invest in its employees to achieve greater loyalty and productivity while retaining its reputation as one of the best places to work in the U.S. Capital One conducts thousands of "experiments" to find the best investments to make in smaller and smaller pools of customers. These and an increasing number of organizations today are combining information and technology to produce the knowledge needed to produce advantageous returns to parties to a relationship, something that has come to be known as value exchange.

Marketers have understood for centuries that value to a customer is relative and unique. It depends on the need as well as the ability and willingness to pay for various product or service features, including the time and place utility associated with convenience. This is why toothpaste sold at the airport is priced more than twice as much as that sold at CVS or Walgreens. Until recently few organizations have been able to take advantage of this, instead offering products and services on a one-price, take-it-or-leave-it basis.

The emergence of information-rich marketing strategies made possible the targeting of smaller and smaller groups of customers, suggesting the ultimate of mass customization and "one-on-one" marketing. Now e-commerce alternatives enable customers to design their own products and purchase terms—whether buying a $1,000 Dell computer, a $100,000 Cisco router, or a $20 book from Amazon.com. Never has so much revenue been generated so fast, although not always profitably.

Most e-commerce strategies provide customers with the power to find sources for solutions to their needs. This reverses a basic tenet of traditional target marketing, which assumes that a vendor seeking to sell products or services on his or her terms to selected customers is in control of a potential commercial relationship. E-commerce typically allows the customer to decide whether the value exchange is right for him. Each customer fashions her own "value exchange," what she gets for what she gives.

Customers have individual unique values to sellers. The value may be measured in terms of money. For example, in some of the early work on value exchange, Loblaw's, a leading Canadian grocery store chain, determined that expanding the customer base by 2% with new primary customers, substituting two store brand items for two national brand items for each customer visit, and reducing the customer defection rate by 5 percentage points would increase the future gross profits of a store by 300% through greater utilization of its fixed investment in stores in what is a very low margin business.[1] This enabled Loblaw's management to beginning fashioning incentives to influence customer behaviors in these ways.

Value may also be measured in terms of information. Dell, Cisco, and Amazon learn something about the customer with every sale that enable them to better meet the future needs of their "do-it-yourself" customers. The "learning architecture," based on pattern recognition techniques, employed by Amazon that enables it to recommend additional books a customer might like (based on selections of customers with similar preferences) has become a well-known example of value exchange from the supplier's standpoint. It has allowed Amazon to price its wares below levels that might be appropriate in a simple transaction. The company is paid in both money and information (on which future sales can be based) by the customer.

Value exchange is the fashioning of offers, including prices, trade terms, and other features of a vendor-customer relationship, in such a way that it provides increased value to both parties to a transaction. It is equally important in crafting the terms of employee relationships as well. It is a first cousin to concepts of customer and employee lifetime value.

The basic tenets of value exchange—that all customers have some value and that all customers and suppliers are created differently—make it a controversial topic, especially since strategies based on value exchange have become more attractive with the emergence of new information technology.

Thanks to some outstanding practitioners of the strategy, we are only beginning to understand the true scope of strategies based on value exchange, one that encompasses every element of the value profit chain. As a result, we are beginning to understand the impact of value exchange as a lever for managing change.

A true pioneer in the practice of value exchange has been the Progressive Corporation under the leadership of Peter Lewis, who literally transformed the company by embracing the concept.

■ A Value Exchange Pioneer: Progressive Insurance

Peter Lewis has always had an intuitive understanding of value exchange.[2] His organization used it years ago to sell "nonstandard" insurance at higher-than-average rates to high-risk drivers, such as motorcycle owners, many of whom Progressive's competitors were not even willing to insure. Progressive's competitors assumed that the practice was a prescription for failure. Those selling nonstandard insurance charged a uniformly high rate, not bothering to do their homework to determine whether pockets of potential customers might represent lower-than-average risks warranting special rates. Lewis's organization took the trouble to find out, for example, that motorcycle owners with children under the age of 15 who garaged their bikes every night represented relatively low risks and high profit under the "one-size-fits-all" actuarial strategies of Progressive's competitors. It also required that Progressive begin collecting more detailed information about potential high-risk applicants for insurance, develop more sophisticated analytic tools, hire some of the brightest people, and conduct actuarial studies that sliced the body of data concerning candidates for nonstandard insurance in many ways. In short, it required that Lewis turn his sleepy little company upside down by means of a mission based on value exchange.

As a result, Progressive designed special contracts for many categories of applicants, many of which carried relatively attractive rates. In the process, it skimmed off a large share of the most attractive segments of the market for nonstandard insurance. It did this while serving many who had been unable to get or afford insurance, often because of bad driving records, at prices reflective of their true risk, building a company with one of the highest long-term returns to investors in the entire list of S&P 500 companies. Today, Progressive occupies a special place in the industry because of its innovative actuarial practices.

Progressive may have been a pioneer in value exchange, but Capital One has taken the concept to a new level.

■ Capital One: The Summit of Value Exchange

Ask credit card company executives and many will say that Capital One is the best in the business. Ask Capital One executives and they will say that their business isn't credit cards, it's IBS (information-based strategies). In less than a decade, they used IBS to build a company literally organized and operated on the value exchange philosophy. How they got there is well worth a few paragraphs.[3]

After studying a big bank's operations for a single day in 1987, consultants Richard Fairbank and Nigel Morris had what Fairbank calls an "epiphany." According to one account, they "decided that the credit-card industry was ripe for revolution. As they saw it, a credit card is not so much a slice of plastic as a formula made up of variables like interest rate, credit line, and cash-advance line, all of which can be changed with a few keystrokes on a computer."[4] So, taking a page out of Progressive's book, they concluded that instead of "rejecting half your potential customers and charging the rest the exact same price, why not use the mountains of data that credit cards produce to design cards with prices and terms to satisfy all sorts of customers?"[5] They proposed the use of information technology to find customers for whom various credit card offerings would be attractive.

CUSTOMER VALUE EXCHANGE

The idea sounded so revolutionary that it was rejected by all the banks the two consultants approached with their idea. All feared the possibility that credit card holders, when comparing rates and terms, would find that theirs differed from those of their friends, creating bad will. Only one company, Signet Bank in Richmond, Virginia, had sufficient banking guts to take on the two entrepreneurs. To do so, Fairbank had to convince a 30-year veteran in the credit card business that, in his words, "We've got to know more about the customers you're rejecting—take everybody."[6] This was especially challenging in view of the fact that this veteran had imposed such strict credit standards that Signet had the industry's lowest bad-debt experience. But Fairbank succeeded.

As charge-offs more than doubled to a 5.9% rate, one of the highest in the industry, and an increasingly impatient cadre of Signet's senior managers began encountering a deteriorating real estate loan business, the Fairbank and Morris team tested hundreds of theories until they hit pay dirt. In this case, pay dirt was the "teaser-rate balance transfer card." It offered potential customers a low initial interest rate if they would consolidate debts from other accounts on the card. The offer was made only to those customers with substantial debt and a good record of making payments. To effect the transfer, customers would submit their debts to Signet for payment on their card. Because of the mountain of data obtained from the original test, Signet began targeting various potential customers with different teaser rates, teaser rate periods, and other features.

The concept was so successful that Signet had to mobilize 100 people in a week to begin mailing checks to pay off cardholders' debts. It inspired continued testing by market analysts—testing that produced a stream of information about literally thousands of other ways in which combinations of credit card terms involving rates, fees, credit lines, rewards, and services (such as pictures of family members or the potential customer's college campus on a card) could be structured to meet the needs of small groups of cardholders.

It's important to pause to note the triggers for change in this case. First, the largest, most successful banking organizations rejected the idea, in part because perceptions of potential problems exceeded perceived benefits. Fairbank and Morris had to find a second-tier bank management with sufficient dissatisfaction with the status quo and present a value-driven model for significant change in a business that had never been central to the bank's strategy.[7]

The success of the IBS-driven strategy was so great that it led to the spin-off of the business through a public offering. As a result, Capital One, with Fairbank and Morris at the helm, was born. They began experimenting with everything about credit cards, including graphics as well as financial terms. They created an organization capable of carrying on an endless experiment, trying hundreds of ideas, keeping those that worked, and in the process building a detailed database about customers' credit card preferences. In short, they built the capability to fashion credit cards for many needs, thereby facilitating "value exchange," even before the growth of the Internet. The vehicle for this growth was IBS, a synonym for value exchange, which they began applying to every element of their company in the manner illustrated in Figure 9-1.

Utilizing a large number of the 50,000 consumer databases widely available today, Capital One established a business analysis department capable of testing the ideas of everyone in the company for effective value exchange.

As Capital One's IBS strategy for credit cards began being emulated and party-going consumers began comparing deals and switched from one card to another, Capital One's marketing analysis shifted from marketing to customer retention efforts, involving tests by its cadre of business analysts, the brains of its value exchange effort. These analysts put to work a massive database on consumers that by 2000 had reached the equivalent of 40 single-spaced pages for every man, woman, and child in America. They used it to profile each customer who might call the company's customer service representatives.[8] How they did this is interesting.

Capital One's business analysts began constructing an experiment to aid in the development of a model of individual cardholder behavior through the process of randomly responding in one of three ways to existing cardholders who called to cancel their cards: matching the supposedly superior terms offered by a competitor, making some kind of counteroffer for rates or fees, or simply rejecting the request. Analysts then waited and watched to see how cardholders behaved. Some switched again, some didn't. Some whose requests were rejected switched, some didn't. As a result, they found out the primary characteristics governing cardholder behavior, and therefore lifetime value. This enabled business analysts to construct models, based on customer char-

■ **Figure 9–1** VALUE EXCHANGE FOR EMPLOYEES, CUSTOMERS, AND INVESTORS

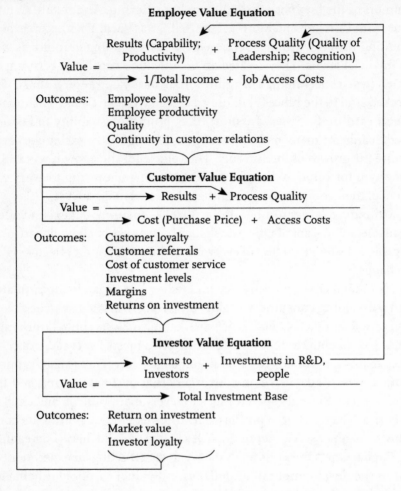

Employee Value Equation

$$\text{Value} = \frac{\text{Results (Capability; Productivity)} + \text{Process Quality (Quality of Leadership; Recognition)}}{1/\text{Total Income} + \text{Job Access Costs}}$$

Outcomes: Employee loyalty
Employee productivity
Quality
Continuity in customer relations

Customer Value Equation

$$\text{Value} = \frac{\text{Results} + \text{Process Quality}}{\text{Cost (Purchase Price)} + \text{Access Costs}}$$

Outcomes: Customer loyalty
Customer referrals
Cost of customer service
Investment levels
Margins
Returns on investment

Investor Value Equation

$$\text{Value} = \frac{\text{Returns to Investors} + \text{Investments in R\&D, people}}{\text{Total Investment Base}}$$

Outcomes: Return on investment
Market value
Investor loyalty

acteristics keyed to individual phone numbers, that provide Capital One's customer service agents as they pick up a phone call with information about (1) the reason for the call, with a 70% accuracy, (2) specific counterterms they might offer a cardholder requesting that his or her card be canceled, based on personalized value exchange calculations including likely customer responses as well as lifetime value, and (3) an actual script to use in negotiating an agreed-on set of terms.[9] To do this, the company has had to recruit, train, and retain very smart people for its battalion of business analysts, which had reached 200 in number by 2000, another task for value exchange.

EMPLOYEE VALUE EXCHANGE

Capital One's extraordinary business analysts, who designed and carried out 45,000 tests of new product or market ideas in 2000, are a product of a meticulous selection and hiring process. For example, senior executives in the company spend 20% of their time in recruiting, much of it with business analysts. Potential analysts are interviewed extensively and asked to analyze business school cases.

Customer service agents, operating out of call centers, undergo a 5 hour battery of primarily psychological and personality tests. The results are compared with profiles of the most successful employees occupying each job, with the objective of replicating those attitudes and capabilities. Because customer service agents are constantly on the lookout for new ideas generated by their conversations with customers—ideas that can be tested by business analysts—they must be carefully selected.

Training is critical. Because much of this business succeeds or fails on the quality of the "handoff" of ideas between business analysts, information technology staff, and customer service representatives, they spend a lot of time working side by side to foster entrepreneurial behavior. Compensation involves a strong incentive to own stock; 40% do. All employees receive performance-based stock options, the only kind the company grants, and managers can trade in compensation for even more options.[10]

In short, careful attention to quality of work life requires that a value exchange be achieved between Capital One and each employee, based on the combined needs of individuals and the team to which they belong. The application of value exchange to the company's relationship with its employees has resulted in Capital One's regularly being identified as one of the top 100 companies to work for in the U.S. and, according to London's *Sunday Times,* third on a list of Britain's best companies to work for.[11]

Investor Value Exchange

To complete the cycle based on value exchange shown in Figure 9-1, it is important to know what kind of value this has produced for investors. At the end of 2000, Capital One was the ninth-largest issuer of MasterCard and Visa cards in the U.S., with 34 million customers and $29.5 billion in cardholder balances.[12] In its first 7 years of existence, the company grew earnings per share at an average cumulative rate of 31%.

■ Extending the Concept to Employees

It's ironic that value exchange for employees is a concept practiced only for those at the top of a typical organization. It results from the negotiations that precede employment or that take place periodically. Too few others in an organization are given the opportunity to craft a customized deal for themselves, even though everyone has special needs and preferences involving everything from compensation to working hours and responsibilities. This flies in the face of our earlier consideration of the lifetime value of even those at the lowest levels of an organization.

The best employers in the eyes of their employees make an effort to shape jobs, hours, and even compensation for all employees. They assume that because needs are not equal, the terms of employment shouldn't be either.

Consider the philosophy that guides human resource management at SAS Institute, a privately owned developer of business software that enables users to access and interpret large masses of data. Even though private, this $1-billion-plus company employing about 8,000 people has attracted a great deal of press for its employee perks, labeled by the company itself "the utopian ideal of the corporate environment."[13] Situated on a bucolic 200-acre campus in Cary, North Carolina, the company was created to reflect the way that one of its founders and its current CEO, James Goodnight, likes to live and work. As a result, it features a number of benefits that have caught journalists' eyes, including on-site day care, an accredited Montessori school, the ability of employees to have lunch with their children in the company's subsidized cafeteria, a 36,000-

square-foot fitness center with daily laundry service, 35-hour work weeks, and first-class medical coverage and services. The list goes on. It does not include the highest salaries, which have been estimated by some as 10% below the market average before they are supplemented by profit sharing and the cost of benefits, which are estimated to be a whopping 7% of revenues.

On the other hand, the SAS voluntary employee defection rate is about one-fifth that for other high-tech knowledge workers in the U.S., something that saves it, not coincidentally, about 7% of revenues. As Goodnight puts it, "So it really comes down to do you want to give your money to recruiters and training expenses and lost productivity or do you want to give that money to your employees. To me, it's a no-brainer."[14]

The company policy most relevant to this discussion, however, is its policy of an unlimited number of sick days, which can be taken either because of personal sickness or sickness in the family. This is perhaps the ultimate example of value exchange for employees, allowing individuals to decide the trade-off between work and attention to medical needs. How do employees manage the trade-off? As David Russo, the SAS head of human resources, points out, "Jim's idea is that if you hire adults and treat them like adults, then they'll behave like adults. . . . If you're out sick for six months, you'll get cards and flowers, and people will come to cook dinner for you. If you're out sick for six Mondays in a row, you'll get fired. We expect adult behavior."[15] The result? In 1999, employees took an average of four sick days apiece.[16]

■ The Underside of Value Exchange

Value exchange and its second cousin, customer lifetime value, are concepts that can backfire when used improperly, unintentionally creating antagonists in the process while ignoring opportunities to convert those loyal to competitors' products and services.

Consider a simple but frequently experienced example perpetrated by airlines, who are some of the strongest adherents to lifetime value and value exchange concepts. Most frequent travelers make efforts, within limits, to accumulate frequent flyer miles on one or two airlines. As miles are accumulated, the privileges afforded such travelers, including personal recognition for their loyalty, also accrue. Perceptions of service, if the system is working, just get better and better.

When, on the odd occasion, it's necessary to fly a seldom-used airline, however, high-value frequent travelers are treated like everyone else—which is to say much worse than they are used to. The reason an alternative airline is being used may be the failure of the preferred carrier, thereby representing a great opportunity to impress a potentially valuable customer. But the airline fails to meet expectations. That's the best that happens; at worst, it creates an antagonist. Airlines do this because of both a fixation on their current customer base and information systems that do not enable them to identify customers loyal to other airlines.

Failure to recognize marketing opportunities, however, probably accounts for only a portion of the growing perception that airline service is deteriorating across the board. Other causes include customer preference programs that are visible to all, thereby alienating those not favored. And of course there is a customer perception, right or wrong, of the misuse—often involving sharing without permission—of the increasing body of data about customers available through increasingly sophisticated data warehousing and analysis techniques available today.[17]

■ Antidotes to Misuses of Customer Profiling

Efforts can be made to avoid the downside of customer profiling resulting from lifetime value estimates while making serious efforts to retain the most valuable customers.

DEVOTING CAREFUL ATTENTION TO TRAINING

Few organizations have been successful in training employees to deliver more than one level of service. Further, few have been able to entrust to frontline employees the estimation of customer value that might lead to differentiated service; this would require both frequent observation of customer behaviors and the kind of acquaintance with individual customers that comes only from long years of employment on the same job in the same place. Organizations that have been able to measure and communicate customer value to employees, such as airlines through their frequent flyer programs, have imposed such rigid restrictions on services for their frequent as opposed to infrequent flyers that they have succeeded only in alienating potentially valuable customers.

There are a few exceptions, of course. Southwest Airlines' frontline employees, who are encouraged to "do whatever you feel comfortable for customers," are able to implement the policy successfully because they can personally recognize a large portion of their frequent customers. Why? Because of their longevity in their jobs.

Southwest has shown us that employee attitude in interacting with customers is often a more compelling way of building customer loyalty than incentives or loyalty programs. The most effective way of attracting potentially desirable customers is to select customer-facing employees primarily on the basis of their attitudes and train them in low-cost ways of parlaying those attitudes into great basic service for everyone. Extraordinary actions may be reserved for the very best customers, but at the same time all will experience high levels of satisfaction at an affordable cost.

DEVELOPING IMPROVED INFORMATION SYSTEMS

A growing body of information is available commercially to identify the purchase frequency, loyalty, viral character, and influential nature not only of an organization's customers but also those of its competitors. Credit or debit card information can be used to track purchasing patterns. Cross-company membership cards providing incentives for all purchases made with card identification can make this available to organizations competing for the same customer. In the future, this information will be used to track highly desired customers in ways that enable an organization to attract new customers by means of a value-sensitive product or service designed to create a highly favorable "first impression."

UTILIZING POSITIVE INCENTIVES

Efforts to induce customers to engage in more profitable buying behavior have, on occasion, backfired because they utilized negative as opposed to positive incentives. Perhaps the most widely known of these were the charges assessed on banking transactions made through the use of a human teller as opposed to automatic teller machine, phone, or the Internet. Such charges produced outcries from heavy users of expensive tellers, typically the elderly and the tech-averse. As a result, their cause attracted the attention of legislators capable of bringing strong pressure to bear for the elimination of such charges.

The same objective can be achieved by providing incentives to those who utilize low-cost methods, whether in doing their banking or in purchasing other products and services. To date, no one has been prohibited from offering such incentives in the form of reduced fees for the utilization of low-cost service or product delivery channels. This is also becoming an especially popular way of marketing a range of travel services through Internet-based direct communication between service providers and consumers.

Exercising Care in "Firing" Customers

Customer profitability is only partially reflected in their loyalty. A loyal customer may nevertheless be very costly to serve. Each transaction may produce little or no profit. Efforts to enhance profitability, such as through service fees, may only risk further alienation. When all else fails, it may make business sense to "fire" customers before their dissatisfaction reaches levels that produce "antagonist" behaviors.

Organizations with outstanding performance and reputations regularly fire customers. Some do it because they are unable to serve a customer adequately and profitably; it often is carried out in the form of both an apology and the recommendation of a competitive source of product or service to the customer. Some fire customers because of their abusive attitudes and actions toward employees. Here, the firing is more often public (if possible, in front of offended employees) and more final. This can produce real dividends in employee attitudes toward an organization willing to stand behind them by the actions of its leadership.

Firing customers can create antagonists, although if properly done this is rarely the case. However, it may be a necessary cost of a strategy aimed at providing the maximum value to a group of targeted clients, those with both purchase potential and the willingness and ability to buy and use products and services in ways that are designed as part of the strategy. To the extent that such clients subsidize the behaviors of those for whom an organization's products and services are not designed, their value exchange is compromised.

APPLYING THE ANTIDOTES

Utilizing several of these antidotes, airlines could correct the problems described at the outset of this section. This would require that an airline combine its databases for passenger experiences, including such factors as flights flown, baggage checked, and complaints registered with its other files regarding flight performance information, such as late arrivals. Armed with this information, any airline could then construct a value exchange system able to fashion individual responses to passengers, recognizing them not only for their loyalty but also for the problems they might have experienced. Such recognition, communicated by email or mail, would not be visible to other customers. Such use of personal information for the benefit of customers would more likely trigger loyalty and commitment—and even ownership—than criticism.

One of us experienced the potential of this several years ago. A flooded roof at O'Hare Airport caused by a sudden summer cloudburst knocked out the monitors directing passengers to flights. Chaos resulted, with planes departing with a fraction of their scheduled passengers, who were hopelessly lost in the airport without gate information. A letter from American Airlines appeared 3 weeks later, acknowledging that one of us had been at O'Hare on the afternoon in question and crediting our frequent flyer account with 2,000 miles in recognition of the inconvenience. The amount was immaterial. The acknowledgment was priceless. Similar opportunities in the intervening years have gone unrecognized, however, by American or any of its competitors.

■ Further Application of Value Exchange

Capital One has sought to diversify the application of IBS, extending its use to other business opportunities.[18] In the process, it has developed a set of negative screens for the application of value exchange. For example, it avoids businesses with infrequent transactions with individual customers that require a long period of time to build a database of customer behavior. It avoids businesses subject to what is known as "adverse selection," the ability of competitors, for whatever reason, to obtain "the right of first refusal" to screen out the best credit risks and cast the rest on the market, creating undue risks for a Capital One. This is characteristic, for example, of the auto finance business, in which captive finance companies have the first chance to offer loans to their customers, a factor leading to the acquisition by Capital One of its own auto finance company.

It avoids businesses in which nearly everything is already known about consumer usage patterns through publicly available data. As Richard Fairbank explains, "What we want are markets where people can see the product being sold but not the algorithms behind it."[19] It avoids businesses in which irrational competitors might quote prices that rapidly erode margins, and it avoids businesses in which regulation inhibits the freedom to test and mass customize offerings.

This leaves a select group of subscription-based businesses in which information about subscriber needs and loyalty patterns can be assembled and analyzed out of the view of competitors and without undue regulation.

■ Questions for Management

In view of the impact that management by value exchange can have on an organization, it is important to keep in mind the following questions:

1. Does value exchange offer an opportunity for differentiation for your organization in its dealings with customers, suppliers, employees, investors, or others?

2. Has your organization accumulated a database that provides the basis for identifying

   a. The lifetime value of customers?

    b. Past customer behaviors in response to offers from the organization?

    c. The nature of the potential customer base for a product or service?

    d. Employee needs and worklife preferences?

3. Do you hire talent capable of generating information from your organization's "data warehouse" and putting it to work in the service of value exchange?

4. Do responses to customer and employee complaints or concerns reflect important value exchange knowledge?

One of the key elements of value exchange is the ability to leverage value over cost for all parties to an organization's activities. Without it, there is little basis for a profitable relationship, and this is our concern in Chapter 10.

Chapter 10

Leveraging Value over Cost

THE 25-MINUTE TURNAROUND, from arrival to departure from the gate at Southwest Airlines is legendary in the airline industry. It contrasts with an average of more than 55 minutes for other U.S. airlines. And does it add value!

Because Southwest's fleet records roughly 2,700 turnarounds per day, this 30 minute advantage saves about 1,350 operating hours for Southwest's fleet each day. Given an average operating time of about 12 hours per day per aircraft in Southwest's fleet, this represents the equivalent of 112 planes that Southwest (in contrast to its competitors) doesn't have to buy or lease to achieve a given level of airlift. At a cost of about $50 million for a Boeing 737–700, Southwest's aircraft of choice, this adds up to a saving in investment of about $5.6 billion for the airline. At an assumed average cost of money of about 10% per year, this represents a $560 million savings in annual interest costs, a figure that was more than half of Southwest's profit before tax in the year 2000. Although it is extreme to conclude that with a 55-minute turnaround time Southwest would have lost money in 2000, it's no overstatement to say that plane turnaround contributed significantly to the airline's profitability.

We doubt that we're the first to run these numbers. In fact, we'd be surprised if all other U.S. commercial airline managements had not run them sometime during Southwest's phenomenal, consistently profitable 30-year operating history in an industry that collectively lost money during the first 70 years of its existence. If so, why aren't others managing their airlines to achieve similar turnaround times and value for passengers, employees, and shareholders like Southwest?

Other airline managers would have to renounce several concepts—hub operations, interline exchange of passengers and baggage, assigned seats, meal service, substantial ticket distribution through agents, and membership in a computerized reservation consortium—that have been advocated and practiced for years in the industry. Further, they would have to adopt a single-aircraft fleet, revamp their route networks to accommodate an average flight length of 90 minutes, operate routes preferably with no fewer than eight flights in each direction per day, and resist expanding service to the dozens of cities requesting it to preserve no more than a 15% annual growth rate for the airline.

This wouldn't suffice. They would also have to hire new employees on the basis of attitude, including their comfort with teamwork, their empathy for others, and their enthusiasm for engaging in afterwork volunteer activities with their colleagues. Then they would have to feature teamwork in training exercises and organize these employees into teams tasked to achieve goals for timely and personable handling of passengers. They would have to renegotiate union contracts to provide unionized employees wide latitude to perform most tasks necessary to achieve the goals. And they would have to reengineer the operation to feature simplicity and effective support systems—standard plane configurations, fewer inventories, more standardized training, and information sharing to support timely operations. All of this would contribute to jobs in which employees, while paid industry wage rates, would be willing to work as many as 20% more hours than at other airlines.

Even if they did all this, however, they would still miss out on an important element of Southwest's formula for creating value. To complete the picture, it would require allowing employees to "do whatever is reasonable to satisfy a customer," often without consulting with anyone else. Products of the creative minds of employees most often would include singing the on-board announcements, leading organized games (from "Who's got the biggest hole in your sock?" to "airline trivia") in both the terminals and on board planes, and celebrating holidays with appropriate costumes. It would require frequent company social events, management by "war stories," and a search for an excuse to recognize employees for every accomplishment and creative act. It would also require that all employees with more than 6 months of service hold ownership stakes in the company.

A clear customer target and marketing strategy would have to be established, in Southwest's case a targeting of frequent business flyers ("road warriors") and budget-minded recreational travelers, with fares for tickets established with the philosophy of charging the lowest fare that still enables the airline to make a profit, reflecting a decision to compete with the automobile, not other airlines. Customers would have to be targeted, selected, and "trained" in the unusual ways of the airline—no assigned seats, no meals, no connections with other airlines. Once selected, or self-selected, however, in or out of Southwest's service "contract" with passengers, such passengers would be receptive to and satisfied with the kind of service delivered by the airline's employees.

In short, it would require shutting down an airline and starting over. This is what it would take to produce the best on-time performance, highest levels of customer satisfaction and loyalty in the industry, fewest bags lost per passenger, regular recognition as one of America's best employers,[1] highest level of employee satisfaction and loyalty in the industry, the lowest costs by far of any major American airline, the most consistent record of profitability of any airline in the world, and a high rate of compounded total return on capital for investors.

Southwest Airlines' management knows how to create value for passengers and communities that benefit from low-cost, low-priced, outstanding service. It knows how to create value for employees, whose value is measured not only in long-term employment but membership in a "cult-like" group that values the concepts of "family" and "fun" and works in teams both on and off the job (in community service). Last but not least, it certainly knows how to create value for investors. What Southwest's management knows can be translated into change-producing processes for other organizations.

■ Identifying "Deep Indicators"

Underlying drivers of results have been termed "deep indicators" by Richard Pascale and his colleagues.[2] Michael Porter refers to them as "higher-order strategic themes" embedded in a set of activities designed to create a strategic position.[3] Jim Collins found that companies going from "good to great" developed "profound insights into their economics," often expressed in terms of just one ratio—profit per employee, per ton of finished steel, per global brand category—expressed in terms of what he calls the "economic denominator."[4]

For Southwest Airlines, the 25-minute turnaround is a deep indicator. Each additional minute required on average to turn a Southwest plane around at the gate costs the company more than $186 million in investment and perhaps $18 million in financing costs. This must be balanced, however, by another deep indicator, customer satisfaction.

At Sears, the discovery that a 5-unit improvement in employee satisfaction produced a 1.3-unit improvement in customer satisfaction and a store-level revenue growth rate 0.5% above the average for all stores provided the retail chain with a set of deep indicators that enabled it to fashion a strategy for turning around the company and its performance, at least for a time. At Capital One and other organizations with similar subscription-based business strategies (such as for credit cards, periodicals, insurance, and to a degree almost anything regularly repurchased by customers), customer retention is a particularly strong deep indicator.

Deep indicators provide a source of focus for complex operating strategies designed to drive change and sustain superior performance. Experience suggests that they are not always immediately obvious—hence their name.

For example, fast turnaround at Southwest Airlines originally was a necessity, not a focal point for a low-cost strategy. The airline was founded with a triangular route structure serving Dallas, Houston, and San Antonio, Texas, with only three planes. To provide frequent service in both directions, Southwest had to turn its planes around rapidly. Later this began to drive decisions, such as not to establish a hub (thereby slowing plane turnarounds), not to operate out of large, congested airports (slowing turnarounds), and to organize in teams charged as a group with getting planes turned within prescribed limits.

Similarly, the airline was born out of the need for a dependable supply of seats on flights between major Texas cities in the early 1970s. Continental, Texas International, and Braniff, the most important airline carriers in the market at the time, planned their flights to fit a national or international route structure. Flights serving Texas cities were often filled with passengers passing through the state on their way to other destinations.

Southwest was founded as a friend of the intrastate Texas traveler. Efforts by major airlines to force it out of business only reinforced its image as an underdog fighting for the needs of its customers. It forged a level of loyalty that became valuable as the airline extended its routes to other U.S. cities. Just as important, it fostered a bonding process among Southwest employees unequaled in the industry, leading to a second set of deep indicators focused on employee satisfaction, loyalty, and productivity.

Sears did not center its strategy around employee and customer satisfaction until it commissioned a study to determine drivers of growth and profit, a study performed by a research group that had already been exposed to value profit chain research. Taking our work further, this group identified cause-and-effect relationships between elements of the value profit chain that came to be identified as deep indicators by at least some of the Sears management.[5]

The founders of Capital One understood clearly the importance of customer retention in the credit card business. Their first efforts were centered on identifying the value exchange needed to attract profitable potential cardholders to the company's cards. It was only later that sophisticated methods were developed to enable value propositions to be developed for individual cardholders automatically.

Note here that deep indicators are rarely financial measures. They are often the drivers of financial performance on which management lavishes so much attention.

■ Deep Indicators: Sources of Leverage

Once understood, deep indicators provide important sources of operating focus. Other elements of an operating strategy can be fashioned around them, as shown for the international furniture retailer and manufacturer, IKEA, in Figure 10-1. Here, six deep indicators are critical to the success of a strategy that relies on the low-cost manufacture and distribution of stylish furniture with a clean design created to appeal to young homemakers: (1) manufacturing cost, (2) sales per square foot of retail selling and storage space, (3) percentage of merchandise in stock in

■ **Figure 10–1**   "Deep Indicators" and Elements of Operating Strategy, IKEA*

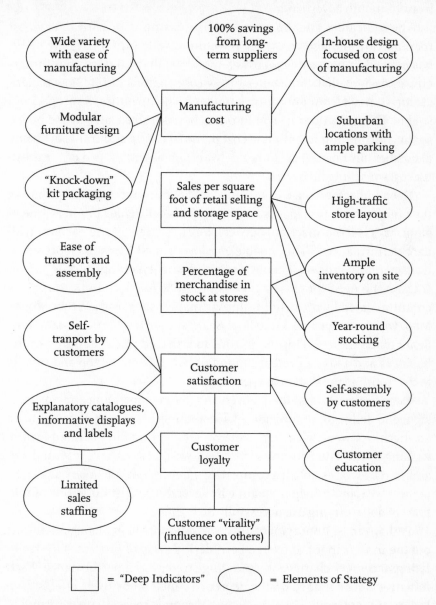

* Adapted from Michael E. Porter, "What is Strategy?" *Harvard Business Review,*
November–December, 1996, p. 71.

stores, (4) customer satisfaction, (5) customer loyalty, and (6) customer word-of-mouth advertising.

The indicators anchor a strategy. For example, to achieve low-cost manufacture and logistics while providing a wide variety of items, IKEA has created in-house design (often modular) that, among other things, creates designs that contributes to low-cost manufacturing. Raw materials are sourced from long-time suppliers. The furniture is shipped and sold in a "knocked-down" condition, to be assembled later by the buyer, again contributing to both low-cost manufacturing and transport while altogether eliminating customer delivery and assembly, two of the greatest costs of selling furniture.

Deep indicators, once understood and communicated to everyone in the organization, provide, as Pascale and his colleagues put it, a "line of sight," a "clear [connection] between a firm's strategy and each individual's performance."[6] They enable employees at all levels in an organization to make knowledgeable decisions and take appropriate action without the need for close supervision. At Sears, deep indicators were communicated by means of training "maps," such as the Sears Money Map, which enabled all 310,000 of Sears employees to understand how Sears made money. This led in turn to a shared understanding of the business and a kind of redistribution of power from the top and middle to the frontline ranks of Sears personnel.[7]

Deep indicators and the focused and tailored operating strategies designed to deliver them provide a hard-to-duplicate source of competitive strength. As we saw earlier, a major, conventionally operated airline wishing to emulate Southwest's strategy would either have to shut down and start over or establish a completely independent subsidiary as a competitive weapon. It helps explain why several have lost hundreds of millions of dollars trying unsuccessfully to do this.

Perhaps most important of all, deep indicators help management sort out the most important from a bewildering array of processes for facilitating necessary changes in operating strategy and performance. Each initiative can be judged on the degree to which it positively affects deep indicators. At Capital One, initiatives designed to calculate the value of the remaining lifetime of an existing cardholder and the kinds of value exchanges that can produce a profitable relationship are priceless to the organization. Similarly, such initiatives as continuous quality improvement, designed to deter cardholders from even questioning their loyalty to a Capital One product, carry a very high value.

This has inspired increased attention to the quantification of the value of actions and their consequences. For example, Roland Rust, Anthony Zahorik, and Timothy Keiningham have developed a method for determining the value, expressed in terms of return on quality (ROQ), of various kinds of quality improvements, providing a basis for determining whether efforts to achieve a particular kind of improvement are worth it.[8]

Their work reflects efforts by British Airways in the early 1990s to identify drivers of revenue lost through customer dissatisfaction.[9] It set out to ascertain this by estimating the frequency of each problem and the proportion of flyers experiencing it who would not repurchase tickets on British Airways. It found that the most revenue was being lost because of (1) overbooking, (2) operational delays, (3) mishandled baggage, (4) food quality, and (5) flight cancellations, in that order. When estimates of costs of remedying sources of dissatisfaction were prepared, the airline's management could then establish priorities for corrective action.

■ Sources of Leverage That Yield Lasting Improvement

Organizations can absorb only so much change. This requires that managers make careful selections from the massive, confusing array of processes, initiatives, and programs designed to deliver operating improvement.[10] Failure to do so, with an attendant proliferation of initiatives, produces a "program of the month" mentality in the ranks, leading to behavior designed to wait out a proposed change until it passes—often with little tangible result.

Sources of leverage that work have several distinctive characteristics: (1) they produce significant behavioral change, (2) they recognize and produce improvements in deep indicators of operating performance, (3) they are organizationwide, or "umbrella-like," in their relevance and application, (4) they reinforce a culture of transparency and boundaryless behavior that encourages individuals to listen continually for the needs of important customers, suppliers, and others and seek solutions and responses to such needs wherever they can be found, and (5) they are sufficiently tested that they are associated with a body of knowledge about how they have been successfully implemented.

Few initiatives meet all these criteria. Each may be appropriate for a given set of conditions, and those applying sources of leverage sometimes lose sight of the criteria. The right initiative, however, applied in response to the right deep indicator in the right manner at the right time will raise the often low probability of success associated with these sources of leverage.

Recall, for example, the Texaco story we recounted earlier. A big problem at Texaco stemmed from a cloistered "not-invented-here" culture that prided itself on careful capacity management and cost control. When a lack of attention to internal process quality and external changes in the competitive environment led to declining performance, steps had to be taken by the company's leadership. They included reorganization into profit centers and the more extensive sharing of internal information. Just as important was an increased emphasis on process quality utilizing, among other things, external benchmarks. For Texaco, the deep indicator was a measure of change in the behavior of management that produced a greater willingness to benchmark the company against its competitors, share best practices within the organization, and in general adopt a broader definition of quality more consonant with that of customers.

Ways in which a sample of popular change initiatives are linked both to deep indicators and important reasons or needs for change are suggested in Figure 10-2. It is worth a brief exploration of each to illustrate the importance of fitting the change initiative to the needs of the organization.

■ Fitting Sources of Leverage to Needs for Change

Among the more commonly applied sources of leveraging value over cost are supply chain restructuring, Workout, Six Sigma Quality, process reengineering, and organization reengineering. Each addresses different combinations of deep indicators and reasons for change, as shown in Figure 10-2.

■ **Figure 10–2**   Matching Sources of Leverage to Reasons for Change (Selected Examples)

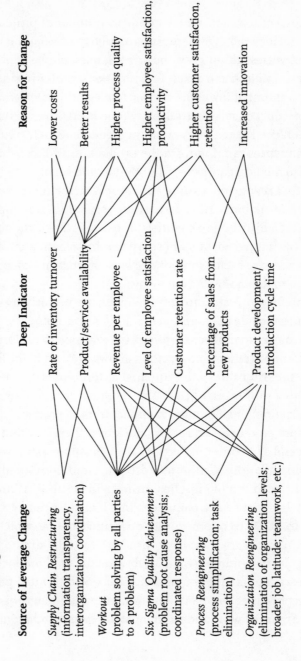

SUPPLY CHAIN RESTRUCTURING

This source of leverage, which applies a number of principles from the field of logistics management, is particularly appropriate for inventory-laden industries, although its basic principles can be applied by service providers as well. It can result in a number of initiatives designed to reduce the amount of inventory needed to meet ultimate demand at a given level of product or service availability (one measure of customer service). It has been used to achieve astounding reductions in inventory in a number of industries ranging from the production and distribution of automobiles to medical equipment, lightbulbs, and soap.

The fuel that powers supply chain restructuring is the faster, more complete availability of information regarding demand and supply throughout a distribution channel. More important is the ability and willingness of channel partners to share that information on a timely basis. This requires the establishment of a level of trust and cooperation that is lacking in many channels even today.

Supply chain restructuring has been an underlying factor in the achievement of "lean" manufacturing.[11] The automobile industry provides perhaps the most comprehensive example. More timely, accurate demand and inventory information allows an auto manufacturer to determine the extent to which finished automobiles can be produced to stock with a minimum of risk. The modular design of products (called modularization) enables auto manufacturers to produce modules (chassis, motors, and drive trains) to stock and then mix and match them upon receipt of an order, a practice called postponement.

The installation of automated equipment combined with the sequenced streaming of supplies for individual units of production has changed the face of auto manufacturing. It enables timely, economic production in EOQs (economic order quantities) of one, which has enabled auto manufacturers literally to produce to individual orders, largely avoiding the inventorying of at least some finished product during periods of heavy demand, particularly of autos with limited popularity. The funneling of timely information from auto manufacturers to their suppliers, combined with relocation of stock nearer the point of manufacture, the use of more dependable methods of transportation, and the application of "lean" manufacturing to suppliers' processes, has also enabled auto parts suppliers to deliver to their customers in a "just-in-time" fashion, thereby reducing inventory investment, clutter, and damage at the point of manufacture.

Supply chain restructuring often requires the leadership of one partner in a channel of distribution, often the one with the most power. Thus, one of the more successful applications of this source of leverage is Wal-Mart's reorganization of the entire channel for products from such major suppliers as Procter & Gamble and GE. It has required changes in the basic logistics practices of all parties to the channel. For Procter & Gamble, its shipments of soap products are triggered by daily demand information supplied by Wal-Mart. Procter & Gamble stores and ships goods in a continual flow to Wal-Mart's distribution centers, where most of the product is "cross-docked," merely moved from the incoming side of the dock to Wal-Mart's store delivery truck fleet. Procter & Gamble generates both the order and an invoice for immediate payment, saving Wal-Mart a number of steps in the process and saving Procter & Gamble working capital. As a result, Wal-Mart's inventory turns on Procter & Gamble's soap products are increased, significantly reducing its investment in inventory and costs of doing business. Thus, even though it may pay the same price for the product as its major rivals, Wal-Mart's total cost of goods landed in its stores is significantly lower than that of its competition. At the same time, Procter & Gamble also enjoys significant revenue and cost benefits from the relationship.

Supply chain restructuring is a response to the need for lower distribution costs, improved product availability (and therefore customer service), and higher customer satisfaction. As shown in Figure 10-2, its success is measured by reduced inventory turn rates, improved product capability, and even higher levels of employee and customer satisfaction. Its implementation requires changes in the ways that channel partners exchange information, ship and store products, and bill and pay for their products. It requires changes in the way that channel partners solve problems when they arise. It explains why Wal-Mart's major suppliers maintain teams of troubleshooters housed at Wal-Mart's headquarters in

Bentonville, Arkansas. At its roots, it requires changes in top management attitudes toward control, cooperation, and trust within a channel of distribution.

WORKOUT

A relatively simple concept of getting all parties to a problem, regardless of organizational loyalty, in the same room for however long it might take to solve a complex, multifunction, multiorganization problem was developed at GE in the late 1980s.[12] Called Workout—getting the work out of processes—it has been applied to all types of needs ranging from increased quality to a faster rate of innovation. As such, it is a somewhat universal process.

Workout is more than a problem-solving process. It requires change in the attitudes and behaviors of people at all levels in an organization. Workout participants are those who are closest to the problem, not their managers, under the assumption that those closest to the problem know best how to resolve it. Participants then make recommendations for ways to resolve problems to those with the authority to approve suggested actions. A manager's performance under Workout is appraised in part on his or her willingness to sponsor the process and to accept and implement all or a portion of the suggestions it produces.

Deep indicators affected by the Workout process vary by the problem addressed by the process. Perhaps the most important is employee satisfaction, resulting from the management confidence in them that the successful application of the process requires. Employees get the message clearly that people closest to a problem are assumed by management to know best how to solve it and that all levels of an organization can be trusted with the information needed to enable them to play a part in effecting important change.

SIX SIGMA QUALITY

Six Sigma is just one of a number of approaches to the improvement of quality based on the notion that a worthy goal of all such efforts is to drive all but 3.4 defects per million "parts" or "events" out of a product, process, or service. Like other approaches, such as continuous quality improvement, it utilizes the analysis of facts to determine root causes of quality problems and then proceeds to eliminate one cause after another. Its application involves many initiatives conducted at all levels of an organization under leaders specially trained in the Six Sigma process. The process itself involves the basic steps of: (1) measurement of end results, such as service or product defects, as well as each of the most important variables influencing the end result, termed CTQs (critical-to-quality) or CTXs (critical-to-costs), (2) analysis of optimal outcomes for discrete, manageable activities to understand how they were achieved in order to establish procedures to make the outcomes routine, (3) improvement through the adoption of new goals, methods, procedures, tools, work environments, tolerances, and measurements, and (4) control to insure that once new processes are in place, high quality levels are maintained.[13]

Many organizations, such as Texaco, as we saw earlier, have improved the quality of their products, processes, and services without the formality of a Six Sigma process. However, Six Sigma has the virtue of imposing discipline on an organization and giving ongoing visibility to an effort that is all too easy to put aside during times of pressing need for other work.

Quality improvement, to the extent that it improves processes as well as products and services, can lead directly to more productive, pleasant work resulting from fewer customer complaints. It speeds response times, thereby satisfying internal needs for timely responses to employee needs. As a result, it can have significant effects on employee satisfaction as well as other deep indicators. In a striking example of the application of Six Sigma Quality at Rapp-Collins, a division of Omnicom, the process time from conception to production of a promotional campaign for a major automobile manufacturing client was reduced from 76 to 17 days. The effort began with such simple "fixes" as starting all meetings on time.

PROCESS REENGINEERING

Breaking down processes into their basic steps, then analyzing each step in terms of its usefulness and combining or discarding steps, tasks, and related activities, came to be known as "reengineering" with the publication in 1996 of a widely read book of the same name by Michael Hammer and James Champy.[14] Neither the hype accompanying the concept nor the disillusionment that has accompanied many subsequent efforts to apply reengineering are fully warranted.

Process reengineering advocates reorienting organizations around important processes as opposed to functions in an organization. The goal is to start with a blank page in redesigning a business process, defined as "a collection of activities that takes one or more kinds of input and creates an output that is of value to the customer."[15] Jobs are combined or eliminated, steps in the process are reorganized into a more logical order, work is performed where it makes the most sense, checks and controls are reduced, and a process manager provides a single point of responsibility and contact. True reengineering requires changing not only processes but also jobs, organization, performance appraisal, and compensation, among other things. Its advocates suggest that reengineering must occur from the top down, reflecting the need for a broad perspective and cross-organizational responsibility and authority among those leading the effort. As a result, it is almost the exact opposite of continuous improvement, which emphasizes incremental change initiated largely from the bottom up, a much more "democratic" concept.

Process reengineering results are seen most often in such deep indicators as employee productivity and measures of speed, such as product development and introduction cycle time, as suggested in Figure 10-2. As a result, it can impact a number of reasons for change shown there.

Reengineering has been criticized for its lack of sensitivity to the needs of workers whose processes and tasks are analyzed. It has been seen as an initiative in which workers reluctant to eliminate their own jobs have not been able to participate. Too many were probably attracted to it primarily because of its dictum that "As few people as possible should be involved in the performance of a process."[16] As a result, it "became a euphemism for mindless downsizing."[17] and has unfairly gained a reputation as the latest in a long line of ways to eliminate jobs, often to the detriment of workers and the shared values of an organization. Clearly, reengineering has not been the right response to all performance problems: in many cases, it was applied too indiscriminately, like a hammer in search of something sticking up.

The fact remains, however, that the reengineering of processes is essential and is carried on every day in many organizations. It is an essential part of quality improvement as well as supply chain restructuring, to mention only two types of initiatives discussed earlier. When applied as intended, it has proven to be effective. Consider, for example, the experiences of one of its strong advocates, Hallmark Cards, Inc., a dominant competitor in the U.S. greeting card industry.[18]

The goal of the effort at Hallmark was to "dramatically (reduce) . . . the time that elapses from noting a new market need to filling it with a card on the retailer's shelf."[19] At the time a process reengineering effort was initiated, this required from 2 to 3 years. It was agreed that everything had to change except Hallmark's dearly held values and beliefs.

As a result of the effort, Hallmark linked its information systems directly to selected retail stores to track demand, developed technology to analyze the data, and grouped people into integrated cross-functional, product development process-oriented teams headed by process managers. Teams reviewed, evaluated, and improved their own work. Well into what became known as "the journey," the time required for new product line development efforts had been more than cut in half.

ORGANIZATION REENGINEERING

Organizations as well as processes can be reengineered. We saw earlier how Taco Bell created fewer, more important jobs by eliminating two levels of management, expanding span of control, and pushing day-to-day decision making lower in the organization.[20] As a result, it was able to hire more capable people for better paying jobs, facilitate more rapid expansion of its "points of distribution," and encourage more teamwork and self-management in its frontline stores.

Organization reengineering asks the basic question of where in the organization each kind of work should be performed and each kind of decision made. Typically, it results in the creation of consulting jobs where command and control functions were formerly performed. This enables a senior manager to assume reporting responsibility for larger numbers of direct reports with day-to-day decision responsibility, thereby fostering a flattening of an organization of given size.

This effort relies heavily on the selection of key managers who believe strongly in the measurement of progress by means of appropriate deep indicators, often requiring basic changes in management philosophy. We saw this earlier at the New York Police Department under Commissioner William Bratton, who required that every one of his 76 precinct commanders "sign on" to an effort to reduce crime—one that would be measured ultimately in terms of their ability to "manage" the rate of major crimes downward, something generally thought previously to be impossible.

■ Reasons for Change Management Failures

Having trumpeted the importance of various ways of leveraging value over cost in the change management effort, it is important to point out that far fewer than half of the initiatives attempted are successful, as measured by the degree to which they meet expectations originally established for them, expectations that often provided the basis for management acceptance of the initiative in the first place. Of course, "overselling" in the form of unrealistic expectations can be blamed for some of this. However, the fact remains that most "failures" are caused by underperformance, for which there are many causes, including those attributable to faulty design and faulty execution.

FAULTY DESIGN

The causes of faulty design may result from a failure to understand the underlying drivers of performance. The most blatant is to target profit improvement as the objective of the effort, a goal that is not only too broad to be actionable but one that focuses on ends versus means.

If contributors to profit performance provide reasons for change, each will have deep indicators that enable managers to mobilize an organization around a small number of targets, several of which may be elements of the value profit chain. Too often, initiatives are designed to do too much, with too many measures of success, not all of them related to a purpose for the change. They become confusing to those entrusted with the task of implementing them.

Initiatives that do not build on previous work are often regarded in the depths of the organization as just another "program of the month." This is the genius of the progression of initiatives established at GE between 1987 and 2000.[21] They began with the establishment of a set of values—including speed, self-confidence, simplicity, and boundarylessness—that helped establish a rationale for a set of deep indicators reflecting these values. In this context, the introduction and rollout of Workout was a natural consequence, with its emphasis on speed in solving complex problems by bringing together people across functional and organizational boundaries. It required self-confidence on the part of GE managers charged with the task of responding in a timely manner to the recommendations agreed on in Workout sessions that often did not even include the managers responsible for seeing to it that recommended problem fixes were implemented.

Once Workout was in place, the establishment of a Stretch process for setting ambitious long-term goals for various deep indicators, such as inventory turnover rates, was a logical next step. With both of these sources of leverage in broad use throughout the GE organization, the implementation of a Six Sigma Quality initiative did not seem so onerous to members of the organization.

The tenacious character of management's approach to change initiatives at GE, with each building on the last rather than replacing it, quickly banished the notion that these efforts were programs of the month.

Even with the proper identification of reasons for change, deep indicators, and sources of leverage—the right initiative for the right reason at the right time—successful change is not guaranteed.

FAILURES OF EXECUTION

Just as many initiatives fail because of poor execution as from poor design. Here, the refrain is familiar and has been explored at length elsewhere,[22] but it is important to recognize several here.

At the outset, change initiatives fail because of lack of sufficient top management commitment and investment, usually resulting from a failure to understand the magnitude of the forces opposing change in most organizations. This is characterized by the absence of highly respected and powerful champions for an initiative. At GE, the investment in Six Sigma Quality, for example, involved hiring 3,000 new executives to replace those placed into training to become Six Sigma leaders. Conservatively, this had to have cost at least $300 million. Few organizations are able or willing to make this kind of commitment to an initiative promising few short-term gains. Yet Six Sigma, 6 years after its initiation, may be enhancing GE's earnings by as much as $1 billion per year, according to company estimates.[23]

Change initiatives fail because of poor communication of the goals and methods associated with the work. Change is threatening, and lack of accurate information adds to the threat. This is a particularly sensitive matter for middle managers, who are often asked to shift decision-making responsibility to subordinates in many of the more popular change initiatives listed in Figure 10-2. They are often the very managers on whom the success of the overall effort depends.

This in turn can lead to an unwillingness on the part of middle managers to give frontline employees the latitude they need to solve problems and produce the results required in most of these initiatives. Because the managers often can't do it themselves, the initiative becomes bogged down.

The failure to set realistic expectations for the magnitude and speed of change often leads to premature disillusionment. It produces an unrealistic impatience for results that reflects the pressures for short-term performance in many organizations today.

Finally, too often persistence is lacking in change ventures. With a waning of interest in an effort that has not yet produced significant results, management turns to the next great idea, not only distracting those responsible for the incumbent change initiative but also communicating the message that both the old and new initiatives are not of primary importance.

Little wonder, then, that most efforts to achieve significant change that leverage results over costs prove to be large disappointments and unnecessary distractions from the day-to-day business of running the organization.

■ Why a Value Profit Chain Focus in Managing Change Raises the Odds of Success

Fortunately, the batting average for initiatives focused on the deep indicators of the value profit chain—employee and customer satisfaction, loyalty, and commitment—is so far higher than that for most other sources of focus.

In examining at least a small sample of such efforts to date, we can reach some preliminary conclusions about why this is so. First, based on a sample of a dozen such efforts, all of them thus far successful, we have concluded that they are meeting their objectives because they (1) have a great deal of surface credibility resulting from the intuitively believable relationships of the value profit chain itself, (2) are simple and easy to understand at all levels in an organization, (3) involve readily accessible measures (deep indicators) of progress, (4) are not dependent on any one of the change initiatives shown in Figure 10-2 but rather benefit to some degree from nearly all of them, and (5) are based on a growing base of evidence that they deliver a wide range of changes described in Figure 10-2.

■ Questions for Management

In examining ways of leveraging value over cost that produce lasting change, a number of questions should be addressed by managers:

1. To what extent do such methods

   a. Effect permanent changes in organization behavior by enabling employees at all levels to make more informed judgments and take appropriate actions?

   b. Enhance performance on deep indicators?

   c. Lend themselves to "umbrella" or organizationwide application?

   d. Encourage "transparency" in measures and boundaryless behavior among organization members?

2. Is there a body of successful experience in application associated with the initiative?

3. Is an effort made to identify and communicate deep indicators, providing a clear connection between an organization's strategy and each individual's performance?

4. Is the initiative selected the one that will produce the greatest improvement in the deep indicator? In short, is it is the right response to the need for change?

5. Is top management prepared for the kinds of actions that informed employees will expect to be able to take under this initiative?

6. Is top management prepared to deal with the intelligent questions that will be raised by increasingly knowledgeable employees under this initiative?

7. Does this initiative build logically on others that have been launched and may still be underway?

This assumes, of course, that questions concerning more generic reasons that many initiatives fail have also been addressed:

1. Has sufficient investment been made up front by management?

2. Is the level of commitment by top management to the initiative sufficiently high to ensure focus, follow-through, and the persistence needed for success?

3. Has middle management been involved from the beginning of the initiative?

4. Have realistic interim and ultimate expectations and goals been set for the initiative?

5. Have both the goals and the methods by which they will be reached been communicated clearly to all levels of the organization?

Several means of leveraging value over cost that meet our criteria for producing useful and lasting change in organizational behavior have been highlighted in this chapter, along with the lessons learned by organizations employing them. They include the coordination of supply chain activities, Workout, Six Sigma Quality, process reengineering, and organization reengineering, often involving the substitution of information for tangible assets and relatively unproductive behavior.

Our purpose here has not been to present comprehensive descriptions of a number of ways of leveraging value over cost. Rather, the objective has been to use several well-known, current, popular strategies for leveraging value over cost as vehicles for exploring how each can create or destroy value, depending on the nature of other elements in a company's strategy and how well they are understood and supported.

Once achieved, the gains from the change management process must be consolidated. This is our next concern.

PART IV

Cementing the Gains

M OST OF THE VALUE claimed in proposals for new initiatives has been counted many times. That's because it was never achieved in the first place. As a result, capital budgeting proposals, for example, have gotten a bad name. Most are intended to correct problems that have been "corrected" before.

Too much management time is spent replowing ground in search of value that was not achieved in previous efforts intended to achieve the same thing. This is often done with varied initiatives, often launched with increasing frequency and frenzy. As a result, jaded middle managers get ready for yet another "program of the month."

The reasons this occurs include insufficient follow-through on the part of top management, little "ownership" in the ranks of middle managers, inadequate measurement of progress, and the lack of incentives and recognition for achieving the goals of such efforts, as well as changes in the environment that represent distractions at least and, in some cases, serious disruptions. Of course, this provides recurring work for consultants who are often hired to undo each others' work or to launch an organization on yet another "exciting" new value-building initiative.

Antidotes to this syndrome are the subject of this part of the book. A "poster organization" for this section is CEMEX, the third largest cement producer in the world, based in Monterrey, Mexico.

We begin in Chapter 11 with the process of identifying and revisiting core values, the basis for an organization's culture. Without them, there is no definition of value and therefore little basis for the development of a vision or strategy. Core values provide an answer to the question of why the organization exists in the first place. One company executive has described the CEMEX culture to us as "the CEMEX nationality," of significance in a company that operates plants and sales offices in 33 countries around the world. This nationality is reinforced by a common language, a common knowledge base, a common technology, and frequent sharing of knowledge and best practice to create "a company that is more global, but also better attuned to local needs; one that is more intensively focused on customer satisfaction, and better able to deliver innovative, customer specific service."* Named the CEMEX Way, it is, in the words of its designers, "about nothing less than reinventing our company and our industry, while creating more value and better opportunities for all of our stakeholders—employees, customers and shareholders alike."† Note the order of stakeholders cited.

Next we consider measurement and recognition efforts in Chapter 12. All organizations keep score in a financial sense. However, for many, this is like recording every fifth play in an athletic contest, given that financial measures may be among the least useful for those leading a value-building initiative. One kind of scorekeeping at CEMEX is largely on financial dimensions. Performance and incentive compensation is based on such factors as shareholder value and return on capital employed. In addition, however, substantial attention is given in individual reviews and promotion decisions to the degree to which a manager's actions and behaviors reflect the CEMEX way, with an emphasis on the sharing of ideas and talent across organizational boundaries.

We then turn in Chapter 13 to ways of achieving what we term "hardwiring performance." This is done primarily through specific commit-

---

*Cemex Way Global Message Guide, October 2001 (company document), p. 5.
† Ibid.

ments made to customers, suppliers, employees, and others that must be fulfilled to ensure the success of the organization. They represent ways that already good performers transform themselves into value-creating machines. CEMEX is perhaps best known for its on-time delivery guarantees on ready-mix concrete that it delivers to builders and contractors in three major Mexican markets. Even though this is admittedly a small portion of the company's total global business, it is characteristic of the innovative thinking fostered throughout the company by the CEMEX way.

CEMEX has changed the nature of the ready-mix concrete business in these selected markets by reducing the "window" of delivery time for the product from 4 hours to 20 minutes, thereby allowing builders to schedule operations knowing that workers will not be left waiting for concrete. This required that CEMEX completely rethink the business, assigning delivery trucks loaded with ready-mix concrete (with a 90-minute "shelf life") to regions rather than routes and sending them out to "roam" while waiting for orders. This strategy was combined with a satellite-based global positioning system that enables CEMEX dispatchers to know where their "inventory" is located at all times. It has "hard wired" its service by guaranteeing "20 minutes or 20 pesos," representing roughly a 5% reduction in price for failure to deliver within the 20 minute window. As a result, employees whose bonuses are based on profitability take actions at a local level necessary to meet the customer-oriented promise.

Note how the efforts just described are meant to be cumulative. To meet this objective, they must have staying power. They have to become second nature to the members of the organization, who are then free to exercise outrageous latitude in delivering value to customers and others. All this requires serious attention to our final topic, knowledge transfer, the core of any effort to create a learning organization, the ultimate vehicle for the creation and sustenance of value through constant change. We turn to it in Chapter 14. In the "CEMEX nation," knowledge transfer is a religion. For example, the guaranteed delivery systems for ready-mix concrete were derived from the visits of a best-practice team to FedEx and the 911 Dispatch Center at the Houston, Texas, Fire Department.

At CEMEX, a manager, regardless of nationality, is selected and prepared to manage anywhere in the world. Transfers, which facilitate knowledge exchange, are frequent. This requires, as we saw in Chapter 7, standard platforms for computer hardware, software, and operating systems that allow managers to function immediately in new operating assignments that may be halfway around the world from their last job. Frequent and relentless formal management education is combined with a global network of mentors assigned to all managers. Transportation budgets to facilitate face-to-face learning are relatively high. The resulting knowledge transfer is an important factor in sustaining one of the most innovative companies in any industry in the world.

This is exciting stuff. It is also some of the hardest to achieve. It can be done, however, as illustrated by organizations we'll look in on as we explore ways in which organizations are cementing the gains of change fostered by value profit chain thinking.

Chapter 11

Identifying and Revisiting Core Values

Thomas J. Watson, Sr., is perhaps the grandfather of corporate cultures comprising values shared by all members of an organization. He crafted a simple set of values addressing the needs of customers and others with whom his brainchild, IBM, did business. These values served the company well until they were literally forgotten by IBM's leadership in the late 1980s, only to be resurrected by a rank outsider several years later.

Johnson & Johnson has ridden its credo to success for decades. One of the first actions of James Burke, upon assuming his job as CEO, was to spearhead an internally controversial effort to revisit the credo (shown in Figure 11-1) through a series of "Credo Challenge" meetings to ensure that everyone understood and believed in it. Burke said at the time that "[The] Credo . . . hangs on the wall . . . and if [it] doesn't mean anything, we really ought to come to that conclusion and rip it off the walls and get on with the job. I think that if it is there as an act of pretension, it's not only valueless but has a negative effect."[1]

Values have mattered a great deal at Cisco Systems, too, even when they could have been regarded as factors contributing to the company's sudden nosedive from the lofty heights of the Internet bubble in late 2000.

■ Importance of Core Values

Corporate culture, as characterized by core values shared throughout the organization, can drive performance. Employees believe it. Customers believe it. And if investors don't focus on it, investment analysts certainly do.

The study by Kotter and Heskett mentioned in Chapter 5 found that nearly every one of 75 leading investment analysts (characterized by gold

■ **Figure 11–1** THE JOHNSON & JOHNSON CREDO

We believe our first responsibility is to the doctors, nurses and patients, to mothers and all others who use our products and services.

In meeting their need, everything we do must be of high quality.

We must constantly strive to reduce our costs in order to maintain reasonable prices.

Customers' orders must be serviced promptly and accurately.

Our suppliers and distributors must have an opportunity to make a fair profit.

We are responsible to our employees, the men and women who work with us throughout the world.

Everyone must be considered as an individual.

We must respect their sense of dignity and recognize their merit.

They must have a sense of security in their jobs.

Compensation must be fair and adequate, and working conditions clean, orderly and safe.

Employees must feel free to make suggestions and complaints.

There must be equal opportunity for employment, development and advancement for those qualified.

We must provide competent management, and their actions must be just and ethical.

We are responsible to the communities in which we live and work and to the world community as well.

We must be good citizens—support good works and charities and bear our fair share of taxes.

We must encourage civic improvements and better health and education.

We must maintain in good order the property we are privileged to use, protecting the environment and natural resources.

Our final responsibility is to our stockholder.

Business must make a sound profit.

We must experiment with new ideas.

Research must be carried on, innovative programs developed and mistakes paid for.

New equipment must be purchased, new facilities provided and new products launched.

Reserves must be created to provide for adverse times.

When we operate according to these principles, the stockholders should realize a fair return.

star ratings, in the parlance of the industry) believed that corporate culture could either enhance or hurt organization performance.[2] Their responses to survey questions are shown in Figure 11-2. The results of the study of which this survey was a part bore out their conclusions.

Not just any set of values, no matter how strongly they are shared, will do. Kotter and Heskett concluded that strong cultures are not enough. What is important is a culture based on a set of values that encourage behaviors that ensure adaptability to the changing needs of employees, customers, and others. An in-depth study of 22 companies in the same industries, all with strong cultures but only 12 with values supporting adaptive behaviors, found that the companies with strong, adaptive cultures outperformed their peers by more than 4 times in revenue growth and more than 12 times in stock price increases over a 10-year period.[3]

Strong, adaptive cultures do not account for 100% of performance, but they provide a strong foundation for successful strategies that deliver value to all important constituencies. Given an organization with strong long-term performance, you will find at its core a set of values that encourage behaviors that remain attuned to the needs of those seeking value in their work, their purchases, and their investments. This is why it

■ **Figure 11–2** INDUSTRY ANALYSTS' VIEW OF CORPORATE CULTURE'S IMPACT ON LONG-TERM ECONOMIC PERFORMANCE

Statements to Which Agreement Was Requested	The 12 Higher-Performing Firms	The 10 Lower-Performing Firms
Culture has helped performance	43 responses	5 responses
Culture has hurt performance	1	29
Culture has both helped and hurt performance	6	10
Culture has had little impact on performance	1	0
Not sure	3	4

*Based on interviews with 75 recognized industry investment analysts, 1989.
Source: John P. Kotter and James L. Heskett, *Corporate Culture and Performance* (New York: The Free Press, 1992), p. 36.

is so critical that the values be formalized at some point in the development of the organization, communicated constantly, and used on a day-to-day basis as guidelines for management decisions and behaviors.

Perhaps most important of all for sustaining a successful value-centered strategy, core values must be revisited periodically to ensure their validity and support by the entire organization. This doesn't mean that they are changed at the whim of senior management; in fact, continuity in shared values provides the context in which everything else near and dear to managers—strategies, policies, processes, and practices—can be changed to meet the shifting demands of the competitive environment.

This perhaps suggests that "changing corporate culture," a daunting task in any event, is an overrated priority for those seeking turnaround in performance. In his study of 11 organizations able to go from "good to great," Jim Collins hardly mentions culture as a factor. Rather, he found a common emphasis on the "culture of discipline," an organizationwide ability to say no to opportunities outside the organization's selected strategy.[4] Others might call this an ability to maintain focus; in any event, it hardly assigns culture change center stage in the rejuvenation process. This is quite appropriate, based on what we know about cultures that foster successful change, but it doesn't follow that this precludes the necessity for periodically revisiting shared values.

When, why, and how shared values are revisited is our primary concern here. The IBM, Johnson & Johnson, and Cisco experiences are instructive in this regard.

■ IBM: Values Forgotten and Remembered

When the name of the Computer-Tabulating-Recording Company (CTR) was changed in 1924, IBM was born. Its leader at the time, Thomas J. Watson, Sr., believed strongly in the importance of corporate culture, comprising both shared values and accepted behaviors. The customer was king. Out of self-respect and respect for the customer, the uniform of the day was the white shirt. Employees were admonished through the ever-present IBM signature logo to THINK. An emphasis on performance combined with respect for the individual pervaded IBM goals, systems, and rewards. Change was embraced, as exhibited by IBM's ability to outdistance its competitors in research and product development. Believers willing to buy into this culture and thrive in it were rewarded handsomely as the company employed these shared values to create a fanatical customer base willing to follow it through eras of calculating, punch-card, and finally electronic computing equipment that fueled the company's growth and success.[5]

IBM's core values, lived but not fully documented, were articulated by Thomas Watson, Jr., in a famous 1961 presentation as only three in number: "major attention to service, respect for the individual, and drive for superiority in all things."[6] They were elegantly spare, easy to communicate throughout a large organization, and supportive of an adaptive culture based on the importance of listening and responsiveness implied in the values.

Over a period of time and during the tenure of several leaders in the 1970s and 1980s, the values became, in the words of one former IBM executive, "more a wall decoration than anything else."[7] Important decisions may or may not have reflected them, as the company's performance continued at a high level, bolstered in the opinions of many by the huge lead in market share that the company had built over its major rivals for computing equipment, a lead so great that most customers elected the safe alternative, IBM, rather than risk recommending a competitor's product and failing to "buy the best."

By 1990, as we saw in Chapter 2, hardware had given way to software as the wave of the future of information technology. IBM's performance reflected this, as the company experienced a loss of nearly $5 billion on $64.5 billion in revenues in 1992. It forced IBM's leadership in late 1992, under CEO John Akers, to announce a dismissal of 25,000 employees, the first in the company's 68-year history under the name of IBM. Worse yet, in 1992, John Akers led an organization at IBM that had forgotten its core values.

Because IBM had become known for never having laid anyone off, the public came to believe that this was a firm IBM policy, even a core value. At a luncheon meeting held with a group of academics in early

1993 that one of us attended, John Akers was asked whether a distressed IBM management had violated one of its core values of lifetime employment by laying off employees for the first time. Akers essentially replied in the affirmative, but asserted that it was necessary under the circumstances. Apparently, Akers himself had forgotten that the relevant core value, crafted by Thomas Watson, Sr., and articulated by his son, made no mention of lifetime employment. It was, instead, an emphasis on "respect for every individual."

It wasn't long before Akers announced his retirement from IBM under pressure from shareholders and directors. His replacement, Louis Gerstner, raised eyebrows because of his complete lack of experience in the high-tech competitive environment. Gerstner, however, who had demonstrated excellent performance at American Express and, more recently, at RJR Nabisco, understood the importance of shared values as a foundation for the effective strategies that might follow. In fact, in his first important meeting with the public, Gerstner eschewed the importance of a vision, saying that he didn't have one for the company.[8] In the meantime, however, an effort was in place to reappraise and communicate those values that had made IBM great, in part a result of Gerstner's self-introduction to the company. This effort resulted in two decisions: (1) to reemphasize the values that had made the company great, and (2) to add to them the value of "restless self-renewal."[9]

Rather than spend his time articulating a vision, Gerstner set out to communicate the revisited values throughout the company. In his words, "If the CEO isn't living and preaching the culture and isn't doing it consistently, then it just doesn't happen."[10]

Having reaffirmed the values and their importance with IBM's leadership, Gerstner could begin to implement strategies, especially those expanding IBM's reach into total solutions with an emphasis on service outlined in Chapter 2, with greater confidence. In this case, it took an outsider to reaffirm the shared values that the insiders had forgotten.

■ Johnson & Johnson: Values in Support of Decentralized Action

Any organization placing a premium on decentralization as an element of a value-creating strategy must have clearly articulated and understood values. No company in the U.S. characterizes this more than Johnson & Johnson. On the surface, J&J appears to be a loose coalition of some 190 operating companies,[11] each pursuing its own strategy with a strong sense of competition, even in relation to each other. Central to J&J's success over the years, in the minds of those who have led it, is its strong emphasis on the decentralization and management independence of its operating subsidiaries, each charged with meeting their own goals in ways deemed best for them by their leaders.

The reason that a decentralized strategy has worked so well for J&J, at least according to its leadership, is its strong reliance on what is called the Credo, shown in Figure 11-1. The credo does not provide much guidance about the kinds of strategies to follow. It contains no mention, for example, of decentralization. It says a lot, however, about how decisions are to be made and implemented—the considerations to be taken into account in day-to-day value-enhancing actions. It has also, on occasion, saved the company from a serious setback and even long-term decline. Consider, for example, the Tylenol tragedy.

The date was September 29, 1982. The event was the cyanide poisoning of bottles of J&J's Extra Strength Tylenol capsules produced by a J&J subsidiary, now known as McNeil Consumer & Specialty Pharmaceuticals, on the shelves of a Jewel Tea grocery store in Chicago, resulting in the nearly immediate deaths of seven people. And it required a lightning-fast response on the part of J&J and McNeil management (whose CEO happened to be traveling in Australia at the time). Jim Burke, then CEO of J&J, literally became a media star as he assured the public in his sincere, straightforward manner about what the company had done and would do to protect its customers. However, he did this only after J&J's management "on the ground" in Chicago had already recommended that the company recall $125 million worth of product, an action that would cost the company a substantial portion of its profit for the year. This was an example of decentralization, J&J style, at work. A recipe for chaos?

Perhaps in most organizations, but not at J&J, thanks to the Credo. As Jim Burke put it, it is important to "give people freedom to do what they are capable of doing and . . . get out of their way. [But you have to have] a moral center that you can recognize and understand. I got to tell you that without that you can swim in chaos. . . . Somehow or other this organization functions the way I think a business institution ought to function. And I think it does because of its value system."[12]

■ Cisco Systems: Constant Values in a Time of Strategic Change

Cisco Systems rode the wave of Internet infrastructure expansion like few other organizations, realizing compounded annual increases of 75 and 69% in revenues and profits, respectively, between 1990 and 2000. In no small part, its successes were based on decisions that reflected the core values of the organization, developed both by the company's founders and early leaders, shown in Figure 11-3. Emphasizing more than just attention to customers' needs, they figuratively shouted Cisco's "dedication to customer success." Cisco as a place to work received its attention as well, with an emphasis on teamwork that "can change the world." The value of partnering was proclaimed as "a business model where companies work together in an open architecture towards a common goal." The value statement also gave some insight into the kinds of behaviors favored by the organization, particularly "frugality . . . doing more with less," something peculiar to many Silicon Valley firms in the heyday of the dot-com boom. This widely shared value at Cisco could be seen in everything from the modest size of executive offices, many without external windows, to the policy that everyone, regardless of rank, travel coach class. Even so, according to customers and competitors, success brought with it a kind of arrogance on the part of Cisco's leadership, arrogance born out of a feeling of invincibility.

The arrogance disappeared quickly with the collapse of the market for telecom equipment and the bankruptcy of many of Cisco's telecom customers, nearly destroying the company's new growth vehicle. It happened so fast that Cisco was actually in the process of building inventories of scarce components to meet its customers' needs at the time the market

■ **Figure 11–3** CISCO SYSTEMS' MISSION AND VALUES

Mission Statement

Shape the future of the Internet by creating unprecedented value and opportunity for our customers, employees, investors, and ecosystem partners.

Cisco Values

Cisco's values drive our business decisions and help create our company culture.

Dedication to Customer Success
Cisco has a chance to lead its customer success by helping our customers' transition to the Internet economy in a way that no other company in the world can. A key component of our strategy for fiscal year 2000 is to move beyond the role of strategic vendor to that of a business partner. A business partner understands a customer's industry, a customer's business strategy within the industry, and how a customer will differentiate itself in the marketplace. A business partner also understands the Web-based applications that will provide the greatest competitive advantage in a customer's industry, and empower the customer with the speed to survive in the Internet economy.

Innovation and Learning
In the Internet revolution, we not only have to stretch ourselves, but also need to work together to stretch our customers, our partners, and governments around the world. This doesn't necessarily mean working harder or being smarter, but asking, "How can I do it differently?" We must continue to adopt new ideas and challenges by accepting change, searching for answers outside, and always evaluating how we can do it better next time.

Partnerships
The Internet ecosystem is a business model where companies work together in an open architecture towards a common goal. Unlike the vertical model where companies take on every aspect of the business themselves, this horizontal model allows each company to focus on what they do best. The ecosystem will ultimately accelerate the transition of companies, countries, and individuals to the New World, enable Cisco to maintain our number one or number two position in each product category, and ensure our customers' success.

Teamwork
Working together as a team, we can change the world. We have great momentum now, but along the way there will be bumps, even an intergalactic battlestar, the horizon. We should all have the confidence that working together as a team, we can handle these future challenges as successfully as we've handled challenges of the past. With good execution and a little Cisco luck, we can truly change the way people work, live, play, and learn—and have fun doing it.

Doing More with Less
As a core component of our culture, frugality is one of the values that has made our company great. It doesn't mean being cheap; it means getting the best value for what we do. I look to all Cisco employees to work with outsource partners on projects that fall beyond our realm of expertise, and to do so effectively. This allows Cisco to continue spending money on the two most important things—our customers and employees.

dried up in a matter of weeks. In addition, its spirit of partnering had led to investments in many of its smaller telecom customers whose fortunes declined as increasing competition fueled rapid price cuts for their services. This resulted in the need to write off $2.5 billion in excess inventories resulting from the fanatical focus on customer needs, as well as devalued investments totaling several billion dollars in 2001.

The resulting implosion of Cisco's stock price and market value by more than 80% dealt a blow to the value of the "currency" it had been using to acquire partners who brought with them the new technologies that enabled Cisco to jump-start its new product development. It led to a decision in mid-2001 to create an in-house product development function, effectively fueling a shift from an "acquisition and development" to a heavier reliance on a more traditional research and development strategy. It also required that the company actually reduce its workforce for the first time, involving a force reduction of 8,500 people, or more than 15%.

All of this may have raised questions in the minds of some about the validity of Cisco's core values, one or two of which could have been perceived as having caused some of the company's problems. But while Cisco's management clearly had made adjustments to the company's strategy, it appeared (as of early 2002) unshaken in its belief in the values that had contributed to its original phenomenal success. As the company's chairman (and former CEO), John Morgridge, put it recently:

> The key to the values is more how they are practiced than what they say. Current key words and phrases (around the company) are customer success, drive change, open communication, fun, empowerment, market transitions, no tech religion, frugality, giving back, stretch goals, and teamwork. Some go back almost to the start and some reflect more what we have been doing all along.[13]

■ Identifying and Revisiting Core Values

The process by which core values are formed follows a reasonably predictable course, according to research by Kotter and Heskett. The process by which they are revisited is becoming much more informed, based on what we are learning from recent experience.

STRONG CULTURES THAT INFLUENCE PERFORMANCE, FOR BETTER OR WORSE

Corporate cultures are spawned by entrepreneurs who often impose their personal values on their creations. This is clearly the case at IBM. It is also true of Johnson & Johnson, whose values were first articulated in the 1940s by General Robert Johnson, Jr. And it characterizes the evolution of Cisco's values from a group of computer scientists who left Stanford University to be able to pursue interests independently of their former employer.

The study of over 200 large organizations in the early 1990s by Kotter and Heskett yielded interesting insights into the patterns by which corporate culture influences performance over time. Early in an organization's history, operating success reinforces the "rightness" of a set of values, further reinforcing adherence to them.[14] If the values are those that encourage adaptability—focused on an understanding of and response to the changing needs for value on the part of those with which the organization deals—an organization may thrive over long periods of time, characteristic of companies qualifying for examination by Collins and Porras in their landmark work, *Built to Last*.[15]

To the extent, however, that a strong culture discourages the acceptance of outside ideas, the internal pooling of assets and knowledge, or effective responses to the needs of customers or employees, performance eventually declines in the face of new competitive challenges, even though an organization may enjoy short-term success.

REVISITING CORE VALUES

The purpose of revisiting core values from time to time is not necessarily to change them but to remind an organization's leadership of their importance. It is not something that needs to be done frequently. There are critical transition points in an organization's development when the exercise can be useful, however.

In the early stages of an organization's development, core values may be "felt" but not articulated. This characterizes the condition of most dot-com start-ups in the 1990s. Many were founded by very bright "rebels" with primary loyalty to ideas rather than organizations and a need for independence in work life. They built their organizations by recruiting others with similar needs and interests. Out of these relationships cultures evolved that helped define shared values, priorities, and accepted behaviors. An interesting aspect of many of these start-ups is the relatively early attention paid to the matter of organizational culture by founders sensitive to the matter and the involvement in the process by all or most employees of these relatively small organizations.

The first natural transition point at which corporate culture is often revisited is the point at which an organization grows to the point that it "feels" too large, a point at which individuals feel too disconnected from one another and at which the leadership no longer knows and relates to everyone. The process is an opportunity to reengage employees in the design of "their organization."

As we saw in the Johnson & Johnson story, a decision to decentralize, conveying greater latitude for decision-making to individual business units, may signal a need to revisit and reinforce core values. This is particularly important when individual units are operating under the umbrella of a common brand or identity that links them through the implications of their individual actions.

A moment of crisis may create the need once again to identify shared values and to assess the way in which they did or did not help the organization through the crisis. This occurred on a national basis, for example, at the time the U.S. faced domestic terrorist attacks in 2001.

A transition of ownership invariably triggers the reaffirmation process. Because the compatibility of cultures is often the most important criterion in the merger or acquisition of organizations, it is a natural time for culture assessment. A change of control may signal a change in relationships between members of an organization, providing an added rationale for review.

Just how the process is carried out reflects the organization's beliefs about the need for breadth of community involvement in such processes. Because it is of vital importance to all members of an organization, however, those interested in the broadest acceptance and communication of the results opt for more rather than less involvement.

Of course, the primary purpose of the process is to identify those beliefs—often few in number—shared most widely by all members of the organization. Other criteria that might be applied to those shared beliefs may also include the extent to which (1) values reflect the needs of all important constituencies for value, (2) they ensure that the organization remains attuned to the changing demands of a constantly changing competitive environment, and (3) they suggest the kinds of behaviors expected of all members of the organization regardless of varying local business unit cultures. In a multi-business organization, a criterion is imposed, that of whether the values provide an umbrella under which a variety of customs and mores attendant to individual business unit cultures can flourish.

If shared values are employed regularly in strategic decision-making, however, more formal revisitation may be less necessary. The organization's culture is tested repeatedly and adjusted when necessary. Thus, a "use it or lose it" mentality is useful here.

■ Putting Core Values to Work: Use 'Em or Lose 'Em

Core values should regularly influence strategic decision making and exert a strong influence on management behaviors (how the organization is managed). To ensure that this happens, organizations sustain their success by giving them high visibility in the performance appraisal and reward process.

Use in Decision Making

Whether core values are a consideration in important decisions within an organization has a lot to do with their simplicity and practicality. This argues for language that is easily understood and highly relevant to those entrusted with their care and use.

For example, the preservation of a focused strategy may be of critical importance to executives at Southwest Airlines, but it is subordinate to the preservation of a very strong culture that addresses the needs of employees, customers, and others. To most, the company's culture is embodied in its cofounder and chairman, Herb Kelleher. Recognizing the danger in wrapping a company in the cloak of a single, mortal person,

Southwest for years has had what has been known as a culture commit-tee, headed by Southwest's current president, Colleen Barrett. The cul-ture committee is entrusted with the tasks of reviewing current strategic decisions to make sure they conform with the values of the organization and devising new initiatives to communicate the organization's values to its rapidly growing body of employees. The unspoken objective of the culture committee is to make sure that the organization is fully able to weather the eventual loss of a person universally known throughout the company as Herb, one of the great personalities of American business.

INFLUENCE ON MANAGEMENT BEHAVIORS

The willingness and ability of a manager to "walk the talk" has become a cliché of the business lexicon. The "talk" in this phrase refers, of course, to shared values that are communicated in part through policy statements to organization members. Whether the talk is walked by management may be the single most important determinant of success in managing change.

The most frequent and critical problem in walking the talk these days appears to be an organization's willingness to part company with man-agers capable of meeting performance goals but not managing by the val-ues. It is cited by Richard Pascale and his coauthors, for example, as one of the important reasons that the transformation of Sears, which looked so promising after the implementation of a value profit chain–based change process, stalled in midstream and eventually proved to be ineffec-tive.[16] What happened?

Having identified the need to achieve higher levels of customer satis-faction by means of improved employee satisfaction and loyalty, Arthur Martinez, Sears' CEO and chief change-agent at the time, instituted an educational effort with the goal of enabling all Sears employees to under-stand the determinants of theirs and the company's success. This was followed by a series of town hall meetings, in which employees at all lev-els were given the opportunity to raise questions that had not been heard previously in the company. They were intended to set the tone for a more open, problem-solving atmosphere in which employees at the customer-facing levels would have greater latitude in responding to customers' needs. However, they proved to be very threatening to some Sears managers, who either didn't believe the talk or couldn't walk it.

At about this time, Sears' encountered what would prove to be important distractions. These included charges that the company had sold used batteries as new and had violated bankruptcy laws with some of its credit and collection practices. Faced with the daunting prospect of driving change down into an organization of 300,000 employees while encountering other more public challenges, Martinez and his colleagues failed to make several decisions critical to the change process. Among the most important was the failure to immediately replace several key managers who were clearly out of step with Martinez' campaign against the command and control management that had characterized the Sears of the past. Eventually they were replaced, but too late. The damage had been done. The message sent to the organization was clear: "We talk greater latitude for you, but we don't walk it."

In contrast, a defining moment in the energizing of GE occurred when, in 1992 for the first time, efforts were made to weed out the so-called type IV manager, one who, in Jack Welch's words, "delivers on all the commitments, makes the numbers, but doesn't share the values— the manager who typically forces performance out of people, rather than inspires it. The autocrat. The tyrant. Too often, we've all looked the other way at these bullies. I know I have."[17] For the first time, type IV managers at GE were asked to leave, the first step in dealing with perhaps the most pervasive problem facing leadership today.

VISIBILITY IN PERFORMANCE APPRAISAL AND REWARD

To begin to weed out the bullies and others simply unable to manage by the values, it is important to ensure that everyone understands what is expected and the nature of the consequences if expectations are not met.

Performance measurements go a long way toward communicating expectations. This is why it's so important that measurements reflect not only the strategies adopted by management but the core values that govern ways they will be achieved. We saw an example of this at Office Depot, described in some detail in Chapter 6.

It's important to make visible not only expectations about managing by the values but decisions concerning those who are unable to do so. Returning to GE and its decision to dismiss type IV managers, then-CEO Jack Welch tried to use the dismissal of managers unable to manage by the values as an opportunity to give visibility to the performance appraisal and reward system. For example, in front of 500 people at GE's most important annual management meeting in 1992, Welch pointed out that there were five notable absences in the audience. As he announced, "One was removed for the numbers, and four were asked to go because they didn't practice our values."[18]

■ The Importance of Values for Value Creation

Process quality is an important element of the value equation for employees, and organization culture is an important determinant on which an organization's internal process quality is judged. If there is inconsistency between shared values and management behaviors, employees perceive this as poor process quality, regardless of the degree to which they are able to achieve the results desired for themselves and their customers. Indirectly, this failure of process quality is communicated by employees to customers, either through excessive defections in the ranks or through the transferral of managerial behaviors they have experienced to their customers, whose resulting expectations for process quality will not be met, either.

■ Questions for Management

The experiences of the organizations profiled in this chapter suggest several important questions for the leadership of an organization:

1. Have you made an effort to identify and communicate values shared by everyone in the organization, unchanging values that provide the bedrock that supports change in everything else—

strategies, organization, policies, processes, and practices—associated with the effective management of the organization?

2. To what extent do the core values of the organization:

   a. Encourage efforts to remain sensitive to the search for value on the part of employees, customers, investors, and other important constituencies?

   b. Ensure that the organization remains attuned to the changing demands of a constantly changing competitive environment?

   c. Suggest the kinds of behaviors expected of all members of the organization, regardless of business unit affiliation?

   d. Provide an umbrella under which desired individual business unit customs and mores may flourish?

3. Are core values taken into consideration when strategic decisions are made, including the most important of all, the selection of successors to the leadership of the organization?

4. Are the core values reflected in performance appraisal processes as well as decisions concerning such factors as personal development plans, compensation, and promotion?

5. Is there a plan in place to revisit, reaffirm, and reemphasize the importance of these core values periodically?

6. Is the process to revisit the core values sufficiently inclusive as to organization participation to assure acceptance and application in day-to-day management?

Core values that do not give sufficient emphasis to the constant monitoring and responsiveness to the needs of core constituencies of an organization can lead to the kind of stasis, even in the presence of strong corporate culture, that may result from short-term success but lead to long-term decline. Values that support efforts to look outside the organization; monitor needs of important customers, suppliers, and others; and scan the competitive environment foster long-term success that results in organizations that are, in the words of Collins and Porras, "built to last."[19] One study has found that such values are most often fostered and underscored most effectively by leaders that are "outsider insiders," that is, managers with sufficient internal experience to foster credibility but whose accomplishments may have been achieved outside the core business activity of the organization.[20]

Success in enhancing long-term value requires that core values shared by everyone in an organization be identified and periodically reaffirmed, if for no other reason than to remind everyone of the reasons for the existence of their organization. Sustainable value enhancement just won't happen without it. CEOs who recognize the importance of culture to their organizations' successes have identified this task as one of the most important elements of their jobs.

The identification, communication, and reaffirmation of an organization's core values provides the foundation on which all other efforts to cement gains are based, including the development of value-centered measurement and recognition, to which we turn next.

Chapter 12

Developing Value-Centered Measurement and Recognition

S EVERAL YEARS AGO, Banco Comercial Português (BCP) developed a separate network of McDonald's-like retail banks to provide fast, consistent customer service and innovative products to a segment of middle-income customers the bank was not serving yet. (BCP had adopted a segmentation approach since its inception in 1985, launching dedicated branch networks to serve each segment, starting with the highest value segments.) This network, called NovaRede (or *"new network"*) immediately began to capture customers from competing banks. Managers, measured and rewarded in part in terms of their increases in revenues and customer account base, rapidly undertook efforts to wean middle income banking customers away from their current banking relationships.

NovaRede was performing quite strongly, but below its full potential. An investigation of the reasons found that many of NovaRede's new customers had only checking accounts and were utilizing free-high-cost channels (such as the teller or the call center). In the meantime, customers' mortgages and other high-profit banking relationships remained with NovaRede's competitors. As a result, the company's cost-to-income ratio exceeded that of best practice European banks by 10% to 15%.

As a result of this finding, a number of initiatives were undertaken. A comprehensive transaction migration program was introduced (leveraging advanced ATM technology, an innovative branch layout, incentives for employees to help customers make transactions at machines, and incentives for customers) to encourage customers to make simple transactions by machine in parallel with a sales stimulation program focused on high value products. An examination of the value equation for NovaRede's customers led to the introduction of such things as modular and bundled product offerings, loyalty schemes, a reduction in tellers and an increase in remote advisors, an Internet platform that went well beyond mere transactional banking, expanded machine availability and functionalities, and even extended opening hours under the "NovaRede everywhere, anytime" concept, all in exchange for premium prices for banking service.

New measures and incentives were established to emphasize not only the continued importance of growth and profitability but also the necessity for increased "depth" of relationship (measured by the number of services offered by the bank that each customer was using) between each branch and its customers. In order to achieve this depth of relationship, employees were encouraged to redouble their efforts to provide good service while being trained to introduce transaction-oriented customers to the bank's full product line. All branches were ranked on their sales and migration performance and recognition was provided to those branches excelling at doing both in addition to enhancing branch profitability, a natural result of success on the other two dimensions.

In part as a result of the introduction of a "scorecard" based on value profit chain measures, NovaRede's profit increases began outpacing its growth of new customer accounts. Today the network is beginning to realize the full potential envisioned for it when it was created. For example, its cost-to-income ratio now ranks among the lowest in Europe, reflecting a very substantial increase in sales, in line with cost containment resulting from more than doubling the percentage of transactions (particularly deposits) in low-cost channels. The NovaRede model has been rolled out internationally by BCP to include the Novabank in Greece and the Millennium chain of banks in Poland.

Harrah's Entertainment has undergone a similar transition, beginning in 1998. At the time, the company's 21 largely-undistinguished, independently operated casinos—in an industry becoming populated by large, increasingly glitzy facilities—were not clearly targeted at any one group of customers. That was when Chairman and CEO Philip Satre decided to build a strategy built upon "customer intimacy."[1] In order to do this, be brought in a new chief operating officer, Gary Loveman, to implement a strategy focused around a standard quality of service throughout the casino network delivered by employees trained to improve customer intimacy, and a Total Rewards program designed to provide incentives for increased loyalty among customers who gambled regularly but did not wager large amounts by industry standards. At the time, they were found to be visiting other casinos more often than Harrah's.

This led directly to a reorganization in which all casino presidents began reporting to Loveman, with each measured on a common set of operating measures, including those associated with customer loyalty, "play" per visit, customer satisfaction, and employee development, satisfaction, and loyalty, reflecting Satre's new definition of value for Harrah's customers. Customer loyalty was increasingly tracked and stimulated through the Total Rewards program centered around a card that customers could use at all Harrah's facilities, thus providing the company with a way of predicting the lifetime value of prospective customers based on four pieces of information: gender, age, where one lives in relation to a Harrah's casino, and what games one likes to play. Once a program member actually visits a Harrah's facility and registers gaming activity by swiping the Total Rewards membership card, each customer's lifetime value profile can be updated.

Today common standards for quality and performance, along with the measurements required to track them, are taken for granted at Harrah's. It is a part of the "woodwork." The fact-based transformation was reinforced by early success. By the end of 1999, the organization could boast that it had 16 million Total Rewards program members in a year in which profits more than doubled over the preceding year. Since then, Harrah's has continued to outperform the industry, building its Total Rewards program membership to 25 million (including both active and inactive card holders) over a network of more than 40,000 gaming machines in 25 casinos in 12 states by early 2002.[2]

In these organizations, many factors have contributed to the desired turnaround. However, measurement, recognition, and reward have played an important role in insuring that gains, once achieved, are maintained.

We wish we could repeat these stories many times over. They describe how organizations have identified factors critical to their value-creation process for customers and others and how they have followed through to build measures, most of them reflecting the management of assets not shown on their balance sheets, to insure that their managements know when and whether planned value is being delivered. These so-called "balanced measurement companies" reflect in their measures and incentives the factors most critical to the successful execution of value-creating strategies. One study of 122 companies fitting this description found that 74% were regarded as industry leaders by executives in competing companies and 83% had financial performance in the top third of companies in their respective industries.[3] Further, they exhibited significantly higher incidence of such effective management behaviors as: (1) agreement among senior management on strategy, (2) good cooperation and teamwork among management, (3) open sharing and communication, (4) effective communication of strategy, and (5) higher levels of self-monitoring by employees than their counterparts not utilizing "balanced measurement" systems.[4]

The problem is that while the number of "balanced measurement companies" is growing, there are all too few such examples of analysis and follow-through in the creation and continued use of value-centered measurement and recognition that really address the value creation process. For example, one recent survey disclosed that while 250 executives ranked "customer satisfaction" and "employee retention" as the two top "measurements of value creation, neither is included in today's formal reporting systems."[5]

This may change significantly in the face of growing interest in a concept known as the "balanced scorecard," resurrected from a concept first developed by the French in the early part of the twentieth century.[6] The fact that entire consultancies are being devoted to providing advice on the creation of balanced scorecards suggests a changing focus for performance measurement systems.

Fortunately, we are learning a great deal that is of value to those either contemplating the implementation of a balanced set of value-based measures of performance or actually in the process of implementing one.

■ Selecting Measures

The move to establish more balanced performance measures to stimulate the value creation process for employees, customers, investors, and others involves much more than a decision to include nonfinancial measures in the process. Those who are making the move are finding that it stimulates a complete reconsideration of all measures, both financial and nonfinancial, providing focus in the management of an organization. It also requires the establishment of criteria by which a small set of critical measures is assembled.

Do They Reflect Core Values?

A real test of management's commitment to an organization's culture is the degree to which shared values are reflected in measurements and recognition.

If a signal value is commitment to customers, then it's quite natural for Harrah's to measure customer satisfaction regularly with their visits to the company's casinos. It also makes sense to track customers' loyalty carefully and their willingness to recommend Harrah's to their best friends, recognizing those who exhibit these characteristics. An interesting side note in this example is that there is little correlation between customer satisfaction levels and their experiences at the gaming tables, suggesting that Harrah's has succeeded in decoupling the two in their patrons' minds through superior levels of service in those areas over which it does have control.

One possible reason why IBM's leadership literally forgot its core values in the process of losing its way in the mid-1980s, as described in Chapter 11, was that efforts to regularly measure and recognize such factors as customer service and respect for the individual, both core values, were allowed to lapse at the operating level.

Do Measures Stand the Test of Fact-Based Analysis?

Literally thousands of measures describe the various activities and accomplishments of an organization, far more than any one individual can usefully employ. Of these, only a few reflect "bundles" of activities of critical importance to the creation of value for employees, customers, investors, and others. By identifying them and verifying them with fact-based analysis, management establishes the credibility necessary to "sell" them to all members of the organization.

For example, Sears managers could speak of the intuitively sensible relationship between employee and customer satisfaction and its impact on sales. But it wasn't until extensive analysis established that a 5-point increase in employee satisfaction led directly to 1.3-point increase in customer satisfaction and a 0.5% increase in sales volume over a period of no more than 9 months that employees became convinced that there might be something powerful in efforts to improve employee satisfaction in the ranks of this large retailing organization.

When Charlie Cawley and his colleagues at MBNA measured the lifetime value of a loyal MBNA credit card holder and compared this to the relatively low level of loyalty exhibited by its cardholders at that time, the task of mobilizing associates to institute policies and procedures designed to extend cardholder life were made much easier. They were quick to respond to a bonus program driven by daily measures of service intended to do just that, something that might have been more difficult to implement on faith.[7]

Do Measures Reflect Causes as Well as Effects?

Most companies only measure and recognize effects—profit, customer satisfaction, and employee turnover. They give too little emphasis to the causes that produced these "symptoms" of good or poor management.

When Merrill Lynch established a direct link between client satisfaction and the number of times per year that clients had contact with their brokers, the measurement of broker contact produced the desired effect on client satisfaction. Limited Brands, a large retailer of fashion and related products, has found that contact with a salesperson increases the "conversion rate," that portion of customers making a purchase at the company's retail outlets, by 34 to 70%, depending on the type of merchandise being sold.[8]

Numerous organizations have found a direct link between the timeliness and quality of performance reviews—one of the least enjoyable and most postponable of all management responsibilities—and employee satisfaction. Full-circle, 360-degree reviews that measure the timeliness and quality of performance reviews in the eyes of those being reviewed have gone some way toward improving the result by dealing with the cause.

Cause-and-effect analysis is at the heart of the task of determining how a for-profit organization makes money. Recently, added attention has been drawn to its importance. As we noted in Chapter 10, Richard Pascale and his associates have cited the importance of understanding the "deep indicators" that drive the performance of the business, presenting as evidence the example of Sears' use of service profit chain drivers of profitability cited earlier.[9]

More recently, Jim Collins' research has called attention to the importance of attaining "deep understanding of the key drivers in [an organization's] economic engine."[10] Every one of the organizations found to have made the successful transition from "good to great" in the Collins sample redefined what he called the economic denominator, the x in the ratio of profit per x. For example, a key "aha" for the leadership at Walgreens, a large retailer of health care and related products, was the shift from an emphasis on profit per store to profit per customer visit. It was based on an analysis that established a close, direct relationship between store success and the ability to capitalize on each customer's visit to a Walgreens store. The rationale was related logically to the company's strategy of establishing high-traffic but expensive store sites, leading directly to an emphasis on the quality of personnel selection and training and requiring high sales per customer visit to defray its high store operating costs within the customer traffic capacity constraints of each store. It also led to a variety of efforts at the store level to increase profit per customer visit that have produced a significantly higher trajectory of sales and profit growth for the company since this transition occurred in 1975.[11]

ARE THE MEASURES PROSPECTIVE?

For years, many measures of performance have reflected the accomplishments of the past that may have little or no relationship to accomplishments of the future. Typical of these are most financial measures. Managers are rewarded for the profits they produced last year, regardless of whether they also took those actions and achieved results that might ensure future profits.

Advocates of a concept called economic value added (EVA) argue that most financial measures are not benign; they are harmful, encouraging decisions that destroy economic value.[12] The reason is that too few economic measures include any charge for capital employed in achieving economic goals. For example, an organization rewarding those who achieve a profit goal without regard to the investment required to produce the profit may be encouraging the destruction of long-term wealth creation, measured by the difference between the market value of a company and the capital that investors have committed to the company. This occurs because investments made in initiatives with returns below the average of past investments (or, more importantly, investor expectations) will eventually affect growth rates, economic performance, and the market value of an organization's stock, an important determinant of economic value.

Of course, measures of employee and customer satisfaction, loyalty, and commitment are foremost among prospective measures for value profit chain advocates. There are others, however, depending on the industry. For example, investments in research and development have been shown to be good predictors of future performance for manufacturers of health care products.

At Capital One, an organization we visited in Chapter 9, the number of experiments in value exchange for the company's credit card and related subscription products is regarded as a good indicator of future performance in an organization that regards itself as totally knowledge based, dependent on its ability to discern the needs of potential clients before its competitors do.

ARE MEASURES CLEAR, UNDERSTANDABLE, AND APPROPRIATELY INFLUENTIAL?

The purpose of measurement and recognition is to influence ongoing management decisions in ways that enhance value. To do this, measures must be limited in number and easy to understand as well as justified by fact.

Managers are only human. They are capable of managing for only so many outcomes, whether such outcomes constitute end goals or ways of achieving them. The number of measures implemented by Office Depot in its balanced scorecard, based on "dimensions" by which performance on values is measured, described in Figure 6-2, probably tests the limits of the number of things that managers can consciously manage and trade off against one another.

The importance of elegance and simplicity in a measurement system increases with the size of the organization. The Sears balanced scorecard, based only on employee satisfaction, customer satisfaction, and sales volume, was particularly attractive for this reason, even though it would have been tempting to expand the list of measures to include important drivers of each of these indicators.

The shift by Walgreens from an emphasis on profit per store to profit per customer visit, cited earlier by Collins, reflected a major shift in the company's strategy. By providing more convenient locations, the company found that it could extract a premium for such convenience, enhancing its margins and its profit per customer visit. To do this, though, it had to blanket an area with more, not fewer, stores. Had it continued to measure and reward profit per store, the influence on decision makers would have been to locate fewer, not more, stores in a given area.[13]

Do Measures Properly Reflect the Organization's Strategy?

Measures, particularly when linked to rewards, are intended to influence the quality of decisions. If biased toward value for only one important constituency—for example, including only measures of profit produced for investors—a measurement system may encourage decisions leading to the destruction of value for employees or customers. This is why the concept of the balanced scorecard is so important.

An example provided by Robert Kaplan and David Norton, resulting from their experiences at Mobil's North American marketing and refining organization in the early 1990s, illustrates this point.[14] The effort resulted from a decision by the organization, after a comprehensive market analysis, to target its efforts primarily to (1) low-cost production of relatively undifferentiated product and (2) product enhancement and marketing efforts targeted to the two-thirds of the retail market seeking quality service at reasonable margins rather than the lowest price. Here, the organization was encouraged to identify first the central objectives of its strategy, then important ways of achieving those objectives, and finally the measures that, if highlighted, would produce decisions supporting the achievement of the strategy.

The overriding objectives identified by Mobil's management included "achieve financial returns (as measured by return on capital employed), delight targeted customers with a great buying experience for food and fuel, develop win-win relationships with dealers and retailers, improve critical internal processes, reduce environmental, safety, and other health-threatening incidents, and improve employee morale."[15] Working from this template, each business unit within Mobil was then encouraged to formulate balanced scorecards reflecting the umbrella objectives. Scorecards emphasizing financial returns at the expense of other objectives were quickly discarded in favor of those encouraging the consideration of trade-offs in decision-making. Delegating scorecard design to the business unit level in this case, just as at Office Depot, provided further opportunity to influence employees in ways supportive of the shared values and strategic objectives of the organization.

DO MEASURES REQUIRE SOME MANAGEMENT JUDGMENT?

Measurement and recognition do not replace the need for management judgment in the assessment of performance. This is particularly true when it comes to assessing managers on their ability to lead according to the shared values established for the organization. Often, behaviors of this kind can only be observed and noted, not measured on any objective scale.

At GE, for example, a Session C review includes a cursory examination of a manager's performance on various economic measures, especially those associated with longer-term, stretch goals concerning such factors as inventory management, cash flows, and quality. Much of the time is spent on the issue of the degree to which a manager's leadership reflects the values of the organization, including its emphasis on, among others, speed, self-confidence, simplicity, the tendency to act in boundaryless ways for the good of the entire corporation, and the degree to which a manager emphasizes and takes satisfaction from the development and successes of others for which he or she might be responsible.

The ultimate result is the preparation of a 3 × 3 matrix profiling each manager's performance and promise.[16]

The need for some degree of subjectivity in the measurement and recognition process creates what may be the most important responsibility of managers, effective evaluation and judgment of others. It can't be evaded. In fact, in outstanding organizations it is elevated beyond art to a "high craft" through a focus on the importance of the task, the careful coaching of those to whom it is entrusted, and follow-up measures of quality, as perceived by those being evaluated.

■ Implementing Measures

The primary question involved in implementing measurement and recognition initiatives is whether they should be tied to rewards. If the answer is positive, this raises issues concerning the relative emphasis to be placed on short- or long-term rewards. There is always the issue of how far into an organization they should be applied. Finally, there is the question of the frequency with which recognition and reward systems should be changed.

TYING PERFORMANCE TO REWARDS

At the outset of any initiative to link performance measurement to the drivers of profitability and growth for the organization, most organizations have found it useful not to use such measures as determinants of rewards immediately. Such measures must first be validated in the eyes of everyone to be measured and then communicated effectively. This may require at least one "cycle" of the performance review process.

Inevitably, compensation based on such measures should comprise more than one driver of organizational success if it is to reflect the complexity of a business. This leads naturally to the idea of the "balanced paycheck" advocated by Robert Kaplan and David Norton.[17] It gives the balanced scorecard clout. It clearly communicates the results expected just as the core values do the way in which the results are to be achieved.

Finally, it forces the consideration of important trade-offs that are present in many strategic decisions.

RELATIVE EMPHASIS ON SHORT- AND LONG-TERM PERFORMANCE

At GE, all senior managers have *stretch goals,* targets that may stretch the imagination and take years to achieve, targets that are orders of magnitude better than current performance, but managers must evidence progress toward those goals in their shorter-term performance. This suggests the importance of identifying longer-term goals on which the measurement of short-term performance is based. However, the value profit chain suggests the nature and importance of short-term, perhaps annual, goals that have long-term impact on the matter most important to investors, profitability.

At Office Depot, measures of improved employee retention may not influence this year's profit figure, but they will certainly do it no harm, and they are critical to long-term performance. At GE, an all-out effort to implement Six Sigma Quality may have cost the company money in the first year of its implementation. Had it not been undertaken, the company would have foregone significant gains in long-term performance.

Clearly, enough "slack" has to be created in budgets and profit plans to accommodate short-term efforts that yield long-term results. This is a creative tension with which leaders in all organizations must deal.

BREADTH, DEPTH, AND NATURE OF APPLICATION

Balanced measures of performance and the reward systems that may accompany them should be implemented, in ways relevant to each type of job, as broadly and as deeply as possible in a transformation based on value profit chain thinking. This often includes frontline employees if the object is to give them the tools to deliver results to customers as well as the latitude (within limits) to do so.

This requires an analysis of the nature of various jobs. Some, such as sales, may warrant individual incentives. Others, such as the information systems support function or a retail store sales force, may suggest team-based incentives. For example, at Office Depot, each shift at each of its 24 distribution centers has goals concerning the accuracy of orders filled. An emphasis has been placed on the importance of solving problems confronted at the distribution centers by employees. As a result, a distribution center performance scorecard contains a number of team-based measures.

At Sears, one of the factors thought to account for the fact that the organization's transformation effort stalled in the mid-1990s was its failure, whether for reasons of management "push-back" or not, to drive its balanced scorecard more deeply than the top 200 managers. As a result, those closest to customers, most notably the Sears cadre of store managers, never participated in the effort.

FREQUENCY OF MEASUREMENT CHANGES

Once designed and implemented, is a balanced performance measurement and reward system carved in stone? Far from it, according to those who have implemented them successfully. First of all, organizations rarely get such systems right the first time. They may require a number of adjustments.

Further, if the primary purpose of such measures is to encourage certain kinds of decision-making behaviors, the emphasis placed on factors influencing decisions may change with the company's strategy. If performance measurement is to be aligned with strategy, it will have to change from time to time.

Of course, there is always a concern that "tinkering" with the performance measurement system will be perceived as an attempt to change the rules of the game by which individuals' efforts are judged. In fact, there is some basis for this. However, necessary changes can be made if they are explained carefully in ways that suggest their importance for the long-run performance of the organization rather than some kind of effort to "one up" those being measured.

■ The Ultimate Ingredient: Leadership

These are complex and controversial questions. Clearly, many things can go wrong in implementing balanced measurement and reward systems.

The single most critical determinant of success appears to be leadership. According to a study by McKinsey & Co., no organization emphasizes leadership at all levels more than the U.S. Marine Corps; it concluded that it "outperformed all other organizations when it came to engaging the hearts and minds of the front line."[18] This is absolutely critical in an organization in which Marine Corps officers, as Robert Kaplan and David Norton point out, "communicate, educate, and train their troops with the goal 'that every private can become a general.'"[19]

The reason that the Marine Corps attracted the attention of Kaplan and Norton was that several of the CEOs they had observed who had been particularly effective in implementing value-driven changes at all levels of their organizations had previously been Marine Corps officers. These former officers were unusually adept and capable of both delegating authority and holding even those in the front lines of their private sector organizations accountable for performance in ways that encouraged them to deliver results to customers while creating value for themselves and those investing in their efforts.

This confirms everything we have observed firsthand. Successful implementation of value-driven performance measurement and reward systems inevitably can be traced back to management understanding, enthusiasm, and support, or a lack of it. It is a primary determinant of the persistence required when distractions arise or results are slow in coming.

■ Questions for Management

Questions implied by experiences we have related here include the following:

1. Do outcomes measured and recognized reflect the shared values of the organization?

2. Do measures and rewards encourage the creation of value for all important constituencies, thereby supporting the self-perpetuation of the value profit chain? How do you know? Have they stood the test of analytic analysis of cause and effect?

3. Are the measures prospective, not retrospective, in nature—reflective of influences on future performance?

4. Are measures sufficiently clear and understandable that they are regularly used to influence major decisions?

5. Are measures sufficiently robust and structured in a manner to encourage managers to make desired trade-offs in their decision-making?

6. Are measures (not necessarily the process by which they are prepared and reported) directly linked to performance review, personal development, compensation, and career advancement? If so,

   a. Are the quantitative measures sufficiently succinct, clear, intuitively logical, and understandable to be credible to those being measured?

   b. Is substantial management judgment employed in qualitatively appraising managers' abilities to manage by the organization's core values?

7. Do recognition and rewards:

   a. Reinforce management behaviors that reflect the shared values of the organization?

   b. Encourage decisions that foster sustainable value enhancement?

   c. Adequately involve managers in sharing the upside rewards and downside risks inherent in a decision on behalf of the organization?

Measures and recognition most often constitute internal methods for encouraging ongoing behavior contributing to both the short- and long-term success of an organization, but market leaders don't stop here. They also seek to involve customers or suppliers in the process of helping them sustain performance gains. They do this by what we call "hard-wiring" performance on dimensions critical to supply chain partners, our next topic.

Chapter 13

Hardwiring Performance

WHEN CEMEX GUARANTEES THE ARRIVAL of needed ready-mix concrete products within 20 minutes of a promised time in the heavy traffic of Mexico City or Monterrey, it is selling its contractor customers building capability rather than cement. At the same time, it enlists its customers in holding its employees to the highest competitive standards in the industry as a means of achieving higher quality and lower operating cost. The result has been not only enhanced growth and profitability, but an added incentive to CEMEX management and employees to come up with new ways of economically delivering building capability.

When Nucor Steel encountered a recession in the early 1970s, instead of releasing its production employees it sent many of them out into the field to help sales representatives generate more demand for the company's products. The effort was so successful, enabling Nucor to avert layoffs and further engender loyalty on the part of its employees, that it began devising processes whereby all members of the organization had the opportunity to come into contact with customers periodically. The result has been amazed customers, a Nucor workforce more sensitized to customer needs, and the actual generation of ideas for new products and services resulting from a broader array of customer contacts, ideas "presold" to those in production and elsewhere who may have had a hand in identifying them.

When GE's leadership challenged its business unit leaders in 1985 to redefine their businesses so that their current share would represent no more than 10%, as described in Chapter 2, many of its manufacturing subsidiaries identified opportunities for expanding presale and after-sale services provided along with products they produced. As a result, GE's Aircraft Engine Group eventually redefined its business in ways that changed the basis on which manufacturers of aircraft engines compete. Instead of selling engines to airframe manufacturers and airlines, leaving them responsible for the costs and risks of engine maintenance, it decided to sell power lift capability and operating time. For example, it entered into a contract with Boeing to take full responsibility not only for the quality of its engines but also the risks associated with failure to perform according to expectations that were written into specific contracts. It required that the Aircraft Engine Group become much more deeply involved in the businesses of ensuring the availability of parts as well as performing various types of maintenance. If performed properly, such businesses could yield higher than normal profits. If performed poorly, they could wipe out profits from the manufacturing as well as the service businesses.

By redefining its aircraft engine business, GE obtained more than merely added business for a line of products that had not distinguished itself up to the time of the decision to sell time and capability versus aircraft engines alone. It committed its employees to a set of standards of performance that would determine the survival of the business and their jobs. This required completely rethinking processes, including those associated with efforts to deliver zero-tolerance, fail-safe quality already in place for many of its components, but also including those related to supply chain management necessary to have critical parts available anywhere in the world on short notice.

By rethinking its business and tying its success to that of its partners, both Boeing and airline operators, the management of GE's aircraft engine business became a strong competitor in a business in which it had been an also-ran. One immediate result was a large contract to become the exclusive supplier of power lift capability to Boeing's new 777 aircraft, something unheard of in the industry.[1] GE effectively had no competition for the business because it had redefined the rules of the game for engine manufacturers.

For the first two decades of its meteoric rise to prominence as one of America's preeminent companies, the Xerox Corporation linked its fortunes directly to those of its customers. It did so through the simple device of leasing rather than selling its copiers to customers, charging them a small fee for every copy produced on the machine. When a copier failed to perform, Xerox felt it directly in its revenues. As a result, the company developed an army of 18,000 service representatives not only to ensure proper ongoing maintenance of its equipment but also fast response in the event a machine failed. It was the largest and finest service organization of its kind at the time, and it was instrumental in helping deliver a stream of constantly increasing revenues and profits to Xerox.

Then in 1985, partly in an effort to supercharge sales and earnings, Xerox management decided to begin giving customers an option to buy or lease equipment.[2] Those who bought became responsible for the maintenance of their equipment, although most signed service contracts with Xerox's service organization. Nevertheless, the risk to Xerox had been decoupled from that of its customers. Machine failures, however critical they might be to customers, did not have quite the same urgency for Xerox's service representatives as they had in the past. Even though service contracts offering varying levels of services (at appropriate prices) were devised, the natural tendency of customers was to skimp on the level of service specified to reduce explicit (not implicit) service costs. Further, it was easier to sell lower-cost service contracts with lower performance standards, regardless of whether they reflected the real needs of customers.

The Xerox decision to sell its equipment was not the only factor contributing to a slow but steady decline in performance that began in 1990. It is more than coincidental that a decline in customer perceptions of Xerox service quality followed not too long after the decision. In addition, there are more than a few Xerox veterans who credit the decision as playing a significant role in the decline of the company. The ultimate result is that today Xerox's name is not heard in discussions of America's leading corporations.

These stories suggest the importance of tying an organization's performance to that of its supply chain partners. Using a term from the world of technology, we call this "hardwiring" the performance of an organization to ensure the creation of value.

■ Hardwiring an Organization's Performance

A practice among those who have lost a key to their automobile, or more commonly among those who steal autos, has involved *hotwiring*, bringing the ignition wire into direct contact with the power source to the starter, bypassing the ignition key. The field of computer hardware and software development has more recently coined a related term, "hardwiring." We think hardwiring describes what leaders in their industries are doing to link the success of their employees so closely to that of customers and others that gains achieved in the past can be more confidently assumed for the future.

Hardwiring can be achieved at several levels, as suggested in Figure 13-1. Each of these levels—transactional, strategic, cultural, and organic—may be most appropriate to a given organization. Those able to achieve organic hardwiring have been able to achieve the most dramatic results from the process.

■ **Figure 13–1**   A Hierarchy of Hardwiring Initiatives

Organic
Developing customers who regard
themselves as owners

Cultural
Linking operational functions—product development
and improvement—to customers or suppliers

Strategic
Repositioning to deliver "solutions"

Transactional
Product warranties
Service guarantees

CREATING PRODUCT OR SERVICE GUARANTEES

The forerunner of current efforts to hardwire performance were the product warranties that became prevalent as early as the nineteenth century as manufacturers sought to build trust in badly abused and skeptical customers, particularly for purchases they perceived as high risk. The practice was given high visibility by auto makers early in the twentieth century. Although the primary motive was marketing—a way of breaking down a barrier to sales—very quickly auto manufacturers and others found that the costs of product warranties required that they address quality problems in their manufacturing processes, attacking value creation at a substantive level as a means of survival.

Product warranties for "big ticket" items provided the model for many of the service guarantees that have become nearly ubiquitous today. It is hard to imagine that when some of the early work was done on service guarantees only two decades ago, they were quite rare.[3] Again, although many organizations instituted service guarantees as marketing devices, they quickly found that their greatest value was in convincing employees of the need for change in processes and behaviors to satisfy customer needs for both results and process quality.

Product and service guarantees have proven valuable in providing a transactional link between an organization and its customers, the most basic kind of hardwiring.

REPOSITIONING TO DELIVER SOLUTIONS

Customers buy solutions, not products or services. Solutions provide much more value. We've said it repeatedly. The power of this idea is reflected in the experiences of GE, IBM, Office Depot, and many other organizations. Its implementation, however, requires the complete rethinking of an organization's strategy, including its organization, policies, processes, controls, and incentives. This kind of repositioning represents strategic hardwiring, the second level of such an effort.

INCORPORATING HARDWIRING INTO THE CULTURE

When Nucor Corporation, the leading operator of minimills for the production of steel from scrap in the U.S., exposes all of its employees to customers and their needs, it incorporates the practice into its culture. It is perhaps more natural for Nucor than for many other organizations because of Nucor's emphasis on "egalitarianism" and absence of hierarchy in its culture, with only four levels of management, a minutely small headquarters, and a compensation and benefit structure that rewards and penalizes everybody according to the organization's performance.[4]

Few companies have hardwired their cultures more directly than Intuit, the producer of financial software for individuals and small businesses. This has accounted for the fact that Intuit has actually expanded its market share to more than 80% in competition with Microsoft since the latter's failed effort to buy Intuit in 1995 for $1.5 billion. This didn't happen by chance. Its founder, Scott Cook, schooled in consumer marketing through his employment at Procter & Gamble, set out to create an organization so closely linked to the fortunes of its customers that it could employ them both to sell and to help develop new product. He set out to do this by designing software distinguished by its ease of use.

He began by hiring software engineers, in his words, "driven to make things simple for users."[5] They were teamed with a creative marketing research team that sought to continually observe people using Intuit's products—Quicken, Turbotax, and Quick Books—both in Intuit's labs and even in their own homes. To strengthen the link between product development and marketing research, software engineers were encouraged to participate regularly in marketing research activities, observing firsthand the results of their efforts. The result was a product so much easier to use than others that Intuit, in an effort to call its work to the attention of the market, offered an unconditional guarantee in which a customer could decide to pay for the product after a free trial period. Word spread so rapidly among customers, who requested the product from their retailers, that Intuit was able to avoid hiring more than a few people to sell it.

The hardwiring didn't stop there. Competitors sought to provide customer service for often confused software users, traditionally at a charge.

■ **Figure 13–2** THE ELIMINATION OF ORGANIZATIONAL "SILOS" AT INTUIT

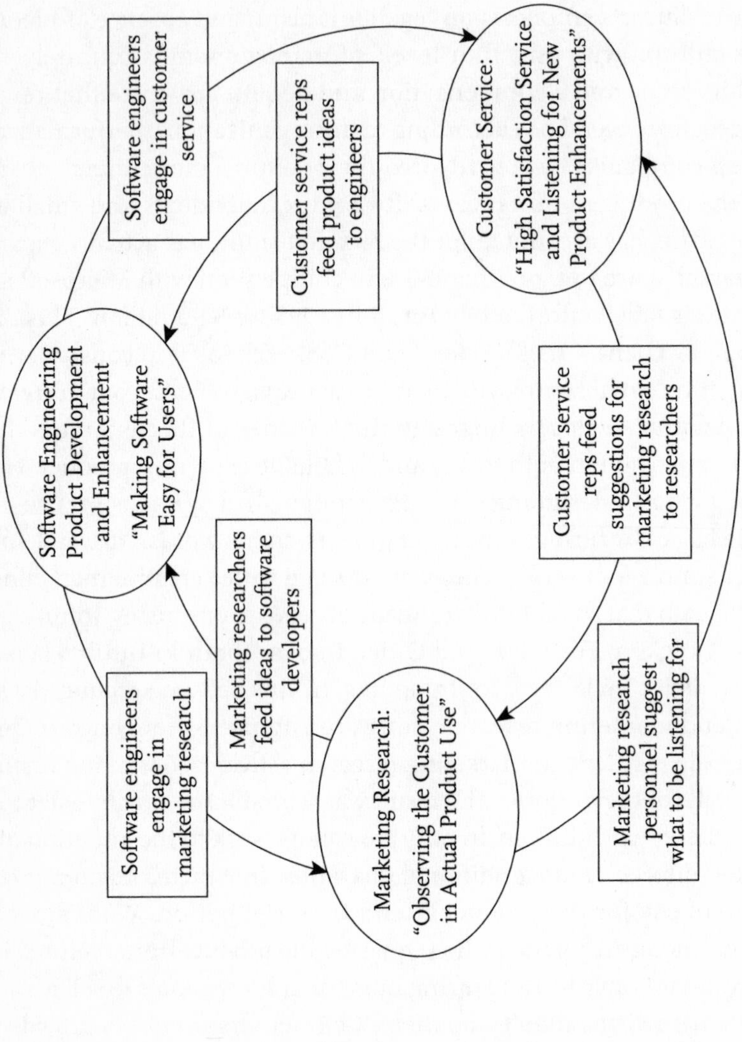

Intuit, in contrast, decided to offer free service, a gutsy move early in the company's development. In addition, the service had to be so good that it captured new product ideas as well as resolved problems for customers. It enlisted customers in the product development effort, leading to frequent product updates and the desire on the part of customers to buy them, creating a stream of revenue and enhancing lifetime value. Both software engineers and marketing researchers were invited periodically to take customer service calls to maintain direct contact with the market. Now the self-reinforcing relationships that hardwired Intuit's organization and culture to the needs of its customers, as diagrammed in Figure 13-2, was complete.

Quicken users are sufficiently devoted and have a sufficient sense of ownership that they frequently provide the source of product improvements that have kept Intuit far ahead of a competitor feared by nearly every other high-tech company.

Scott Cook and his associates at Intuit have achieved cultural hardwiring, the third level in our hierarchy. They have done it in part by encouraging a sense of partnership between Intuit's employees and customers. An organization that has generated a true feeling of "ownership" among customers that is characteristic of our fourth level of hardwiring is one that vaulted to nearly universal acclaim just a few short years ago.

FOSTERING CUSTOMER OWNERSHIP

If you talk with Scott Cook, he will refer to eBay, the online trading site, as the "ultimate killer app" as a way of describing the degree to which eBay was made for the Internet and, in fact, couldn't function without it.[6] From its very beginnings, it was recognized for its genius, an enterprise that could be scaled in size with little effort and minimum cost on the part of its management.

A cursory look at eBay suggests that it is a veritable money machine, collecting very small charges from every buyer connected with a seller on its site. A deeper look suggests the importance of client ownership in the nearly unique e-commerce success of this child of the Internet.

Those putting things up for auction describe their own offerings, posting them to the eBay site. Buyers can then scan the offerings and make bids up to a time determined by the seller. The process takes place without any direct intervention by eBay's staff, except to interdict contraband or other socially unacceptable offerings. Together, sellers and buyers build a network with increasing value to everyone as it expands—a recipe for sustainability and competitive advantage.

When Pierre Omidyar founded eBay in 1995, he had big dreams, but even he probably didn't foresee the possibility that his company would realize a billion dollars in revenue and $150 million in profits only 7 years later. It took him several months to come up with the idea that has really put eBay on autopilot and hardwired it to its customers, the idea of the Feedback Forum, in which buyers were given an opportunity to rate sellers, thereby ensuring the integrity of sellers and enhancing eBay's quality image among prospective buyers. Thus, eBay's customers were not only put in charge of sales, they were also given responsibility for quality control. This has resulted in an incidence of fraud of less than 1 in 10,000 transactions, far below that experienced by credit card issuers.

To some, hardwiring may resemble tightrope walking, involving both great rewards and risks. What does it require? Under what circumstances does it work best?

■ Requirements for Hardwiring

Hardwiring is a method of preserving gains and staking out a long-term competitive position, not a way of turning around a poorly performing organization. As Jack Welch would say, "Not everyone can play this game." You have to ask if your organization is good enough. Why? Because of the requirements for a successful hardwiring initiative.

PROVEN SUCCESS AND RESULTS

All levels of hardwiring are based on a certain amount of trust between an organization, its customers, and its employees. Trust is built from a base of credibility, the sum of past actions and successes, and a reputation for not only capability but also integrity. A product warranty from General Motors means much more than one from a competitor with a poorly regarded dealer and service network. The promise of operating capability provided by 24-hour worldwide availability for replacement parts for construction and earth-moving equipment means much more coming from Caterpillar than from a much smaller competitor. The guarantee of delivery for ready-mix concrete to builders within a 20-minute time window in the sometimes chaotic traffic of Mexico City is more credible coming from CEMEX than other of its more traditional competitors operating under conventional "out and back" systems of order acceptance, production, and delivery. None of these organizations built their capabilities and reputations overnight.

Hardwiring puts employees under the gun to perform up to the promises made by the organization to its customers. In a sense, they risk severe exposure for failure to perform. The positive side is that it encourages a great deal of acceptance of responsibility for delivering improved results and process quality on the part of employees. The downside is that failure to perform may place them at risk. This requires a careful approach to handling failure in the hardwiring process. It requires an emphasis on retraining, when desirable, rather than the creation of negative incentives or the threat of dismissal. Above all, employees must perceive the organization as treating them fairly.

A WILLINGNESS TO PUT THE BUSINESS ON THE LINE

In guaranteeing satisfaction with its product at an early stage in its development, Intuit's management literally put the business on the line. Failure to deliver on the company's promise of easy-to-use software could have resulted not only in loss of revenue but also in excessively expensive product returns, one reason dissatisfied customers were encouraged not to return the product. The most important cost of all would have been that resulting from customer dissatisfaction, which meant that there would have been very little word-of-mouth promotion for the product, the only kind that the company could afford at the time.

It was a moment of truth for Intuit that Scott Cook will never forget.[7] As it turned out, it provided the breakthrough from which Intuit never turned back in its domination of its competition. However, it could have spelled the end of the company.

HIGHLY SENSITIVE LISTENING DEVICES

Organizations that hardwire themselves to their customers must listen better than others. At the same time, the process naturally turns up the volume on the feedback loudspeaker. Consider the eBay experience. eBay has developed several of its new trading sites merely by watching trends in trading behavior. According to one account, "After noticing random car sales (on its site), eBay created a separate site called eBay Motors in 1999, with special features such as vehicle inspections and shipping. This year [2001], eBay expects to gross some $1 billion worth of autos and parts—many of them sold by dealers."[8]

An attitude of ownership on the part of customers, however, carries with it the expectation that owners will be heard. As a result, eBay regularly organizes Voice of the Customer meetings at which selected buyers and sellers on the site are given a chance to provide feedback. New site revisions are posted on the Internet so that potential users can test them and provide feedback; in one recent case, 10,000 responded, many with suggestions for the proposed revision. eBay executives, led by CEO Meg Whitman, are regularly encouraged to put things up for sale on the company's auction site in order to sensitize themselves to how it is working. Even so, eBay's users often spot problems before its management. As Maynard Webb, president of its technology unit, says "They catch things we don't. The community actually moves faster than we do."[9] When it does, it sometimes exposes eBay's management to criticism.

IF NECESSARY, REORGANIZE

Both Procter & Gamble and General Electric have altered their organizations to partner with Wal-Mart. In both cases, newly formed teams of managers were established near Wal-Mart headquarters to manage nearby inventories as well as other issues of coordination that arose in the administration of their partnerships.

At a more fundamental level, organizations have had to eliminate "silos," barriers to the cross- and interorganization coordination required in most hardwiring initiatives. The silos never arose at Intuit, because the company was organized from the outset around the three core functions shown in Figure 13-2.

Expectations for the boundaryless behavior required of all employees if Intuit was to succeed in building necessary levels of loyalty and lifetime value required of its customers were thus established early in the company's existence.

Psychological "silos" were eliminated at Nucor Steel out of the necessity to respond to a severe recession in the demand for product. They have been discouraged ever since.

A PARTNERING MENTALITY: A WILLINGNESS TO BE "OWNED"

The kind of partnering forged by hardwiring initiatives sounds logical and straightforward, but it has rarely proved so, because it often requires a high degree of trust as well as assurances that the trust will not be violated. For example, FedEx has built a substantial business by taking responsibility for the integrated supply chain management of some of its clients, literally assuming responsibility for meeting inventory and customer service goals.[10]

Many FedEx clients have come to it out of a sense of desperation and the knowledge that they have failed at the task. Others, upon seeing the potential advantages of superior supply chain coordination that might result from hardwiring, have been willing to engage in the exchange of employees, the reassignment of responsibilities, and the development of incentives designed to bring the needs of both partnering organizations into alignment required by the process.

Those who use eBay's services have assumed such a sense of ownership that eBay has come to be known as The People's Company, one operated under a stated corporate goal of creating a "global economic democracy."[11] The benefits have been priceless. It has held management to a high standard of behavior, though, in addressing the needs of users ranging from the occasional purveyor of junk from the attic to a large corporation, such as Disney, using eBay as an alternative channel for its merchandise.

■ The Payoff

The real impact of actions like those just described is to engineer lasting change in the way in which, for example, managers choose customers, select employees, organize work, and are measured and compensated. This helps sustain the gains in value achieved by an organization, regardless of leadership succession or a changing competitive environment.

The rewards from hardwiring can far outpace the risks. Without it, organizations like eBay and Intuit, both with roughly 80% market share in their respective industries, wouldn't exist today. The GEs and IBMs would exist, but with fewer ways to bring their enormous resources and capabilities to bear on customer relationships that establish long-lasting competitive advantage, and FedEx would only be in the increasingly competitive package delivery business.

Returning to the example with which we began this chapter, hardwiring has paid off handsomely for CEMEX in enabling it to differentiate itself in that portion of its business, the production and delivery of ready-mix concrete, that is fraught with the challenges of providing dependable delivery for a product that can be made in 8,000 combinations that has a 90-minute shelf life in the rotating barrel on the back of the delivery truck. It is worth examining the experience in more detail.[12]

Enamored by the idea of providing greater value to its customers, the CEMEX team set about rethinking what that would require in an operating environment in which hundreds of trucks with rotating bins full of concrete plied traffic-clogged routes under undependable conditions, including some created by customers. First, it would require improved communication, both to and from trucks. Next, it would require completely reconceptualizing the business from a fixed-based operation to one centered around an inventory constantly on the move on the backs of its trucks. Dispatchers would have to be able to track every truck constantly. Further, incentives for employees would have to be changed to reflect the new objective of delivering results instead of merely product or service. Drivers and dispatchers alike would have to trained to understand the demands of the new business definition and philosophy. Unions would have to be persuaded that required changes in work rules would lead to more jobs. In the end, of course, the customer would be calling the shots in a combination of policies, practices, and processes designed to enable the company to live with chaos.

All this was achieved, but over a period of more than 2 years. An artificial intelligence system was created to enable CEMEX dispatchers to match moving trucks with orders and mixing plants, at the same time taking into account traffic patterns and delivery delays at various times of day. Two-way communication capability was installed in all trucks. A global positioning satellite system was introduced to enable dispatchers—and the artificial intelligence system—to determine the location of all trucks at all times. Union work rules were renegotiated. Dispatchers and drivers alike were enrolled in weekly classes spanning a 2 year period in customer services.

These actions enabled CEMEX to become "good enough" to implement a service guarantee designed to distance its value offering permanently from that of its competitors: "20 x 20," a 20-peso (about 5%) discount per cubic meter if the load failed to arrive at its destination within 20 minutes of the appointed time. This required not only that incentives be instituted to reward employees meeting the guarantee but that teams be created to continue searching for ways to become even more effective in meeting the guarantee.

For any student of value profit chain thinking, the results could be predicted. The guarantee attracted attention and customers. CEMEX found itself failing to meet the guarantee in less than 2% of all orders. The efficiencies resulting from new technology, new policies, new practices, new processes, and new incentives led directly to a 30% improvement in vehicle utilization, providing CEMEX with a margin of improvement sufficient to support an even more attractive guarantee if it might become necessary. Needless to say, given the range of value-enhancing changes it has produced, it hasn't become necessary to provide more competitive prices.

■ Questions for Management

Hardwiring an organization for continued outstanding performance is one of the most important strategic decisions a manager can make. The following questions are among the most important to be taken into consideration in making the decision:

1. Will hardwiring the organization create a significant advantage that competitors will find it difficult to emulate?

2. What exactly does hardwiring mean in your business:

   a. Redefining the business to deliver solutions (versus products or services) to customers?

   b. Creating self-reinforcing customer feedback cycles for use in results-oriented product or service improvement?

   c. Directly linking employee and customer (or supplier) performance and rewards?

   d. Creating a sense of ownership among customers requiring extremely sensitive organizational responses to their needs?

   e. Creating business systems that provide total access and transparency among supply chain partners?

3. Is your organization performing well enough to "put the business on the line"?

4. Are the requirements for highly sensitive listening and responding mechanisms demanded by the partnership in place?

5. Are you willing to change such factors as organization, performance measurement, and reward structures in support of a hardwiring initiative?

Hardwiring is an opportunity that presents itself only to those companies who are making the most of information and technology to distance themselves from their competition. Information and technology alone won't do it. It takes leadership able to see the opportunities inherent in such a strategy for learning and innovation. These are special people, not always at the top of their organizations. This is why it is important for us to understand more about how organizations are "wired" to learn and innovate and the kinds of people who lead such efforts. We turn to these matters next.

Chapter 14

Leading the Organization to Learn and Innovate

THE KNOWLEDGE ECONOMY of the twenty-first century will reward most handsomely those organizations best able to acquire, develop, and share knowledge, organizations that do more than merely learn, organizations that also remember, connect seemingly unrelated information to predict the future, and so engage their employees in the acquisition and utilization of ideas for new products, services, processes, and solutions that they transform the individual as well as the collective work experience. Lew Platt, when he was CEO of Hewlett-Packard, said "If HP knew what HP knows, we would be three times as profitable."[1]

The waste of organizational knowledge is the greatest deterrent to value creation. It results from the failure to develop information from available data, encourage the development of individual knowledge and capability, and facilitate the retention of such knowledge and its transfer from one part of the organization to another. It is the most important challenge addressed by leadership in organizations competing primarily on the basis of information and knowledge.

■ Forms That Knowledge Takes

Knowledge takes several forms, at the most basic level of differentiation encompassing what has been termed "explicit" and "tacit" knowledge, as suggested in Figure 14-1. Explicit knowledge is more easily captured and exchanged. It is relatively simple, observable in use, often schematic in nature, documented, and relatively easy to communicate. It resides near the bottom of the "organization learning hierarchy" shown in Figure 14-1.

"Tacit" knowledge, on the other hand, is complex, hard to observe in use, rich and often undocumented, hard to teach, and difficult to com-

■ **Figure 14–1** The Organizational Learning Hierarchy*

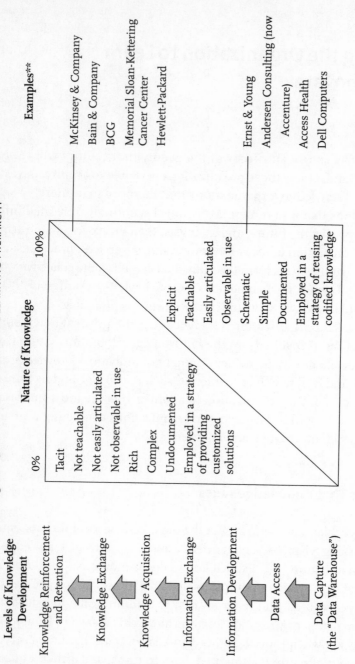

Source: Adapted from material in Sidney G. Winter, "Knowledge and Competence as Strategic Assets," in David J. Teece, ed., *The Competitive Challenge* (Cambridge, MA: Ballinger, 1987), p. 1970.

** Concepts linking strategy to organizational learning as well as specific examples are drawn from Morton T. Hansen, Nitin Noria, and Thomas Tierney, "What's Your Strategy for Managing Knowledge?" *Harvard Business Review,* March–April, 1999, pp. 106–116.

municate even by the best technology. It often is not shared without a culture of learning and specific incentives supplied by leadership.

THE MANY FACES OF KNOWLEDGE-BUILDING INITIATIVES

When USAA, a large provider of financial services, offers its employees a curriculum of more than 200 courses taught in 75 classrooms at its San Antonio headquarters, it is fostering one aspect of a learning organization. When the U.S. Marine Corps benchmarks selected supply chain activities against similar initiatives at Wal-Mart, it is engaged in one of a number of ways of learning. When Olive Garden, a large restaurant chain operated by Darden Restaurants, Inc., encourages the managers of its worst-performing stores to consult with managers of its best-performing stores, it is encouraging a kind of learning. When SAS Institute, the privately owned developer of software applications that we visited in Chapter 7, spends $55,000 per year for 22.5 tons of M&M candies, which are dispensed every Wednesday at popular employee meeting points, it is fostering yet another kind of learning.[2] The objective is to coordinate various individual learning initiatives into a coherent whole by the encouragement of activities that build on one another.

■ The Organization's Brain

Just as learning takes place in complex ways in individual brains, it occurs as well in what we like to think of as the "organization's brain," as shown in Figure 14-2. Just as we are told that the brain functions by the firing of electrical impulses between synapses in the human brain, organization learning occurs through the figurative firing of these synapses between elements of a learning strategy, indicated by arrows in Figure 14-2. At the center of this activity are knowledge leaders.

A learning organization requires leadership not only willing to embrace change, but also to mobilize organizations to take advantage of it. Richard Tedlow, in his in-depth study of seven immensely successful corporate leaders, found that the trait that they shared most strongly was their ability to embrace change.[3] Not all were able to energize their orga-

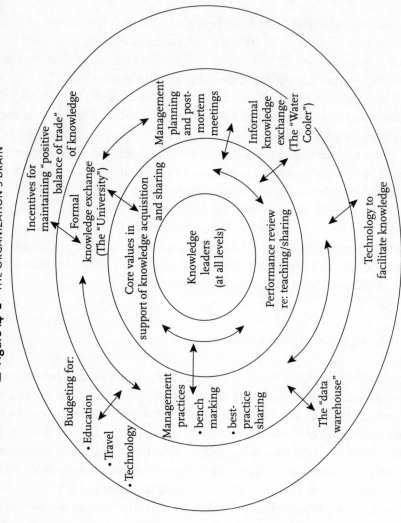

■ **Figure 14-2** THE ORGANIZATION'S BRAIN

nizations to take advantage of it, but one, George Eastman, was one of the first to build what we today call a "learning organization" at Eastman Kodak, beginning in 1887. He did this by hiring well-educated employees, creating a basic research effort, and networking with universities.[4]

An in-depth example suggests what we are getting at when we speak of the organization's brain.

■ Organizational Learning at Omnicom

Tom Watson occupies several roles at Omnicom, a $6.2-billion provider of advertising, public relations, marketing, and other services to a wide range of clients in a hundred countries through several hundred operating companies.[5] Nominally, he is executive vice president of the Omnicom Group. He also goes by the title of vice chairman of Diversified Agency Services (DAS), a major component of Omnicom. When June and July arrive each year, however, he enthusiastically embraces the title of dean of Omnicom University. If he were a member of a more formal academic institution, he would have the title of university professor, with a free rein to wander anywhere throughout the organization where he might be accepted.

Watson came to these roles through long preparation in the industry beginning as a marketing/media planning manager with the advertising agency BBDO in 1966 after several years of selling health care products. In addition, his close relationship with John Wren, CEO of Omnicom, with whom he teamed to helped build Omnicom through numerous acquisitions has provided him with added credibility as a "go-to guy" as well as latitude in carrying out his duties. Over time, his curiosity, amiable behavior, interest in other people, controlled ego, and general likeability have brought him into contact with literally thousands of members of Omnicom organizations. It provides him with knowledge of who knows what, where knowledge is located, and how to unlock it. His willingness to share this knowledge brings an increasing number of colleagues to the door of his office at company headquarters in New York. He can be counted on to put the right people with the right ideas together. Although he knows "where the bodies are buried" at Omnicom, he has built a high level of trust by his care in maintaining confidences. He spends a great deal of time giving other people credit for various accomplishments in which he has played a role. And he would deny most of what we have just said, characterizing it as a vast overstatement. All of this has put him at the center of an extended internal and external Omnicom learning network.

A natural result of these interests was Watson's proposal to establish Omnicom University in 1995, an endeavor in which roughly 100 of the most senior Omnicom executives participate in a 6 day "undergrad" program in their first year and a 4 day "grad" program in their second year. The curriculum for both programs is based largely on case studies, most of which are developed from the experiences of participants who are required to propose and carry out "initiatives" between the first and second years of their classroom study. Initiatives typically involve the application of ideas brought to the university through cases from outside and inside Omnicom as well as participant interchange of best practice. They may involve the implementation of new employee selection procedures, compensation systems, client selection procedures, pricing, Six Sigma Quality, or knowledge transfer initiatives in their respective companies. The results of these initiatives, tracked and shared by the class, quite likely more than defray the costs of the university. Thus, the university's curriculum reflects needs perceived by Omnicom's managers as well as materials brought from outside Omnicom by the university's faculty.

As dean of Omnicom University, Tom Watson has now seen more than 500 of the company's most talented managers at close hand. As an outgrowth of the "initiatives," he is as familiar with a broad sweep of management initiatives within the company as anyone, including CEO John Wren. Because he is perceived as an all-knowing, benevolent Dean, the university reinforces his ability to connect people and ideas, something he enjoys best.

Nor are the results of these efforts totally intangible. University participants have half the defection rate of non-participants, estimated to have saved Omnicom $13 million. This does not include the value of new client business developed among the university's "students" as a result of their involvement in the program. Watson can point as well to a wide range of management initiatives, such as Six Sigma Quality, emanating from the university that have become part of the "woodwork" in Omni-

■ **Figure 14–3** THE OMNICOM "BRAIN"

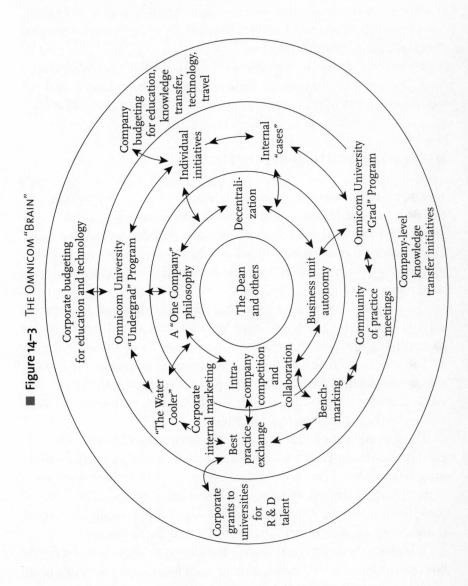

com's operating companies. He can match hundreds of names with the faces and ideas of Omnicom's best talent. And he is able to lend his credibility and support to the development of sophisticated knowledge-sharing technology as well as the incentives needed to induce people throughout the organization to share knowledge willingly with the assurance that there will something in it for them.

He is at the center of the "Omnicom Brain" diagrammed in Figure 14-3. There is a strong belief at Omnicom that its brain contributed significantly to a sevenfold increase in net income between 1992 and 2000.

■ Organizational Learning and Strategy

Few organizations rely more heavily on learning than those providing professional services, health care, and information technology. In an in-depth study of a small sample of such firms, however, Morton Hansen, Nitin Nohria, and Thomas Tierney found that they pursued two very different approaches to organizational learning depending on the extent to which their respective strategies depended on customization and innovation.[6]

One strategy, centered on providing relatively high-cost, customized solutions, called for a heavy reliance on face-to-face knowledge exchange of "tacit" knowledge with such characteristics as those shown in Figure 14-1. Examples of firms in their research sample pursuing such strategies were strategy consultants McKinsey & Co., Bain & Company, and BCG; a health care provider, the Memorial Sloan-Kettering Cancer Center, and the high-tech firm Hewlett-Packard.

The second strategy, one that Hansen, Nohria, and Tierney called the codification strategy, in which individuals contribute to a central database material capable of being codified and later extracted by others, was typical of those firms offering lower-cost, less-customized solutions. Examples of these firms advanced by the researchers were Ernst & Young, Andersen Consulting (now Accenture), Access Health, and Dell Computer.

The researchers observed that all organizations they studied utilized both strategies to some degree, but the most successful relied primarily on one strategy, avoiding what has commonly become known as getting "caught in the middle." They characterized this as an "80:20 split," with

For our purposes, it is important that a leader be able to appreciate the importance of continuous teaching and learning and to do this either informally on a day-to-day basis or formally. Beyond this, leadership for learning and innovation requires an appreciation and allocation of the resources needed to support knowledge acquisition and sharing at all levels in an organization.

TEACHING AND LEARNING

Bill Pollard, when he was chairman and CEO of ServiceMaster, probably enjoyed nothing more than the planning of educational activities within the company. A former college-level instructor, he never really left the classroom. Furthermore, both board members and senior managers were constantly bombarded with reading assignments and ideas for further thought. At one meeting one of us attended, Pollard not only chaired the meeting but played a major role in selecting in advance the five books and two articles that were assigned to all participants. As if this were not enough, he then crafted questions to be used by discussion leaders in the small groups organized to discuss the various readings, leading one of the groups himself.

It's probably no surprise that a bookcase is a piece of furniture found in the office of nearly every ServiceMaster manager, regardless of level. All managers are encouraged to learn and teach, including subjects from philosophy to new methods for lawn care or pest control that are constantly developed in the laboratories of the ServiceMaster subsidiary companies that provide these services.

This naturally provides a supportive attitude toward expenditures for basic learning for ServiceMaster employees. English-language training, for example, enables many ServiceMaster employees to communicate their ideas to others in need of them.

PROVIDING SUPPORT FOR LEARNING

Other leaders of organizations that learn and innovate supp̱ process in less explicit ways, perhaps because they don't trust ̓ teaching skills in a more formal setting. Nevertheless, the

80% of the investment in and reliance on one strategy or the other,
gested by the placement of their examples in the diagram in Figure 1

■ The Role of Leadership

Certain leadership behaviors foster organizational learning, as we have
seen in the case of Omnicom's Tom Watson and his associates. Many of
these behaviors are characteristic of what Jim Collins has termed level 5
leadership. Level 5 leadership, characterized by all of those leading their
organizations from good to great, combines what Collins terms "professional will," combining a resolve "to do what must be done to produce
the best long-term results," with "personal humility," including an absence of boastful behavior as well as "quiet, calm determination" and a
reliance on "inspired standards, not inspiring charisma, to motivate."[8]
The level 5 leader distributes much of the credit for success to others and
avoids attributing responsibility for poor results . . . [to] other people, external factors, or bad luck."[9]

Based on our own observations, such leaders have strong but carefully controlled egos combined with a clear sense of self, resulting in a
high degree of self-confidence. In a sense, they have little to prove to
themselves but a strong desire to ensure the long-term success of the organization. They often combine these traits with the abilities and willingness to teach and learn, identify with the work of others, and enjoy the
success and personal development of others in the service of the organization or a given objective. No matter their level in an organization, they
observe the common courtesies that make life more pleasant and do it in
a natural, not a contrived, way.

It may seem like a small thing, but when, without a second thought, Bill
Pollard (then chairman and CEO of ServiceMaster) cleans up spilled coffee
on the floor in front of his board members; Bill Marriott habitually picks up
trash in the lobbies of hotels operated by his company; or Paul O'Neill (as
U.S. Treasury Secretary) naturally helps a cleaning woman pick up supplies she has dropped, all are exhibiting several symptoms of the kind of
leadership behaviors that may also support organizational learning.[10] With
leaders like these, there is little artifice. What you see is what you get.

learn on the job every day, listening more than they talk, considering and often accepting ideas from others, and encouraging the transfer of the ideas from one part of the organization to another. They put money behind their priorities, making the necessary investments in information technology, education, and travel needed to ensure knowledge acquisition and innovation.

■ Fostering a "Favorable Balance of Trade" in Knowledge: The McKinsey Experience

The greatest challenge in knowledge transfer has little to do with implementing the right technology. It is not even the training required to instruct people in how to extract knowledge from a common base. Rather, it involves getting people to contribute to the knowledge pool in the first place. Whether rushed for time, impatient to move on to the next project or challenge, or unwilling to conduct a postmortem of past accomplishments, participants in a knowledge exchange too often neglect to document their accomplishments for others. This creates a kind of "unfavorable balance of trade" that, if allowed to continue, will bring knowledge transfer to an eventual halt.

Organizations have gone to great lengths to encourage contributions to the pool of knowledge. Some organizations have established incentives for contributions to the knowledge bank. In some extreme cases, individuals have been restricted from extracting knowledge from the pool without making contributions of their own to it. However, this is a challenge best addressed with both a carrot and a stick. The carrot may take the form of examples set by an organization's leadership as well as various incentives. The stick, on the other hand, is probably best applied through the vehicle of the performance review that encourages knowledge sharing.

Experiences at McKinsey & Company, the strategy consulting firm, under its managing directors Fred Gluck and his successor, Rajat Gupta, suggest that a multi-faceted approach is necessary to foster knowledge transfer. Although operated under a "one firm" philosophy in which consultants were known for cooperative effort and the sharing of knowledge from its founding, efforts to develop knowledge were redoubled, beginning with the creation of the McKinsey Staff Paper series in 1978. The preparation of Practice Bulletins, two-page summaries of useful ideas gained from client engagements, was encouraged. In 1987, a Knowledge Management Project was launched under the leadership of Fred Gluck. It involved a commitment to build a common database of knowledge gained from client engagements and the hiring of "practice coordinators" for each of McKinsey's major consulting groups to serve as "intelligent switches" for the transfer of knowledge between clientele sectors and centers of competence created by the firm.

As a result, a Practice Development Network (PDNet), stocked with documents contributed by consultants, was created. It is important to note that it was not introduced until consultants had completed the task of "begging, cajoling and challenging each practice to develop and submit" 2,000 documents.[11] It helped ensure that PDNet would hold so much value for future users that they would be willing to contribute their ideas as well, thus assuring an effective balance of trade in the sharing of ideas. This was also accompanied by the publication of a highly successful Knowledge Resource Directory (KRD), a virtual "Yellow Pages" to "who is doing what" within McKinsey.

When Gupta took over from Gluck in 1994, he created several additional initiatives to supplement his predecessor's efforts. These included the creation of a series of regional competitions, called Practice Olympics, at which teams of consultants shared their ideas and best practices. The McKinsey Global Institute, the firm's research center, was expanded. A change center intended to spearhead the injection of new ideas into the organization was created.

One might argue that an organization in the business of selling knowledge is hardly a typical example for other organizations. In fact, as knowledge becomes the sine qua non for competition in all endeavors, it is important to look to those with the greatest experience in its development. Further, as the efforts of McKinsey illustrate, there is no one golden key to unlock an organization's knowledge. The effort must be multifaceted and reflect both an organization's strategy and the temperament and character of those who will be participating in the knowledge development effort.

■ Making the Pieces Mesh: Knowledge Transfer and Learning at GE

Six Sigma Quality has produced dramatic results for GE in recent years, but the story behind the story—that of the process by which the entire GE organization of more than 300,000 employees was motivated to learn about how to implement Six Sigma Quality both from within as well as from other world-class practitioners—is of greater interest to us. It's one of the best examples we know of how all elements of the corporate brain can be brought together with all synapses firing to achieve a remarkable amount of learning, leading, in this case, to multibillion-dollar profit improvements.

The story unfolds at several places and events. One was a meeting of GE's top 30 executives, called the Corporate Executive Council (CEC), in 1995 which was addressed by "alumnus" Larry Bossidy. Bossidy by that time was CEO of the Allied-Signal Corporation and so strongly advocated Six Sigma Quality (no more than 3.4 defects per million "opportunities") that he convinced GE's top management that it should attempt to achieve it.

The groundwork for the process by which the entire GE organization would "learn" Six Sigma Quality began much earlier. In some ways, it began with the rejuvenation in the early 1980s of GE's threadbare management development center, a group of buildings situated on a 52-acre campus in Ossining, New York, which had lost its luster in the minds of GE managers.[12] With the support of the company's CEO, Jim Baughman, the head of the center at the time, kicked off a $46 million renovation of facilities and programs that would involve between 5,000 and 10,000 GE executives, customers, and others per year. One innovation added to the curriculum was that of "action learning," introduced by Baughman's Crotonville academic director, Noel Tichy. It involved GE managers in work on actual problems facing GE as part of their course requirements, with the expectation of direct payout to the company.

The road to Six Sigma Quality also began with the initiation of boundaryless behavior in 1990, spearheaded by CEO Jack Welch, as an all-important soft measure of manager performance at GE. To exhibit boundarylessness, managers were expected to search everywhere for new ideas and talent and be willing to share them with others in the GE family. When told by business unit managers about new ideas or initiatives being implemented in their respective business units, senior executives began responding, "That's great. Who else have you told about this?" It wasn't long before business unit managers, proud of their accomplishments, knew that the right answer was not "no one."

Next the scene shifts several years later to the electrical products business and its VP of manufacturing, Lloyd Trotter. As Welch described it,[13]

> Lloyd told us about a "matrix" he had created that helped to capture the best practices from each of his 40 factories. Lloyd first came up with 12 measurements and processes common to all plants. Then he asked the managers of each factory to rate themselves on each one, from inventory turns to order fulfillment.

After each manager had provided the ratings, Trotter then circulated the completed matrix showing how each of them had rated themselves, encouraging all those with 1's and 2's to find out how those with 4's and 5's did it. According to Welch,[14]

> Lloyd's operating margins increased from 1.2% in 1994 to 5.9% in 1996 and 13.8% in 2000. . . . The "Trotter matrix" became a hot tool all around GE. I've never seen a case . . . when the matrix failed to generate a significant improvement in performance.

One might add that the performance often occurred with very little top management intervention; managers knew they were expected to initiate the best practice exchange without being asked to do so. The Trotter matrix was to become a centerpiece for the effort to implement Six Sigma Quality, according to Steven Kerr, head of Crotonville in 1995, who next picked up the story.[15]

Each year, Crotonville's two most extensive executive programs for senior managers involves roughly 200 managers per year in programs designed to convey the latest in management concepts before sending teams of "students" out for a postprogram "action learning" exercise to study topics of interest to the corporation and report recommendations to the Corporate Executive Council. In one of the 1995 programs, the topic for field study was "the things you have to be good at to achieve Six Sigma Quality." To collect them, teams fanned out around the world to visit world-recognized leaders in Six Sigma Quality, such as Toyota, Motorola, and other U.S. and European companies.

The results of the field study were used to begin constructing a Scorecard. Scorecards are used to disseminate best practice and are created on an ad hoc basis to support the implementation of a "big" idea, such as Six Sigma Quality. Crotonville, which has the responsibility for "making good ideas portable," manages the Scorecard process. It is regarded as a "proactive" means of communicating best practice as opposed to the "reactive" process of sharing ideas in which Crotonville must wait for a communication from someone desiring to share an idea.

A Scorecard looks a lot like a Trotter matrix. For Six Sigma Quality, it listed "the things you have to be good at" to achieve it down the left-hand side of the matrix. Business units or regions were listed across the top of the matrix. Each business manager was then asked to assess his organization against each of these areas of excellence. The entries for each area were 1, not doing it; 2, working on it; 3, pretty good at it; and 4, we think we are at best practice level. The responses were sent to the staff at Crotonville. All 4's were checked out by those who were most expert in the practice (not on Crotonville's staff). If it was confirmed that a business indeed had a best practice, the 4 on the Scorecard was changed to a 5 ("confirmed"). These best practices, when possible, were confirmed against an outside standard.

Scores from all businesses or regions were then combined into one matrix. The full matrix was distributed to all managers. Those with 1's or 2's could see who was performing at the level of 5 on a particular practice. They could call and arrange to exchange the information necessary to improve their own operations. All managers knew that progress would be assessed in various business reviews.

The Scorecard also led to innovative behavior. For example, Senior Executive Program teams identified supplier capability as an important element of Six Sigma Quality. GE top management had assumed that it had to "get its own house in order before trying to help suppliers."[16] The SEP teams were told by companies in which they did their benchmarking that this was a recipe for disaster. So now the best practice in a business at GE is to lend "black belt" quality experts to supplier organizations for whatever length of time is necessary to help them improve their quality.

Another surprise in the Six Sigma Quality effort was the need to view quality through the eyes of the customer. Most people assumed that customers rated a business low on quality because of technical problems. Just as often, when customers were consulted, it was found that billing problems, for example, were the most important cause of poor perceptions of quality.

While Six Sigma best practice ideas were being exchanged throughout the organization, GE corporate was doing its part. This effort involved, among other things, committing at least $300 million per year to the massive task of finding replacements for 3,000 GE managers chosen to be trained to become "black belts," those who would lead the implementation of Six Sigma Quality throughout GE.

This example conveys both the complexity of transferring implicit knowledge in a huge organization as well as the genius of interrelated efforts coming together to make it happen, as suggested in Figure 14-4. Every element of the organization brain was at work here, including an effort led by the CEO and other thought leaders at GE; a "one-company" mentality supported by a high value placed on boundaryless behavior in combination with a decentralized business operating strategy; formal education (the university); less formal learning activities, such as benchmarking and best-practice sharing (the "water cooler"); ample budgets for training, travel, and technology; and incentives for the exchange of knowledge.

The payoff reflects the magnitude and genius of the effort. By the end of 2000, Six Sigma Quality was delivering what was estimated to be in excess of $1 billion annually, enabling GE to exceed investment analysts' expectations for several quarters in a row.[17]

■ Questions for Management

Questions posed here for management recognize the importance of formal, mechanistic processes for the transfer of what has been termed explicit knowledge. They also reflect our belief in the much greater value

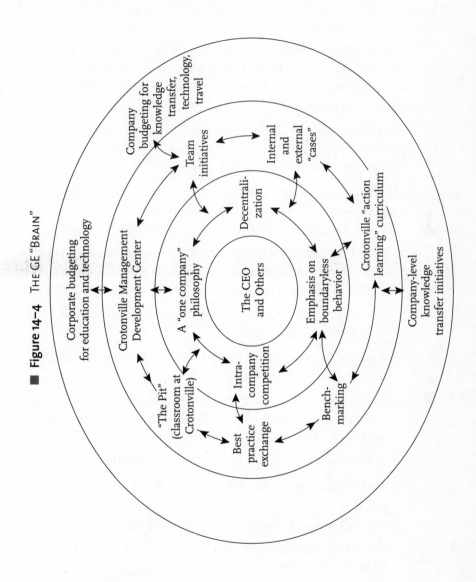

Figure 14–4 THE GE "BRAIN"

Corporate budgeting for education and technology

Company budgeting for knowledge transfer, technology, travel

Crotonville Management Development Center

Team initiatives

Internal and external "cases"

A "one company" philosophy

Decentralization

"The Pit" (classroom at Crotonville)

The CEO and Others

Crotonville "action learning" curriculum

Intracompany competition

Emphasis on boundaryless behavior

Best practice exchange

Benchmarking

Company-level knowledge transfer initiatives

that results in those efforts to capture and expand tacit knowledge, efforts that are hard to quantify and reward. The questions include the following:

1. Is your organization's "explicit" data structured in such a way that individuals can extract and manipulate it in ways that provide answers to their questions about customer, supplier, or competitor behavior?

2. What kinds of incentives do you provide to those outside the organization possessing knowledge regarding products, services, and processes to share it with employees?

3. How do you recognize members of the organization who "buy, beg, or borrow" knowledge from each other and from outside sources? Are individuals recognized for their ability to do this?

4. Which of the following mechanisms, among others, are in place to encourage knowledge transfer, especially that of "tacit" knowledge, within the organization:

   a. An expectation, evidenced in performance appraisals, that knowledge will be shared?

   b. A liberal transportation budget to bring far-flung colleagues into periodic face-to-face contact?

   c. The creation of frequent occasions, ranging from management meetings to educational programs, designed to encourage the sharing of ideas?

   d. Formal benchmarking and best practice initiatives?

   e. Technology that facilitates the exchange of ideas and knowledge?

   f. An incentive system providing "credits" for contributors to the knowledge bank and "debits" for those extracting knowledge without contributing?

   g. The creation of a work environment that naturally brings employees into frequent social as well as business contact with each other?

5. Do you select leaders based on

    a. Their willingness and ability to teach and learn?

    b. The degree to which they credit the work of others and obtain satisfaction from the development and success of others?

6. Does your organization have someone who naturally plays the role of Chief Knowledge Officer, someone who

    a. Seems to know everyone worth knowing in the organization?

    b. Knows where relevant information is "buried" in the organization?

    c. Spends most of his or her time linking people, ideas, and information throughout the organization?

    d. May spearhead the organization's formal educational efforts, which are regarded not only as an educational opportunity but also a way of creating networks for the exchange of knowledge?

We've covered a great deal of ground in exploring ways in which value profit chain thinking can be employed in the transformation of an organization and its performance. At this point, we owe it to you to pull together the various strands of this discussion in one place. At the same time, we probably need to clarify where we stand on an important issue or two. These are our objectives in the Afterword.

WE HAVE FOCUSED our attention on how value is measured, perceived, and created for employees, customers, investors, suppliers, and others. More important, we have explored how these ideas can be used to lead and manage change in organizations. As we have seen, it requires making sure that the right people, culture, values, vision, and strategy—all elements of the performance trinity—are in place. Not only does this require that they be aligned with each other but also that they reflect the demands of the competitive, legal, social, and economic environment in which organizations function.

The process begins by building dissatisfaction with the status quo through methods that not only suggest the possible but also highlight gaps between the possible and the actual through such means as the estimation of customer and employee lifetime value, internal best practice comparisons, and benchmarking against other organizations. This may disclose important gaps in the way goals are set, resources are deployed, values are articulated and adhered to, and capability is developed in the organization, including everything from the selection of people to the way in which they are recognized and rewarded for creating value. It may even disclose gaps in the quality of management needed to move the performance "needle" from the actual to the possible.

The creation of value requires an understanding of value profit chain relationships as well as the components of value for employees, customers, investors, and others, only a portion of which are measured in monetary terms. With this knowledge as a foundation, important ways of leveraging value over cost can be developed, leading ultimately to greater value for all of an organization's constituents. Increasingly, this will require understanding the needs of individuals, as we saw in our discussion of value exchange. It will be facilitated by the acquisition, storage, and analysis of increasing volumes of information, all made possible by new generations of information technology and those who understand its use. It requires, however, a vision centered around value profit change. And, of course, it requires visionaries able to communicate its importance, able to formulate strategies for achieving it, and able to lead the change itself.

Once achieved, value-focused change can produce remarkable results. There are forces, however, that make this a challenging task—forces that most often are internal to the organization—including loss of the focus that produced the change, complacency, and even arrogance, all ironically products of success. Combating these forces requires not only constant reminders of potential threats to continued success but also mechanisms by which organizations can sustain their gains. These include revisiting the values on which success was built: making sure the right measures and incentives for continued performance are in place; tying the success of an organization to that of its customers, suppliers, or others; and ensuring that the organization is able to learn and innovate, raising the probability of continued value-focused change.

You may wonder why we didn't devote more space to ways in which technologies help shape these phenomena. There is little disagreement that technology has made possible many of the strategies described in this book and is a lever for change. Take, for example, our discussion of Speedpass, the use of information technology to speed purchases of gasoline and other products at service stations. It represents the first major breakthrough in decades in the battle to combat the necessary evil of refueling a vehicle.

For that matter, how about the transformation that has occurred in airline reservation and ticketing processes over the past two decades, beginning with the development of an airline reservation and information system called SABRE? It is a transformation accompanied by an equally amazing increase in airline capabilities to price individual seats in an effort to maximize the revenue for a given flight. None of this would have been possible without advances in information technology.

Technology has contributed significantly to the creation of value, but it has rarely proven to be a source of continued competitive advantage for anyone but its creators. Sophisticated users have long since concluded that it is useless to fashion a strategy based on long-term competitive advantage through the differential in value resulting from the deployment of technology. Rather, they have concluded that long-term differentiated value results from an understanding and use of information assembled and analyzed by means of technology. As a result, the inventors of Speedpass decided to make available the technology to others, banking on their ability to get more retailers to adopt the Speedpass alternative in order to build a large network of Speedpass users (and accepters) faster than others who license the technology. They concluded that value for customers and retailers is created through the size of the network, not a technology that would likely be replicated anyway in a few months by competitors.

Based on much the same thinking, those responsible for SABRE have sold access to both its information processing capabilities and the database it represents, even to competitors. They have bet that they can make more creative use of the information than competitors who might be buying into the system. They assumed that it was only a matter of time before the technology would be replicated anyway.

Harlan Cleveland pointed out years ago that in an age of information (versus material things), not only would it be more difficult to hoard ideas, but that it would also be more difficult to keep secrets.[1] We have seen all too many instances in which this has proved to be the case. It applies to technology as well. Technology, like information, leaks. In fact, it's in the interest of purveyors of technology to make it as widely available as possible. For these reasons alone it is a poor basis for sustainable competitive advantage. In the hands of those who can put together the right value package for employees, customers, and investors to go along with effective technology—as FedEx has proved—it can contribute to long-term success. This, of course, brings us back to the focus of this book.

We have not said enough about the ways in which value is distributed among an organization's important constituencies. In this matter, markets are not perfect. Over long periods of time, there are market mechanisms for ensuring that employees, customers, and investors receive adequate value from their relationships with an organization. Otherwise, organizations find it difficult to attract the right kind of talent, markets dry up, and investors may turn elsewhere for their expected returns.

The way in which value is distributed varies among the world's major markets. For example, employees are compensated in relation to their managers much more handsomely in Europe than in the U.S. Much of the value received by European employees may be in the form of benefits, but the fact remains that the ratio of compensation for managers compared to that for employees is much lower in Europe than in the U.S.

Until recent years, European and Japanese investors endured much lower rates of return on their investments or invested their money in the U.S. In fact, flows of funds are one of the best indicators of investors' perceptions of value.

As we prepare this book for publication, questions are being raised regarding the methods of executive compensation in the U.S., whether they deliver too large a share of the total value generated by the organization to its leaders rather than its employees, customers, or investors. Some may argue that this is a reflection of the scarcity of good management. Others maintain that it is a product of the constant benchmarking in executive salaries that is encouraged by compensation consultants. Still others cite an implicit "pact" between executives and those on their boards of directors responsible for their compensation. And yet others suggest that the incentives built into compensation packages today are so great that they encourage executives to make goals at all costs, including methods that require the subsequent restating of earnings with predictably adverse effects on an organization's market value.

However relevant the topic, it is much too large for us to tackle here. We suspect that the current concerns are with short-term imperfections in "markets" for talent, customers, and money that have led to imbalances in the attribution of value to various constituents of the organization. If this is the case, they will be corrected, either by the markets themselves or by outside forces.

All of this assumes, of course, that value is properly measured and accounted for. This is what provides the basis of trust on which value can be created most effectively. Those responsible for the preservation of this trust—managers, accountants, and others responsible for oversight—thus play a critical role in the creation of value. As we see being played out in organizations like Enron, the abuse of trust can lead to the rapid destruction of value that reaches far beyond the confines of a single organization.

What we have attempted to highlight here are the remarkable ways in which value is being created today in organizations large and small, for-profit and not-for-profit, service-producing and manufacturing. In the process, we have raised many questions for managers while seeking to provide possible responses through descriptions of best practice. These questions are organized in the form of a self-audit in Appendix B. The self-audit can be used as an economic form of benchmarking. It can be used as a vehicle for fostering discontent with the status quo as a prelude to instituting change. It can also be used as a means of sharing information with other organizations in an organized manner.

It is only by understanding how value is created that one can seek the kind of change in people, values, and strategies that can lead to more effective value creation. Change is a constant in business life. It might as well enhance value.

Compendium of Value Profit Chain Research (Ordered by Value Profit Chain Component)

VPC Components	Source	Size/Nature of Sample	Findings and/or Conclusions
Employee loyalty and growth and profit	L. Barber, S. Hayday, S. Bevan, "From people to profits," *The Institute for Employment Studies*, IES Report 355, 1999.	Employee, customer, and sales performance data collected by a major retailer over a period of 2 years.	"A one point increase in employee commitment could lead to a monthly increase of up to £200,000 in sales per store."
Employee satisfaction (and quality of work life)	Susan G. Cohen, Lei Chang, and Gerald E. Ledford, Jr., "A hierarchical construct of self-management leadership and its relationship to quality of work life and perceived work group effectiveness," *Personnel Psychology*, Summer, 1997.	390 self-managing and 412 traditionally managed employees and 94 external leaders from 58 self-managing and 60 traditionally managed teams in a large telephone company	The study looked at self-managing work teams versus traditionally managed groups. Findings supported the theory that self-managing leadership is a valid construct. Other findings in the research included: (1) although self-managing leadership behaviors were not found to be significantly greater in the self-managing versus the traditionally managed teams, self-managing leadership behaviors were found to positively correlate to quality of work life (employee satisfaction; (2) self-managing teams were not found to produce significantly different outcomes than traditionally managed teams.

Topic	Source	Sample	Findings
Employee satisfaction and employee loyalty	J. M. Carsten, and P. E. Spector, "Unemployment, job satisfaction and employee turnover: a meta-analytic test of the Muchinsky model," *Journal of Applied Psychology*, vol. 72, 1987.	Existing studies from 1947 to 1983, collected from bibliographies of comprehensive reviews; data used was collected throughout U.S., Canada, and parts of Europe and across many occupations and industries; sample sizes ranged from 40 to 6,000 employees	Authors tested correlation of employee satisfaction and turnover during times of high unemployment and times of low unemployment. During times of high unemployment, the correlation between satisfaction and turnover was lower than during times of higher unemployment, supporting their hypothesis that economic conditions impact satisfaction-turnover correlations.
Employee satisfaction, loyalty and productivity	Tom Davis and Michael Landa, "The Story of Mary: How the 'organization culture' can erode bottom-line profitability," *The Canadian Manager*, Winter 2000.	1999 study of Canadian workplaces, public and private companies ranging from small to large businesses	Research focused on the importance of culture as opposed to compensation in determining outcomes of VPC components. It suggests how organization culture can have an adverse effect on bottom-line profitability.
Employee satisfaction and return to shareholders	"100 Best Companies to Work For," *Fortune*, January 8, 2001, pp. 148–168.	Statistical analysis of 3-, 5-, and 10-year annualized return to shareholders, *Fortune* survey's 100 best companies to work for vs. the S&P 500	Analysis of shareholder value of two samples of companies indicates that the 100 best companies to work for in 2000 had roughly double the annualized return to shareholders for 3-, 5-, and 10-year periods leading up to the survey.
Employee satisfaction and loyalty and profit growth	Adrian Gostick, "They do recognition right," *Workspan*, October, 2000.	KFC restaurants nationwide for the period 1998–1999	KFC found that employee recognition helps to achieve employee satisfaction. Employee recognition fosters employee loyalty. Employee satisfaction helps to achieve profitability.

VPC Components	Source	Size/Nature of Sample	Findings and/or Conclusions
Employee satisfaction and loyalty	Stephen J. Havlovic, "Quality of work life and human resource outcomes," *Industrial Relations*, Vol. 30, 3.	Unionized midwestern heavy manufacturing firm from 1976 to 1986; 50 union members volunteered to participate in quality-of-work-life program	Study looked at impact of quality-of-work-life (QWL) programs on absenteeism, turnover and grievances. Findings suggested that "Employers can expect to see reductions in minor accident, grievance, absenteeism, and turnover rates with the installation and institutionalization of a QWL process (worker participation program)." The authors recommend that future research should have a control group as well as control for economic variables.
Employee capability, satisfaction, and productivity and growth and profit	Mark A. Huselid, "The impact of human resource management practices on turnover, productivity, and corporate financial performance," *Academy of Management Journal*, June, 1995.	968 senior human resource managers in firms with more than 100 employees, none of which were foreign owned, holding companies, or publicly held business units or divisions of larger firms	This study researched the magnitude of the returns for investments in high performance work practices on employee turnover, productivity and corporate performance. "I [the author] found considerable support for the hypothesis that investments in such practices are associated with lower employee turnover and greater productivity and corporate financial performance."
Employee satisfaction, loyalty, capability, and productivity and growth and profits	R. S. Lau, "Quality of work life and performance—ad hoc investigation of two key elements in the service profit chain model," *International*	Companies with reputation for high quality of work life contrasted with a control group from the S&P 500	The study showed that service organizations that emphasized quality of work life for their employees tended to have better sales growth, asset growth, and return on asset growth over a five-year period when contrasted to other S&P

	Journal of Service Industry Management, Vol. 11, Issue 5, 2000.	500 firms. While this research did not differentiate among firms regarding their average profitability, it is generally recognized that "profitability suffers from accounting distortions and is generally not a useful measure for cross-industry comparisons. . . . The observed performance growth relationships with QWL are consistent with the service [value] profit chain model's expectation of 'increased employee loyalty' and 'share of wallet.'"
Employee satisfaction, commitment, retention, and shareholder value	Bruce N. Pfau and Ira T. Kay, *The Human Capital Edge* (New York: McGraw Hill, 2002).	Results of responses from 7,500 workers in Watson Wyatt's *WorkUSA 2000* survey and Human Capital Index. Employee satisfaction and retention have positive impact on company market value. Companies with high employee commitment produce a total 3-year return to shareholders nearly 50% greater than companies with low employee commitment.
Employee capability and productivity and profits	Aleda V. Roth, "Performance dimensions in services: An empirical investigation of strategic performance," *Advances in Services Marketing and Management*, Vol. 2, 1993, pp. 1–47.	140 banking executives (11.3% response rate); data collected through 1991 Survey of Retail Banking Strategy and Performance, administered biannually to probability samples of retail banks. The author focuses on identifying which service factors are related to performance and measuring them. "Market performance was associated with the simultaneous development of multiple capabilities." Those capabilities were business process performance (quality of customer interface, productivity, innovation, and quality of work life), competitive capabilities (total of nine factors, including service quality and technological leadership), and business unit viability (traditional financial measures).

VPC Components	Source	Size/Nature of Sample	Findings and/or Conclusions
Employee satisfaction and loyalty	Roland T. Rust, Greg L. Stewart, Heather Miller, and Debbie Pielack, "The satisfaction and retention of frontline employees," *International Journal of Service Industry Management*, Vol. 7, Issue 5.	Low-paid, certified nursing assistants from six nursing homes; half were from urban areas and the other half from rural; 326, or 81.5% of the selected sample of CNAs, completed surveys	Study examines the measurement of employee satisfaction and retention through means of customer satisfaction surveys. Authors say that employees are customers, especially as qualified employees are becoming harder to find. There is the underlying assumption throughout the article that there is a ripple effect from satisfied employee to satisfied and loyal customers (although that is not the focus of this study).
Employee satisfaction and loyalty (retention)	John E. Sheridan, "Organizational culture and employee retention," *Academy of Management Journal*, December, 1992.	904 college graduates in six accounting firms over a 6-year period	Author looks at impact of organizational culture on employee satisfaction and employee retention. Findings were that "professionals hired in the companies that emphasized interpersonal relationship values stayed 14 months longer (45 months in total) than those in the firms emphasizing the work task values."
Employee satisfaction and growth and profits	Silvestro Rhian and Stuart Cross, "Applying the service profit chain in a retail environment," *International Journal of Service Industry Management*, Vol. 11, 3, 2000.	A small sample of stores in one of the U.K.'s leading grocery retail chains	Does not support value profit chain theory in its entirety. The research involved an exploratory study of service profit chain relationships applied to a single organization. The results showed correlations between profit, customer loyalty, customer satisfaction, service value, internal service quality, output quality and productivity. However, there was a

Topic	Citation	Study / Sample	Findings
			strong correlation between employee dissatisfaction and store profitability. This paper calls into question the "satisfaction mirror" between employees and customers.
Employee satisfaction and loyalty	R. P. Steel, and N. K. Ovalle II, "A review and meta-analysis of research on the relationship between behavioral intentions and employee turnover," *Journal of Applied Psychology*, Vol. 69, 1984.	34 published and unpublished works that reported on relationships between behavioral intentions and employee turnover	Authors conclude that there is a stronger correlation (and thus better predictor) between behavioral intentions to quit and employee turnover (loyalty) versus affective mechanisms including overall job satisfaction, satisfaction with the work itself, and organizational commitment.
Employee capability and productivity and profitability	Richard A. Swanson, "Demonstrating the financial benefit of human resource development: Status and update on the theory and practice," *Human Resource Development Quarterly*, Fall, 1998.	Cites studies the author has done as well as others to support argument that core financial analysis (CAM) method works; samples include (1) 20 grocery store baggers, (2) 139 "old" and 92 "new" clothing machine operators, (3) 68 company managers in an adult education program, (4) 136 Onan Corp. employees in a truck assembly plant	The author examines the core financial analysis method (CAM), which since the 1980s has been useful for many human resource development programs in forecasting and evaluating the financial effectiveness of their programs. He concludes that employee training can lead to increased employee productivity and capability and many times increased firm profitability.

VPC Components	Source	Size/Nature of Sample	Findings and/or Conclusions
Employee satisfaction, customer satisfaction and growth and profit	William Copulsky, "Balancing the needs of customers and shareholders," *Journal of Business Strategy,* November/December 1991.	Merck, Xerox, General Motors Saturn plant, among others	Stakeholders include employees, customers, and shareholders, not just shareholders. Author concludes that if we pay attention to employees and customers, then profits will follow.
Employee satisfaction and customer satisfaction	Patricia A. Denzer, "Conducting internal service audits," *Healthcare Executive,* July/August, 1999.	Naval Medical Center in San Diego; twice per year surveys of employees and customers analyzed; a range of employee and customer satisfaction issues surveyed	This study establishes relationships between dimensions that the authors label as professionalism, teamwork, courtesy, promptness, employee satisfaction, and customer satisfaction.
Employee satisfaction and customer satisfaction	Daniel J. Koys, "The Effects of Employee Satisfaction, Organizational Citizenship Behavior, and Turnover on Organizational Effectiveness: A Unit-Level Longitudinal Study." *Personal Psychology,* Vol. 54 (2001) pp. 101–114.	Regional restaurant chain with 28 stores conducted over 2 years (year 1, 774 hourly employees and 64 managers; year 2, 693 hourly employees and 79 managers); 50% response rate; 5,565 customer responses in year 1 and 4,338 responses for year 2	Employee satisfaction predicts customer satisfaction and therefore supports VPC relationship. Customer satisfaction can influence employee satisfaction. The study could not prove that employee dissatisfaction significantly affects customer satisfaction.
Employee satisfaction, quality and client focus, and profitability	David H. Maister, *Practice What You Preach: What Managers Must Do to Create a High Achievement Culture* (New York: The Free Press, 2000).	5,500 employees in 139 offices operated by 29 marketing service firms	The author concludes that financial performance was driven primarily by quality and client focus, which in turn was a function most importantly of employee satisfaction and standards of excellence in work.

Topic	Citation	Company/Data	Findings
Employee satisfaction, customer satisfaction, and growth and profit	Michael J. McDermott, "Satisfaction guaranteed," *Chief Executive*, February, 2001.	PNC Financial Services Group	Supports relationship between employee satisfaction, customer satisfaction, and revenue growth for a short period from 1999 to 2000. Report implies the existence of empirical data, although none are supplied.
Employee loyalty, customer loyalty, and growth and profits	Frederick F. Reichheld, "Loyalty-based management," *Harvard Business Review*, March–April 1993.	Cites several case studies, including (1) MBNA (customer retention), (2) Olive Garden (employee retention), (3) State Farm Insurance (customer retention and loyalty, (4) USAA (insurance for military—customer retention), (5) Entenmann's Bakeries (customer retention), (6) Honda (customer retention), (7) Leo Burnett (employee retention)	Employee retention helps ensure customer retention and both contribute to greater profits versus competitors who do not focus on these value profit chain elements.
Employee satisfaction, employee capability, and customer value (service quality)	Leonard A. Schlesinger and Jeffrey Zornitsky, "Job satisfaction, service capability, and customer satisfaction: An examination of linkages and management implications," *Human Resource Planning*, 14, 2.	1,277 employees and 4,269 customers of a personal lines insurance organization	(1) Employee perceptions of service quality are related to job satisfaction and self-perceived service capability. (2) Job satisfaction, service capability and employee perceptions of service quality rise over employee's tenure. (3) Difference between employee perceptions of service quality and customer satisfaction are negatively related to employee job satisfaction and service capability. (4) Service capability is an important promoter of job satisfaction, and several organizational attributes are related to both.

VPC Components	Source	Size/Nature of Sample	Findings and/or Conclusions
Employee satisfaction, customer satisfaction, and growth	Anthony Rucci, Stephen P. Kirn, and Richard T. Quinn, "The employee-customer-profit chain at Sears," *Harvard Business Review*, January–February, 1998.	820 full-line Sears department stores collecting data over a 2-year period	A 5-point increase in customer satisfaction at the store level in quarter 1 was found to produce a 1.3-point increase in customer satisfaction in quarter 2 and a revenue growth rate 0.5% higher than the national average for all stores in quarter 3.
Employee satisfaction and customer satisfaction	Michael A. Spinelli and George C. Canavos, "Investigating the relationship between employee satisfaction and guest satisfaction," *Cornell Hotel and Restaurant Administration Quarterly*, December, 2000.	6 metropolitan full-service hotels surveyed in 1994; 240 employees responded to questionnaire; approximately 100 hotel guests responded	"In summary, a satisfied employee is one who is involved in decision making, received adequate training and benefits, and has an effective general manager. . . . A happy employee does influence the guest's attitude toward the hotel."
Employee satisfaction, customer satisfaction, and growth and profit	Priscilla S. Wisner and Hollace A. Feist, "Does teaming pay off?," *Strategic Finance*, February, 2001.	45 Bell Atlantic call centers, staffed with 6,000 sales consultants. Half were in a control group and the other half implemented a teaming approach; the study was conducted over a 2-year period	Employee satisfaction and productivity were higher with teaming. They were positively correlated with customer satisfaction, market share, and additional revenues.

VPC Components	Source	Size/Nature of Sample	Findings and/or Conclusions
Customer satisfaction and loyalty	Eugene V. Anderson and Mary W. Sullivan, "The antecedents and consequences of customer satisfaction for firms," *Marketing Science*, Vol. 12, No. 2, Spring, 1993.	22,300 customers of 114 companies in 16 major product and service industries in Sweden	This study showed that high-quality products produce more satisfied customers and, moreover, customers that are likely to be retained. According to the authors, "If it is more costly to add new customers than to maintain relationship with current customers, then such firms should enjoy greater profitability in the long run." The relationship with profitability, however, is not examined.
Customer satisfaction and growth and profit	Eugene V. Anderson and Vikas Mittal, "Strengthening the satisfaction-profit chain," *Journal of Service Research*, November, 2000.	Data provided from 125 firms comprising the Swedish Customer Satisfaction Barometer at the University of Michigan	The authors argue that value profit chain elements affect each other in a nonlinear, rather than a linear fashion. They conclude that "On average a 1% increase in customer satisfaction is associated with a 2.37% increase in ROI, whereas a 1% decrease in satisfaction is associated with a 5.08% drop in ROI. This suggests that on average, a decrease in customer satisfaction is two times more deleterious than the benefit associated with an equivalent increase in satisfaction."

VPC Components	Source	Size/Nature of Sample	Findings and/or Conclusions
Customer satisfaction and growth and profit	K. N. Bernhardt, N. Donthu, and P. Kennett, "A longitudinal analysis of satisfaction and profitability," working paper, Georgia State University, December, 1999.	National chain of fast-food restaurants; 342,308 consumer responses; 3,009 employee responses collected over a year	Time series data reveals that there is a positive impact on profits with a positive change in customer satisfaction over the long run (which can be obscured in the short run). The study also found that there is a positive correlation between employee satisfaction and customer satisfaction at any given period of time ("satisfaction mirror").
Customer satisfaction and loyalty	Manfred Bruhn and Michael A. Grund, "Theory, development and implementation of national customer satisfaction indices: The Swiss Index of Customer Satisfaction (SWICS)," *Total Quality Management*, September, 2000.	20 industries within 6 sectors. 7,436 telephone interviews with 3,845 respondents in German-speaking part of Switzerland for average of 17 minutes with each respondent; each industry had roughly 300–500 respondents (with roughly 1,000 for health insurance)	The authors conclude that customer satisfaction is crucial for customer loyalty. They distinguish between customer satisfaction and customer dialogue. The more comparable products and services are, the more important is customer dialogue for customer loyalty.
Customer satisfaction, loyalty, and value	Bob Evans, "So, what makes you loyal?," *Informationweek*, March 26, 2001.	Study by *Informationweek* research group consisted of extensive discussions with 500 IT and business managers	According to the authors, "how IT vendors work with their customers and . . . the nature and degree of that collaboration directly impacts the loyalty those customers feel toward their vendors."

Topic	Citation	Sample / Details	Findings
Customer satisfaction and loyalty and growth and profit	Joe Flower, "Relationship tech," *Health Forum Journal*, September/October, 1999.	A sample of patients and service providers at Kaiser Permanente, Northwestern Medical Faculty Foundation, Community Hospitals of Indiana, and Elements Wellness (a health insurance provider)	These conclusions were stated without empirical evidence: increased relationships with customers, even through relatively impersonal means (mailings that appear personalized), can improve service/quality while at same time reducing costs; more personal-touch service up front can reduce back-end, higher cost interactions, such as surgery and expensive visits.
Customer satisfaction and loyalty and growth and profit	Roger Hallowell, "The relationships of customer satisfaction, customer loyalty, and profitability: an empirical study," *International Journal of Service Industry Management*, Vol. 7, Issue 4, 1996.	12,000 retail-banking customers at 59 divisions of a bank; sample represented 73% of all households served by the bank; all divisions had been part of the bank for at least a year	The author's findings support the conclusion that value profit chain elements are related. However, this study does not prove that a satisfied customer unquestionably means a loyal customer and therefore a profitable customer.
Customer satisfaction and loyalty	Christopher W. L. Hart and Michael D. Johnson, "Growing the trust relationship." *Marketing Management*, Spring, 1999.	Study by Jeffrey Dyer of Wharton and Wujin Chu of Seoul University School of Management of 8 largest auto manufacturers in Japan, South Korea, U.S., and 435 of their suppliers is cited; objective was to determine trust levels and the consequences; the purchase volume by the highest trust automaker was double that of the least trusted manufacturer	Article focuses on how to achieve customer "total trust" versus merely satisfaction.

VPC Components	Source	Size/Nature of Sample	Findings and/or Conclusions
Customer satisfaction and growth and profit	Reported in "India: Stress on customer relationship," *Businessline*, March 25, 2001.	Study done by Accenture of the impact of customer relationship management on financial performance; 500 executives in 250 North American companies participated	The study concludes that "The percentage of variance between average and high performance, explained by customer relationship management capabilities, was 64% in electronics and high tech, 52% in chemical, 50% in communication and 47% in pharma."
Customer satisfaction, value and loyalty and growth and profit	Jukka Laitamaki and Raymond Kordupleski, "Building and deploying profitable growth strategies based on the waterfall of customer value added," *European Management Journal*, Vol 15, No. 2, April, 1997.	Two unidentified companies in capital goods industry	The article aims to expand knowledge of the key drivers of customer satisfaction and business process excellence and to strengthen skills in developing profitable growth strategies based on customer value added (CVA). The findings reflect relationships in the value profit chain.
Customer satisfaction and growth and profit (shareholder value)	L. Biff Motley, "Why satisfying the customer is good business," *Bank Marketing*, April, 2000.	A study of customer satisfaction in the U.S. based on 164 companies in most major industries	The study showed that in 2000 firms that scored in the top 50% in overall customer satisfaction created over $24 billion in shareholder value, but the lower 50% created only $14 billion. Since 1994, there has been a positive correlation between customer satisfaction and stock prices.

Topic	Citation	Sample	Findings
Customer satisfaction and growth and profit	Karin Newman, Alan Cowling and Susan Leigh, "Case study: Service quality, business process re-engineering and human resources: A case in point?" *International Journal of Bank Marketing*, Vol. 16, Issue 6, 1998.	Northbank, a major U.K. bank with 650 branches	The bank underwent corporate transformation and also strived to improve service quality. The 5 year project focused specifically on employee communications, the redesign of work, recruitment and reward processes, and introducing consumer research-based national quality standards. The bank was rated number 1 in 3 consecutive years in service quality surveys following all the changes. However, during this period, while customer satisfaction and retention was rising, employee satisfaction was declining. The author concludes as well that an improved definition of service quality should be pursued.
Customer loyalty and growth and profit	Frederick F. Reichheld, and Earl Sasser, Jr., "Zero defections: quality comes to services," *Harvard Business Review*, September–October, 1990.	MBNA, Domino franchise, Staples, Mastercare (Bridgestone/Firestone), Great-West Life Assurance Company	The authors conclude that, in their sample companies, a "5 percentage point improvement in defection rates increases average customer value by from 25% to 125%."
Customer value and growth and profit	Aleda V. Roth and William E. Jackson, III, "Strategic determinants of service quality and performance: Evidence from the banking industry," *Management Science*, Vol. 41, No. 11, November, 1995.	Data collected under the Retail Banking Futures Project, a collaborative research study between the Bank Administration Institute and the Kenan-Flagler Business School, University of North Carolina at Chapel Hill	This paper focuses on a service management strategy called the "operation capabilities-service quality-performance (C-SQ-P) triad. Insights from the research that pertain to value profit chain theory include: (1) generic operations capabilities affect service quality and performance, although the relationships are not always direct, and (2) the effects of technologi-

VPC Components	Source	Size/Nature of Sample	Findings and/or Conclusions
			cal leadership and market acuity on service quality are moderated by the absorptive capacity of employees to recognize and exploit their potential. Hence investments in people are critical to success.
Customer value and growth and profit	Roland T. Rust, Anthony J. Zahorik, and Timothy L. Keiningham, "Return on quality (ROQ): Making service quality financially accountable," *AMA,* April, 1995.	A national hotel chain; 7,882 individual responses collected over a year	Authors developed and tested model to determine where quality improvements should (and shouldn't) be made to positively impact firm profitability. They cite several examples of Malcolm Baldrige winners who shortly after winning went bankrupt. The authors believe there is a point at which additional spending on quality is not profitable.
Customer satisfaction and loyalty	Donald J. Shemwell, J. Joseph Cronin, and William R. Bullard, "Relationship exchange in services: An empirical investigation of ongoing customer service–provider relationships," *International Journal of Service Industry Management,* Vol. 5, Issue 3, 1994.	A sample of population of primary care physicians, automobile mechanics, and hairstylists; the study provides data tables and significance levels for findings	Study findings include (1) the higher the level of trust in the customer relationship, the greater the probability that the customer will continue the relationship and the lower the level of perceived risk in the relationship; (2) females seek more trust and commitment than do males; and (3) in general, consumers place more trust and are more committed to their hairdresser and doctor than to their mechanic.

VPC Components	Source	Size/Nature of Sample	Findings and/or Conclusions
Customer loyalty and growth and profit	Joseph Schlesinger, Miles Cook, Darrell Rigby, and Julian Chu, "Order fulfillment: Delivering the e-promise," *Ivey Business Journal*, July/August, 2001.	Bain/Mainspring study of on-line retail customers Webvan, Wal-Mart, Amazon, Tesco, L.L. Bean, J. Crew, Lands' End, UPS	The authors studied (1) order fulfillment performance and (2) customer repeat purchases. They base their conclusions regarding the direct relationships between customer loyalty, growth, and profit on the success or failure of each on-line retailer.
Customer satisfaction, value, and loyalty	Scott Shrake, "Studies find loyalty pinned (loosely) to satisfaction, value," *Target Marketing*, September, 1999.	Harte-Hanks market research study of consumer loyalty of 2,000 credit-worthy individuals and W.A. Dean & Associates behavioral study of 1,400 catalog shoppers	These studies concluded that only select rewards programs will move a satisfied customer to a loyal one. Cash rebates, airline miles, and discounted merchandise work. Personalized communication is the top loyalty builder, along with thank-yous with gifts.
Customer satisfaction and loyalty	Youjae Yi, "A critical review of consumer satisfaction," *Review of Marketing*, 1990.	Cites 160 articles in current customer satisfaction research review, some of which report empirical research	This survey seeks to understand current consumer satisfaction research (definition, antecedents, and consequences) and to suggest future areas for research. The author concludes that consumer satisfaction will influence purchase intention and postpurchase attitude.

■ VPC COMPONENTS IV: CUSTOMER VALUE, CUSTOMER LOYALTY, AND EMPLOYEE PRODUCTIVITY

VPC Components	Source	Size/Nature of Sample	Findings and/or Conclusions
Customer loyalty, employee productivity, and customer value	Moira Clark, "Modelling the impact of customer-employee relationships on customer retention rates in a major UK retail bank," *Management Decision*, Vol. 35, Issue 4, 1997.	Major U.K. retail bank; looked at two similar branches with 75 and 60% retention rates; interviewed employees and customers	Findings reveal that employee and customer perceptions of service quality are related to customer retention rates and employee and customer perceptions of service quality are related to each other.

The Value Profit Chain Audit

■ Suggested Use

This audit can be used to identify management perceptions of how well an organization is doing in applying concepts from the value profit chain. Although it can be administered at all levels of a management hierarchy, it is most effective when used to identify perceptions at each level, thereby providing an assessment of the extent to which concepts are communicated and applied at each level.

When administered to a department or division within a much larger organization, it is important that respondents understand clearly whether they are being asked to describe the department or division of which they are a member or the organization as a whole. If time permits, it is most useful to ask them to complete an audit for both. When time is limited, it is usually most relevant for them to describe in their responses only the department or division of which they are a member.

To calibrate responses to the audit questions, it is first useful to ask respondents to judge the importance of each dimension of the audit to the organization. Next, they can be asked to judge how well the organization is doing on each dimension. Those items with the largest gap between importance and actual performance provide the highest priorities for future attention.

Items with little or no relevance to the organization can be deleted before administering the audit. Less relevant portions of the audit may be deleted completely.

By ensuring that responses to the audit will not be associated with individual respondents, more objective appraisals of actual performance are obtained, especially on questions concerning the organization's leadership.

■ The Value Profit Chain Audit

The following are a number of statements about the organization of which you are a member. Please respond to each with perceptions of *(your department or division) (the entire organization) (first your department or division, then the entire organization)* by circling the number that most closely responds to your current opinion.

Although you have been asked to place your name and your affiliation on the audit, the results will be tabulated and none will be identified with your name.

References to customers include both those external and internal to the organization. Thus, if your department primarily provides support to other departments in the organization, those whom you serve should be regarded as customers for the purposes of this audit.

In providing responses to each of the following statements, please do it by *first providing your assessment of the relative importance of each dimension to your organization* by circling the number in the first "bank" of numbers that most closely corresponds to your assessment of importance. However, to learn more about your opinion regarding the relative priority of each of the dimensions, please give your highest priority (circling 7) to no more than 20 of the statements, your next highest priority to no more than 20 (by circling 6), and so forth.

Then return to the first statement and complete your assessment of the performance of your organization by circling the most appropriate number in the second "bank" of numbers.

The statements are as follows:

A. (Re)defining and (Re)positioning the Business

	Highest Importance → No Importance	Agree Completely → Disagree Completely
1. Customers targeted by my organization are clearly defined in terms of whom we do and whom we do not seek to serve.	7 6 5 4 3 2 1	7 6 5 4 3 2 1
2. The needs of targeted customers, and hence the mission of my organization, are defined in terms of elements of the customer value equation (results, process quality, access costs, and price), not products or services.	7 6 5 4 3 2 1	7 6 5 4 3 2 1
3. Every effort is made to ensure that these needs are identified and reassessed from time to time.	7 6 5 4 3 2 1	7 6 5 4 3 2 1
4. Those associated with my organization, from leadership to frontline management ranks, understand the needs of targeted customers.	7 6 5 4 3 2 1	7 6 5 4 3 2 1
5. Those associated with my organization, from leadership to frontline management ranks, understand how we propose to meet the needs of targeted customers.	7 6 5 4 3 2 1	7 6 5 4 3 2 1

6. Leadership has clearly positioned the organization to meet each of the needs of targeted customers better than competitors.

7 6 5 4 3 2 1

7 6 5 4 3 2 1

7. The results and process quality that my organization seeks to deliver are clearly communicated to customers in ways that differentiate it from competitors.

7 6 5 4 3 2 1

7 6 5 4 3 2 1

8. My organization has identified the core values shared by all or nearly all of the members of the organization.

7 6 5 4 3 2 1

7 6 5 4 3 2 1

9. My organization has developed an operating strategy—comprising organization, policies, practices, procedures, and processes—that reinforces the values shared by all or nearly all of its members.

7 6 5 4 3 2 1

7 6 5 4 3 2 1

10. My organization's value delivery system—including facilities, locations, information systems, networks—provides outstanding support in enabling it to leverage value to customers over costs.

7 6 5 4 3 2 1

7 6 5 4 3 2 1

11. A very small number of primary means have been identified by which value to customers is leveraged over costs to the organization.

7 6 5 4 3 2 1

7 6 5 4 3 2 1

12. Indicators of performance, so-called "deep indicators," reflect the primary means by which value to customers is leveraged over costs to the organization.

7 6 5 4 3 2 1   7 6 5 4 3 2 1

13. People in my organization are rewarded on the basis of how they perform on "deep indicators" of performance.

7 6 5 4 3 2 1   7 6 5 4 3 2 1

14. Measures of performance include nonfinancial elements of the value profit chain, such as employee satisfaction and commitment (willingness to recommend the firm or its products and services to others), as well as customer satisfaction and commitment.

7 6 5 4 3 2 1   7 6 5 4 3 2 1

15. People in my organization are rewarded on the basis of how they perform on non-financial elements of the value profit chain (such as employee satisfaction and commitment as well as customer satisfaction and commitment) as well as financial measures.

7 6 5 4 3 2 1   7 6 5 4 3 2 1

B. Managing Levers for Change

1. From time to time, my organization estimates the lifetime value of its most important customers.

   7 6 5 4 3 2 1   7 6 5 4 3 2 1

2. Customer lifetime value is widely communicated within the organization as a means of sensitizing employees to the importance of a single customer.

   7 6 5 4 3 2 1   7 6 5 4 3 2 1

3. Customer lifetime value is an important determinant of investments in initiatives aimed at customer retention.

   7 6 5 4 3 2 1   7 6 5 4 3 2 1

4. In estimating customer lifetime value, an effort is made to identify antagonists, hostages, mercenaries, loyalists, viral loyalists, and apostle/owners in the customer base and to establish a value for each.

   7 6 5 4 3 2 1   7 6 5 4 3 2 1

5. As a result of estimates of customer lifetime value:

   a. Training programs for frontline employees have been altered.

   7 6 5 4 3 2 1   7 6 5 4 3 2 1

   b. Employees have been given greater latitude to deliver results to customers.

   7 6 5 4 3 2 1   7 6 5 4 3 2 1

   c. Employees in customer-facing jobs have been given greater recognition and performance incentives.

   7 6 5 4 3 2 1   7 6 5 4 3 2 1

6. In recent years, more than 20% of the marketing budget has been devoted to the retention of highly valued customers as opposed to attracting new customers.

7 6 5 4 3 2 1

7. My organization regularly tracks employee satisfaction, loyalty (planned and unplanned turnover rates), and commitment (willingness to recommend the organization to prospective employees) for important job categories.

7 6 5 4 3 2 1

8. Total costs associated with the replacement of employees in selected job categories (including those of recruitment, training, the cost of damaged customer relationships, wage escalation, and the general impact on the effectiveness of the organization) are regularly estimated for important job categories.

7 6 5 4 3 2 1

9. My organization has estimated and communicated widely throughout its management ranks the bottom-line impact of a 1-percentage point increase in employee retention.

7 6 5 4 3 2 1

10. My firm endeavors to strengthen relationships along all three sides of the Bermuda Triangle linking the firm, its customers, and its customer-facing employees.

7 6 5 4 3 2 1

11. Estimates of employee value have directly influenced efforts to extend employee "life" on the job.

7 6 5 4 3 2 1

12. Shared values at the core of my organization's culture emphasize the importance of activities—listening to customers and employees, innovation, and continuous value creation, among others—that ensure productive change.

7 6 5 4 3 2 1

13. Carefully selected organizationwide "umbrella" initiatives, such as customer relationship management or continuous quality improvement (versus the "program of the month"), effectively encourage continuous change.

7 6 5 4 3 2 1

14. Through such methods as leadership by example and the core values of the organization, complacency and arrogance, especially toward customers, are avoided while pride in the organization and its activities is maintained.

7 6 5 4 3 2 1

C. Engineering Value Profit Change

1. Before launching performance-enhancing initiatives, my organization regularly ensures that the right leaders are in place.

7 6 5 4 3 2 1   7 6 5 4 3 2 1

2. My organization has been successful in creating dissatisfaction with the status quo as a prelude to major change.

7 6 5 4 3 2 1   7 6 5 4 3 2 1

3. Our leadership has a clear vision and sense of direction for the management of change in our organization.

7 6 5 4 3 2 1   7 6 5 4 3 2 1

4. Important "umbrella" initiatives periodically provide the high-quality "processes" important for useful change.

7 6 5 4 3 2 1   7 6 5 4 3 2 1

5. "Soft" elements of the performance trinity—adherence to values, support for the culture, and provision of effective leadership and management—are regularly taken into consideration in appraising performance and rewarding managers in my organization.

7 6 5 4 3 2 1   7 6 5 4 3 2 1

6. Managers unable to manage by the values, regardless of their ability to make their numbers, regularly are dismissed *in a timely manner* in my organization.

7 6 5 4 3 2 1   7 6 5 4 3 2 1

7. Members of my organization are compensated on the basis of a "balanced paycheck," reflecting performance on some or all dimensions of the value profit chain.

7 6 5 4 3 2 1   7 6 5 4 3 2 1

8. My organization has a database (or "warehouse") that enables marketing managers to fashion "value exchanges" that appeal to individual customers and are profitable to the organization.

7 6 5 4 3 2 1   7 6 5 4 3 2 1

9. "Value exchange" is a concept that is also applied to relationships with individual employees in my organization.

7 6 5 4 3 2 1   7 6 5 4 3 2 1

10. Responses to customer and/or employee complaints reflect important value exchange knowledge and the calculation of value in my organization.

7 6 5 4 3 2 1   7 6 5 4 3 2 1

11. My organization regularly engages in the following initiatives designed to encourage "transparency" and the exchange of knowledge:

a. External benchmarking against practices among world-class practitioners   7 6 5 4 3 2 1

b. Internal "best practice" comparisons   7 6 5 4 3 2 1

c. Performance comparisons designed to encourage the exchange of ideas   7 6 5 4 3 2 1

12. For the most part, my organization has been prepared to deal openly with intelligent questions raised by increasingly knowledgeable employees that come with greater "transparency."   7 6 5 4 3 2 1

13. An effort is made to identify and communicate "deep indicators" that provide clear connections between the organization's strategy and each individual's performance.   7 6 5 4 3 2 1

14. My organization's management regularly selects initiatives that will yield the greatest improvement in "deep indicators"; in short, the right initiatives are selected for the right reasons.   7 6 5 4 3 2 1

15. By and large, new initiatives for change implemented by my organization build logically on others that have been launched, whether or not they are still underway.

7 6 5 4 3 2 1

16. In the vast majority of important initiatives launched by my organization,

a. Sufficient investment has been made at the outset of the initiative by management to educate everyone about what to expect and gear up for the initiative itself.

7 6 5 4 3 2 1

b. Management has had a high enough level of commitment to ensure focus and follow-through and the persistence needed for success.

7 6 5 4 3 2 1

c. Middle management has been involved from the beginning of the initiative.

7 6 5 4 3 2 1

d. Realistic interim expectations and goals have been set for the initiative.

7 6 5 4 3 2 1

e. Both the goals and the methods by which they will be reached have been communicated clearly to all levels of the organization.

7 6 5 4 3 2 1

D. Treating Employees Like Customers

1. My organization facilitates the "self-selection" process by communicating clearly focused values to both current and potential employees.

7 6 5 4 3 2 1   7 6 5 4 3 2 1

2. As many as 20% of our new employees are recommended by existing (committed) employees.

7 6 5 4 3 2 1   7 6 5 4 3 2 1

3. Employee needs are regularly assessed in my organization.

7 6 5 4 3 2 1   7 6 5 4 3 2 1

4. Whether or not it has resulted from an assessment of employee needs, my organization:

a. Takes special steps to emphasize among managers the importance of hiring, recognizing, promoting, and dismissing the right employees.

7 6 5 4 3 2 1   7 6 5 4 3 2 1

b. Regularly rewards those managers who are most effective in recognizing the accomplishments of those who report to them.

7 6 5 4 3 2 1   7 6 5 4 3 2 1

c. Has established a substantial employee development program offering both job-related and non–job-related training.

7 6 5 4 3 2 1   7 6 5 4 3 2 1

d. Has increased the latitude among customer-facing employees to deliver results for valued customers.

7 6 5 4 3 2 1   7 6 5 4 3 2 1

e. Makes every effort to ensure that "winners" are working with "winners."

7 6 5 4 3 2 1   7 6 5 4 3 2 1

f. Has, over the past few years, created fewer, higher paying, more important jobs for its employees.

7 6 5 4 3 2 1   7 6 5 4 3 2 1

5. My organization hires and promotes with a disproportionately large amount of "A player" input.

7 6 5 4 3 2 1   7 6 5 4 3 2 1

6. My organization measures and rewards well the delivery of results to important constituencies.

7 6 5 4 3 2 1   7 6 5 4 3 2 1

7. Every effort is made to reduce unplanned management defections.

7 6 5 4 3 2 1   7 6 5 4 3 2 1

8. When it has been necessary, we have been able to move fast in reengineering the organization, generally resulting in fewer reporting relationships and bigger jobs.

7 6 5 4 3 2 1   7 6 5 4 3 2 1

9. The organization dismisses unneeded or unwanted employees in ways that produce useful feedback and encourage the continued loyalty of both those leaving and those staying.

7 6 5 4 3 2 1   7 6 5 4 3 2 1

E. Treating Customers as Employees

1. My organization has explicit criteria for selecting customers.

7 6 5 4 3 2 1

2. On the basis of established criteria, my organization regularly rejects customers not fitting the targeted profile.

7 6 5 4 3 2 1

3. We regularly observe customers employing products or services produced by my organization to ensure that they have the knowledge necessary for proper use.

7 6 5 4 3 2 1

4. As a result of regular assessment, customers are provided the training and support needed to properly use the products and services produced by my organization.

7 6 5 4 3 2 1

5. Customers have easy access to the customer training and support provided by my organization.

7 6 5 4 3 2 1

6. Valued customers are regularly recognized and rewarded and made to feel that they are valued members of a "club" or "community."

7 6 5 4 3 2 1

7. My organization has procedures in place for disengaging from unproductive or even destructive customer relationships.

7 6 5 4 3 2 1

8. Customer-facing employees have a voice in decisions about whether to disengage from undesirable customers.

7 6 5 4 3 2 1

F. Cementing the Gains

1. The core values of the organization are revisited and reaffirmed and their importance reaffirmed from time to time.

7 6 5 4 3 2 1

2. Core values are regularly taken into consideration when strategic decisions are made.

7 6 5 4 3 2 1

3. In reappraising the core values of the organization, an effort is made to keep in mind the importance of the following:

a. Encouraging efforts to remain sensitive to the search for value (as defined by needs) on the part of employees, customers, investors, and other important constituencies.

7 6 5 4 3 2 1

b. Ensuring that the organization will remain at-tuned to the changing demands of a constantly changing competitive environment.

7 6 5 4 3 2 1

7 6 5 4 3 2 1

c. Suggesting the kinds of behaviors expected of all members of the organization, regardless of business unit affiliation.

7 6 5 4 3 2 1

7 6 5 4 3 2 1

d. Providing an umbrella within which desired individual business unit customs and mores may flourish.

7 6 5 4 3 2 1

7 6 5 4 3 2 1

4. Core values are regularly reflected in performance appraisal processes as well as decisions about personal development plans, compensation, and promotion.

7 6 5 4 3 2 1

5. Measures and rewards used in my organization encourage the creation of value for all important constituencies.

7 6 5 4 3 2 1

7 6 5 4 3 2 1

6. Some measures employed are prospective in nature, reflective of influences on future performance.

7 6 5 4 3 2 1

7 6 5 4 3 2 1

7. Measures used are sufficiently clear and understandable that they are regularly used to influence major decisions.

7 6 5 4 3 2 1

7 6 5 4 3 2 1

8. For those measures linked directly to performance review in my organization:

a. The quantitative measures are sufficiently succinct, clear, intuitively logical, and understandable to be credible to those being measured.

7 6 5 4 3 2 1

b. Substantial management judgment complements quantitative measures in appraising managers' abilities to manage by the organization's core values.

7 6 5 4 3 2 1

9. Recognition and rewards in my organization:

a. Reinforce management behaviors that reflect the shared values of the organization.

7 6 5 4 3 2 1

c. Adequately involve managers in sharing the upside rewards and downside risks inherent in a decision.

7 6 5 4 3 2 1

10. My organization has taken advantage of many opportunities to "hardwire" its performance to that of its customers. It has done this by

a. Redefining the business to deliver solutions (versus products or services) to customers.

7 6 5 4 3 2 1

b. Making it easy for customers to provide feedback for use in results-oriented product or service improvement.

7 6 5 4 3 2 1

c. Directly linking employee, customer, and supplier performance to rewards.   7 6 5 4 3 2 1   7 6 5 4 3 2 1

d. Creating a sense of "ownership" among customers and employees.   7 6 5 4 3 2 1   7 6 5 4 3 2 1

11. My organization is performing well enough to put its efforts "at risk" through a hardwiring initiative.   7 6 5 4 3 2 1   7 6 5 4 3 2 1

12. The highly sensitive listening and responding mechanisms demanded by a hardwiring partnership are in place.   7 6 5 4 3 2 1   7 6 5 4 3 2 1

13. My organization's management is willing to change such factors as organization, performance measurements, and reward structures if that's what is needed to support an important hardwiring initiative.   7 6 5 4 3 2 1   7 6 5 4 3 2 1

14. Leaders are selected in my organization on the basis of:

a. Their willingness and ability to teach and learn.   7 6 5 4 3 2 1   7 6 5 4 3 2 1

b. The degree to which they credit the work of others and obtain satisfaction from the development and success of others.   7 6 5 4 3 2 1   7 6 5 4 3 2 1

15. My organization has someone who naturally plays the role of chief knowledge officer, whether any official designation is given to the role or not.

7 6 5 4 3 2 1

16. My organization's "explicit" (easily communicated) data is structured in such a way that individuals can extract and manipulate it in ways that provide answers to questions about customer, supplier, and employee behavior.

7 6 5 4 3 2 1

17. Members of the organization are regularly recognized for "buying, begging, or borrowing" knowledge and sharing it with one another.

7 6 5 4 3 2 1

18. Adequate incentives are in place to encourage the development and sharing of knowledge among members of the organization.

7 6 5 4 3 2 1

For tabulating purposes only, please provide your name and department/division/ business affiliation:

Name: _____

Department/division/business affiliation: _____

Methods of Estimating Customer Lifetime Value

IN ESTIMATING CUSTOMER lifetime value, the first question to be addressed is the purpose of the estimate. Efforts can be made to carefully estimate lifetime value on a periodic basis for the purposes of (1) allocating marketing effort, (2) assessing the impact of new product development and introduction, and (3) designing marketing efforts that reflect the "life cycle" of a customer of, for example, financial products. One of the more important uses of customer lifetime value concepts is in convincing top management of the importance of efforts to retain and develop existing customers as well as attract new ones. This requires a much less accurate and often a one-time measurement of the type described here. Regardless of the purpose, the assumptions used in and information required by the calculations are the same.

A second set of questions deals with the nature of the product or service for which customer lifetime value is being estimated. Products or services with high perceived purchase risk resulting from personal, economic, or social importance—such as medical services, an automobile, or living room furniture, respectively—are more likely to be purchased to a greater extent on the recommendations of others whom we have characterized as viral loyalists or apostle/owners. They may actually encourage more viral activity on the part of satisfied or dissatisfied customers. Products or services for which there is little or no competition will, for example, count among their customers a larger number of customers we have called hostages. Some portion of them may be dissatisfied with their plight. In general, this set of questions is addressed through the assumptions that one makes in estimating lifetime value.

Lifetime value can be estimated for an individual customer or a portfolio of customers. Both approaches are demonstrated here.

The calculation requires estimates (based on either evidence or assumptions) of various kinds. These include: (1) the type of customer being profiled—antagonist (highly dissatisfied with tendencies to share the dissatisfaction with other current and potential customers), hostage (dissatisfied, but with no other alternatives, somewhat inclined to share dissatisfaction with others), mercenary (someone who purchases a portion of total needs from a single source, usually motivated by low price), loyalist (a highly satisfied customer purchasing all or most products or services from a single source, with much less price sensitivity than the mercenary), viral loyalist (a highly satisfied customer with characteristics similar to the loyalist, but with a greater tendency to share the satisfaction with others), or apostle/owner (a viral loyalist who has credibility sufficiently high to convince others of the desirability of switching to the product or service), as described in Chapter 3, (2) the length of the life of the customer, (3) the acquisition cost of the customer, (4) the pattern of purchase of a portfolio of products or services over time, recognizing the fact that loyalists, viral loyalists, and apostles/owners tend to increase their purchases of standard and new products over time, (5) the margin associated with the pattern of purchases, including recognition of both the fact that loyal customers tend to be less price sensitive and less costly to serve, resulting in higher margins on sales over time, (6) successful referrals of new customers by viral loyalists and apostles, (7) the type of customer gained through such referrals, and (8) the discount rate to be associated with cash flows resulting from a customer relationship.

The following example of Acme Home Products illustrates these ideas. It is a fictional case based on a composite of data obtained from actual research.

Results of the exercise of estimating lifetime value of two customers—one a mercenary and one an apostle/owner—at Acme Home Products are shown in Figure C-1. They are based on the following assumptions:

1. A customer life of 5 years for the mercenary and 10 years for the apostle/owner.

2. A level of purchases for the apostle that is six times that of the mercenary in year one and increases at the rate of 10% per year. That of the mercenary remains constant at the year 1 level over the entire 5-year period.

■ **Figure C-1** Estimated Lifetime Value, Expressed in Margins Realized on Sales, for Two Acme Home Products Customers[a]

Year	Mercenary (In Units of "x")	Apostle/Owner, Without referrals (In Units of "x")	Apostle/Owner, With Referrals (In Units of "x")
0[b]	(.25x)	(.25x)	(.25x)
1	.25x	1.80x	1.80x
2	.25	2.11	4.41
3	.25	2.47	7.28
4	.25	2.87	10.75
5	.25	3.34	14.59
6	—	3.82	16.61
7	—	4.21	18.31
8	—	4.63	19.87
9	—	5.09	21.59
10	—	5.60	23.37
11[c]	—	—	19.53
12[c]	—	—	15.32
13[c]	—	—	10.69
14[c]	—	—	5.60
	1.00x	35.69x	189.47x
Present value of Total[d]	.74x	22.32x	102.62x

[a]Based on assumption regarding buying behavior described in the text to this appendix.
[b]Representing customer acquisition costs.
[c]Residual value of customers attracted by the apostle/owner in years 2 though 5.
[d]Assuming an 8% annual discount rate.

3. A margin on sales to the apostle in year 1 of 30%, increasing by two percentage points per year in succeeding years. A margin on sales to the mercenary of 25%, remaining constant over a 5-year period. (This pattern is based on the assumptions that mercenaries are highly price-sensitive and purchase low-margin products and services from several suppliers, remaining relatively expensive for any one supplier to serve, while less price-sensitive apos-

tle/owners buy high-margin as well as low-margin products and services, concentrate their purchases, and thereby become less expensive to serve, as reflected in growing margins from the relationship.)

4. A customer acquisition cost equal to 25% of the first year's revenue from mercenary (or .25x).

5. No revenue or margin from referrals by the mercenary. A pattern of referrals by the apostle/owner that results in three new customers per year between years two and five, two of whom become mercenaries and one of whom becomes an apostle/owner.

6. A discount rate for the time value of cash flows associated with acquisition costs and margins on sales of 8%.

Indexing the estimates for both the mercenary and the apostle/owner, we begin with a first-year sales estimate of 1x for the mercenary and 6x for the apostle. The acquisition cost of each is estimated to be 0.25x. Sales and margin flows associated with the basic purchases of both the mercenary and apostle, given the assumptions listed above, are shown in Figure C-1. When the cash flows associated with referrals are factored in, as shown in Figure C-1, the value of the apostle in relation to the mercenary is enhanced further. Adjusting the acquisition costs and flows of margin from both of these customers by the 8% discount rate produces a total value for the apostle/owner that is 102.62x, or nearly 139 times that of a mercenary, as shown in Figure C-1. This suggests that (1) mercenaries carry little value to Acme, and (2) significant amounts of money can be invested by Acme's management in efforts either to identify potential apostle/owners among the organization's mercenaries and convert them or to recruit new apostle/owners to the customer base.

Similar efforts can be made to profile an entire customer base. It begins with the identification of the proportion of total customers falling into each of the categories of antagonists, hostage, mercenaries, loyalists, viral loyalists, and apostle/owners, as shown in Figure C-2. Assumptions similar to those used above have to be estimated for each category of customer, depending on the nature of the business and what is known about

■ **Figure C-2** Estimated Lifetime Value, Expressed in Margins Realized on Sales, for a "Portfolio" of One Hundred Acme Home Products Customers[a]

Category of Customer	Lifetime Value (In Units of "x")[b]	Number in "Portfolio"	Total Lifetime Value, for Category (In Units of "x")[b]
Apostle/Owner	102.62x	3	307.86x
Viral Loyalist	49.14	5	245.70
Loyalist	22.07	12	264.84
Mercenary	.74	72	53.28
Hostage	11.82	4	47.28
Antagonist	(45.18)	4	(180.72)
Total		100	653.40

[a]Based on assumptions rergarding buying behavior described in the text to this appendix.
[b]Discounted for present value at the rate of 8% per year.

customer behavior. For the purposes of the estimates for Acme Household Products, the following assumptions were used:

1. Acquisition costs for all categories of customers buying from Acme for the first time are the same. However, customers acquired through referrals by existing viral loyalists and apostle/owners have no acquisition costs.

2. Antagonists stop purchasing after the first year, during which their purchases yield a 30% margin. However, they continue to discourage others from purchasing Acme's products at the rate of two customers per year for three years after they discontinue purchasing themselves. The value lost to Acme through this phenomenon is represented by a weighted average of the lifetime value of all mercenaries, loyalists, viral loyalists, and apostle/owners.

3. Hostages continue to purchase product at a constant rate of six times that of a mercenary (6x) and a 30% margin over a 10-year period. They attract no new customers during their ten-year lifetime.

4. Mercenaries purchase products at a constant rate of "x" at a 25% margin to Acme over a period of 5 years.

5. Loyalists purchase initially at six times the rate of mercenaries (6x in the first year), increasing their purchases by 10% over a 10-year period, with margins on their purchases beginning at 30% and increasing at the rate of 2 percentage points per year in years two through five.

6. Viral loyalists exhibit the same characteristics as loyalists, but in addition they attract (through referral) one additional customer per year during years two through five of their 10-year life. This referred customer base is composed of two mercenaries for every loyalist.

7. Apostle/owners exhibit the purchasing, loyalty, viral, and persuasive characteristics described above over a period of ten years.

Application of these assumptions produces the lifetime value estimates for Acme Household Products' customer portfolio shown in Figure C-2 in this appendix and Figure 3-3 of the book. In addition to the extraordinary difference in value between apostle/owners and mercenaries noted earlier, it suggests some remarkable characteristics that are nevertheless not unusual in actual practice, among them the following:

1. Loyalists, viral loyalists, and apostle/owners, representing only 20% of the customer portfolio, nevertheless produce more than 100% of the margin on sales. Margins realized from mercenaries and even from some loyalists merely compensate for those lost through relationships with antagonists and hostages.

2. Significant amounts of money can be invested in identifying and attracting loyalists, in inducing loyalists to become more viral, and in developing apostle/owners by providing them with information that enables them to become more credible in their viral activities.

Preface

1. See "Gallup Path Economics," The Gallup Organization, 2001.

2. In order, these books were: James L. Heskett, *Managing in the Service Economy* (Boston: HBS Press, 1986); James L. Heskett, W. Earl Sasser, Jr., and Christopher W. L. Hart, *Service Breakthroughs: Changing the Rules of the Game* (New York: The Free Press, 1991); and John P. Kotter and James L. Heskett, *Corporate Culture and Performance* (New York: The Free Press, 1992).

3. See James L. Heskett, Thomas Jones, Gary Loveman, W. Earl Sasser, Jr., and Leonard A. Schlesinger, "Putting the Service Profit Chain to Work," *Harvard Business Review,* November–December, 1994, pp. 164–174, and James L. Heskett, W. Earl Sasser, Jr., and Leonard A. Schlesinger, *The Service Profit Chain* (New York: The Free Press, 1997).

4. James C. Collins and Jerry I. Porras, *Built to Last* (New York: HarperCollins, 1997), p. 44.

5. A study with similar objectives but somewhat different kinds of conclusions is described by Jim Collins in *Good to Great* (New York: HarperCollins, 2001).

Chapter 1

1. Material in this chapter concerning the Vanguard Group, in addition to personal conversations with John Bogle, is drawn from John C. Bogle, *Common Sense on Mutual Funds* (New York: John Wiley & Sons, 1999), Robert Slater, *John Bogle and the Vanguard Experiment* (Chicago: Richard D. Irwin, 1996), and Roger Hallowell, *Dual Competitive Advantage in Labor-Dependent Services* (Boston: Harvard Business School Doctoral Dissertation, 1997).

2. Presentation by John Bogle to a Harvard Business School class, December 7, 1999.

3. Material in this chapter concerning Wal-Mart is based on personal observations reported in James L. Heskett, *Confidential Memorandum,* Case No. N1-396-270 (Boston: HBS Publishing, 1996); Sam Walton with John Huey, *Made in America* (New York: Doubleday, 1992); Stephen P. Bradley and Pankaj Ghemawat, *Wal-Mart Stores, Inc.,* Case No. 9-794-024 (Boston: HBS Publishing, 1996); and Roger Hallowell, *Dual Competitive Advantage in Labor Dependent Services* (Boston: Harvard Business School Doctoral Dissertation, 1997).

4. Sam Walton with John Huey, *Sam Walton: Made in America* (New York: Doubleday, 1992), pp. 229–230.

5. *Ibid.,* p. 221.

6. John Bogle, *op. cit.* See also Richard Teitelbaum, "The Greatest Hits of the Index King," *The New York Times,* October 8, 2000, p. 24BU.

7. Roger Hallowell, *op. cit.*, p. 216.

8. Jay O. Light and James E. Sailer, *The Vanguard Group, Inc. (A)*, Case No. 9-293-064 (Boston: HBS Publishing, 1992), p. 13.

9. Michael Porter refers to these relationships as activity systems. See, for example, his article, "What Is Strategy," *Harvard Business Review,* November–December, 1996, pp. 61–78, especially pp. 71–73.

10. For the measures and their format, we are indebted to Roger Hallowell, who first presented this format in his doctoral dissertation, *Dual Competitive Advantage in Labor Dependent Services* (Boston: Harvard Business School, 1997). We have updated some of his data.

11. John C. Bogle, *Common Sense on Mutual Funds* (New York: John C. Wiley & Sons, 1999), p. 423.

12. *Ibid.,* p. 430.

13. "Rating the Stores," *Consumer Reports,* November 1994, pp. 4 and 8.

14. For example, see Douglas J. Tigert, Stephen J. Arnold, and Terry W. Cotter, *K-Mart, Target & Wal-Mart: The Battle Is Joined in the Big Cities*, Babson College Retailing Research Reports, Report No. 7, Vols. 1–3.

15. *BrandPulse* reports periodically prepared by Planet Feedback, an online customer-monitoring service.

16. Jay L. Johnson, "We're All Associates" and "How Wal-Mart's People Make a Difference," *Discount Merchandiser,* August, 1993, p. 62.

17. *Ibid.,* p. 50.

18. Sam Walton and John Huey, *op. cit.*, p. 21.

19. *Ibid.,* p. 129.

20. Michael L. Golstein and Lili Lynton, *The Future of the Money Management Industry* (New York: Sanford C. Bernstein & Co., 1991), p. 44.

Chapter 2

1. See, for example, Barnaby J. Feder, "Retrenchment, Not Retreat," *The New York Times,* January 24, 2001, pp. C1 and C6.

2. David Rocks, "IBM's Hottest Product Isn't a Product," *Business Week,* October 2, 2000, pp. 118 and 120.

3. Judith H. Dobrzynski, "Rethinking IBM," *Business Week,* October 4, 1993, p. 89.

4. Barnaby J. Feder, *op. cit.*, p. C6.

5. See, for example, Thomas J. Watson, Jr., *A Business and Its Beliefs: The Ideas That Helped Build IBM* (New York: McGraw-Hill, 1963). The three values, of

which the first was cited by Watson as most important, are (1) respect for the individual, (2) the best customer service of any company in the world, and (3) pursuit of all tasks with the idea that they can be accomplished in a superior fashion.

6. Barnaby J. Feder, "Independence in Computers Is I.B.M. Goal," *The New York Times,* April 27, 2001, pp. C1 and C4.

7. For a graph of historical trends in employment in various sectors, see, for example, James L. Heskett, *Managing in the Service Economy* (Boston: Harvard Business School Press, 1986), p. 180.

8. See, for example, Christopher Lovelock, *Product Plus: How Product + Service = Competitive Advantage* (New York: McGraw-Hill, 1994).

9. *2001 Annual Report,* Hewlett-Packard, p. 47.

10. Otis Elevator Company sales brochure, 2001.

11. http://www.ge.com/corporate/innovation/flash.html, July 25, 2001.

12. http://globalbb.onesource.com/SharedScripts/Functions/OTFR/MISC/QuickListOTFR.asp?SortVar=SAUSD, July 25, 2001.

13. For a more extensive discussion of this process, see Jack Welch, *Jack: Straight from the Gut* (New York: Warner Business Books, 2001), especially pp. 105–120.

14. Claudia H. Deutsch, "Five Questions for John F. Welch Jr.: Dominate Markets, but Cast a Wide Net," *The New York Times,* March 18, 2001, Section 3, p. 7.

15. Jack Welch, *op. cit.,* p. 201.

16. *Ibid.,* p. 202.

17. Robert Gavin and Greg Jaffe, "Boeing Revamp Cuts Ties to Seattle, Puts Focus on New Services," *The Wall Street Journal,* March 22, 2001, p. A1.

18. Henry Tricks, "High Tech Strengthens the Mix," *The Financial Times,* November 16, 2000, p. 19.

19. http://www.nyc.gov/html/nypd/pdf/chfdept/cslist.pdf, April 23, 2002. See also James L. Heskett, *"NYPD New,"* Case No. 9-396-293 (Boston: HBS Publishing, 1997).

Chapter 3

1. Carl Sewell and Paul B. Brown, *Customers for Life* (New York: Doubleday Currency, 1990).

2. Quoted from a presentation by Philip Bressler to a Harvard Business School class, November 1985.

3. For one of the best examples of this work, see Roland T. Rust, Valarie A. Zeithaml, and Katherine N. Lemon, *Driving Customer Equity: How Customer Lifetime Value Is Reshaping Corporate Strategy* (New York: The Free Press, 2000).

4. See, for example, David E. Bowen, "Managing Customers as Human Resources in Service Organizations," *Human Resource Management*, Fall 1986, pp. 371–383, and C. A. Lengnick-Hal, "Customer Contributions to Quality: A Different View of the Customer-Oriented Firm," *Academy of Management Review*, July 1996, pp. 791–824.

5. S. J. Grove and R. P. Fisk, "The Impact of Other Customers on Service Experiences: A Critical Incident Examination of 'Getting Along'," *Journal of Retailing*, Spring, 1997, pp. 63–85.

6. Dwayne D. Gremler and Stephen W. Brown, "The Loyalty Ripple Effect: Appreciating the Full Value of Customers," *International Journal of Service Industry Management*, Vol. 10, No. 3, 1999, pp. 271–291.

7. *Ibid.*, pp. 275–276.

8. *Ibid.*, pp. 282–284.

9. Frederick F. Reichheld and W. Earl Sasser, Jr., "Zero Defections: Quality Comes to Services," *Harvard Business Review*, September–October, 1990, pp. 1–8.

10. This information is excerpted from James L. Heskett, *PlanetFeedback: The Voice of One . . . The Power of Many (A)*, Case No. 9-901-051 (Boston: Harvard Business School Publishing, 2001). In 2001, the company merged with Intelliseek; Heskett is a director of the company.

11. Email communication with Tinesha Ross, Investor Relations/Media Relations, MBNA, July 31, 2001.

12. Activity-based costing requires the identification of all important activities required to make, market, sell, and deliver products or services. For example, in calculating relationship costs, relevant measures might include average order size, number of orders placed, and number and intensity of customer contacts, with an attendant cost assigned to each activity as it occurs. For a more extensive exploration of activity-based costing, see Robert S. Kaplan and Robin Cooper, *Cost & Effect: Using Integrated Cost Systems to Drive Profitability and Performance* (Boston: Harvard Business School Press, 1997).

13. Harvard Business School class presentation of Philip Bressler, *op. cit.*

14. John P. Morgridge and James L. Heskett, *Cisco Systems: Are You Ready? (A)*, Case No. 9-901-002 (Boston: HBS Publishing, 2000).

Chapter 4

1. Presentation by Andrew Fromm, The Service Management Group, March 23, 1999. The study involved tens of thousands of employees employed in thousands of stores operated by several major retail chains. Controllable profit growth for organizations with high employee satisfaction was 10.60% year after year. That for organizations with low employee satisfaction was 5.54%.

2. Melanie Trottman, "Amid Crippled Rivals, Southwest Again Tries to Spread Its Wings," *The Wall Street Journal,* October 11, 2001, pp. A1 and A10.

3. Correspondence from Cliff Ehrlich, Senior Vice President of Human Relations, Marriott Corporation, November 15, 1989.

4. Presentation by Andrew Fromm, The Service Management Group, *op. cit.*

5. Frederick F. Reichheld, *The Loyalty Effect* (Boston: HBS Press, 1996), pp. 98 and 105.

6. Robert Levering & Milton Moskowitz, "The 100 Best Companies to Work For," *Fortune,* February 14, 2002, p. 72.

7. Devon Spurgeon, "Fast-Food Industry Pitches 'Burger-Flipping' as Career," *The Wall Street Journal,* May 29, 2001, pp. B1 and B16.

8. Robert S. Kaplan and David P. Norton, *The Strategy-Focused Organization* (Boston: Harvard Business School Press, 2001), p. 212. The term is also used to express an organization's commitment to its employees. See, for example, Dave Ulrich and Dale Lake, *Organizational Capability* (New York: John Wiley & Sons, 1990), pp. 107–108.

9. Presentation of Andrew Fromm, The Service Management Group, *op. cit.*

Chapter 5

1. This account relies heavily on Almar Latour, "A Blaze in Albuquerque Sets off Major Crisis for Cell-Phone Giants," *The Wall Street Journal,* January 29, 2001, pp. A1 and A8.

2. *Ibid.,* p. A1.

3. *Ibid.,* p. A1.

4. *Ibid.,* p. A8.

5. *Ibid.*

6. John P. Kotter and James L. Heskett, *Corporate Culture and Performance* (New York: The Free Press, 1992).

7. Much of the following information about Texaco is based on interviews with James Kinnear, at the time Texaco's CEO, by James Heskett in October 1990 as reported in Roger Hallowell and James L. Heskett, "Texaco, Inc.," Case No. 9-392-076 (Boston: HBS Publishing, 1992).

8. *Ibid.,* pp. 2–3.

9. From interviews conducted as part of their research by John P. Kotter and James L. Heskett as inputs to their book, *Corporate Culture and Performance,* op. cit.

10. Roger Hallowell and James L. Heskett, op. cit. p. 16.

11. David Altany, "Share and Share Alike," *Industry Week,* 240 (1991), p. 12.

12. Faith Keenan, "The Marines Learn New Tactics—From Wal-Mart," *Business Week,* December 24, 2001, p. 74.

13. See, for example, Robert C. Camp, *Benchmarking: The Search for Industry Best Practices That Lead to Superior Performance* (ASQC Quality Press: Milwaukee, 1989); Ken Stork and James P. Morgan, *Benchmarking: In Theory and Practice* (Boston: Cahners Business Information, 1999); and Robert C. Camp (ed.), *Global Cases in Benchmarking: Best Practices from Organizations Around the World* (Milwaukee: ASQC Quality Press, 1998).

14. *Ibid.*

15. "MCI-Gallup Survey Reveals Technology and Responsiveness as Keys to Competition," *PR Newswire*, May 16, 1997.

16. Reported in Geoffrey Colvin, "Earnings Aren't Everything," *Fortune*, September 17, 2001, pp. 58–59.

17. James C. Collins and Jerry I. Porras, *Built to Last: Successful Habits of Visionary Companies* (New York: Harper Business, 1994).

18. James L. Heskett, W. Earl Sasser, Jr., and Leonard A. Schlesinger, *The Service Profit Chain* (New York: The Free Press, 1997).

Part III Introduction

1. Adapted from an equation that first appeared in Michael Beer, *Organization Change and Development: A Systems View* (Santa Monica, CA: Goodyear Publishing, 1980).

2. Claudia H. Deutsch, "Healing From Executive Trauma," *The New York Times*, March 18, 2001, Section 3, p. 2.

Chapter 6

1. Quote verified by David Glass, April 10, 2002.

2. Michael Porter, *Competitive Strategy: Techniques for Analyzing Industries and Competitors* (New York: The Free Press, 1980). In Porter's later writings, he has recognized the importance of other elements of the "performance trinity." See, for example, "What is Strategy," *Harvard Business Review*, November–December, 1996, pp. 61–78.

3. Edgar Schein, *Organization Culture and Leadership* (San Francisco: Jossey-Bass, 1985).

4. John P. Kotter and James L. Heskett, *Corporate Culture and Performance* (New York: The Free Press, 1992).

5. "New Math for a New Economy," *Fast Company*, December 14, 1999.

6. See, for example, Jack Welch, *Jack: Straight from the Gut* (New York: Warner Business Books, 2001), especially pp. 105–108.

7. James L. Heskett, W. Earl Sasser, Jr., and Christopher W. L. Hart, *Service Breakthroughs: Changing the Rules of the Game* (New York: The Free Press, 1991).

8. Jim Collins, *Good to Great* (New York: HarperCollins, 2001), p. 13.

9. Andrea Jung, private interview, November 2001.

10. Much of this section is based on Dan Maher, Dan O'Brien, Jeffrey Rayport, and Tom Watson, "What You Need, What You Need to Know." (A): Office Depot, Inc., Case No. OU-081A (New York: Omnicom University and the Omnicom Group Inc., 2002), as well as personal interviews at the company. James Heskett is a director of and an investor in the company.

11. For a description of this effort, see Anthony Rucci, Steven P. Kirn, and Richard T. Quinn, "The Employee-Customer-Profit Chain at Sears," *Harvard Business Review,* January–February 1998, pp. 83–97.

12. For a description of this process, see Robert H. Miles, *Leading Corporate Transformation* (San Francisco: Jossey-Bass, 1997).

13. For an analysis of the Sears experience, see Richard T. Pascale, Mark Millemann, and Linda Gioja, *Surfing the Edge of Chaos* (New York: Crown Business, 2000), especially p. 57.

14. For a discussion of how GE faces this challenge, see Jack Welch, *Jack: Straight from the Gut* (New York: Warner Business Books, 2001), especially pp. 158–162.

15. For an extended discussion of these ideas, see Leonard A. Schlesinger and James L. Heskett, "The Service-Driven Service Company," *Harvard Business Review,* September–October 1991, pp. 1–20.

16. Miguel Ochoa and James Heskett, *CEMEX: The CEMEX Way*, in preparation.

17. See James L. Heskett, *NYPD New*, Case No. 9-396-293 (Boston: HBS Publishing, 1999).

18. Leonard A. Schlesinger and James L. Heskett, *op. cit.*

19. See, for example, Marcus Buckingham and Curt Coffman, *First, Break All the Rules* (New York: Simon & Schuster, 1999), pp. 110 and 132.

20. This practice is described in "The Lifetime Value of Customers," *Service Profit Success* (Boston: Harvard Business School Productions, 1994).

21. Leonard A. Schlesinger and James L. Heskett, *op. cit.* See p. 9 for a hypothetical example illustrating this.

22. The data in this paragraph was supplied on April 12, 2002, by Robert Nelson, VP Financial Planning and Analysis of General Electric. Data for GE Capital, because of the distinctly different nature of this business from all others at GE, has been excluded from computations in this paragraph.

23. For an eloquent explanation of this strategy, see the 1995 General Electric Annual Report.

24. Christopher Bartlett, ed., *General Electric Company 1981–1999*, Videotape No. 1107 (Boston: Harvard Business School, 1999).

25. Based on data from *Compustat,* analyzed by our research associate, Laura Coleman.

26. James C. Collins and Jerry I. Porras, *Built to Last* (New York: Harper-Collins, 1997), p. 44.

27. *Ibid.*

Chapter 7

1. Hal F. Rosenbluth and Diane McFerrin Peters, *The Customer Comes Second* (New York: Morrow Quill, 1992).

2. Hoovers Online. Other references to Cisco Systems in this chapter are based on John P. Morgridge and James L. Heskett, *Cisco Systems: Are You Ready? (A)*, Case No. 9-901-002, (Boston: HBS Publishing, 2000).

3. Michael Lewis, "O'Neill's List," *The New York Times Magazine*, January 13, 2002, p. 24.

4. Information about this organization is based on Leonard A. Schlesinger and James Mellado, *Willow Creek Community Church (A)*, Case No. 9-691-102 (Boston: HBS Publishing, 1991).

5. In the most recent nationwide study, Cisco ranked 15 among all employers in 2001, according to "The Best Companies to Work for in America," *Fortune*, January 4, 2002, pp. 72–90.

6. Scott Thurm, "Under Cisco's System, Mergers Usually Work; That Defies the Odds," *The Wall Street Journal*, March 1, 2000, at p. A1.

7. See, for example, John A. Byrne and Ben Elgin, "Cisco Behind the Hype," *Business Week*, January 21, 2002, pp. 54–60.

8. For more information about the CEC, see Philip Anderson, Vijay Govindarajan, Chris Trimble, and Katrina Veerman, *Cisco Systems (A), Evolution to E-Business* (Hanover, NH: Center for Global Leadership, Dartmouth College, 2001).

9. Michael Lewis, *op. cit.*, p. 24.

10. Based on data obtained from *Yahoo! Finance*, February 2002.

11. Leonard A. Schlesinger and James Mellado, *op. cit.*

12. For a description of this effort, initiated by Leonard Schlesinger, see W. Earl Sasser, Jr., and Lucy Lytle, *Au Bon Pain Partner/Manager Program*, Case No. 9-687-063 (Boston: HBS Publishing, 1987).

13. Some of the information in this story is drawn from James L. Heskett and Kenneth Ray, *Fairfield Inn (A)*, Case No. 9-689-092 (Boston: HBS Publishing, 1989), In 1990, Marriott began franchising the Fairfield Inn concept for the first time. The operating strategy described here did not necessarily apply to franchised as opposed to company-owned units.

14. For a discussion of disruptive technologies and how to combat them, see Clayton M. Christensen, *The Innovator's Dilemma* (Boston: HBS Press, 1997).

15. For a more detailed description of the use of "life themes" in the hiring

process, see Leonard A. Schlesinger, "How to Hire by Wire," *Fast Company,* November, 1993, pp. 86–91.

16. See, for example, Paul C. Weiler, Howard W. Hiatt, Joseph P. Newhouse, William G. Johnson, Toryen A. Brennan, and Lucien L. Leape, *A Measure of Malpractice* (Cambridge, MA: Harvard University Press, 1993).

17. This study, reported in detail in Marcus Buckingham and Curt Coffman, *First, Break All the Rules* (New York: Simon & Schuster, 1999), was based on in-depth interviews with over 80,000 managers in more than 400 companies.

18. *Ibid.*

19. Jack Welch, *Jack: Straight from the Gut* (New York: Warner Business Books, 2001), pp. 188–189.

20. *Ibid.,* p. 57.

21. *Ibid.,* p. 388.

22. William M. Carley, "Looking Ahead: CEO's Heart Surgery Is Giving GE a Case of Succession Jitters," *The Wall Street Journal,* May 24, 1995, p. A1.

23. Information about the company is drawn from Miguel Ochoa and James L. Heskett, *CEMEX: The CEMEX Way,* in preparation.

24. David H. Maister, *Practice What You Preach: What Managers Must Do to Create a High Achievement Culture* (New York: The Free Press, 2001). This study examined feedback from more than 5500 respondents from 139 offices operated by 29 separate firms owned by the same publicly held marketing communications company.

25. For a more extensive discussion of these findings, based on data from nearly 1300 employees and more than 4000 customers of a personal lines insurance company, see Leonard A. Schlesinger and Jeffrey Zornitsky, "Job Satisfaction, Service Capability, and Customer Satisfaction: An Examination of Linkages and Management Implications," *Human Resource Planning,* Vol. 14, No. 2, pp. 141–149.

26. Mike McNamee, "Credit Card Revolutionary," *Stanford Business,* May, 2001, p. 23.

27. Tom Watson, Dan Maher, and Dan O'Brien, *Nailing Jelly to the Ceiling: Developing The Most Interesting Workplace in Town,* Case No. GM-021 (New York: Omnicom University, 2000).

28. Maister, *op. cit.,* p. 19.

29. *Cisco Systems: Are You Ready? (A), op. cit.,* p. 10.

30. James L. Heskett, *ServiceMaster Industries, Inc.,* Case No. 9-388-064 (Boston: HBS Publishing, 1987), p. 6.

31. Marcus Buckingham and Curt Coffman, *First, Break All the Rules* (New York: Simon & Schuster, 1999).

32. Email communication with Jamie Priestley, December 2001.

Chapter 8

1. See, for example, Seth Godin, *Permission Marketing: Turning Strangers into Friends, and Friends into Customers* (New York: Simon & Schuster, 1999).

2. Email communication with Mark Doherty, Head of Advisor Practice Development, ING-USFS Marketing, April 26, 2002.

3. Much of this section is based on Keith H. Hammonds, "Pay As You Go," *Fast Company*, November, 2001, pp. 44–46.

4. See, for example, Regis McKenna, *Relationship Marketing* (Reading, MA: Addison-Wesley, 1991).

5. This work was first reported widely in A. Parasuraman, Valarie A. Zeithaml, and Leonard Berry, "SERVQUAL: A Multiple-Item Scale for Measuring Consumer Perceptions of Service Quality," *Journal of Retailing*, Spring, 1988, pp. 12–40.

6. A discussion of the results of this work can be found in Marcus Buckingham and Curt Coffman, *First, Break All the Rules* (New York: Simon & Schuster, 2000), especially pp. 128–132.

7. For products and services representing low levels of financial, psychological, or physical risk or payoff, brands provide much of the assurance needed to foster loyalty, underscoring the importance of advertising and image for products and services with roughly similar and adequate levels of performance and quality. Important as they are, they are not the focus of our concern here.

8. Everett Rogers, *The Diffusion of Innovations* (New York: The Free Press, 1962), p. 264.

9. Tom Watson, Dan Maher, and Dan O'Brien, *Merkley Newman Harty*, Case No. GM-012 (New York: Omnicom University, 2000), p. 1.

10. *Ibid.*, p. 2.

11. See, for example, Valarie A. Zeithaml, A. Parasuraman, and Leonard L. Berry, *Delivering Quality Service: Balancing Customer Perceptions and Expectations* (New York: The Free Press, 1990).

12. Roger Hallowell and James L. Heskett, *Southwest Airlines 1993*, Case No. 9-394-126 (Boston: HBS Publishing, 1993).

13. Email communication with Peter Blackshaw, co-founder of PlanetFeedback, March 4, 2002.

14. Videotaped interview with Herbert D. Kelleher, *"Service Profit Chain"* Tape #1942 (Boston: Harvard Business School Productions, 1994).

15. Address by Jack Welch to the graduating class of the Harvard Business School, June 2001.

16. Email correspondence from Arkadi Kuhlmann, president and CEO of INGDirect, April 16, 2002.

17. Email from Jamie Priestley, December 2001.

18. John P. Morgridge and James L. Heskett, *Cisco Systems: Are You Ready? (A)*, Case No. 9-901-002 (Boston: HBS Publishing, 2000), p. 11.

19. Email, Jamie Priestley, December 2001.

Chapter 9

1. Alan W. H. Grant and Leonard A. Schlesinger, "Realizing Your Customers' Full Profit Potential," *Harvard Business Review,* September–October, 1995, pp. 59–72.

2. Much of the information in this section is based on James L. Heskett, *Progressive Corporation Transportation Group (A),* Case No. 9-693-033 (Boston: HBS Publishing, 1995).

3. Among other sources for this section, we relied on Bharat Anand, Michael G. Rukstad, and Christopher H. Paige, *Capital One Financial Corporation,* Case No. 9-700-124 (Boston: HBS Publishing, 2000).

4. James Surowiecki, "The Credit-Card Kings," *The New Yorker,* November 27, 2000, p. 74.

5. Mike McNamee, "Credit Card Revolutionary," *Stanford Business,* May 2001, p. 17.

6. *Ibid.*

7. This is quite typical of ways in which so-called "disruptive technologies" that change the face of entire industries are introduced. This process is described in Clayton M. Christensen, *The Innovator's Dilemma* (Boston: HBS Press, 1997).

8. Bharat Anand, Michael G. Rukstad, and Christopher H. Paige, *op. cit.,* p. 10.

9. The Capital One approach to customer retention, which relies heavily on tech-formulated responses delivered by customer service agents with limited latitude to customize responses, contrasts with that of competitor MBNA, which relies on greater latitude for customer service representatives, who must interpret customer profiles provided by the company's online information system.

10. Much of this information was obtained from Mike McNamee, *op. cit.,* p. 23.

11. Capital One 2000 Annual Report, p. 22.

12. *Ibid.,* pp. 1 and 25.

13. News release by SAS Institute, Inc., 2001.

14. Emery P. Dalesio, "Quiet Southern Software Giant Is Ready to Shout Technology," *Los Angeles Times,* May 9, 2001.

15. Charles Fishman, "Making IT with the Golden Rule," *Fast Company,* February 15, 1999.

16. Leslie Gross Klaff, "Companies Make Magazine's Family-Friendly List," *Charlotte Observer,* September 6, 2000.

17. For a description of the kind of customer backlash resulting from the application of customer profiling techniques, see Diane Brady, "Why Service Stinks," *Business Week,* October 23, 2000, pp. 118–128.

18. This section is based on Bharat Anand, Michael G. Rukstad, and Christopher H. Paige, *op. cit.*, pp. 12–13.

19. *Ibid.*, p. 13.

Chapter 10

1. Southwest's name has appeared at or near the top of the list in every year through 2000. Since then, Southwest's management has chosen not to compete in the judging.

2. Richard T. Pascale, Mark Millemann, and Linda Gioja, *Surfing on the Edge of Chaos* (New York: Crown Business, 2000), p. 234.

3. Michael E. Porter, "What is Strategy?" *Harvard Business Review,* November–December, 1966, p. 71.

4. Jim Collins, *Good to Great* (New York: HarperBusiness, 2001), pp. 104–108.

5. Unfortunately, potential changes in performance suggested by these indicators were not fully realized at Sears because top management, according to several accounts (including Pasquale *et al., ibid.*, p. 235), failed to convince middle managers of their importance, became distracted by other needs of the business, and did not implement performance measures and rewards necessary to sustain initial performance improvements.

6. This and other observations can be found in Pascale *et al., op. cit.*, pp. 232–235.

7. For a more extensive description of this effort, see Anthony Rucci, Steven P. Kirn, and Richard T. Quinn, "The Employee-Customer-Profit Chain at Sears," *Harvard Business Review,* January–February 1998, especially pp. 94–95.

8. Roland Rust, Anthony Zahorik, and Timothy Keiningham, "Return on Quality (ROQ): Making Service Quality Financially Accountable," *Journal of Marketing*, April, 1995, pp. 58–70.

9. W. Earl Sasser, Jr., and Norman Klein, British Airways: Using Information Systems to Better Service the Customer, Case No. 395-065 (Boston: HBS Publishing, 1994), p. 13.

10. For one study of the kinds of management tools and techniques currently employed by a large sample of managers, see Darrell Rigby, "Management Tools and Techniques: A Survey," *California Management Review,* Winter, 2001, pp. 139–160.

11. James P. Womack and Daniel T. Jones, *Lean Thinking: Banish Waste and Create Wealth in Your Corporation* (New York: Simon & Schuster, 1996).

12. For a description of the application of Workout at GE, see Jack Welch, *Jack: Straight from the Gut* (New York: Warner Basic Books, 2001), especially pp. 182–189.

13. For a description of how Motorola has applied Six Sigma Quality, see Hal

Plotkin, "Six Sigma: What It Is and How to Use It," HBR Management Update, June 1999, pp. 3–4.

14. Michael Hammer and James Champy, *Re-engineering the Corporation: A Manifesto for Business* (New York: HarperBusiness, 1993).

15. *Ibid.*, p. 31–33.

16. *Ibid.*, p. 144.

17. Michael Hammer and Steven Stanton, "How Process Enterprises *Really* Work," *Harvard Business Review,* November–December, 1999, p. 108.

18. This example is described in some detail in Michael Hammer and James Champy, *op. cit.*, pp. 158–170.

19. *Ibid.*, p. 160.

20. This process is described in greater detail in Leonard A. Schlesinger and James L. Heskett, "The Service-Driven Service Company," *Harvard Business Review,* September–October, 1991, pp. 2–20.

21. This progression is described in James L. Heskett, *GE: We Bring Good Things to Life (A),* Case No. 9-899-162 (Boston: HBS Publishing, 2000).

22. For a discussion of the nature of the challenge and possible responses see, for example, Michael L. Tushman and Charles A. O'Reilly III, "Ambidextrous Organizations: Managing Evolutionary and Revolutionary Change," *California Management Review,* Summer, 1996, pp. 8–30.

23. James L. Heskett, *GE: We Bring Good Things to Life (B),* Case No. 9-899-163 (Boston: HBS Publishing, 2000).

Chapter 11

1. Francis J. Aguilar, ed., *J&J Credo Challenge Meeting 1976,* Videotape No. 1448 (Cambridge, MA: Harvard Business School, 1983).

2. John P. Kotter and James L. Heskett, *Corporate Culture and Performance* (New York: The Free Press, 1992), especially pp. 35–36.

3. *Ibid.*, p. 78. This study tracked company performance from 1977 to 1988.

4. Jim Collins, *Good to Great* (New York: HarperBusiness, 2001), especially pp. 120–143.

5. For a colorful description of Thomas J. Watson, Sr., and the early development of IBM, see Richard S. Tedlow, *Giants of Enterprise* (New York: HarperBusiness, 2001), pp. 187–245.

6. Thomas J. Watson, Jr., *A Business and Its Beliefs: The Ideas That Helped Build IBM* (New York: McGraw-Hill, 1963), p. 39.

7. From an interview conducted by one of the authors with a former IBM executive in 1989.

8. Robert Slater, *Saving Big Blue* (New York: McGraw-Hill, 1999), p. 109.

9. *Ibid.*, pp. 97–107.

10. *Ibid.*, p. 87.

11. As reported on the Johnson & Johnson Web site (www.jnj.com), February 2002.

12. "J&J Credo Challenge Meeting 1976," *op. cit.*

13. John P. Kotter and James L. Heskett, *op. cit.*, p. 57.

14. James C. Collins and Jerry I. Porras, *Built to Last* (New York: Harper-Collins, 1997).

15. Richard T. Pascale, Mark Millemann, and Linda Gioja, *Surfing the Edge of Chaos* (New York: Crown Business, 2000), especially pp. 43–57.

16. Jack Welch, *Jack: Straight from the Gut* (New York: Warner Business Books, 2001), p. 188.

17. *Ibid.*, p. 189.

18. Jim Collins and Jerry Porras, *Built to Last.*

19. John P. Kotter and James L. Heskett, *op. cit.*, pp. 83–93.

Chapter 12

1. Joe Ashbrook Nickell, "Welcome to Harrah's," *Business 2.0*, April 2002, pp. 49–54 at p. 52.

2. *Ibid.*, p. 50. The information in parentheses is based on interviews with company executives in May 2002.

3. J. H. Longle and W. A. Shieman, "From Balanced Scorecards to Strategic Gauges: Is Measurement Worth It?" *Management Review*, March, 1996, pp. 56–62.

4. *Ibid.*

5. Richard E. S. Boulton, Barry D. Silbert, and Steven M. Samek, *Cracking the Value Code* (New York: HarperBusiness, 2000), pp. 17–19.

6. See, for example, Robert S. Kaplan and David P. Norton, *The Balanced Scorecard: Translating Strategy into Action* (Boston: HBS Publishing, 1996).

7. This is described in James L. Heskett, W. Earl Sasser, Jr., and Leonard A. Schlesinger, "The Lifetime Value of Customers," *People Service Success* (Boston: Harvard Business School Management Productions, 1994).

8. "Aligning Your Culture with Your Brand," internal company document, The Limited, September 2000.

9. Richard T. Pascale, Mark Millemann, and Linda Gioja, *Surfing the Edge of Chaos* (New York: Crown Business, 2000), p. 234.

10. Jim Collins, *Good to Great* (New York: HarperBusiness, 2001), p. 104.

11. *Ibid.*, pp. 92–93 and 104–105.

12. See, for example, Al Ehrbar, *Stern Stewart's EVA: The Real Key to Creating Wealth* (New York: John Wiley & Sons, 1998), especially pp. 41–53.

13. Jim Collins, *op. cit.*, pp. 104–105.

14. Robert S. Kaplan and David P. Norton, *The Strategy-Focused Organization: How Balanced Scorecard Companies Thrive in the New Business Environment* (Boston: Harvard Business School Press, 2001), especially pp. 29–63.

15. *Ibid.*, pp. 44–45.

16. Jack Welch, *Jack: Straight from the Gut* (New York: Warner Business Books, 2001), pp. 162–165.

17. Robert S. Kaplan and David P. Norton, *op. cit.*, pp. 253–271.

18. J. R. Katzenbach and J. A. Santamaria, "Firing up the Front Line," *Harvard Business Review*, May–June, 1999, p. 108.

19. Robert S. Kaplan and David P. Norton, *op. cit.*, p. 351.

Chapter 13

1. Jack Welch, *Jack: Straight from the Gut* (New York: Warner Business Books, 2001), p. 419.

2. David Kearns, *Prophets in the Dark* (New York: HarperBusiness, 1992), pp. 110–113.

3. See, for example, Christopher W. L. Hart, "The Power of Unconditional Service Guarantees, *Harvard Business Review,* July–August, 1988, pp. 54–61.

4. See, for example, Ken Iverson, *Plain Talk* (New York: John Wiley & Sons, 1998), pp. 54–59.

5. Videotaped interview with Scott Cook, 1991, Tape No. 3741, Harvard Business School.

6. Interview with Scott Cook, February 2000.

7. See John Case, "Customer Service: The Last Word," *Inc.*, April, 1991, pp. 88–93.

8. Robert D. Hof, "The People's Company," *Business Week*, December 3, 2001, p. EB21.

9. *Ibid.*, p. EB20.

10. This process is described in some detail in Gary Loveman and Robert Anthony "Laura Ashley and Federal Express Strategic Alliance, Case No. 9-693-050 (Boston: HBS Publishing, 1992 revised 1996)

11. See Robert D. Hof, "The People's Company," *Business Week*, December 3, 2001, pp. EB14–EB21, at p. EB16.

12. Based on personal interviews with CEMEX executives resulting in a case by James L. Heskett and Miguel Ochoa, *The CEMEX Way* (in preparation), and material in Thomas Petzinger, Jr., *The New Pioneers* (New York: Simon & Schuster, 1999).

Chapter 14

1. Thomas H. Davenport and Laurence Prusak, *Working Knowledge* (Boston: HBS Publishing, 1998), p. xii. The origins of quotations are sometimes murky. For

example, Carla O'Dell based the title of her book, *If We Only Knew What We Know,* on a quotation, "If TI only knew what TI knows," attributed to Jerry Junkins, the late chairman of Texas Instruments. See Carla O'Dell and C. Jackson Grayson, Jr., *If We Only Knew What We Know* (New York: The Free Press, 1998), p. ix.

2. Kevin Mancy, "SAS Gets off on Right Foot with Workers," *USA Today,* May 23, 2001, p. B3.

3. Richard Tedlow, *Giants of Enterprise: Seven Business Innovators and the Empires They Built* (New York: HarperBusiness, 2001), p. 9.

4. *Op. cit.,* pp. 72–117.

5. "Omnicom Group, Inc.," Hoover's Company Profile, 2001.

6. Morton T. Hansen, Nitin Nohria, and Thomas Tierney, "What's Your Strategy for Managing Knowledge?" *Harvard Business Review,* March–April, 1999, pp. 106–116.

7. *Ibid.,* pp. 112–113.

8. Jim Collins, *Good to Great* (New York: HarperBusiness, 2001), p. 36.

9. *Ibid.*

10. The first example is based on our personal observations; the second was reported to us by Marriott managers; the third was described in Michael Lewis, "O'Neill's List," *The New York Times Magazine,* January 13, 2002, pp. 20–25.

11. *Ibid.,* p. 7.

12. See Jack Welch, *Jack: Straight from the Gut* (New York: Warner Business Books, 2001), especially pp. 169–184.

13. *Ibid.,* p. 195.

14. *Ibid.,* p. 196.

15. Interview with Steven Kerr, September 29, 1999.

16. *Ibid.*

17. James L. Heskett, *GE: We Bring Good Things to Life (B),* Case No. 9-899-163 (Boston: HBS Publishing, 1999).

Afterword

1. See Harlan Cleveland, "Information as a Resource," *The Futurist,* December, 1982, pp. 34–39, and "The Twilight of Hierarchy: Speculations on the Global Information Society," *Public Administration Review,* January–February, 1985, pp. 185–195.

Access Health, 276, 282
Accuracy, customer need for, 170, 171
Acitivity-based costing, 67
Acquisition costs, 66–67
Advice, customer need for, 170–171
A.G. Edwards & Sons, Inc., 80
Akers, John, 36, 231–232
Alcoa, 136, 140
Allocating resources, 72–73
"Alumni" networks, 164
Amazon.com, 185
American Airlines, 197
American Cyanamid Company, 41, 48
American Express credit cards, 176
Anderson Consulting, 276, 282
Antagonists, 58, 59, 72
"A player" input, hiring and promoting with, 130
Apostle-like behavior, 55
Apostle/owners, 58–62, 69, 72, 73
Application service providers, 42–43
Attitude, hiring and firing for, 148–150
Au Bon Pain, 129, 142
Authority, customer need for, 170
Automobile dealerships, 41–42
Availability, customer need for, 170, 171

Bain & Company, 276, 282
Balanced measurement, 247–248. See also Performance measurement and recognition
Balanced paycheck concept, 255
Balanced scorecard method, 120, 122–123, 131, 248, 252–254
Banco Commercial Português (BCP), 245–246
Barret, Colleen, 174, 240
Baughman, Jim, 287
BCG, 276, 282

Beck, Barbara, 160
Benchmarking, 103–105, 125, 126
Berkshire Hathaway Inc., 10
Bermuda Triangle of employee-customer relations, 80–82
Berners-Lee, Tim, 117
Best practice, internal, 105–106
Blackshaw, Pete, 64–65
Boeing, 46, 261
Bogle, John, 5, 6, 15, 16, 30–31
Bossidy, Larry, 287
Brain, organization's, 277–282
    defined, 277, 278
    General Electric example, 287–291
    Omnicom example, 279–282
Bratton, William, 46, 128
Bressler, Phil, 53, 70
British Airways, 207
Brown, Stephen, 56
Buckingham, Marcus, 149–150, 162, 170
Buffett, Warren, 10
Built to Last (Collins and Porras), 107, 134, 237
Burke, James, 227, 233, 234
Business mission, focused, 147–148
Business redefinition. See Rethinking the business
Business-to-business customer profiling, 62–63

Camp, Robert, 103–104
Capital One:
    deep indicators at, 203, 204, 206–207
    employee opportunities for ownership in organization at, 162
    recruiting at, 159
    value exchange at, 184, 187–192, 197–198, 252
Cause-and-effect analysis, 250–251

Cawley, Charlie, 250
C2B (consumer to business) "feed-
    back spaces," 64–65
CEMEX:
    change in management behaviors
        at, 129
    creation of fewer, more significant
        jobs at, 128
    hardwiring performance at, 260,
        269, 272–273
    support systems at, 152
    transition from products and ser-
        vices to results at, 46
Champy, James, 214
Cisco MarketPlace Internet site, 180
Cisco Systems, Inc.:
    core values at, 227, 234–237
    employee opportunities for owner-
        ship in organization at, 162
    employee relationship manage-
        ment (ERM) at, 136
    firing decision at, 160
    identifying and tracking customer
        behavior at, 71
    promises at, 161
    recognition of value of continuity
        at, 157
    treating employees like customers
        at, 137–139
    value exchange at, 185
    vendor relationship management
        at, 180
Claydon Heeley Jones Mason
    (CHJM):
    dismissal of clients at, 179
    facilitation of self-selection at, 159–
        160
    impact of weak economic environ-
        ment on, 181–182
    procedures for employment
        turnover at, 164
Cleveland, Harlan, 297
"Clicks," 11
Coffman, Curt, 149–150, 162, 170
Colley, Jerry, 118

Collins, James, 106–107, 134, 202–
    203, 230, 237, 251, 253, 283
Commitment, employee. See Em-
    ployee commitment
Commoditization, 39
Communication:
    of lifetime value, 70
    of values, vision, and strategy at
        Office Depot, 121
Comparative yardsticks. See Yard-
    sticks, comparative
Compensation:
    high-capability employees and,
        156–158
    as part of value package, 162
    paying more in order to pay less,
        131–132
Competitive Strategy (Porter), 114
Computer-Tabulating-Recording
    Company (CTR), 230
Consumer customer profiling,
    63–65
Consumer Reports, 25
Control, spans of, 127–128
Cook, Scott, 265, 267, 269
Core values, 227–242
    at Cisco Systems, 227, 234–237
    decision making and, 239–240
    at IBM Corporation, 227, 230–232,
        237, 249
    importance of, 227–230
    influence on management behav-
        iors, 240–241
    at Johnson & Johnson, 227, 228,
        233–234, 237
    patterns of influence on perfor-
        mance, 237
    performance measurement and re-
        ward and, 241–242, 249
    revisiting, 237–239
    value creation and, 242
Cost, leveraging value over. See Lever-
    aging value over cost
Cost estimates of employee defec-
    tions, traditional, 79–80

Cost increases, employee continuity and commitment and, 83
Cost reductions:
  customer lifetime value and, 56, 57
  employee commitment and, 82–86
  estimating employee value and, 89–91
Coughlan, Tom, 8–9
Culture, organization. *See also* Core values
  as brand, 158–164
    achieving organization continuity, 162–163
    compensating fairly, 162
    encouraging managers to listen, learn, teach, serve, and communicate, 161
    facilitating self-selection into or out of organization, 159–160
    procedures for employee turnover, 163–164
    setting high standards and expectations, 160
    trust and promises, 161–162
  as component of performance trinity, 113–116
  hiring and promoting with "A player" input, 130
  at Office Depot, 119–120
  employee relationship management (ERM) and, 139
  impact on long-term economic performance, 227–230
  incorporating hardwiring into, 265–267
  strong, mobilizing for value-focused change. *See* Strong cultures, mobilizing for value-focused change
Customer behaviors, hierarchy of, 54–55
Customer Comes Second, The (Rosenbluth and Peters), 136

Customer commitment:
  customer satisfaction surveys and, 63–64
  in hierarchy of customer relations, 54, 55
Customer defections, employee continuity and commitment and, 83
"Customer facing" premium, 90–91
Customer lifetime value, 53–73, 76
  actions based on, 70–73
    allocating resources, 72–73
    communicating lifetime value, 70
    identifying and tracking customer behavior, 70–71
    organizing for customer relationship management, 71–72
  concept of, 53–54
  factors contributing to, 56, 57
  hierarchy of relationships with customers, 54–55
  measuring, 66–70
    acquisition costs, 66–67
    example of, 338–343
    length of relationship, 66
    margins on related sales, 67–68
    relationship costs over time, 67
    value of referrals, 68–69
    value of suggestions, 69–70
  profiling the customer portfolio, 62–65
    business-to-business, 62–65
    consumer, 63–65
  value in a portfolio of customers, 57–62
Customer loyalty:
  customer lifetime value and:
    in portfolio of customers, 57–62
    product or service recommendations and, 56
  hierarchy of customer needs and, 170–171
  in hierarchy of customer relations, 54, 55

Customer loyalty (*cont.*)
  Vanguard Group and, 21, 25
  Wal-Mart and, 23, 25
Customer needs, hierarchy of, 170–171
Customer ownership behavior, 54–55, 267–268
Customer profiling:
  antidotes to misuses of, 194–197
  business-to-business, 62–65
  consumer, 63–65
Customer relationship, length of, 66
Customer relationship management (CRM), 76–77, 166–182
  customer value equation, 167–169
  evaluation, 175–176
  firing, 177–179
  hierarchy of customer needs and, 170–171
  impact of weak economic environment on, 180–182
  organizing for, 71–72
  recognition and reward, 176–177
  selection and self-selection, 171–173
  training and support, 173–175
Customers:
  treating like employees. *See* Customer relationship management (CRM)
  vendor relationship management, 169–170, 179–180
Customer satisfaction:
  customer lifetime value and, 57–62
  employee lifetime tenure and, 93
  in hierarchy of customer relations, 54, 55
  surveys, 63–64
  Vanguard Group and, 21, 25
  Wal-Mart and, 23, 25
Customer "sweet spot," 61
Customer value equation, 167–169
Customer value exchange, 187–191

Darden Restaurants, Inc., 277
Decision making, core values and, 239–240
Deep indicators:
  identifying, 202–204
  as sources of leverage, 204–207
Defections:
  customer, employee continuity and commitment and, 83
  employee:
    at Cisco Systems, 139
    traditional cost estimates of, 79–80
  management, unplanned, reducing, 131
Dell Computer:
  organizational learning at, 276, 282
  value exchange at, 185
Dependability, customer need for, 170
Design, faulty, 216–217
Differentiation, 11
Discipline, culture of, 230
Dismissal. *See* Firing
Domino's Pizza, 70

Eastman, George, 279
Eastman Kodak Company, 279
eBay, 267–268, 270–272
E-commerce, 174–175, 184–185
E-commerce software, 42
Economic value added (EVA) measures, 51, 251–252
Ehrlich, Cliff, 76
Empathy, customer need for, 170
Employee commitment, 30
  as barometer of future performance, 93
  defined, 82
  impact on employee lifetime value and profitability, 82–87
    cost reduction, 82–86
    referrals, 82–86
    revenue enhancement, 82, 83, 86

value of planned turnover, 86
at Vanguard Group, 24
at Wal-Mart, 24
Employee continuity:
as barometer of future performance, 93
impact on employee lifetime value
and profitability, 82–87
cost reduction, 82–86
referrals, 82–86
revenue enhancement, 82,
83, 86
value of planned turnover,
86–87
importance of, 76–78
recognition of value of, 157
two faces of, 78–79
Employee defections, traditional cost
estimates of, 79–80
Employee lifetime value:
as barometer of future performance, 93
changing assumptions regarding,
80–82
impact of employee continuity and
commitment on, 82–87
cost reduction, 82–86
referrals, 82–86
revenue enhancement, 82,
83, 86
value of planned turnover,
86–87
Employee loyalty, 30
at Vanguard Group, 20
at Wal-Mart, 22, 24–25
Employee productivity, 30
at Vanguard Group, 20, 24
at Wal-Mart, 20, 24–25
Employee relationship management
(ERM), 77, 136–164
breaking the cycle of mediocrity,
142–153
example of, 142–147
steps in, 147–153

organization culture as brand, 158–
164
achieving organization continuity, 162–163
compensating fairly, 162
encouraging managers to listen,
learn, teach, serve, and communicate, 161
facilitating self-selection into or
out of organization, 159–160
procedures for employee
turnover, 163–164
setting high standards and ex-
pecting a lot, 160
trust and promises, 161–162
treating employees like customers:
at Alcoa, 140
at Cisco Systems, 137–139
at Willow Creek Community
Church, 140–142
value equation for employees, 157–
158
what employees want, 153–157
Employee retention, value of a
1-percentage-point change in,
89–90
Employees, reducing number of,
127–128
Employee satisfaction, 30
as barometer of future performance, 93
profit growth and, 75
referrals and, 83–84
varying patterns in, 79
at Wal-Mart, 24
Employee turnover rates. *See*
Turnover rates
Employee value, 75–93
changing assumptions regarding employee lifetime value,
80–82
employee satisfaction, continuity,
and commitment as barome-
ters of future performance, 93

Employee value (*cont.*)
    estimating rules of thumb, 88–93
      "customer facing" premium,
        90–91
      management premium, 91–92
      replacement costs per employee,
        89
      top management premium,
        92–93
      value of a 1-percentage-point
        change in employee retention,
        89–90
    factors in estimating, 87–88
    impact of employee continuity and
      commitment on lifetime value
      and profitability, 82–87
      cost reduction, 82–86
      referrals, 82–86
      revenue enhancement, 82, 83, 86
      value of planned turnover, 86–87
    importance of employee continuity,
      76–78
    traditional cost estimates of defec-
      tions, 79–80
    two faces of employee continuity,
      78–79
Employee value equation, 157–158
Employee value exchange, 191–193
Enron, 298
Ernst & Young, 276, 282
Evaluation of customers, 175–176
Execution, failures of, 217–218
Expectations, high, 160
Explicit knowledge, 275, 276

Fact-based analysis, 249–250
Fairbank, Richard, 159, 187–190
Fairfield Inn division, Marriott Inter-
    national, 142–148
Fairness of managers, 155, 157, 158
FedEx, 127–129, 271, 272, 297
"Feedback spaces," C2B (consumer to
    business), 64–65
"Fewer/better" employee phenome-
    non, 84, 85

Fiat Corporation, 180
Firing:
    customers, 177–179, 195–196
    employees:
      for attitude, 148–150
      creating winning procedures for,
        163–164
Focus groups, 71
Franchise value, 115
Fuente, David, 117

Gallup Organization, 104, 143–144, 170
Gap analysis, 107
General Electric Company:
    continuity at, 162
    core values at, 241, 242
    employee opportunities for owner-
      ship in organization at, 162
    firing at, 177
    firing for attitude at, 150
    hardwiring performance at, 260–
      261, 270
    organizational learning at, 287–291
    performance measurement at,
      254–255
    performance trinity at
      delivering value from the center,
        132–133
      internal best practice, 105–106
      paying more in order to pay less,
        132
      results, 133–134
    planned turnover at, 79
    servicing activities of, 43, 46
    Six Sigma Quality achievement at,
      217, 218, 256, 287–290
    stretch goals at, 256
    transition from products and ser-
      vices to results at, 45–46
    Wal-Mart's supply chain restructur-
      ing and, 9, 16, 211, 270
    Workout at, 212, 217
General Electric Financial Services, 43
General Motors Corporation, 268–
    269

Gerstner, Louis, 34–38, 232
Giordana, Joe, 167
Giroux, Mimi, 138
Glass, David, 113, 127
Gluck, Fred, 285–286
Goodnight, James, 192
Gremler, Dwayne, 56
Group behavior norms, 114
Growth, 48
    at Cisco Systems, 138, 139
    reengineering of performance
        trinity and, 133–134
    at Vanguard Group, 21, 25
    at Wal-Mart, 23, 26
    at Willow Creek Community
        Church, 141–142
Gupta, Rajat, 285, 286

Hallmark Cards, Inc., 215
Hallowell, Roger, 15–16
Hamel, Gary, 104
Hammer, Michael, 213–214
Hansen, Morton, 282–283
Hardwiring performance, 260–273
    customer ownership, 267–268
    defined, 262–263
    hierarchy of initiatives, 263
    impact of, 272–273
    incorporating into the culture, 265–
        267
    product or service guarantees,
        264
    repositioning to deliver solutions,
        264
    requirements for, 268–271
        listening devices, 270
        partnering mentality, 271
        proven success and results, 268–
            269
        reorganization if necessary, 270–
            271
        willingness to put business on
            the line, 269
Harley-Davidson Motor Company,
    The, 73

Harrah's Entertainment, 246–247,
    249
Hay, Edward N., 87
"Hay points," 87
Heavy users, 57
Heskett, James L., 227–229, 236,
    237
Hewlett-Packard Company, 39, 275,
    276, 282
Hiring:
    with "A player" input, 130
    for attitude, 148–150
Hiring costs. *See* Replacement costs
Hostages, 58–60, 62, 72
Hybels, Bill, 137, 140–141

IBM Corporation:
    core values at, 227, 230–232, 237,
        249
    poor performance in the 1980s of,
        100
    promises at, 161
    value-focused transformation at,
        34–38, 48
Identifying customer behavior,
    70–71
IKEA, 204–206
Immelt, Jeffrey, 151, 162
Individual factors in estimating
    employee value, 87
Industry leadership, 30–31
Information, value measured in, 185
Information-based strategies (IBS),
    187–189, 197–198
Information systems, as antidote to
    misuses of customer profiling,
    195
ING Direct, 177–178
ING's U.S. Financial Services Group,
    166, 167
Intangibles, 115
Internet-based profiling, 63–65, 71
Internet shopping, 174–175, 184–185
Intuit, 265–267, 269–272
Investor value exchange, 192

Job factors in estimating employee value, 87
Johnson & Johnson, 227, 228, 233–234, 237
Jung, Andrea, 116

Kaplan, Robert, 82, 253–255, 258
Keiningham, Timothy, 207
Kelleher, Herb, 177, 239
Kerr, Steve, 288
Kinnear, James, 100
Knowledge. *See also* Learning, organizational
forms of, 275–277
Korhonen, Pertti, 95
Kotter, John P., 227–229, 236, 237
Kuhlmann, Arkadi, 178

Labor market, targeting, 148
Latitude to deliver results, 130–131, 152–153
Leadership, 30–31
as component of performance trinity, 113–116
at Office Depot, 118–119
organizational reengineering of, 125–134
benchmarking and, 125, 126
creating fewer, more significant jobs, 127–128
delivering value from the center, 132–133
forcing change in leadership and management behaviors, 128–130
giving the jobs only to those who buy into performance trinity, 128
hiring and promoting with "A player" input, 130
measuring and rewarding delivery of results, 130–131
moving fast, 133
paying more in order to pay less, 131–132
productivity, growth, and profitability and, 133–134
reducing unplanned management defections, 131
performance measurement and recognition and, 257–258
role in organizational learning, 283–285
"Lean" manufacturing, 210
Learning, organizational, 275–291
"favorable balance of trade" in knowledge, 285–286
forms of knowledge, 275–277
organization's brain, 277–282
defined, 277, 278
General Electric example, 287–291
Omnicom example, 279–282
role of leadership in, 283–285
strategy and, 282–283
Lev, Baruch, 115
Level 5 leadership, 283
Leveraging value over cost, 200–219
deep indicators:
identifying, 202–204
as sources of leverage, 204–207
odds of success and, 219
reasons for change management failure, 216–218
sources of leverage:
characteristics of, 207–208
organization reengineering, 209, 215–216
process reengineering, 209, 213–215
Six Sigma Quality achievement, 209, 212–213, 217, 218
supply chain restructuring, 209–212
Workout, 209, 212, 217
at Southwest Airlines, 200–202
Lewis, Peter, 186
Lifetime value. *See* Customer lifetime value; Employee lifetime value
Limited Brands, 250

Listening posts, 63, 71
Loblaw Companies Ltd., 185
Lovelock, Christopher, 145
Loveman, Gary, 246, 247
Loyalists, 58, 60, 61, 69, 72–73
Loyalty:
  customer. *See* Customer loyalty
  employee, 30
    at Vanguard Group, 20
    at Wal-Mart, 22, 24–25
Loyalty ripple effect, 56
Luechtefeld, Monica, 117
LUVLines, 153

Maister, David, 153–155
Malcolm Baldrige National Quality
    Awards, 103, 106
Management:
  as component of performance
    trinity, 113–116
  encouraging to listen, learn, teach,
    serve, and communicate, 161
  influence of core values on behav-
    ior of, 240–241
  at Office Depot, 118–119
  organizational reengineering of,
    125–134
    benchmarking and, 125, 126
    creating fewer, more significant
      jobs, 127–128
    delivering value from the center,
      132–133
    forcing change in leadership and
      management behaviors, 128–
      130
    giving the jobs only to those who
      buy into performance trinity,
      128
    hiring and promoting with "A
      player" input, 130
    measuring and rewarding deliv-
      ery of results, 130–131
    moving fast, 133
    paying more in order to pay less,
      131–132

  productivity, growth, and prof-
    itability and, 133–134
  reducing unplanned manage-
    ment defections, 131
Management premium, 91–92
Margins:
  customer lifetime value and, 56, 57
  on related sales, 67–68
Marketing strategies, 184–185
Marquee accounts, 63
Marquee effect, 61
Marriott, Bill, 143, 283
Martinez, Arthur, 240, 241
MBNA, 66, 130–131, 250
McAllister, Dan, 8–9
McKinley, John, 100
McKinsey & Company, 258, 276, 282,
    285–286
McKinsey Global Institute, 286
McNeil Consumer & Specialty Phar-
    maceuticals, 233
Mediocrity, breaking the cycle of:
  example of, 142–147
  steps in, 147–153
Membership, customer need for,
    176–177
Memorial Sloan-Kettering Cancer
    Center, 276, 282
Mercenaries, 58–60, 62, 72
Merkley Newman Harty, 171–173,
    175–176
Merrill Lynch & Company, Inc., 176,
    250
Microsoft Corporation, 164
Mobil:
  North American marketing and re-
    financing organization, 253–254
  Speedpass, 167–169, 296
Mobilizing for change. *See* Strong
    cultures, mobilizing for value-
    focused change
Money, value measured in, 185
Monsanto Company, 45
Morgridge, John, 236
Morris, Nigel, 187–190

Nelson, Bruce, 118, 119, 121
New York Police Department, 46, 128, 150, 216
Nohria, Nitin, 282–283
Nokia Corporation, 95–97, 101–102
Norton, David, 82, 253–255, 258
"Not invented here" syndrome, overcoming, 98–101
NovaRede, 245–246
Nucor Steel, 260, 265, 271

O. M. Scott & Sons, 45, 48
Office Depot:
    balanced scorecard method of, 120, 122–123, 131, 252–253
    emphasis on long-term performance at, 256
    emphasis on solving problems at distribution centers at, 256–257
    performance trinity at, 116–125, 129
        communication and implementation of values, vision, and strategy, 121
        culture and values, 119–120
        leadership and management, 118–119
        results of, 121, 124–125
        vision and strategy, 120, 122–123
Olive Garden, 277
Omidyar, Pierre, 268
Omnicom, Inc.:
    customer relationship management at, 166
    organizational learning at, 279–282
O'Neill, Paul, 136, 140, 283
Operating strategy. See Strategy
Organization reengineering, 125–134
    benchmarking and, 125, 126
    creating fewer, more significant jobs, 127–128
    delivering value from the center, 132–133
    forcing change in leadership and management behaviors, 128–130
    giving the jobs only to those who buy into performance trinity, 128
    hiring and promoting with "A player" input, 130
    leveraging value over cost with, 209, 215–216
    measuring and rewarding delivery of results, 130–131
    moving fast, 133
    paying more in order to pay less, 131–132
    productivity, growth, and profitability and, 133–134
    reducing unplanned management defections, 131
Otis Elevator Company, 40–41, 48
Outcomes, prescribing, 130–131
Outsourcing, 138–139
Ownership behaviors, customer, 54–55, 267–268

Partnering mentality, 271
Partnership, customer need for, 170–171
Pascale, Richard, 202, 206, 240, 251
Peer group profiling, 102
Performance, hardwiring. See Hardwiring performance
Performance-based reward systems, 130–131
Performance measurement and recognition, 245–258
    balanced scorecard method, 120, 122–123, 131, 248
    core values and, 241–242, 249
    criteria for selecting measures, 248–255
        cause-and-effect analysis, 250–251

clear, understandable, and
appropriately influential
measures, 252–253
core values, 249
fact-based analysis, 249–250
management judgment, 254–255
prospective measures, 251–252
reflection of organization strategy, 253–254
examples of, 245–247
implementing measures, 255–257
breadth, depth, and nature of
application, 256–257
frequency of measurement
changes, 257
relative emphasis on short- and
long-term performance, 256
tying performance to rewards,
255–256
leadership and, 257–258
Performance trinity, 113–134
components of, 113–116
defined, 113
at Office Depot, 116–125, 121
communication and implementation of values, vision, and
strategy, 121
culture and values, 119–120
leadership and management,
118–119
results of, 121, 124–125
vision and strategy, 120, 122–123
organizational reengineering of,
125–134
benchmarking and, 125, 126
creating fewer, more significant
jobs, 127–128
delivering value from the center,
132–133
forcing change in leadership and
management behaviors, 128–
130
giving the jobs only to those who
buy into performance trinity,
128

hiring and promoting with "A
player" input, 130
measuring and rewarding delivery of results, 130–131
moving fast, 133
paying more in order to pay less,
131–132
productivity, growth, and profitability and, 133–134
reducing unplanned manage-
ment defections, 131
Personal development, opportunity
for, 156–158
Peters, Diane McFerrin, 136
P&G Interactive, 64–65
Philips Electronics NV, 95, 97
PlanetFeedback, 65, 174–175
Planned turnover, 79, 86–89
Platt, Lew, 275
Pollard, Bill, 161, 283, 284
Porras, Jerry, 107, 134, 237
Porter, Michael, 114, 202
Portfolio of customers, value in,
57–62
Priestly, Jamie, 159–160, 164, 179,
181–182
Problem solving, opportunity for,
156–158
Process quality, 47
Process reengineering, 209, 213–215
Procter & Gamble
"Alumni" networks at, 164
importance of viral customers at, 64
value exchange at, 184
Wal-Mart's supply chain restructur-
ing and, 9, 16, 211, 270
Product guarantees, 264
Product improvement, customer rec-
ommendations for, 56, 57
Productivity:
estimating employee value and, 89
reengineering of performance
trinity and, 133–134
at Vanguard Group, 20, 24
at Wal-Mart, 22, 24–25

Products:
shift in emphasis to results from,
38–43
shift in emphasis to services from,
38–43
Profiling:
customer:
antidotes to misuses of, 194–197
business-to-business, 62–65
consumer, 63–65
peer group, 102
Profitability, 48
customer lifetime value and, 56, 57
employee relationship management (ERM) and, 153–155
employee satisfaction and, 75
impact of employee continuity and
commitment on, 82–87
cost reduction, 82–86
referrals, 82–86
revenue enhancement, 82, 83,
86
value of planned turnover, 86–87
organizational continuity and, 93
reengineering of performance
trinity and, 133–134
at Vanguard Group, 25–26
at Wal-Mart, 23, 26
Progressive Corporation, 186–187
Project Eliza, 37–38
Promises, 161–162
Promotion, with "A player" input, 130
Prospective performance measures,
251–252
"Pygmalion effect," 160

Quicken, 265, 267

Rapp-Collins, 213
Recognition:
of customers, 176–177
of employees, 153, 155, 157, 158.
See also Performance mea-
surement and recognition

Recruiting costs. See Replacement
costs
Redfield, Carl, 180
Reengineering:
organization, 125–134
benchmarking and, 125, 126
creating fewer, more significant
jobs, 127–128
delivering value from the center,
132–133
forcing change in leadership and
management behaviors, 128–
130
giving the jobs only to those who
buy into performance trinity,
128
hiring and promoting with "A
player" input, 130
leveraging value over cost with,
209, 215–216
measuring and rewarding delivery of results, 130–131
moving fast, 133
paying more in order to pay less,
131–132
productivity, growth, and profitability and, 133–134
reducing unplanned management defections, 131
process, 209, 213–215
Referrals:
customer lifetime value and, 56, 57,
68–69
employee commitment and, 82–86
records of, 63
Referral value, 58
Relationship costs over time, 67
Replacement costs, 76, 79–82
estimating rules of thumb, 88–93
"customer facing" premium,
90–91
management premium, 91–92
top management premium,
92–93

value of a 1-percentage-point change in employee retention, 89–90
per employee, 89
Repositioning to deliver solutions, 264
Research, compendium of, 301–317
Resource allocation, 72–73
Results:
latitude to deliver, 130–131, 152–153
measuring delivery of, 130–131
recognition for, 153, 155, 157, 158
as requirement for hardwiring, 268–269
rewarding, 130–131, 153
shift in emphasis from products and services to, 43–46
shift in emphasis to value from, 47
Rethinking the business, 34–48
patterns in organizational behavior, 48
from products and services to results, 43–46
from products to services, 38–43
from results to value, 47
value-focused transformation at IBM, 34–38, 48
Revenue enhancement:
employee commitment and, 82, 83, 86
estimating employee value and, 89, 90
Revenue reduction, employee continuity and commitment and, 83
Rewards:
breadth, depth, and nature of application and, 256–257
core values and, 241–242
for customers, 176–177
performance-based systems, 130–131
for results, 130–131, 153
tying performance to, 255–256

Ritz-Carlton Hotel Company, 152–153
Rosenbluth, Hal, 136
Russo, David, 193
Rust, Roland, 207

SABRE, 296, 297
Sales, margins on, 67–68
Sales information, 62
SAS Institute:
organizational learning at, 277
value exchange at, 184, 192–193
Satisfaction:
customer:
customer lifetime value and, 57–62
employee lifetime tenure and, 93
in hierarchy of customer relations, 54, 55
surveys, 63–64
Vanguard Group and, 21, 25
Wal-Mart and, 23, 25
employee:
as barometer of future performance, 93
profit growth and, 75
varying patterns in, 79
at Wal-Mart, 24
Satre, Philip, 246
Schein, Edgar, 114
Sears, Roebuck and Company
core values at, 240–241
deep indicators at, 203, 204
fact-based analysis at, 249–250
failure of transformation effort, 120, 241, 257
Selection, customer, 171–173
Self-auditing, 106–107
Self-selection:
customer, 171–173
employee, 159–160
Service guarantees, 264
Service improvement, customer recommendations for, 56, 57

Service Management Group, The, 79, 83
ServiceMaster, 161, 284
Services:
  improvement of, customer recommendations for, 56, 57
  shift in emphasis from products to, 38–43
  shift in emphasis to results from, 43–46
Sewell, Carl, 53
Shared values, 100–101
Signet Bank, 188
"Silver bullet" policy for firing customers, 177
Six Sigma Quality achievement, 209
  defined, 212–213
  at General Electric, 217, 218, 256, 287–290
  at Omnicom, 280, 282
SMMS, Inc., 166–167
Soderquist, Don, 7, 28
Solutions, repositioning to deliver, 264
Southwest Airlines:
  core values at, 239–240
  customers' sense of "ownership" at, 73
  customer training at, 174
  deep indicators at, 203–204
  employee attitude in interacting with customers at, 195
  employee opportunities for ownership in organization at, 162
  employee value at, 75–76
  firing of customers at, 177
  focused business mission of, 147–148
  latitude to deliver results at, 153
  leveraging value over cost at, 200–202
  recognition of results at, 153
Spans of control, 127–128
Speedpass, Mobil's, 167–169, 296
Standards, high, 160

Staples, 116, 117
Strategic value vision:
  defined, 11–12
  operating strategy, 11, 13–17
  target market, 11–14
  value concept, 12–15
  value delivery system, 11, 13, 14, 18
Strategy, 11, 13–17. *See also* Leveraging value over cost
  as component of performance trinity, 113–116
  at Office Depot, 120, 122–123
  organizational learning and, 282–283
  performance measures and, 253–254
Stretch goals, 256
Strong cultures, mobilizing for value-focused change, 95–107
  developing comparative yardsticks, 101–107
    benchmarking, 103–105
    identification of symptoms, 101–102
    internal best practice, 105–106
    self-auditing, 106–107
    Nokia vs. Ericsson example, 95–97, 101–102
    overcoming the "not invented here" syndrome, 98–101, 114–115
Success:
  cycle of, 153–155
  as requirement for hardwiring, 268–269
  strong cultures and, 98–101
Successful Money Management Seminars program, SMMS, Inc., 166–167
Suggestions, value of, 69–70
Supply chain restructuring, 209–212
Support systems, 151–152
Symptoms, identification of, 101–102

Tacit knowledge, 275–277
Taco Bell:
  attitude towards change of managers at, 150
  creation of fewer, more significant jobs at, 127–128, 215
  hiring for talent at, 129
  paying more in order to pay less at, 131–132
Talent, hiring for, 149–150
Tangible evidence, customer need for, 170
Target market, 11–14
Teaching, 284
Technology, 296–297
Tedlow, Richard, 277
Telefon AB L.M. Ericsson, 95–97, 101–102
"Terrorists," 86, 196
Texaco Inc., 99–100, 208, 213
Tierney, Thomas, 282–283
Timeliness, customer need for, 170
Top management premium, 92–93
Total rewards program, Harrah Entertainment, 246–247
Tracking customer behavior, 70–71
Training:
  careful attention to, as antidote to misuses of customer profiling, 194–195
  customers, 173–175
  for the job and for life, 150–151
Training costs. See Replacement costs
Trotter, Lloyd, 288
Trust, promises and, 161–162
Turnover:
  creating winning procedures for, 163
  planned, 79, 86–89
Turnover rates:
  employee satisfaction and, 75
  estimating employee value and, 88
  low, costs of, 78–79
  at Vanguard Group, 20
  at Wal-Mart, 22, 24–25

Unilever, 103
UPS, 103
U.S. Justice Department, 43
U.S. Marine Corps, 103, 258, 277
U.S. Securities and Exchange Commission, 25
U.S. Social Security Administration, 156
USAA, 66, 277

Value, 10–32
  delivering from the center, 132–133
  distribution of, 297–298
  industry leadership and, 30–31
  leveraging over cost. See Leveraging value over cost
  shift in emphasis from results to, 47
  strategic value vision:
    defined, 11–12
    operating strategy, 11, 13–17
    target market, 11–14
    value concept, 12–15
    value delivery system, 11, 13, 14, 18
  value equation. See Value equation
  value profit chain, 19–26
    customer satisfaction and loyalty, 21, 23, 25
    defined, 19
    employee satisfaction, commitment, loyalty, and productivity, 20, 22, 24–25, 30
Value concept, 12–15
Value delivery system, 11, 13, 14, 18
Value equation, 26–29
  customer, 167–169
  employee, 157–158
Value exchange, 184–198
  antidotes to misuses of customer profiling, 194–197
  at Capital One, 187–192, 197–198, 252
  defined, 185
  for employees, 191–193

Value exchange (*cont.*)
  at Progressive Corporation, 186–187
  underside of, 193–194
Value profit chain, 19–26
  achievement of. *See* Rethinking the business; Vanguard Financial Group; Wal-Mart Stores
  customer satisfaction and loyalty, 21, 23, 25
  defined, 19
  employee satisfaction, commitment, loyalty, and productivity, 20, 22, 24–25, 30
  growth and profitability, 21, 23, 25–26
  performance trinity and. *See* Performance trinity
Value profit chain audit, 318–337
Values:
  as component of performance trinity, 113–116
    at Office Depot, 119–120
  core. *See* Core values
Vanguard Group, The:
  as advocate for the investor, 5–6
  industry leadership and, 30–31
  similarities with Wal-Mart Stores, Inc., 31–32
  strategic value vision at:
    operating strategy, 13, 15–16
    target market, 12, 13
    value concept, 12, 13, 15
    value delivery system, 13, 18
  value equation of, 26–27
  value profit chain performance of, 19–22, 25–26
    customer satisfaction and loyalty, 21, 25
    employee satisfaction, commitment, loyalty, and productivity, 20, 22, 24
    growth and profitability, 21, 25–26
Vendor relationship management, 169–170, 179–180

Verizon, 42–43
Viking International, 118
Viral behavior, 58, 70, 72–73
Viral character, 61, 63–65, 68
Viral loyalists, 58, 59, 61, 69
Vision:
  as component of performance trinity, 113–116
  at Office Depot, 120, 122–123
  strategic value:
    defined, 11–12
    operating strategy, 11, 13–17
    target market, 11–14
    value concept, 12–15
    value delivery system, 11, 13, 14, 18

Walgreens, 251, 253
Wal-Mart Stores, Inc., 103
  as agent for the customer, 6–10
  industry leadership and, 30
  similarities with The Vanguard Group, 31–32
  strategic value vision at:
    operating strategy, 14, 16–17
    target market, 12, 14
    value concept, 14, 15
    value delivery system, 14, 18
  supply chain restructuring at, 9, 16, 211–212, 270
  value equation of, 27–29
  value profit chain performance of, 19, 22–26
    customer satisfaction and loyalty, 23, 25
    employee satisfaction, commitment, loyalty, and productivity, 22, 24–25
    growth and profitability, 23, 26
Walton, Helen, 30
Walton, Sam, 8, 30
Walton Institute, 7
Warriner, Mel, 142–147, 148
Watson, Thomas J., Sr., 227, 230–232

Watson, Tom, 279–282
Webb, Maynard, 270
Welch, Jack, 45, 133, 151, 177, 241, 242, 287, 288
Whitman, Meg, 270
Willow Creek Community Church, 137, 140–142
"Winners," working with, 155–158
Workout, 209, 212, 217
Wren, John, 279, 280

Xerox Corporation:
    attitude towards change of managers at, 150
    benchmarking at, 103–104
    creation of fewer, more significant jobs at, 127–128
    hardwiring performance at, 261–262
    hiring for talent at, 150

Yardsticks, comparative, 101–107
    benchmarking, 103–105
    identification of symptoms, 101–102
    internal best practice, 105–106
    self-auditing, 106–107

Zahorik, Anthony, 207
Zambrano, Lorenzo, 46, 152

About the Authors

JAMES L. HESKETT is Baker Foundation Professor at the Harvard Business School and co-author with Earl Sasser and Leonard Schlesinger of the landmark bestseller *The Service Profit Chain*.

W. EARL SASSER, JR., is UPS Foundation Professor of Service Management at the Harvard Business School and chairman of the board of Harvard Business School Interactive.

LEONARD A. SCHLESINGER was the George F. Baker Jr. Professor of Business Administration at the Harvard Business School and professor of sociology and public policy at Brown University before assuming his current role as Chief Operating Officer of Limited Brands. He has also served as Chief Operating Officer of Au Bon Pain Co. Inc.